Global Governance of Labour Rights

LEUVEN GLOBAL GOVERNANCE

Series Editor: Jan Wouters, *KU Leuven, Belgium*

The Leuven Global Governance series comprises high-quality monographs and edited volumes dedicated to innovative research on global governance. The series focuses particularly on the following themes: European Union and global multilateral governance; trade and sustainable development; peace and security studies; human rights, democracy and the rule of law; space governance; and comparative federalism. In full recognition of the complex issues involved, the series favours studies approaching global governance from a multidisciplinary, multi-level and multi-actor perspective.

Titles in the series include:

China, the European Union and Global Governance
Edited by Jan Wouters, Tanguy de Wilde, Pierre Defraigne and Jean-Christophe Defraigne

Private Standards and Global Governance
Economic, Legal and Political Perspectives
Edited by Axel Marx, Miet Maertens, Johan Swinnen and Jan Wouters

The Governance of Climate Relations between Europe and Asia
Evidence from China and Vietnam as Key Emerging Economies
Edited by Hans Bruyninckx, Qi Ye, Nguyen Quang Thuan and David Belis

Indirect Expropriation in International Law
Sebastián López Escarcena

China, the European Union and the Developing World
A Triangular Relationship
Edited by Jan Wouters, Jean-Christophe Defraigne and Matthieu Burnay

Global Governance and Democracy
A Multidisciplinary Analysis
Edited by Jan Wouters, Antoon Braeckman, Matthias Lievens and Emilie Bécault

The Contribution of International and Supranational Courts to the Rule of Law
Edited by Geert De Baere and Jan Wouters

Global Governance of Labour Rights
Assessing the Effectiveness of Transnational Public and Private Policy Initiatives
Edited by Axel Marx, Jan Wouters, Glenn Rayp and Laura Beke

Global Governance through Trade
EU Policies and Approaches
Edited by Jan Wouters, Axel Marx, Dylan Geraets and Bregt Natens

Global Governance of Labour Rights

Assessing the Effectiveness of Transnational Public and Private Policy Initiatives

Edited by

Axel Marx

Deputy Director, Leuven Centre for Global Governance Studies, KU Leuven, Belgium

Jan Wouters

Full Professor of International Law and International Organizations, Jean Monnet Chair ad personam *EU and Global Governance, and Director, Leuven Centre for Global Governance Studies and Institute for International Law, KU Leuven, Belgium*

Glenn Rayp

Professor in International Economics, Department of Economics, University of Ghent, Belgium

Laura Beke

Doctoral Researcher, KU Leuven, Belgium

LEUVEN GLOBAL GOVERNANCE

EE Edward Elgar PUBLISHING

Cheltenham, UK • Northampton, MA, USA

Published by
Edward Elgar Publishing Limited
The Lypiatts
15 Lansdown Road
Cheltenham
Glos GL50 2JA
UK

Edward Elgar Publishing, Inc.
William Pratt House
9 Dewey Court
Northampton
Massachusetts 01060
USA

A catalogue record for this book
is available from the British Library

Library of Congress Control Number: 2015943140

This book is available electronically in the Elgaronline
Law subject collection
DOI 10.4337/9781784711467

MIX
Paper from responsible sources
FSC® C013056

ISBN 978 1 78471 145 0 (cased)
ISBN 978 1 78471 146 7 (eBook)

Typeset by Servis Filmsetting Ltd, Stockport, Cheshire
Printed and bound in Great Britain by TJ International Ltd, Padstow

Contents

List of figures vii
List of tables viii
List of contributors ix

1 Protecting labour rights in a globalizing world: an introduction 1
Axel Marx, Jan Wouters, Laura Beke and Glenn Rayp

2 The protection of international labour rights: a longitudinal analysis of the protection of the rights of freedom of association and collective bargaining over 30 years in 73 countries 13
Axel Marx, Jadir Soares and Wouter Van Acker

3 The EU's social dimension and its external trade relations 42
Samantha Velluti

4 Divided we stand: the European Parliament's position on social trade in the post-Lisbon era 63
Lore Van den Putte

5 Asian and US perspectives on labor rights under international trade agreements compared 83
Ronald C. Brown

6 EU economic governance and labour rights: diversity and coherence in the EU, the Council of Europe and ILO instruments 118
Frank Hendrickx and Pieter Pecinovsky

7 Trade unions and collective bargaining power in global labor governance 150
Sigrid Koch-Baumgarten and Melanie Kryst

8 The rapprochement of ILO standards and CSR mechanisms: towards a positive understanding of the 'privatization' of international labour standards 170
Ruben Zandvliet and Paul van der Heijden

9 Between the dragon's gift and its claws: China in Africa and the (un)civil fostering of ILO's Decent Work Agenda 190
Abdul-Gafar 'Tobi' Oshodi

10 On the transformative capacity of private fair labour arrangements 209
Ceren Pekdemir, Pieter Glasbergen and Ron Cörvers

11 Compliance opportunities and the effectiveness of private voluntary standard setting – lessons from the global banana industry 230
Dennis Klink

12 The 'Accord for Fire and Building Safety in Bangladesh' in response to the Rana Plaza disaster 257
Juliane Reinecke and Jimmy Donaghey

13 The International Labour Organization, multinational enterprises, and shifting conceptions of responsibility in the global economy 278
Yossi Dahan, Hanna Lerner and Faina Milman-Sivan

14 Conclusion: which way to enforcement? 306
Glenn Rayp, Axel Marx and Jan Wouters

Index 315

Figures

2.1	Evolution of FACB protection: 1985–2012	21
2.2	Evolution protection of FACB rights by country income level	22
2.3	Trends on FACB rights protection: difference in protection by law and by practice	27
2.4	Determinants of workers' rights protection: summary of the literature	31
4.1	Qualitative assessment of the political groups on the non-trade issue vs. trade issue distinction	74
4.2	Qualitative assessment of the political groups on the competitiveness frame vs. human rights frame distinction	76
4.3	Qualitative assessment of the political groups on the economic development frame vs. social development frame distinction	78
11.1	The global banana industry at a glance	232
11.2	Implementation of GLOBAL GAP on supplier plantations	236
11.3	Transnational CSR as a multi-level top-down process	237
11.4	Public regulations and GLOBAL GAP implementation on supplier farms	241
11.5	Compliance culture and GLOBAL GAP implementation on supplier farms	243
11.6	CSR-sensitive groups and GLOBAL GAP implementation on supplier farms	246
11.7	Education and professionalization and GLOBAL GAP implementation on supplier farms	247
12.1	Regimes of global labour governance	259

Tables

2.1	List of countries included in the sample	19
2.2	Relationship between different human rights indicators	20
2.3	Protection of FACB rights: country scores	24
2A.1	Kucera's template for measuring FACB rights violations	35
2A.2	Correlation of FACB rights and other labour rights measures	38
5.1	East Asian Free Trade Agreements (ASEAN+3 countries)	102
5.2	Free Trade Agreements involving countries in East Asia (ASEAN+6 countries)	103
8.1	Reference to labour practices in CSR codes	177
8.2	Usage of ILO standards and concepts in the GRI Implementation Manual	180
8.3	Usage of ILO standards and concepts in the UN Draft Norms	183
11.1	CSR standard adoption by MNCs	235
11.2	Institutional mechanisms and measurement	240
11.3	Favorable and unfavourable institutional environments for the implementation of CSR standards	249

Contributors

Laura Beke is a PhD Researcher at KU Leuven, Belgium.

Ronald C. Brown is a full Professor of Law at the University of Hawaii Law School and served as the University's Director of the Center for Chinese Studies from 2000 to 2006.

Ron Cörvers is Director of the International Centre for Integrated assessment and Sustainable development (ICIS) and Associate Professor in Governance and Sustainable Development at Maastricht University, the Netherlands.

Yossi Dahan is a Professor of Law at the Academic Center of Law & Business Ramat-Gan, Israel, where he is the Director of the Human Rights program.

Jimmy Donaghey is Professor of Industrial Relations and Personnel Management at Warwick Business School, UK.

Pieter Glasbergen is Honorary Professor at Maastricht University (International Centre for Integrated assessment and Sustainable development [ICIS]) and Emeritus Professor of Environmental Studies, Policy and Management at Utrecht University and the Dutch Open Universiteit, the Netherlands.

Frank Hendrickx is Full Professor of Labour Law at the Faculty of Law at KU Leuven, Belgium. He is also a part-time Professor of European Labour Law at Tilburg Law School, the Netherlands, hosted at the ReflecT Institute.

Dennis Klink is a researcher at Öko-Institut Berlin and a graduate of the doctoral program Berlin Graduate School for Transnational Studies (BTS), Germany.

Sigrid Koch-Baumgarten is Professor of Political Science, in the Department of Social Sciences and Philosophy at Philipps-University of Marburg, Germany.

Melanie Kryst is a doctoral student at Philipps-University of Marburg, Germany.

Hanna Lerner is a Senior Lecturer in Political Science at Tel Aviv University, Israel.

Axel Marx is Deputy Director and Senior Researcher at Leuven Centre for Global Governance Studies, KU Leuven, Belgium.

Faina Milman-Sivan is an Assistant Professor of Law at the University of Haifa, Israel.

Abdul-Gafar 'Tobi' Oshodi is a PhD researcher at the Centre for Research on Peace and Development (CRPD), KU Leuven, Belgium.

Pieter Pecinovsky is a PhD researcher at the Institute for Labour Law, KU Leuven, Belgium.

Ceren Pekdemir is a PhD researcher at the International Centre for Integrated assessment and Sustainable development (ICIS) at Maastricht University, the Netherlands.

Glenn Rayp is Professor in International Economics at the Ghent University, Belgium.

Juliane Reinecke is Professor of Organizational Behaviour at Warwick Business School and a member of the Industrial Relations Research Unit at the University of Warwick, UK.

Jadir Soares is an Associate Fellow of the Leuven Centre for Global Governance Studies, KU Leuven, Belgium.

Wouter Van Acker is a PhD researcher at the Leuven Public Governance Institute, KU Leuven, Belgium.

Lore Van den Putte is a PhD researcher and fellow of the Research Foundation Flanders (FWO) at the Centre for EU Studies at Ghent University, Belgium.

Paul van der Heijden is a Professor of International Labour Law and has served six years as President and Rector Magnificus of Leiden University and five years as Rector Magnificus of Amsterdam University, the Netherlands. He is Chair of the ILO Committee on Freedom of Association.

Samantha Velluti (LLB, LLM, PhD) is Reader in EU Law at Lincoln Law School, UK.

Jan Wouters is Jean Monnet Chair *ad personam* EU and Global Governance, Full Professor of International Law and International Organizations, and founding Director of the Institute for International

Law and of the Leuven Centre for Global Governance Studies, KU Leuven, Belgium.

Ruben Zandvliet is a PhD researcher at the Grotius Centre for International Legal Studies at Leiden University, the Netherlands.

1. Protecting labour rights in a globalizing world: an introduction

Axel Marx, Jan Wouters, Laura Beke and Glenn Rayp

Stories and images of collapsed factories, burned down sweatshops, imprisoned migrant workers, abused child workers, violent suppression of peaceful labour protests and many other violations of internationally recognized labour rights continue to spread across the globe. This is nothing new. Nor is the recognition that addressing these issues is not the sovereign and sole responsibility of a state. Many labour rights violations take place in the context of transnational and global economic transactions, and there has long been a widespread consensus that international action and coordination are necessary to address labour rights violations. International labour regulation, as a result, has a long history. Attempts to internationally coordinate the improvement of labour conditions date back from 1919, when the International Labour Organization (ILO) was established to develop international policies and norms on a range of labour-related issues. Since its creation in 1919, The International Labour Organization (ILO) has introduced a system of international labour standards aimed at 'promoting opportunities for women and men to obtain decent and productive work, in conditions of freedom, equity, security and dignity'.[1] The basic idea, in 1919, was to prevent a deterioration of labour standards and promote their adoption in a world recovering from war, based on the principle of social justice as an 'indispensable condition for universal and lasting peace',[2] whereby 'the failure of any nation to adopt humane conditions of labour is an obstacle in the way of other nations which desire to improve the conditions in their own countries'.[3] The latter specifically referred to the increase in volumes of trade and the resulting international

[1] See: http://www.ilo.org/global/standards/introduction-to-international-labour-standards/lang--en/index.htm

[2] First Recital of the Preamble, ILO Constitution.

[3] Third Recital of the Preamble, ILO Constitution.

economic competition which was intensifying between countries in the context of rapid industrial development. This competition led some countries to pursue a strategy of either not installing or lowering labour standards to gain a competitive advantage in producing goods, since the protection of labour standards was assumed to increase production costs.

The need to balance the benefits from international trade and investment with the protection of workers was further developed in the ILO's Philadelphia Declaration, which was adopted in 1944 and annexed to the 1919 Constitution. The Declaration aimed to balance trade and labour concerns and over time has led to the adoption of many labour-rights-related conventions within the context of the ILO. So far, the ILO has put forward 189 conventions, six protocols and 203 recommendations,[4] and has consistently promoted four core labour standards since the adoption of the 1998 Declaration on Fundamental Principles and Rights at Work. This Declaration on Fundamental Principles and Rights at Work covers the core rights and standards laid down in four principles and eight conventions. These principles are: (1) freedom of association and the effective recognition of the right to collective bargaining; (2) elimination of all forms of forced or compulsory labour; (3) effective abolition of child labour; and (4) elimination of discrimination and respect for employment and occupation. As stipulated by the ILO the 'Declaration makes it clear that these rights are universal, and that they apply to all people in all States – regardless of the level of economic development'.[5]

Testifying to its scaling-up efforts not only to advance ratification but also to foster the effective enforcement of core labour standards in its 185 member states, the ILO adopted its Declaration on 'Social Justice for a Fair Globalization' in 2008, promoting the decent work agenda and stressing the 'need for a strong social dimension to globalization' (ILO, 2008, p. 1). This was again emphasized in the 2010 Action Plan (ILO, 2009, p. 1). In addition, other intergovernmental initiatives were developed to further promote the protection of labour rights through addressing multinational enterprises. These include, for example, the ILO Tripartite Declaration of Principles concerning Multinational Enterprises and Social Policy (MNE Declaration) and the OECD Guidelines for Multinational Enterprises. The MNE Declaration, adopted by the ILO's Governing Body in 1977, is currently laid down in its fourth edition of 2006. The Declaration tries to

[4] http://www.ilo.org/dyn/normlex/en/f?p=NORMLEXPUB:1:0, accessed on 7 March 2015.

[5] See http://www.ilo.org/declaration/thedeclaration/lang--en/index.htm, accessed on 7 March 2015.

encourage MNEs to participate in creating economic and social welfare and highlights the role which firms play in safeguarding labour and human rights. The OECD Guidelines for Multinational Enterprises were adopted in 1976 and updated for the fifth time in 2011. The OECD Guidelines provide for a global framework for responsible business conduct, covering areas such as human rights, employment and industrial relations, environment, combating bribery, consumer protection, science and technology, competition and taxation. Finally, the United Nations Global Compact (the Compact), launched on 26 July 2000, aims to bring together a wide variety of stakeholders, including civil society organizations, trade unions and academic scholars, in order to enable businesses to pursue a corporate social responsibility agenda based on ten principles, including human rights declarations, labour rights declarations, environment declarations and the anti-corruption convention.

However, confronted with many labour rights violations across the world, despite the widespread ratification of ILO conventions, the World Bank (2012, pp. 32–33) recently expressed the concern that 'ratification on its own is not sufficient'. Indeed, many academic scholars have focused on the so-called 'enforcement' and 'compliance gap', showing that ratification of international conventions is not a sufficient condition for compliance. Hafner-Burton (2013, p. 3) plots for nine protected rights under the UN Covenant on Civil and Political Rights, the number of states which have ratified the Covenant and, for those states who have ratified the Covenant, the number of states in which there are reported violations of these rights or which are known to abuse those rights. The analysis shows that for worker rights the number of states which abuse workers' rights is almost as high as the number of states which have ratified the Covenant, indicating that for almost every state which has ratified the Covenant there are still abuses. Beth Simmons (2009, 2013) also identified this compliance gap and so-called false positives, i.e. countries which ratify international treaties without the intention of really enforcing them. Recognizing the limits of multilateral enforcement through international agreements, several state and non-state actors have developed a range of policy tools which aim to enforce compliance with labour rights.

These initiatives have proliferated through the last decade and take many forms. Most notably, labour rights are increasingly governed through a variety of unilateral and bilateral governmental initiatives and via different non-state initiatives. Over recent years these initiatives have received increasing attention in the literature. These include: the integration of labour rights in the unilateral (Yap, 2013) and bilateral trade policies (ILO, 2013) of governmental actors; the rise of unilateral action by firms in the form of corporate social responsibility (Vogel, 2005); the conclusion of International Framework Agreements between multinational enterprises and global union federation (Niforou, 2012) and the emergence of non-state regulatory initiatives which monitor and enforce labour rights (Marx and Wouters, 2015; forthcoming). This volume aims to take stock of these developments, map the different initiatives, assess the current forms they take, and highlight the potential and limitations of these forms of global labour governance.

OUTLINE OF THE BOOK

The volume starts off with an empirical contribution on the evolution of the protection of two fundamental labour rights and rights which are generally considered to be two key enabling rights for other rights, namely freedom of association and collective bargaining. Marx, Soares and Van Acker build on the work of David Kucera (2001, 2002) and Layna Mosley (2011) to analyse the protection of the rights of freedom of association and collective bargaining in 73 countries over 30 years. Their chapter offers new empirical evidence that the protection of these rights has declined over the last three decades. The decline is less marked for OECD countries, but even in these countries one can observe a decline in the protection of these rights, based on an index which takes 37 items into account. The authors extensively discuss the main results and delve deeper into the possible explanations for this decline. Their contribution shows that despite the commitment, through ratification, of many countries to these two international ILO conventions, these rights are increasingly not protected – quite the reverse. A similar analysis is not available for many other labour rights since the data is lacking. As the authors show, the existing human rights indicators are only a weak proxy to measure the protection of labour rights. Without extrapolating these results to other labour rights it is safe to assume that the protection of labour rights is under stress. Consequently several state and non-state initiatives are developed to further strengthen the enforcement of labour rights. The other contributions in this volume focus on these initiatives.

A first set of chapters concentrates on the governance of labour rights through trade. Non-trade objectives, such as the protection of labour rights, are increasingly pursued through trade policies. This shift to the use of trade as a policy instrument has received scholarly attention in recent times. In an early contribution, Meunier and Nicolaïdis (2006) coined the idea of governing through trade in reference to external relation policies pursued by the European Union (EU). Governing *through* trade refers to the fact that the EU uses *inter alia* its trade policy to 'export' its laws, standards, values and norms. This governing *through* trade can take many forms, including via regulatory measures, unilateral trade measures and/or bilateral trade agreements (for an elaborate discussion see Wouters et al., 2015). Samantha Velluti in 'The EU's Social Dimension and its External Trade Relations' provides a comprehensive discussion of how the EU uses its Common Commercial Policy (CCP) to pursue non-trade objectives. She argues that by injecting a normative approach into its external relations through Articles 3(5) and 21 of the Treaty on the European Union, the EU is clearly attempting to establish itself as a global human rights actor. The chapter explores the role which the EU has committed itself to in relation to the promotion of social rights and international labour standards in its CCP. In particular, it examines the EU's practice of promoting social standards through the Generalized System of Preferences ('GSP' – in its three main variants, i.e. the 'general GSP' scheme, the 'GSP +' incentive scheme, and the 'Everything but Arms' (EBA) scheme) and its bilateral and regional trade agreements. The analysis includes a critical review of how labour provisions have been incorporated into trade agreements and the various goals pursued in combination with the mechanisms employed to achieve them.

In order to better understand the politics behind these developments of integrating labour rights into common commercial policies, we need to unravel the political processes behind this push for a social dimension to trade. In 'Divided We Stand: The European Parliament's Position on Social Trade in the Post-Lisbon Era' Lore Van den Putte aims to do this, and concentrates on the political processes in the European Parliament. She starts from the observation that several ideologically opposed political actors do not quarrel significantly over the necessity of integrating labour rights considerations in trade policy instruments. Van den Putte interestingly finds that the European Parliament (EP) has shown a great interest in linking social issues to trade policy, as measured by the number of EP resolutions on this topic. What is interesting about the EP's dealings with labour rights is that it has focused more on how social norms should be included in trade agreements, rather than on why. Indeed, little to no debate in the EP has been devoted to why social norms as such should be included in EU trade agreements, which is very surprising given the wide variety of ideological positions in the EP. Social trade seems to be a taken-for-granted issue among a large majority within the EP. Van den Putte argues that while it is indeed true that the EP as a whole is strongly in favour of a social clause, different ideas lie beneath this policy consensus. These different interpretations explain the current success of the concept of social trade within the EP. While at first sight these coalitions might share the same thoughts about the 'problem', a closer look reveals that they have different interpretations of it, which also connects to their respective social and cognitive commitment to it. On a deeper level, the discourse on social trade reveals contradictory interpretations. Van den Putte's chapter aims to unveil the different conceptions behind the social emphasis of the EP.

Ronald C. Brown in 'Asian and US Perspectives on Labor Rights under International Trade Agreements Compared' then discusses and explores how labour rights are included in non-EU trade agreements and bilateral investment treaties. He shows that what all have in common is the central role of the International Labour Organization's core labour standards. His chapter explores, via carefully selected cases such as the US-Korea Free Trade Agreement, how the US and Asian countries engage with labour rights in free trade agreements (FTAs). This example is used as an illustration of the nature and parameters of the new US model of social dimension provisions being negotiated with labour protections. The author then turns to the Asian perspective and actually notes that this encompasses a very wide diversity of approaches and countries. He tries to identify some common threads, starting from the observation that the number of ratified FTAs involving at least one country from the region is more than 100, resulting in a 'convoluted "noodle bowl" of overlapping free trade agreements', which take many different forms ranging from bilateral to mega-regional ones. The author shows that in contrast to the FTAs in which the 'Global North' countries and actors such as the EU and the US are involved, the Asian FTAs pay little attention to labour issues. This might be a temporary state which could evolve, as Brown notes in his conclusion, into a situation in which labour rights are increasingly taken on board.

Frank Hendrickx and Pieter Pecinovsky shift the focus from external trade and investment policies to broader economic policies of the EU and their impact on labour rights in the context of the new EU (austerity) initiatives. In 'EU Economic Governance and Labour Rights: Diversity and Coherence in the EU, the Council of Europe and ILO Instruments', they discuss the tension between the EU's economic policies and its commitment to fundamental labour rights. This tension not only emerges within the EU's own legal order, but also in relation to policies pursued by the Council of Europe and the ILO. Hendrickx and Pecinovsky analyse this tension by means of the concept of internal and external coherence. They argue that coherence problems exist both within the EU's legal and governance system as well as in relation to international instruments. They highlight and extensively discuss problems related to internal and external coherence. In relation to internal coherence, the authors note that, within the EU, the relationship between the economic and social dimension is unbalanced. As long as there is an imbalance between economic and social policies in the EU, there will remain good reasons for criticism directed at economically motivated EU measures which are designed to have a (negative) impact on labour rights and welfare systems. Concerning external coherence, the authors observe inconsistencies and contradictory outcomes from different enforcement mechanisms at the international level (the EU, Council of Europe and ILO). Given these inconsistencies, the authors raise the question of which level has the authority to induce others to correct their views or approaches. In the current situation, it seems that neither the ILO nor the Council of Europe is capable of imposing their views on the EU. Moreover, the Union's member states are bound by the ILO's conventions, the European Social Charter and the ECHR, but the EU is not bound by them directly. In exploring answers to this question Hendrickx and Pecinovsky assess different possibilities, including the accession of the EU to the European Convention of Human Rights and shifting from hierarchical perspectives on nested legal orders to network approaches of autonomous co-existing legal orders.

Besides a range of trade and economic policies pursued by governmental and inter-governmental actors to protect labour rights, we also observe the emergence and further development of initiatives by non-state actors. They take different forms elaborated in different contributions. The next two contributions look at either side of the 'employment relation', namely unions and firms. The first contribution, 'Trade Unions and Collective Bargaining Power in Global Labor Governance' by Sigrid Koch-Baumgarten and Melanie Kryst, focuses on the action of one of the most obvious non-state actors in labour relations, namely the trade unions in the context of a shift in labour governance from the national to the international level and the emergence of new non-state actors such as labelling organizations and NGOs. Their chapter examines the importance of trade unions in this evolving context and how their corporate and economic power in collective bargaining helps to regulate, implement and monitor labour rights and labour protection in a global economy. They focus on specific actions, resources and potential power that trade unions can bring to transnational labour governance. In this context specific attention is given to International Framework Agreements (IFAs) as a key instrument used by unions. These are, according to the ILO (2007), 'instruments negotiated between a multinational enterprise and a Global Union Federation (GUF) in order to establish an ongoing relationship between the parties and ensure that the company respects the same standards in all the countries where it operates'. IFAs are based on social dialogue or collective bargaining with workers' representatives on a global or regional multinational enterprise level, and often include the four fundamental principles and rights at work, making specific reference to ILO conventions. These IFAs should not be regarded as substitutes for new forms of global labour governance but as a complement to them. In this way, as Koch-Baumgarten and Kryst argue, unions strengthen and complement new forms of labour governance by bringing collective bargaining power and transnational networks to the fore. They illustrate this further via case studies such as trade union regulation of the maritime industry and an analysis of the Clean Clothes Campaign (CCC), an example of NGOs cooperating with trade unions to defend labour rights transnationally.

The second contribution provides a perspective from the firm and investigates the corporate social responsibility (CSR) policies firms are developing, framed in the context of an internationally agreed upon set of labour rights and standards. The purpose of the chapter by Ruben Zandvliet and Paul van der Heijden, 'The Rapprochement of ILO Standards and CSR Mechanisms: Towards a Positive Understanding of the "Privatization" of International Labour Standards', is to examine the relevance of international labour law in the context of corporate social responsibility, and it specifically analyses the consequences of the so-called privatization of public norms. The chapter analyses to what extent international labour law, including the work of the ILO supervisory bodies, is relevant in the context of corporate social responsibility. It first analyses the use of ILO standards by other fields of public international law and notes a trend towards more reliance on ILO standards by a variety of bodies. This analysis lays the groundwork for the observation that ILO standards are globally diffusing through different mechanisms. Next, the authors turn to the interaction between international labour law and CSR and the possible privatization of international law. The authors argue that contrary to some other perspectives, privatization of public standards should not be equated with private standards that lack this public underpinning. Contemporary CSR practice shows a trend towards more complete and more specific references to international labour law. Secondly, they argue that privatization of public norms might be necessary to further strengthen their enforcement. Thirdly, they note that privatization is usually accompanied by public regulation and hence does not necessarily lead to a hollowing out or weakening of the state.

Moving away from the traditional non-state actors in employment relations, the next four chapters focus more specifically on new non-state actors involved in global labour governance. Abdul-Gafar 'Tobi' Oshodi in 'Between the Dragon's Gift and its Claws: China in Africa and the (Un) civil Fostering of ILO's Decent Work Agenda' analyses China's labour practices in Africa vis-à-vis struggles for the incorporation of the ILO's Decent Work Agenda across the continent. The chapter highlights the 'points of exit' of African governments and the 'points of engagement' of African non-state actors in the fostering of the Decent Work Agenda in Chinese companies in Africa. With several examples, the chapter not only identifies the civil contexts of non-state points of engagement, but most importantly warns against the possibility of increased uncivil confrontations as a reaction to the exit of African governments in the prioritization of the Decent Work Agenda. The chapter illustrates the potential dangers of non-state engagement since it might 'hollow out' state-led commitments.

In 'On the Transformative Capacity of Private Fair Labour Arrangements' Ceren Pekdemir, Pieter Glasbergen and Ron Cörvers focus on the role of private labour monitoring initiatives which aim to govern global supply chains. These initiatives may be multi-stakeholder when they are partnerships that include actors from both civil society and the business domain or initiatives springing solely from civil society or the market domain. These arrangements are involved in regulatory activities that are voluntary in nature and encompass setting standards, providing training for businesses, monitoring the implementation of standards, certifying factories, and accrediting certification programmes. Many of these schemes have recently been criticized for not being very effective. After introducing these different forms of private governance, the authors engage with the debate on effectiveness and argue that the ineffectiveness of initiatives should not be understood as a consequence of individual arrangements, but as originating from some characteristics of the system of arrangements as a whole, which impairs the transformative capacity of private arrangements. The authors define transformative capacity as the ability to bring about substantial change in unfair labour practices. Their chapter provides further food for thought on the potential but also, and especially so, the limitations of private initiatives to govern labour standards.

The issue of the potential and limitations of private governance is further explored by Dennis Klink in 'Compliance Opportunities and the Effectiveness of Private Voluntary Standard Setting – Lessons from the Global Banana Industry'. He focuses on private labour governance in an agricultural sector and analyses the different adoption rates of private certification schemes. He starts from the observation that all multinational firms trading bananas have endorsed and committed themselves to various voluntary social and environmental certification systems at the central company level. These private systems often form the cornerstone of their corporate social responsibility policies. However, when comparing the adoption statistics of different banana-producing countries, Klink observes significant differences, despite the fact that these countries are integrated into the global supply chains of firms. This finding draws attention to the importance of domestic political conditions in individual supply-chain countries for the effectiveness of these schemes as measured by their adoption rate. Klink further elaborates on this and develops an analytical framework to better understand these domestic conditions. This framework focuses on four conditions: public business regulations; compliance culture; labour market characteristics; and education of the workforce. He applies this framework to GlobalGAP certification in two countries (Ecuador and Costa Rica) and concludes that institutional characteristics in producing countries are of key importance in understanding the effectiveness of voluntary standards.

A final contribution on non-state actors focuses on the outcomes of the Rana Plaza disaster. On 24 April 2013, a ready-made garment factory collapsed in Dhaka, Bangladesh. As an estimated 1,129 casualties were mourned in the aftermath of the Rana Plaza disaster, the debate on the need for international action was soon revived. This resulted *inter alia* in the Accord for Fire and Building Safety in Bangladesh, which is an independent, legally binding agreement between brands and trade unions designed to work towards a safe and healthy Bangladeshi ready-made garment industry. The contribution by Juliane Reinecke and Jimmy Donaghey, 'The "Accord for Fire and Building Safety in Bangladesh" in Response to the Rana Plaza Disaster', uses the case study of the response to Rana Plaza to examine how production and consumption-based power interact to produce private labour governance in global supply chains. They argue that the Accord is unprecedented in its binding nature and hence constitutes a very interesting case study to further analyse the potential of a specific form of private governance which focuses on safety issues. Their findings indicate how the complementarity of production and consumption-based power contributed to making an agreement binding which includes a significant number of international and brand-name firms. The research shows how the production–consumption interface may provide leverage to improve labour standards in global supply chains.

Many of these contributions show the potential of some of these initiatives, but also point to their limitations, often implicitly, or even explicitly, hinting at the importance of a strengthened multilateral approach with a stronger enforcement mechanism. This brings us back to the International Labour Organization. Indeed, throughout all the contributions the International Labour Organization plays an important role, since it provides the legal framework for the protection of labour rights which is used in these non-multilateral approaches. Founded almost a century ago in a world which differs greatly from today's, its role might change and shift in the context of these evolving governance dynamics.

Building on the previous chapters and starting from this observation Yossi Dahan, Hanna Lerner and Faina Milman-Sivan submit proposals of what this shift might entail. The central claim in 'The International Labour Organization, Multinational Enterprises, and Shifting Conceptions of Responsibility in the Global Economy' is that the ILO should rethink its understanding of the very concept of responsibility, which currently rests on an outdated conception that is unsuited to the structure of the global economy. According to this outdated conception, the nation state is either the sole or primary agent bearing responsibility towards workers within member states' jurisdictions. As becomes clear in the other chapters in this volume, recent economic, political and legal developments across the globe have changed the context in which the ILO operates. Hence the ILO should not only allocate responsibility for workers' rights to states but also empower private non-state actors. The authors propose that the ILO adopts a novel conception of *shared* responsibility, which they term *the labour connection model of shared responsibility*. In this model, the responsibility for remedying unjust working conditions in the global labour market is borne by a complex set of agents and institutions that participate in global production, including multinational enterprises.

In a concluding chapter we assess the different contributions via the red thread of enforcement. What do we learn from the different contributions in terms of the enforcement of international labour rights? In answering this question we hope to contribute to a better understanding of how labour rights can be protected in a globalizing world.

REFERENCES

Hafner-Burton, E. (2013) *Making Human Rights a Reality*. Princeton: Princeton University Press.

ILO (International Labour Organization) (2007) 'International Framework Agreements: A Global Tool for Supporting Rights at Work', http://www.ilo.org/global/about-the-ilo/newsroom/news/WCMS_080723/lang--en/index.htm

ILO (International Labour Organization) (2008) *ILO Declaration on Social Justice for a Fair Globalization*, adopted by the International Labour Conference at its Ninety-seventh Session, Geneva, 10 June.

ILO (International Labour Organization) (2009) 'Plan of Action (2010–2016). Towards Widespread Ratification and Effective Implementation of the Governance Conventions: Labour Inspection, Employment Policy and Tripartite Consultation', adopted by the Governing Body of the International Labour Organization at its 306th Session, November.

ILO (International Labour Organization) (2013) *Social Dimensions of Free Trade Agreements*. Geneva: International Institute for Labour Studies and International Institute for Labour Studies.

Kucera, D. (2001) 'Measuring Fundamental Rights at Work', *Statistical Journal of the United Nations*, 18: 175–186.
Kucera, D. (2002) 'Core Labour Standards and Foreign Direct Investment', *International Labour Review*, 141(1–2): 31–69.
Marx, A. and J. Wouters (2015) 'Competition and Cooperation in the Market of Voluntary Standards Sustainability Standards', in Delimatsis, P. (ed.) *International Standardization – Law, Economics and Politics*. Cambridge: Cambridge University Press.
Marx, A. and J. Wouters (forthcoming) 'Redesigning Enforcement in Private Labor Regulation: Will it Work?', *International Labor Review*.
Meunier, S. and K. Nicolaïdis (2006) 'The European Union as a Conflicted Trade Power', *Journal of European Public Policy*, 13(6): 906–925.
Mosley, L. (2011) *Labor Rights and Multinational Production*. Cambridge: Cambridge University Press.
Niforou, C. (2012) 'International Framework Agreements and Industrial Relations Governance: Global Rhetoric Versus Local Realities', *British Journal of Industrial Relations*, 50(2): 352–373.
Simmons, B. (2009) *Mobilizing for Human Rights: International Law in Domestic Politics*. Cambridge: Cambridge University Press.
Simmons, B. (2013) 'From Ratification to Compliance: Quantitative Evidence on the Spiral Model', in Risse, T., Ropp, S. and Sikkink, K. (eds) *The Persistent Power of Human Rights: From Commitment to Compliance*. Cambridge: Cambridge University Press, pp. 43–59.
Vogel, D. (2005) *The Market for Virtue: The Potential and Limits of Corporate Social Responsibility*. Washington, DC: The Brookings Institution.
World Bank (2012) *World Development Report 2013 on Jobs*. Washington, DC: World Bank.
World Commission on the Social Dimension of Globalization (2004) *A Fair Globalization: Creating Opportunity for All*. Geneva: ILO.
Wouters, J., A. Marx, D. Geraets and B. Natens (eds) (2015) *Global Governance through Trade*. Cheltenham, UK and Northampton, MA, USA: Edward Elgar Publishing.
Yap, J. (2013) 'Beyond "Don't Be Evil": The European Union GSP+ Trade Preference Scheme and the Incentivisation of the Sri Lankan Garment Industry to Foster Human Rights', *European Law Journal*, 19(2): 293–301.

2. The protection of international labour rights: a longitudinal analysis of the protection of the rights of freedom of association and collective bargaining over 30 years in 73 countries

Axel Marx, Jadir Soares and Wouter Van Acker

1. INTRODUCTION[1]

Since its creation in 1919, The International Labour Organization (ILO) has introduced a system of international labour standards aimed at 'promoting opportunities for women and men to obtain decent and productive work, in conditions of freedom, equity, security and dignity'.[2] During this long path, many standards related to labour rights have been developed. The ILO's Declaration on Fundamental Principles and Rights at Work (1998)[3] covers the core rights and standards laid down in four principles and eight conventions. These principles are: (1) freedom of association and the effective recognition of the right to collective bargaining;[4] (2) elimination of all forms of forced or compulsory labour;[5] (3) effective

[1] The authors thank Glenn Rayp for helpful comments on a first draft of this chapter. They acknowledge support by the European Commission under the FRAME FP7 Project (grant agreement €320,000).

[2] See: http://www.ilo.org/global/standards/introduction-to-international-labour-standards/lang--en/index.htm

[3] See: http://www.ilo.org/declaration/thedeclaration/textdeclaration/lang--en/index.htm

[4] Freedom of Association and Protection of the Right to Organize Convention, 1948 (No. 87) and Right to Organize and Collective Bargaining Convention, 1949 (No. 98).

[5] Forced Labour Convention, 1930 (No. 29) and Abolition of Forced Labour Convention, 1957 (No. 105).

abolition of child labour;[6] and (4) elimination of discrimination in respect of employment and occupation.[7]

The importance of these rights was reiterated in the 2004 report by the World Commission on the Social Dimension of Globalization (WCSDG), *A Fair Globalization: Creating Opportunities For All*, which stated 'There is wide international agreement on the essentials which we must all urgently strive for . . . a vibrant civil society, empowered by freedom of association' (p. xii).

Since 1995 the ILO has invested in efforts to make the ratification of these eight conventions universal. These efforts have resulted in a widespread adoption of the four principles and the eight related conventions. By January 2014, over 1,200 ratifications succeeded, representing 86 per cent of the possible number of ratifications. In addition, many public and private actors have used these core labour rights in their policies (for an overview see Levi et al., 2013). They have been integrated in several unilateral (GSP+) and bilateral trade policies (Free Trade Agreements) (ILO, 2013) and private certification schemes and codes of conduct (Fransen, 2012; Marx et al., 2012).

However, relatively little data is available to assess whether these labour standards have had any real impact on the situation on the ground at the country level. Several general human rights indicators and indexes exist and have been used in previous studies to assess the protection of human (and labour) rights, such as Freedom House and the Cingranelli-Richards (CIRI) Human Rights indicators (i.e., Elkins et al., 2013; Hafner-Burton, 2005; Simmons, 2009). Although these measures include labour rights they also include other aspects not related to labour rights, such as freedom of the press and religious freedom, which limits the validity for an analysis specifically focused on labour rights. The use of composite indicators in such cases makes them vulnerable to ecological fallacy type of errors (Robinson, 1950), i.e. drawing conclusions from observations on the level of the composite indicator which might not hold for its components separately. In addition, especially in relation to the Cingranelli-Richards indicators, the measurement of indicators is relatively 'rough' and the transformation of information in a three order ordinal scale generates a significant loss of information and variation which would be interesting for those seeking a more fine-grained analysis.

---

[6] Minimum Age Convention, 1973 (No. 138) and Worst Forms of Child Labour Convention, 1999 (No. 182).

[7] Equal Remuneration Convention, 1951 (No. 100) and Discrimination (Employment and Occupation) Convention, 1958 (No. 111).

In order to address these limitations David Kucera (2001, 2002) developed a new indicator, which specifically aims to capture the degree to which two specific core labour conventions are protected, namely ILO Convention 87 (Freedom of Association and the Protection of the Right to Organize Convention) and ILO Convention 98 (Right to Organize and Collective Bargaining). Combined, Kucera calls these indicators the FACB-index. Layna Mosley used this index to develop a time series, from 1985 to 2002, on the protection of freedom of association and collective bargaining (hereafter FACB). Her study showed that the protection of FACB rights was declining on a global scale, raising doubts about the global protection of at least two core labour conventions for the period of 1985 to 2002.

The aim of this chapter is to report on a data collection effort in order to extend the time-series initially developed by Kucera and Mosley. By gathering new, up-to-date data for a sample of 73 countries over the period 2003–2012, this chapter provides a better understanding of global, long-term labour rights trends. The methodology described in this chapter follows the one applied by David Kucera and Layna Mosley, in order to keep the data comparable. The coding of data for an additional ten years allows for an analysis of trends over a period of almost 30 years. The chapter shows a continued, although less strong, downward trend of the protection of FACB in the 73 countries that were analysed. The chapter proceeds as follows. First we introduce the construction of the FACB rights index and our sample. Next, we present the main results in general, by country groupings and by distinguishing between the protection of FACB rights in law and in practice. In a third section, we explore possible explanations for the observations and point to future research. The chapter ends with some concluding and critical remarks, a discussion on our findings, as well as suggestions for further research.

2. FACB INDEX: DATA COLLECTION AND SAMPLE

The principle of freedom of association and the effective recognition of the right to collective bargaining is laid down in two conventions. The Freedom of Association and Protection of the Right to Organize Convention (ILO Convention No 87) came into force on 4 July 1950 and was, in 2014, ratified by 153 states. It refers to the right of workers to create or participate in organizations of their choice without interference or reprisal (ILC, 2008). The right to freedom of association is also recognized as a basic human right in the Universal Declaration of Human

Rights (article 20). Linked to the right of freedom of association is the right to collective bargaining. The convention concerning the application of the principles of the right to organize and collective bargaining (ILO Convention No. 98) came into force on 18 July 1951 and has so far been ratified by 164 states. In a nutshell, this right allows workers to freely negotiate their working conditions.

David Kucera (2001, 2002) developed an index of freedom of association and collective bargaining, based on 37 evaluation criteria considering both *de jure* and *de facto* violations of these two labour rights. The author identified the 37 evaluation criteria based on the two ILO conventions: Freedom of Association and the Protection of the Right to Organize Convention (No. 87) and the Right to Organize and Collective Bargaining (No. 98). The analysis, carried out following Kucera's FACB-index, is based on a content analysis of three distinct sources: the International Confederation of Free Trade Unions' Annual Survey of Violations of Trade Union Rights, the US State Department's Country Reports on Human Rights Practices, and the International Labour Organization's (ILO) Reports of the Committee on Freedom of Association.[8]

The strength of this measure lies in its fine graded framework (composed of 37 issues related to FACB rights – see annex 1), and in the use of three sources to collect information, which minimizes the bias from specific sources. A limitation of Kucera's measure is its cross-sectional nature (only one single measure for each country summarizing data collected from text reports between 1993 and 1997), which does not allow for a longitudinal analysis. To fill this gap, Mosley (2011) used Kucera's template to code FACB rights from 1985 to 2002. Layna Mosley used this time series in an analysis of the determinants of labour standards, considering both the overall measure and two derived measures of rights in law and in practice.

The indicators developed by Kucera and Mosley show that a more fine-grained indicator for specific labour rights can generate different results from the Freedom House and CIRI indexes, and hence the ecological fallacy and rough measurement problems are relevant in the context of analysing the protection of specific labour rights. As an illustration of the problem of the ecological fallacy problem, consider Cyprus in 2000. In 2000 Cyprus had the best possible score on civil liberties (1), but its score on freedom of association and collective bargaining (from Mosley, 2011) was below the average (6.35). As an illustration of the rough measurement problem, consider the cases of Peru and Lithuania. In 2000, workers'

[8] For more discussion on the sources, see annex 2.

rights were occasionally violated in Peru and Lithuania according to the CIRI dataset (both score 1 out of scale going from 0 to 2). However, if we look at the Mosley index of FACB rights, violations were much more common in Peru (score of 3.5) than in Lithuania (score of 7.4).

2.1 Data Collection and Methodology[9]

The basis of the data collection, following Kucera and Mosley, lies in an analysis of three sources, per year, per country. These sources are the annual Human Rights Reports by the US State Department,[10] the ILO Freedom of Association cases[11] and ILO Supervising Reports,[12] and finally the International Trade Union Confederation's (ITUC) Annual Reports on the Violation of Trade Union Rights.[13] These sources are used to code a 37-category coding template which was developed on the basis of ILO Conventions 87 (Freedom of Association) and 98 (Right to Collective Bargaining). Within the above-mentioned sources the coders[14] looked for any references to violations of the 37 items for each of the countries and years identified (see annex 1). Violations on each of the 37 items were measured as a dummy variable. When one or more of the sources reported a violation for a specific country, a '1' was given to that country. If none of the three sources provided indications for a violation a '0' was given.

Each category was also assigned a specific weight, since some violations are more serious than others. The weight depends on how severe a violation is, usually ranging from 1 to 2. Three severe types of violation have an especial weight of 10: the ban on all unions (category 6), the absence of any union activity due to social/economic breakdown (category 7), and the general prohibition of collective bargaining (category 24).[15] As a result, the score for a given country and year is the sum of all scores (0 or 1) for each of the 37 categories multiplied by the weight for the specific category. Theoretically, the highest score on this scale is 86.5. However, the highest

---

9 For more on coding see annex 2.

10 http://www.state.gov/j/drl/rls/hrrpt/

11 http://www.ilo.org/dyn/normlex/en/f?p=NORMLEXPUB:20030:0::NO:::

12 http://www.ilo.org/dyn/normlex/en/f?p=1000:11000:0::NO:::

13 The ITUC's sources were gathered with the help of the ITUC itself: 2003 and 2004 were available in a paper format only, 2006, 2007 and 2013 were available online, and the others were sent to us as pdf files.

14 The authors coded the violations. In case of doubt, the authors decided on how to code a specific instance. A list of decisions of doubt is included in the methodological note available in annex 2.

15 There is a small difference between Kucera and Mosley on using the weights. We follow the procedure followed by Mosley.

score observed in the research population was 29.75, for Turkey in 2007. The lowest theoretical score, 0, was observed several times.

In order to make the results more easily and visibly understandable we reversed the scores and re-scaled them on a 0–10 scale. This means that a higher score (10 or close to 10) refers to better labour rights situations with fewer violations on FACB, and a lower score indicates more severe violations. In other words, an upward trend indicates an improvement in the protection of FACB, a downward trend a deterioration.

In order to further refine the analysis we made a distinction between two groups of categories: categories covering violations in law on the one hand and violations in practice on the other hand.[16] The categories covering violations in law regard the incorporation of labour rights (derived from ILO Conventions 87 and 98) into domestic law; for example, the absence of the legal right to strike (category 32), the absence of the right to collective bargaining (24) or a restriction on the foreign financial contributions a union is allowed to receive (23). The situation in practice is measured by the remaining practice-categories, covering issues such as trade union members who are fired for union activities (10) or an employer limiting the agenda in collective bargaining (28). This distinction between law and practice becomes relevant when we analyse the results. Some countries turn out to have a spotless record in law, but have a contrasting situation on the ground. Another potential important difference between the two types of category concerns the dynamics. The score on violations in practice changes more profoundly under the influence of domestic disturbances or economic downturns. At the same time, changing existing law can take a long time, therefore resulting in a much more stable score for violations in law.

2.2 Sample

Our sample differs from Kucera and Mosley. While these authors worked with a global sample, this was not possible for this research project due to time and resource limitations. Instead, data was collected for only a number of countries, mainly EU member states and all countries that have ratified Free Trade Agreements (FTA) which contain labour rights clauses, based on a recent study prepared for the ILO (2013).[17] Table 2.1

---

[16] The law-categories are: 6, 8, 13, 14, 15, 16, 18, 19, 20, 21, 22, 24, 25, 26, 29, 30, 32, 33, 34, 35 and 37. The practice-categories are: 1, 2, 3, 4, 5, 7, 9, 10, 11, 12, 17, 23, 27, 28, 31 and 36.

[17] This selection is mainly based on the purpose of the wider research project on which this chapter is based, namely the impact of FTAs on the protection of labour rights.

Table 2.1 List of countries included in the sample

Algeria	Cyprus	Jordan	Singapore
Antigua & Barbuda	Czech Republic	Latvia	Slovakia
Argentina	Denmark	Libya	Slovenia
Australia	Dominica	Lithuania	South Africa
Austria	Dominican Republic	Luxembourg	South Korea
Bahrain	Ecuador	Macao (SAR)	Spain
Barbados	Egypt	Malta	Sweden
Belgium	Estonia	Mexico	Switzerland
Belize	Finland	Morocco	Taiwan
Brazil	France	New Zealand	Thailand
Brunei	Germany	Norway	The Bahamas
Bulgaria	Greece	Oman	The Netherlands
Canada	Hong Kong (SAR)	Palestinian Territories	Tunisia
Chile	Hungary	Panama	Turkey
China	Iceland	Peru	United Kingdom
Colombia	Ireland	Poland	United States
Costa Rica	Israel	Portugal	Uruguay
Croatia	Italy	Romania	Venezuela
	Japan		

provides an overview of all countries included in the sample. It is important to note that our sample is biased in that it mostly contains high income countries and almost no least developed or low income countries. Hence, the results, to a degree, apply to the top tier in the class.

2.3 Relationship with Other Human Rights Indicators

As noted in the introduction, several general human rights indicators and indexes exist and have been used in previous studies to assess the protection of human (and labour) rights, such as Freedom House Civil Liberties (FH – CL) and the Cingranelli-Richards (CIRI) human rights indicators. When we compare the FACB index for our sample with these indicators (see Table 2.2) we see that they are correlated, but that these correlations are not that high as to assume that the indicators measure the same thing. This means that countries can score differently on the different indicators and that the FACB index captures different realities than the composite indicator. One could even argue that the overall correlation is rather surprisingly low given that OECD countries are a substantial component of the sample and they skew the correlation upwards since they tend to score

Table 2.2 Relationship between different human rights indicators

		FACB Rights	FACB Rights Law	FACB Rights Practice	CIRI_INDEX WORKER RIGHTS	FREEDOM HOUSE
FACB Rights	Correlation	1	.850*	.845*	.572*	−.554*
	N	2,037	2,037	2,037	1,600	1,622
FACB Rights Law	Correlation	.850*	1	.437*	.511*	−.583*
	N	2,037	2,037	2,037	1,600	1,622
FACB Rights Practice	Correlation	.845*	.437*	1	.460*	−.358*
	N	2,037	2,037	2,037	1,600	1,622
CIRI_ WORKER	Correlation	.572*	.511*	.460*	1	−.601*
	N	1,600	1,600	1,600	1,600	1,539
FH_CL	Correlation	−.554*	−.583*	−.358*	−.601*	1
	N	1,622	1,622	1,622	1,539	1,622

Note: * Significant at 0.01 level.

highly on most indexes. Note also that Freedom House and Cingranelli-Richards do not perfectly correlate.[18]

3. FACB RIGHTS PROTECTION – TRENDS SINCE 1985

Figure 2.1 presents the main results of the data collection and plots the protection of FACB rights over a 30-year period for all 73 countries in the sample (average of all countries per year). The figure shows a clear downward trend on FACB rights over the whole period. The FACB index is scaled 0–10, where 0 represents the worst case (more violations reported), and 10 represents the theoretical maximum of no violations. To avoid differences caused by the different sample of countries, the Mosley index was re-scaled considering only the 73 countries included in our sample.

The average scores for the period 1985–2002 (measured by Mosley) are plotted in black and the average scores for the period 2003–2012 (FRAME) are plotted in light grey. Figure 2.1 also includes three trend lines (linear approximation),[19] one for each period and one for the whole

[18] Note that the negative relationship with the Freedom House indicator is the result of the fact that Freedom House uses a reverse scale in which high scores (range from 1 to 7) indicate a high violation of rights.

[19] Note that the time series do exhibit a degree of non-linearity and there is substantial variation between years. The trend-line aims to capture the overall

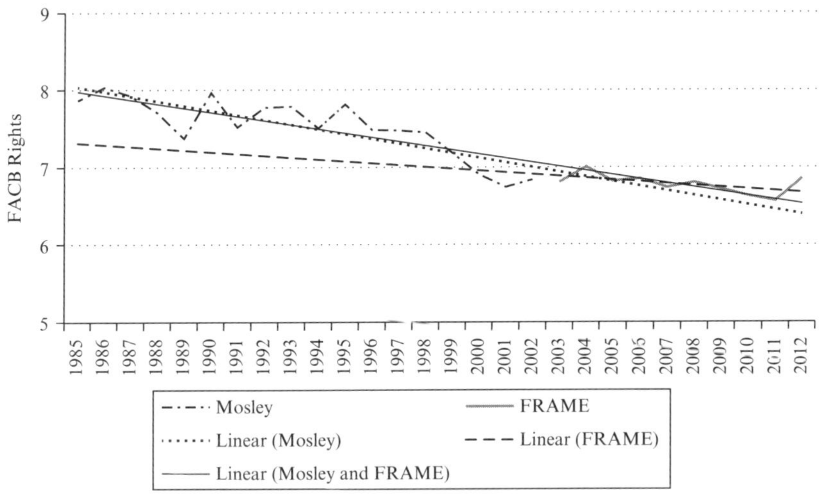

Source: Mosley (2011) 1985–2002 + authors' own calculations 2003–2012.

Figure 2.1 Evolution of FACB protection: 1985–2012

period 1985–2012. Although the negative trend for the period 2003–2012 is less outspoken in comparison with the previous period, the trend for the whole period (thin black line) is clearly negative, indicating that FACB rights are less protected over the last three decades for the average of almost all countries in the sample.

Next, we differentiate the trend between five categories of countries: EU countries, OECD countries, high income non-OECD countries, higher middle-income countries and lower middle income countries, all based on World Bank categorizations (Figure 2.2).[20] We also include the linear trend coefficient to indicate the strength of the trend. Figure 2.2 reveals three interesting facts. First, it shows that the downward trend on FACB rights is independent of the countries' income level, as can be seen by the negative coefficient in all linear equations. Although the EU averages the highest score, their coefficient reveals that FACB rights are decreasing faster in the EU compared to OECD countries (note that there is overlap in membership, meaning that the Non-EU OECD countries

trend over the studied period. Yearly fluctuations would require more in-depth research at the country level.

[20] A t-test on the mean to capture statistically significant differences confirms that the OECD is higher than 'high income non-OECD' mean, and that the mean of these two groups are higher than the mean of middle income countries.

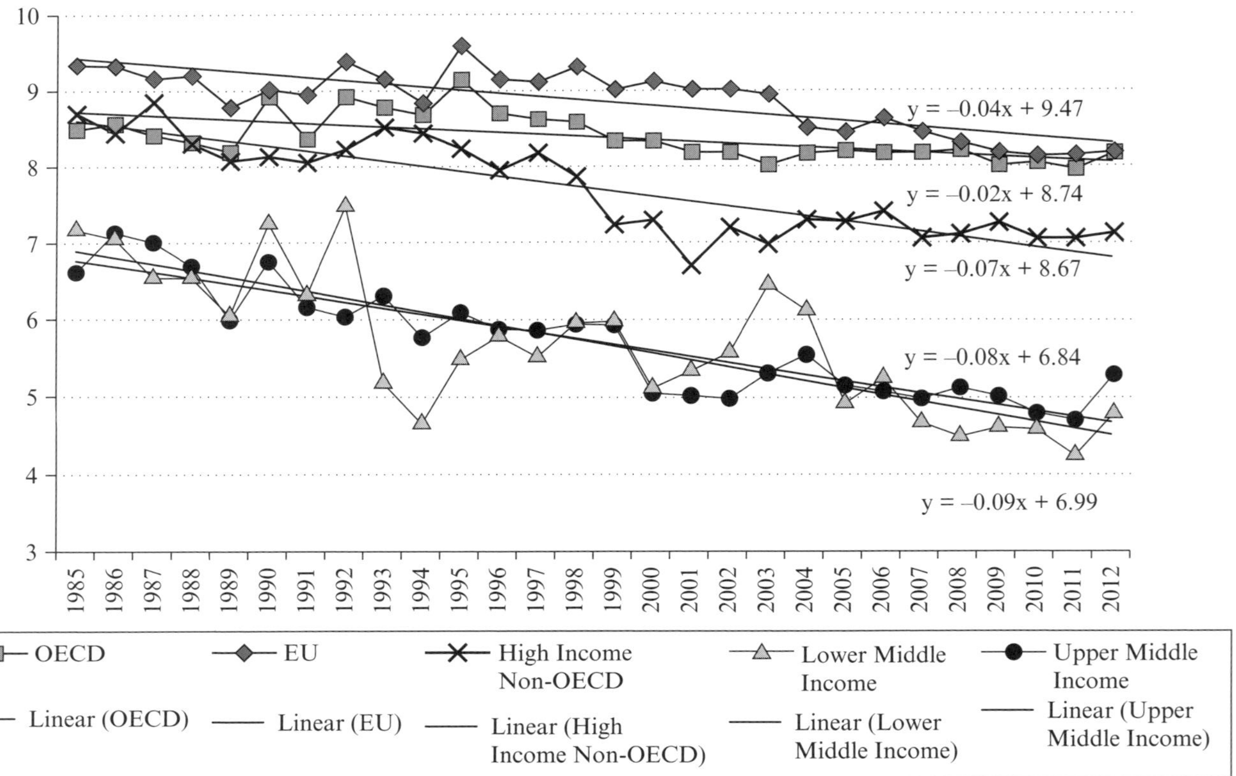

Source: Authors' calculations.

Figure 2.2 Evolution protection of FACB rights by country income level

significantly raise the trend-line to a more stable pattern). Second, the figure also shows that there are substantial differences in FACB rights protection between different groups of countries. The EU and OECD members score highest for the whole period. Other high-income countries that are not OECD members also score highly until the end of the 1990s, but their scores decreased substantially since then. The average scores of lower- and upper-middle income countries are substantially lower than high income countries indicating, as could be expected, that the protection of FACB in lower income countries is lower. Third, while the trends for OECD countries point to stability, decreasing very slowly, trends for lower- and upper-middle income countries shows that FACB rights in these countries have deteriorated much faster, mainly for the group of lower-middle income countries, whose average dropped from 7.2 in 1985 to 4.8 in 2012. The overall trend-line differs as much as four times between groups. This sharp downward trend for developing countries raises great concerns. For these countries the drop in FACB protection is very significant.[21]

We further explore the trends and changes at the country level. The average scores for the whole sample or groupings of countries hide quite substantial variation between countries. Table 2.3 summarizes this data. The first column presents the country; the second column the average FACB index for the period 2003–2012, with the standard deviation in parentheses; the third column the average FACB index for the period 1985–2002, with the standard deviation in parentheses; the fourth column the difference in average scores for the two periods (a plus indicating improvement and a minus indicating deterioration); the fifth column the date of ratification of Convention 87; and the sixth column the date of ratification of Convention 98.

Table 2.3 orders countries from the highest to the lowest average score for the 2003–2012 period. Austria, with an average of 9.9, is the country where FACB rights were most protected during the period 2003–2012. Austria is closely followed by Ireland and Iceland, whose average score is

---

[21] Looking at these downward trends, one should be aware that these negative trends could be, in theory, a consequence of successful efforts made by unions and NGOs to report all sorts of violations in a country, instead of more actual violations. These efforts for more precise reporting would be more relevant in new democracies, in which activists now have more freedom to act, than in stable democracies, where activists were free to report violations during the whole period of our analysis, and where the degree of FACB rights has been more stable and far less dire. However, as Figure 2.2 shows, the downward trend is evident in every type of country.

Table 2.3 Protection of FACB rights: country scores

Country	Average Score (std) 2003–2012		Average Score (std) 1985–2002		Change	Date Rat. C087	Date Rat. C098
Austria	9.9	(0.2)	9.5	(0.5)	0.4	1950	1951
Ireland	9.8	(0.2)	9.8	(0.4)	0	1955	1955
Iceland	9.8	(0.3)	9.6	(0.5)	0.2	1950	1952
Finland	9.6	(0.1)	9.9	(0.3)	−0.3	1950	1951
Denmark	9.6	(0.4)	9.0	(0.5)	0.6	1951	1955
Norway	9.6	(0.0)	9.3	(0.4)	0.3	1949	1955
Sweden	9.6	(0.5)	10.0	(0.1)	−0.4	1949	1950
Netherlands	9.5	(0.3)	9.1	(0.5)	0.4	1950	1993
Luxembourg	9.5	(0.3)	9.8	(0.3)	−0.3	1958	1958
Italy	9.1	(0.7)	9.7	(0.3)	−0.6	1958	1958
Slovenia	9.1	(0.3)	8.9	(1.3)	0.2	1992	1992
Slovakia	9.1	(1.0)	7.8	(2.4)	1.3	1993	1993
Dominica	9.0	(0.5)	9.6	(0.5)	−0.6	1983	1983
France	9.0	(0.8)	9.9	(0.2)	−0.9	1951	1951
New Zealand	8.9	(1.1)	9.0	(0.5)	−0.1		2003
Uruguay	8.7	(0.8)	8.7	(1.1)	0.0	1954	1954
Greece	8.6	(0.8)	8.0	(0.8)	0.6	1962	1962
Barbados	8.5	(0.5)	9.4	(0.4)	−0.9	1967	1967
Portugal	8.4	(0.6)	9.1	(0.6)	−0.7	1977	1964
Malta	8.4	(0.9)	9.0	(1.1)	−0.6	1965	1965
Cyprus	8.4	(1.0)	8.5	(1.4)	−0.1	1966	1966
Antigua and Barbuda	8.3	(0.1)	9.3	(0.4)	−1.0	1983	1983
European Union	8.2	(1.4)	8.5	(1.6)	−0.3	–	–
Belgium	8.1	(0.4)	9.3	(0.5)	−1.2	1951	1953
Israel	8.1	(0.6)	8.1	(1.2)	0.0	1957	1957
Germany	8.0	(0.6)	9.2	(0.6)	−1.2	1957	1956
Hungary	7.9	(0.6)	8.3	(1.1)	−0.4	1957	1957
Estonia	7.7	(0.3)	8.9	(1.4)	−1.2	1994	1994
Switzerland	7.6	(0.5)	9.7	(0.4)	−2.1	1975	1999
United Kingdom	7.6	(0.5)	7.4	(0.8)	0.2	1949	1950
Latvia	7.6	(0.9)	8.6	(1.3)	−1.0	1992	1992
Spain	7.5	(0.5)	8.7	(1.2)	−1.2	1977	1977
Lithuania	7.5	(0.6)	7.4	(1.4)	−0.1	1994	1994
South Africa	7.4	(0.6)	6.3	(2.2)	1.1	1996	1996
Brunei Darussalam	7.2	(0.2)	8.9	(0.8)	−1.7		
Palestinian Territories	7.1	(1.2)	7.6	(0.9)	−0.5		
Japan	7.0	(0.7)	8.1	(0.9)	−1.1	1965	1953
Hong Kong SAR	7.0	(0.6)	7.7	(1.4)	−0.7		

Table 2.3 (continued)

Country	Average Score (std) 2003–2012		Average Score (std) 1985–2002		Change	Date Rat. C087	Date Rat. C098
Belize	7.0	(0.6)	9.0	(0.9)	−2.0	1983	1983
United States	6.8	(0.6)	7.9	(1.2)	−1.1		
Macao SAR	6.8	(0.9)	8.8	(1.1)	−2.0		
Croatia	6.8	(0.4)	7.3	(1.7)	−0.5	1991	1991
Libya	6.5	(0.9)	5.5	(2.0)	1.0	2000	1962
Czech Republic	6.5	(0.5)	6.8	(2.0)	−0.3	1993	1993
Australia	6.4	(0.6)	8.7	(1.0)	−2.3	1973	1973
Poland	6.1	(0.6)	6.3	(1.9)	−0.2	1957	1957
Bahamas	6.0	(1.1)	9.3	(0.6)	−3.3	2001	1976
Canada	6.0	(0.5)	7.6	(0.8)	−1.6	1972	
Tunisia	5.8	(1.0)	7.1	(1.1)	−1.3	1957	1957
Oman	5.8	(1.4)	5.0	(1.8)	0.8		
Argentina	5.7	(0.5)	6.8	(1.8)	−1.1	1960	1956
Costa Rica	5.6	(0.7)	6.1	(1.4)	−0.5	1960	1960
Bulgaria	5.5	(0.6)	6.9	(1.1)	−1.4	1959	1959
Chile	5.5	(0.6)	6.1	(2.0)	−0.6	1999	1999
Bahrain	5.4	(1.4)	4.8	(1.7)	0.6		
Peru	5.4	(0.9)	4.2	(1.6)	0.8	1960	1964
Mexico	5.3	(0.6)	6.1	(2.1)	−0.8	1950	
Romania	5.1	(0.7)	5.2	(1.8)	−0.1	1957	1958
Singapore	5.0	(0.6)	7.5	(1.3)	−2.5		1965
Morocco	5.0	(1.1)	6.1	(1.3)	−1.1		1957
Algeria	4.3	(0.7)	6.8	(1.2)	−2.5	1962	1962
Venezuela	4.3	(0.9)	7.8	(1.7)	−3.5	1982	1968
Colombia	4.2	(0.5)	3.5	(1.6)	0.7	1976	1976
Brazil	4.1	(0.9)	5.8	(1.3)	−1.7		1952
Dominican Republic	4.1	(0.6)	5.9	(1.4)	−1.8	1956	1953
China	4.0	(0.4)	4.3	(1.0)	−0.3		
Jordan	4.0	(0.8)	7.1	(1.1)	−3.1		1968
Taiwan	3.9	(1.1)	6.1	(1.4)	−2.2		
Thailand	3.5	(0.7)	5.6	(1.7)	−2.1		
Panama	3.3	(1.0)	5.0	(1.8)	−1.7	1958	1966
Korea, Republic of	3.2	(0.4)	3.8	(0.8)	−0.6		
Egypt	3.0	(0.5)	4.5	(1.6)	−1.5	1957	1954
Ecuador	3.0	(0.6)	4.4	(1.5)	−1.4	1967	1959
Turkey	2.3	(0.8)	2.2	(1.2)	0.1	1993	1952

9.8, and then by Finland, Denmark, Norway and Sweden, with a score of 9.6. At the bottom of the table, Turkey reached an average score of only 2.3, being the country where FACB rights were most violated during this period. Close to Turkey, Ecuador and Egypt present an average score of 3.0. Surprisingly, the fourth-worst score belongs to an OECD country, the Republic of Korea, whose average is only 3.2.

Table 2.3 clearly shows the significant variation between countries and the fact that some countries' scores are very low. It also shows the divergent dynamics between countries in which some states significantly improve the protection of FACB over the 30-year period (comparing average scores of the two periods), while other countries protect FACB rights significantly less. In 16 countries the protection of FACB rights improved when we compare the 2003–2012 period with the 1985–2002 period, in three countries there was no change and in 54 countries the situation deteriorated. In some cases, such as Jordan and Venezuela, the situation deteriorated very significantly.

The results presented above report on the protection of FACB rights in general and might bias results upward since the measurement includes the protection of FACB rights on paper (legal protection). Several authors have argued that countries sometimes ratify international conventions and adopt legislation concerning FACB but do not respect these rights in practice (Hafner-Burton, 2013; Mosley, 2011; Simmons, 2009). In order to explore this further we make a distinction between protection of FACB in law and in practice and analyse these differences. Figure 2.3 presents the average scores of FACB rights in law and practice for five groups. For all groupings, rights are better protected in law than in practice. Among OECD members, EU member states, and other high income countries, the differences between the protection in law and the protection in practice are small, around 10 per cent, indicating a relatively small enforcement gap. However, the differences between rights in law and in practice are higher for lower and upper-middle income countries, reaching, in some years, 4 points in a scale of 0–10. One explanation for these differences could be, as discussed by Levi et al. (2013), the lack of state administrative and regulatory capacity to enforce contracts and protect rights. Another possible reason is that governments in countries with low regulatory quality and low rule of law can create regulations that they do not intend to respect, as a short-term response to international or domestic pressure (Levi et al., 2013). Note the strong increase in the protection of rights in practice for low middle-income countries in the last year which probably is caused by changes in reporting methods of ITUC.

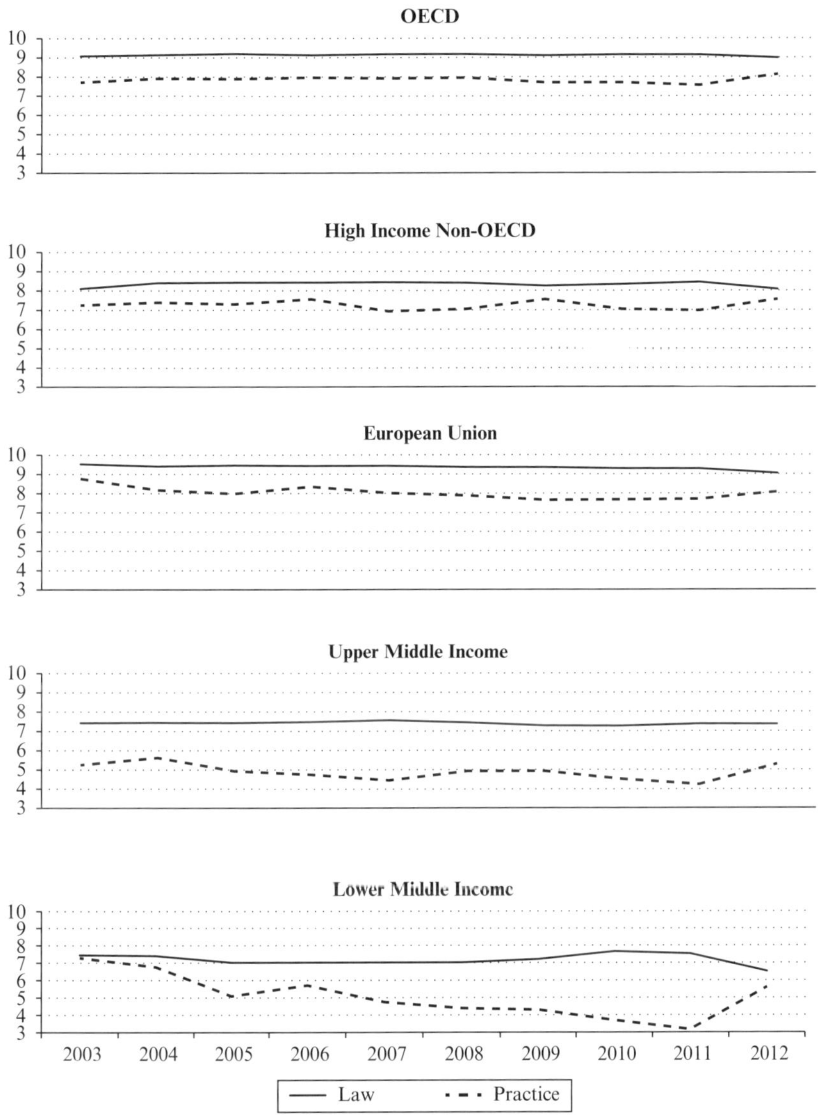

Source: Authors' calculations.

Figure 2.3 Trends on FACB rights protection: difference in protection by law and by practice

4. DISCUSSION

We observe a decrease in the protection of FACB rights. How should we make sense of this evolution? We briefly explore three explanations which can shed light on this development.

A first explanation might be found in the data-collection process. The data on violations is based on *reported* violations in three different sources. One possibility could be that over time more and more violations get reported. This can be the result of several dynamics. First of all this may be due to increased attention paid to the protection of freedom of association and collective bargaining (because they are included in so many agreements, arrangements, etc.), so that awareness is raised and several stakeholders are more likely to report violations. Second, due to developments in information technology and news sharing, stakeholders can more easily report violations. Third, and interrelated, the increase in the number of international NGOs, watchdogs, etc. contributes to better spotting and reporting of violations. Hence, it is reasonable to think that these three factors are contributing to a more accurate and increased reporting of violations, resulting in more reported violations, and not necessarily in a real increase in violations in the countries observed.

However, it should be noted that the way in which the FACB index is constructed the number of violations is not important. It is actually one of the weaknesses of the index. We do not count the number of violations in one country, but whether one violation of one of the 37-item questionnaire occurred. If a violation occurred it is coded as a violation for that item for that country. If in that country many more violations are reported, this will not affect the score. The arguments above mainly influence the reported number of violations but not necessarily the reporting of single violations. With this in mind, the influence of the above three factors might not be too substantial. However, relatively high scores for countries such as Brunei Darussalam might indicate that the measurement could be subject to external influences such as NGOs. The method might under-report violations in countries with low levels of civil society organizations.

A second related explanation focuses on the fact that the observation of an increase in reported violations could be attributed to the fact that in the last decades the number of (international) monitoring mechanisms has increased significantly. This increased monitoring might reveal more violations and hence generate an increase in reported violations. The implementation of the two ILO conventions is monitored via different mechanisms. First of all, the ILO Declaration itself has a follow-up mechanism that requires states that have not ratified the conventions to report on the steps they are taking to ratify the conventions. In addition, the ILO has a Committee of Experts on the Application of Conventions and Recommendations (CEACR), which monitors compliance with ratified conventions. Furthermore, the ILO has three complaint mechanisms, which help to monitor the enforcement of the standards and conventions (Zandvliet and van der Heijden, Chapter 8, this volume). Secondly, in a proliferating number of bilateral, trilateral or multilateral (economic and trade) agreements social clauses that directly refer to the relevant ILO conventions have been taken on board (see contributions by Velluti (Chapter 3) and Brown (Chapter 5) in this volume). In a recent publication, the ILO (2013) provided a full overview and discussion of social clauses in trade and economic partnership agreements. In addition, they identify the monitoring and sanctioning mechanisms for non-compliance. Thirdly, reference to the two ILO conventions can also be found in many other international or regional agreements and conventions such as the International Convention on Civil and Political Rights, the International Convention on Economic, Social and Cultural Rights, the European Social Charter, European Convention on Human Rights, etc. Each has its own enforcement and monitoring mechanism. Some of them are stringent since courts, which can offer binding rules, are linked to these agreements and conventions. As Karen Alter (2014) showed in her recent book, an increasing number of international and regional courts are emerging which use international conventions in their ruling. Finally, one can also observe an increasing number of private regulatory mechanisms which aim to enforce and monitor these rights (Abbott and Snidal, 2009; Marx, 2011; Pekdemir et al., Chapter 10, this volume). Many of these private governance and monitoring systems are diffusing globally. It is plausible that these different monitoring systems contribute to an increase in reporting of violations.

A third explanation for the downward trend starts from the assumption that the trend is real and that we need to understand what drives it. A plausible explanation could be that increased economic globalization and trade openness drives this negative trend.[22] As Mosley and others have argued, trade openness and the need to participate in an increasingly global supply-chain world might put downward pressures on the protection of labour rights. Over the last half century the growth of international trade has been spectacular. With an almost 30-fold increase over 50 years it has truly transnationalized economic activities (Hoekman, 2014). In addition, and more fundamentally, the nature of international trade is changing. As Bernard Hoekman notes:

[22] For an extensive discussion on globalization see Potrafke (2014).

> [M]uch of the recent growth in world trade comprises intermediate inputs, components and services of various kinds. Steadily declining costs of trade and information and telecommunications have permitted firms to geographically splinter their 'production lines', designing international supply chains that allocate different parts of the production process to firms in different countries. International supply chains and production networks are the mechanisms through which this process of specialization is organized, with goods being processed – and value being added – in multiple countries that are part of the chain. (2014, p. 15)

These developments might generate downward pressures on the protection of labour rights. The conventional argument holds that higher labour standards in general will inhibit competitiveness and growth due to increasing costs and reducing flexibility of labour markets. Several dynamics play out here. At the start, labour standards may increase cost and lead to decreased competitiveness (and export). As a result, manufacturing might move from one country to another due to the fact that companies will source from countries with the lowest level of costs. Countries might be played out against one another not to enforce labour standards, especially in a context of short-term ownership and mobility of factories. Within several manufacturing industries some factories, or capital sustaining them, are highly mobile, searching constantly for locations with the lowest input costs (Levi et al., 2013). Hence, as Levi et al. note, 'When challenged by workers forming unions or pressured by MNCs trying to induce compliance with private regulatory schemes, many factories will simply shut their doors without paying severance to workers and re-locate' (2013, p. 22).

These dynamics provide incentives for countries to not strictly enforce standards especially in relation to freedom of association and collective bargaining in order to attract business opportunities. As Levi et al. (2013) identify, states fail to comply with labour standards for at least three interrelated reasons. The first is opposition by state actors to enforce compliance with labour standards. The state may oppose compliance because it would lose some measure of authority, be obliged to expend resources, or no longer be able to promote certain export sectors by ignoring labour standards violations. The second explanation is opposition by private actors who have captured state policy: domestic and multinational businesses may oppose compliance to reduce costs and preserve flexibility. Finally, the state may lack the capacity to implement; many developing countries face 'a severe dearth of the requisite scientific, technical, bureaucratic, and financial wherewithal to build effective domestic enforcement systems' (Chayes and Chayes, 1993, p. 194).

Future research can explore this further. However, it should be noted that when one reviews the literature several domestic and international

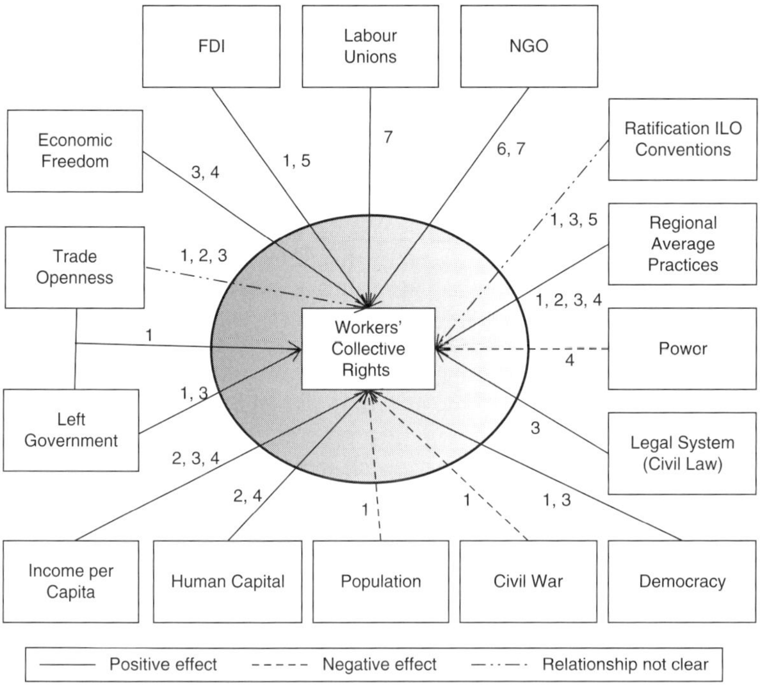

Sources: Based on: (1) Mosley; (2011); (2) Busse (2004); (3) Neumayer and De Soysa (2006); (4) DeLoach et al. (2006); (5) Mosley and Uno (2007); (6) Neumayer (2005); (7) Murillo and Schrank (2005).

Figure 2.4 Determinants of workers' rights protection: summary of the literature

factors which drive the protection of FACB rights can be identified. Figure 2.4 identifies the different explanatory conditions which have been significantly (positively or negatively) associated with the protection of labour rights in the literature. In the figure, continuous lines indicate a positive effect of the variable on the protection of labour rights, while dashed lines indicate a negative effect. The third type of line, which alternates dashes and dots, represents relationships that are still unclear according to the reviewed literature, i.e., while some studies reveal a positive significant effect, others reveal a negative significant effect. The numbers on the arrow refer to the studies in which these effects have been identified. It is clear that many factors influence the protection of labour rights/FACB rights. Additional research needs to further disentangle the different drivers for FACB protection and violations.

5. CONCLUSION

Ten years ago, in 2004, the WCSDG underlined the importance of freedom of association and collective bargaining in order to reach a fairer globalization.

> Labour market institutions, including appropriate legal frameworks, freedom of association, and institutions for dialogue and bargaining are also essential in order to protect the fundamental rights of workers, provide social protection and promote sound industrial relations. Social dialogue is an important component of good governance, and an instrument for participation and accountability. (2004, p. 56, see also pp. 62, 91)

The analysis in this paper showed that the rights of freedom of association and collective bargaining are potentially under stress. Over the almost 30-year period we observe a clear downward trend as measured by our FACB Index. This trend is stronger in the first 18 years but still present in the last ten years. Especially in middle-income countries, the protection of FACB rights is deteriorating significantly. Given the fact that our sample is biased towards high- and middle-income countries this also raises concerns about trends in non-observed countries, especially the least developed countries. The decline in protection is both observed in law as well as in practice. Concerning the former this means that countries are reforming legislation in order to provide less protection of FACB rights.

The discussion of the observed trends, however, also highlighted that these observed trends can be linked to several distinct explanations, some of which point to the way the data is collected. Other explanations focus on the domestic and international drivers of these changes. Future research should focus on these possible explanations and further assess their possible effects.

REFERENCES

Abbott, Kenneth W. and Snidal, D. (2009). 'Strengthening International Regulation Through Transnational New Governance: Overcoming the Orchestration Deficit', *Vanderbilt Journal of Transnational Law*, 42, 2, pp. 501–578.

Alter, Karen (2014). *The New Terrain of International Law: Courts, Politics, Rights*. Princeton: Princeton University Press.

Busse, Matthias (2004). 'On the Determinants of Core Labour Standards: The Case of Developing Countries', *Economics Letters*, 83, pp. 211–217.

Chayes, A. and Chayes, A.H. (1993). 'On Compliance', *International Organization*, 47(2), pp. 175–205.

Cingranelli, David L. and Richards, David L. (1999). 'Respect for Human Rights after the End of the Cold War', *Journal of Peace Research*, 36, 5, pp. 511–534.
Cingranelli, David L. and Richards, David L. (2008). *The Cingranelli-Richards (CIRI) Human Rights Data Project Coding Manual Version 2008.3.13*. Available at: http://ciri.binghamton.edu/documentation/ciri_coding_guide.pdf (accessed 10 January 2014).
DeLoach, Stephen B., Das, Jayoti and Conley, Lindsey (2006). 'Power Politics and International Labour Standards', *International Advances in Economic Research*, 12, pp. 51–66.
Elkins, Zachary, Ginsburg, Tom and Simmons, Beth Ann (2013). 'Getting to Rights: Treaty Ratification, Constitutional Convergence, and Human Rights Practice', *Harvard International Law Journal*, 54, 1, pp. 61–95.
Fransen, L. (2012). *Corporate Social Responsibility and Global Labour Standards*. New York: Routledge.
Freedom House (2013). *Freedom in the World 2013: Democratic Breakthroughs in the Balance*. Available at: www.freedomhouse.org (accessed 9 January 2014).
Gibney, M., Cornett, L., Wood, R. and Haschke, P. (2012). *Political Terror Scale (PTS) 1976–2012*. Available at: http://www.politicalterrorscale.org/ (accessed 14 January 2014).
Hafner-Burton, Emilie M. (2005). 'Trading Human Rights: How Preferential Trade Agreements Influence Government Repression', *International Organization*, 59, 3 (Summer), pp. 593–629.
Hafner-Burton, Emilie M. (2013). *Making Human Rights a Reality*. Princeton: Princeton University Press.
Hoekman, Bernard (2014). *Supply Chains, Mega-Regionals and Multilateralism: A Road Map for the WTO*. London: CEPR Press.
International Labor Conference (2008). *Freedom of Association in Practice: Lessons Learned. Report of the Director-General. Global Report under the Follow-up to the ILO Declaration on Fundamental Principles and Rights at Work*, 97th Session 2008 Report I. Geneva: International Labor Office Available at: http://www.ilo.org/wcmsp5/groups/public/---dgreports/---dcomm/documents/publication/wcms_096122.pdf
International Labour Organization (2013). *Social Dimensions of Free Trade Agreements/International Labour Organization; International Institute for Labour Studies*. Geneva: ILO.
ITUC (International Trade Union Confederation) (2011). *Annual Survey of Violations of Trade Union Rights*. International Trade Union Confederation, Brussels.
Kucera, David (2001). 'Measuring Fundamental Rights at Work', *Statistical Journal of the United Nations*, 18, pp. 175–186.
Kucera, David (2002). 'Core Labour Standards and Foreign Direct Investment', *International Labour Review*, 141, 1–2.
Kucera, David (2004). *Measuring Trade Union Rights: A Country-Level Indicator Constructed from Coding Violations Recorded in Textual Sources*. Working paper No. 50. Geneva: International Labour Office, Statistical Development and Analysis Unit.
Levi, Margaret, Adolph, Christopher, Berliner, Daniel, Erlich, Aaron, Greenleaf, Anne, Lake, Milli and Noveck, Jennifer (2013). *Aligning Rights and Interests: Why, When and How to Uphold Labor Standards*. Background Paper for the World Development Report 2013. Available at:

http://siteresources.worldbank.org/EXTNWDR2013/Resources/8258024-1320950747192/8260293-1320956712276/8261091-1348683883703/WDR2013_bp_Aligning_Rights_and_Incentives.pdf (accessed 13 June 2014).
Marx, Axel (2011). 'Global Governance and the Certification Revolution', in D. Levi-Faur (ed.) *Handbook of the Politics of Regulation*. Cheltenham, UK and Northampton, MA, USA: Edward Elgar Publishing.
Marx, Axel (2014). 'Varieties of Legitimacy: A Configurational Institutional Design Analysis of Eco-labels', *Innovation: European Journal for Social Science Research*, 26, 3, pp. 268–287.
Marx, Axel, Maertens, Miet, Swinnen, Jo and Wouters, Jan (eds) (2012). *Private Standards and Global Governance: Interdisciplinary Perspectives*. Cheltenham, UK and Northampton, MA, USA: Edward Elgar Publishing.
Mosley, Layna (2011). *Labour Rights and Multinational Production*. New York: Cambridge University Press.
Mosley, Layna and Uno, S. (2007). 'Racing to the Bottom or Climbing to the Top? Economic Globalization and Collective Labour Rights', *Comparative Political Studies*, 40, 8, pp. 923–948.
Murillo, V. and Schrank, A. (2005). 'With a Little Help from My Friends? Partisan Politics, Transnational Alliances, and Labour Rights in Latin America', *Comparative Political Studies*, 38, pp. 971–999.
Nardo, Michela, Saisana, Michaela, Saltelli, Andrea, Tarantola, Stefano, Hoffman, Anders, and Giovannini, Enrico (2005). *Handbook on Constructing Composite Indicators: Methodology and User Guide*. OECD Statistics Working Paper, August. Available at: http://www.oecd.org/std/research
Neumayer, Eric (2005). 'Do International Human Rights Treaties Improve Respect for Human Rights?', *The Journal of Conflict Resolution*, 49, 6 (Dec), pp. 925–953.
Neumayer, Eric and De Soysa, Indra (2006). 'Globalization and the Right to Free Association and Collective Bargaining: An Empirical Analysis', *World Development*, 34, 1, pp. 31–49.
Potrafke, Niklas (2014). 'The Evidence on Globalisation', *World Economy*, doi: 10.1111/twec.12174.
Robinson, W.S. (1950). 'Ecological Correlations and the Behavior of Individuals', *American Sociological Review*, 15, 3 (June), pp. 351–357.
Simmons, Beth A. (2009). *Mobilizing for Human Rights: International Law in Domestic Politics*. Cambridge: Cambridge University Press.
World Commission on the Social Dimension of Globalization (WCSDG) (2004). *A Fair Globalization: Creating Opportunities For All*. Geneva: ILO.
Wood, Reed M. and Gibney, Mark (2010). 'The Political Terror Scale (PTS): A Re-introduction and a Comparison to CIRI', *Human Rights Quarterly*, 32, 2 (May), pp. 367–400.

ANNEX 1

Table 2A.1 Kucera's template for measuring FACB rights violations

Category	Description	Weight
	Freedom of association/collective bargaining related liberties	
1	Murder or disappearance of union members or organizers	2
2	Other violence against union members or organizers	2
3	Arrest, detention, imprisonment, or forced exile for union membership or activities	2
4	Interference with union rights of assembly, demonstration, free opinion, free expression	2
5	Seizure or destruction of union premises or property	2
	Right to establish and join union and worker organizations	
6	General prohibitions	10
7	General absence resulting from socio-economic breakdown	10
8	Previous authorization requirements. *Does not include requirements that unions register with governments, unless these requirements are deemed onerous by the ILO*	1.5
9	Employment conditional on non-membership in union	1.5
10	Dismissal or suspension for union membership or activities. *Includes dismissal for strike activities*	1.5
11	Interference of employers (attempts to dominate unions)	1.5
12	Dissolution or suspension of union by administrative authority	2
13	Only workers' committees and labour councils permitted	2
14	Only state-sponsored or other single unions permitted. *Includes allowing only one union per industry or sector*	1.5
15	Exclusion of tradable/industrial sectors from union membership	2
16	Exclusion of other sectors or workers from union membership. *Includes exclusion of public sector workers from union membership. Excluding 'essential services' is acceptable, provided the definition of 'essential services' is not excessively broad (i.e. following ILO guidelines, limitations on armed forces' union membership are acceptable)*	2
17	Other specific de facto problems or acts of prohibition	1.5
18	(No) Right to establish and join federations or confederations of unions	1.5
19	Previous authorization requirements regarding above row	1
	Other union activities	
20	(No) right to elect representatives in full freedom. *Includes requirement that union leaders must work full time in a given industry*	1.5

Table 2A.1 (continued)

Category	Description	Weight
	Other union activities	
21	(No) right to establish constitutions and rules	1.5
22	General prohibition of union/federation participation in political activities. *Includes limits on union contributions to political parties*	1.5
23	(No) Union control of finances. *Includes situations in which unions receive a substantial portion of financing from government sources, or rules that unions may not receive financial contributions from abroad or from certain groups*	1.5
	Right to collectively bargain	
24	General prohibitions	10
25	Prior approval by authorities of collective agreements	1.5
26	Compulsory binding arbitration. *Includes systems in which compulsory binding arbitration is necessary before a (legal) strike may be called*	1.5
27	Intervention of authorities. *Includes unilateral setting of wages by authorities*	1.5
28	Scope of collective bargaining restricted by non-state employers	1.5
29	Exclusion of tradable/industrial sectors from right to collectively bargain	1.75
30	Exclusion of other sectors or workers from right to collectively bargain. *Includes the exclusion of civil servants or all public sector workers. Excluding 'essential services' is acceptable, provided the definition of 'essential services' is not excessively broad*	1.75
31	Other specific de facto problems or acts of prohibition. *Includes 'no legal right' to bargain collectively (but no legal prohibition on doing so)*	1.5
	Right to strike	
32	General prohibitions	2
33	Previous authorization required by authorities. *Includes requirement for official approval prior to strike. A requirement to notify officials prior to a strike is not coded as a violation*	1.5
34	Exclusion of tradable/industrial sectors from right to strike	1.5
35	Exclusion of other sectors or workers from right to strike. *Includes the exclusion of civil servants or all public sector workers. Excluding 'essential services' is acceptable, provided the definition of 'essential services' is not excessively broad*	1.5
36	Other specific de facto problems or acts of prohibition	1.5

Table 2A.1 (continued)

Category	Description	Weight
	Export processing zones	
37	Restricted Rights in EPZs. *Includes export processing zones, free trade zones, and/or special economic zones*	2

Source: Kucera (2002). Weights according to Mosley (2011).

ANNEX 2: SOURCES AND CODING

Sources

The State Department reports are prepared by US embassy personnel, with input from several local and US actors. They then get reviewed by the State Department Bureau for Democracy, Human Rights and Labour with input from other State Department Bureaus and outside experts, after which they are submitted to Congress. The reports cover a range of issues, amongst which are two specific sections on freedom of association for labour organizations and collective bargaining rights.

The ILO's Freedom of Association cases are handled by the Committee on Freedom of Association (CFA). The Committee has nine members, three from each part: governments, employers and workers. If a complaint against a government violating ILO Convention 87 or 98 is lodged, the Committee first looks to see if it is relevant. If it is considered relevant, the Committee then consults with the government for a response. When the Committee finds that a violation has occurred, it finally writes and publishes a report outlining ways to resolve the conflict.

The ILO's Supervising Reports are produced by the CEACR (Committee of Experts on the Applications of the Conventions and Recommendations). It only supervises the conventions a given country has actually ratified (in contrast to the CFA who can accept complaints about countries who have ratified neither 87 nor 98). The CEACR's reports on ILO Convention 87 or 98 come out whenever the Committee makes relevant observations on the country's application of core labour standards.

The last source is The International Trade Union Confederation (ITUC, formerly ICFTU), the largest global trade union federation, which reports on collective labour right violations in almost all countries. These reports, the Survey of Violations of Trade Union Rights, are published annually (although recently changed into a regularly updated blog-format), and are based on information by the ILO, NGOs, member organizations and their own observations. Although this is the source with the biggest potential bias, it is also the most elaborate and detailed one.

Coding

One should take into account that, although following the same methodology, the codification process includes the interpretation of text documents made by different coders. Then, distinct coders could interpret FACB rights violation in distinct ways, resulting in a kind of coder bias. To avoid this problem, beyond following the same methodology as applied by Layna Mosley, multiple coders were used in this task, and, for a random sub-sample of country-years, more than one person codified the same country-year for comparison of results. All issues identified as possible sources for different interpretations were discussed (see below).

In addition, systematic coding differences could arise between our coding and the coding of Mosley. In order to spot systematic differences we correlate our index and that of Mosley with external measures. If differences are systematic, the index should correlate differently with other external measures (Nardo et al., 2005), i.e., if there are significant differences in interpretation between FACB rights codified for the period 1985–2002 and FACB rights codified for the period 2003–2012, these measures most probably would not correlate in the same way with other measures that are not affected by the coders employed in the codification of FACB rights. To check this potential bias, Table 2A.2 presents the correlation of these measures of FACB rights with two other measures of labour rights discussed before: the Freedom House Civil Liberties and the Workers' Rights index provided by Cingranelli and Richards. The correlation of FACB rights with the CIRI workers' rights is 0.60 for the period 1985–2002 and 0.55 for the period 2003–2012. The correlation of FACB rights and civil liberties is −0.55 for the period 1985–2002 and −0.60 for the period 2003–2012. In

Table 2A.2 Correlation of FACB rights and other labour rights measures

	2003–2012	1985–2002
CIRI Workers' rights	.60*	.55*
FH Civil Liberties	−.55*	−.60*

Note: * Correlation is significant at the 0.01 level (2-tailed).

both cases, the correlations with the external indexes with FACB rights before and after 2002 point to the same direction and the differences are not substantial (only 0.05). Based on this evidence, it does not seem that there are systematic coding differences. Consequently, we consider these measures comparable over time.

During the coding process we noted some issues related to coding which we discuss. First, it is not possible in practice to add up the number of observations of different violations within the same category. The sources with which we work are regrettably not as systematically constructed to get an accurate and reliable picture of the complete number of violations that take place. It is, however, possible to get a reliable and valid picture of the different types of violations that occur within a certain country. In this way, a global picture of the labour rights situation in any given country is extracted. To this purpose, when a similar violation was observed several times, these observations still count as one violation. As a result, all violations are coded as being either present (1) or absent (0) (dichotomous). This means that cases in which single, solitary events occur are weighted equally as systematic abuses of the same category. A case in point would be category '2': 'Other violence against union members or organizers'. When for example one employee in Belgium in 2009 was threatened with a knife to step down as a trade union leader, this was an isolated incident. This however clearly constitutes a violation of category 2, and was coded as such. In the same year in Colombia there were numerous reports of (death) threats and structural physical violence by employers towards striking or negotiating employees. This was coded in the same way as the Belgian case, even though in Colombia these violations are more common practice, while in Belgium they constitute an exception.

Secondly, even though Kucera's template is elaborate and refined, and Mosley adds a number of coding notes to the template, problems still arise in practice when the observations and coding starts. Some cases fall in between categories, or do not seem to fit any description. Other observations can be interpreted in several ways. In the spirit of full transparency and consistency, we list below all the problems encountered, and explain how we dealt with them during the coding process.

- Violations in sub-national regions, states, provinces, etc., within countries are coded as violations for the country as a whole (e.g. Canada, reported in ITUC (2011, p. 84)).
- When relevant, and given that there is enough information, (semi-) autonomous regions are observed apart from the country they form a part of (e.g. Macau and Hong Kong with regard to China).

- If a government is a party in a collective agreement (e.g. in negotiations with civil servants) the unilateral changing of terms, negotiable terms, etc. are considered a violation '27' (e.g. Hong Kong, reported in ITUC (2011, p. 139)).
- The requirement to get approval of a negotiated agreement by the government is not seen as a violation (e.g., Brazil, reported in ITUC (2011, p. 83)). The requirement to get approval to start negotiations on the other hand is a violation.
- If a government or a mediator proposes 'binding' solutions to a conflict, but the parties both have the possibility to reject them, it is not seen as a form of compulsory and binding arbitration (e.g., Uruguay, reported in ITUC (2011, p. 114)).
- Threats, death threats and harassment are considered to be a '2' violation ('Other violence').
- Violation '37' (regarding EPZs) is only coded if there are less rights in the EPZs (it is a law-variable, not a practice-variable).
- 'Yellow' or 'Parallel' unions are considered a violation 11. A pro-management union, taking over the position formerly held by an independent union, is a de facto act of interference by the employer (e.g., Mexico, reported in ITUC (2011, p. 103)).
- Blacklisting union members is considered a violation 9, since the list consists of union-members and organizers in order to shut them out of other jobs (e.g., Macau, reported in ITUC (2011, p. 155)).
- If one sector is allowed to have 'workers' councils' instead of unions (e.g. South Korea), it is considered a violation 16.
- If one sector is allowed only one union (e.g., Spain, reported in ITUC (2011, p. 219)), it is considered a violation 17.
- The freezing of union assets after a strike (e.g., Malta, reported in ITUC (2011, p. 316)) is considered a violation 36 due to its direct link with the strike.
- One allowed state-sponsored union confederation, with only semi-autonomous sub-unions (e.g. Jordan, in ITUC (2011, p. 241)) is considered a violation 14.
- A requirement to notify the management of a union meeting, and a cap on the number of hours per year a union can meet during working-hours (e.g. Portugal, reported in ITUC (2011, p. 211)) is not considered a violation.
- In the information for category 16 it is noted that limitations on armed forces' union membership are acceptable. However, the ILO makes an exception for armed forces and the police. Throughout the coding we have followed Mosley's codebook, and have accepted the armed forces as the only limitation on the right to union mem-

bership, instead of the ILO definition. The other 'sector exclusion categories' do not mention the ILO definition, but only speak of 'essential services' not being defined too broadly. Here we have used the ILO definition that it concerns sectors, which have an impact on the immediate health and security of the people and society.

3. The EU's social dimension and its external trade relations

Samantha Velluti

1. INTRODUCTION

In the past decade the European Union (EU) has been at the forefront of attempts to strengthen and promote the social dimension of globalization through trade, focusing chiefly on the promotion of labour standards internationally through increased cooperation with the International Labour Organization (ILO) and through its external trade policies.

The injection of a social dimension in the EU's external trade policy raises many complex questions in relation to competence, coherence, effectiveness and legitimacy of the EU as a global actor. This analysis is particularly prominent and made necessary by fundamental changes introduced by the 2009 Treaty of Lisbon (TL) in relation to the constitutional design of EU External Relations, and in particular the Common Commercial Policy (CCP), as well the conferral of the same legal value of the Treaties to the EU Charter of Fundamental Rights (EUCFR). By injecting a normative approach into its external relations through Articles 3(5) and 21 TEU[1] and, in particular, by including social and environmental goals into its trade policy, the EU is clearly attempting to assert itself as a global human rights actor.

The chapter explores the role the EU has committed itself to in relation to the promotion of social rights and international labour standards in its CCP. In particular, it examines the EU's practice of promoting social standards through the Generalized System of Preferences ('GSP' – in its three main variants, that is the 'general GSP' scheme, the 'GSP +' incentive

[1] For a discussion of normative approaches in EU external trade policy, see Aurora Voiculescu, 'Human Rights, Corporate Social Responsibility and the Shaping of the European Union's Linkage Strategy: "A Peaceful Revolution"?' in Tamara Takács, Andrea Ott and Angelos Dimopoulos (eds), *Linking Trade and Non-Commercial Interests: The EU as a Global Role Model?* CLEER Working Paper 2013/4, 49–64.

scheme, and the 'Everything but Arms' (EBA) scheme) and its bilateral and regional trade agreements. In this context, the chapter seeks to assess the extent to which recent developments at European level indicate an increased commitment of the EU to pursuing social objectives more vigorously, in the broader framework of the EU's 'deep trade agenda', namely the push for further trade liberalization focusing on the removal of domestic non-tariff regulatory measures. The analysis includes a critical review of how labour provisions have been incorporated into trade agreements and the various goals pursued in combination with the mechanisms employed to achieve them. The chapter concludes with some considerations on the future trajectory of social and labour rights in EU external trade relations.

2. THE TRADE–LABOUR LINKAGE

2.1 The Debate

Discussions concerning the nature of the relationship between labour and trade and, in particular, the role played by social policies in the furthering of trade liberalization and what type of trade should be promoted (i.e. should we ensure 'fair' and not only 'free' trade?) both at multilateral and regional levels, has been, to varying degrees, at the centre stage of political and legislative agendas since the early nineteenth century.[2] There are a number of rationales for including labour provisions in trade agreements, namely, social, economic and human rights rationales.[3] The social rationale reflects a concern for safeguarding social protection. The economic rationale is premised on the idea of using labour provisions as tools against unfair competition. The human rights rationale uses labour provisions as a means for ensuring respect for labour-related human rights that reflect values universally accepted by the international community

---

[2] Bob Hepple, *Labour Laws and Global Trade* (Hart 2005), Chapter 2; André Sapir, 'The Interaction between Labour Standards and International Trade Policy' (1995) 18(6) *The World Economy* 791.

[3] ILO, Report on *The Social Dimensions of Free Trade Agreements*, 6 November 2013, 6–7, http://www.ilo.org/global/research/publications/WCMS_228965/lang--en/index.htm (accessed 25 July 2014); see also European Commission, Final Report on *The Use, Scope and Effectiveness of Labour and Social Provisions and Sustainable Development Aspects in Bilateral and Regional Free Trade Agreements*, 15 September 2008, Chapter 2, http://ec.europa.eu/social/main.jsp?catId=89&furtherNews=yes&langId=en&newsId=480 (accessed 10 December 2014).

and also for improving labour standards generally. In the EU context three broad forces have maintained and increased the demand for EU social measures linked to globalization and transnational trade processes: the pace of globalization itself; the risk of trade policy failure, and linked to that, adjustment measures and changes in the institutional framework of key international organizations.

2.2 Labour and the WTO

Attempts to establish the connection between trade liberalization and labour rights during the Uruguay Round (1986–1994), which resulted in the creation of the World Trade Organization (WTO), failed. The quest for a 'social' clause at the WTO had been driven by ethical and unfair competition concerns between industrialized and developing countries as well as concerns for the ILO's limited ability in enforcing its Conventions.[4] It is now well documented that the majority of developing countries have fiercely opposed the proposal of the insertion of a 'social' clause because of the latter being perceived as an expression of veiled protectionism undermining their comparative advantage in terms of labour costs.[5] Renewed attempts in favour of a trade–labour linkage were made at the first WTO Ministerial Conference in Singapore in 1996 without receiving any consensus. Nevertheless, delegates committed themselves to a declaration to observe internationally recognized core labour standards (CLS), accepting that the ILO would be the competent body to set and supervise such standards.[6] At the third WTO Ministerial Conference in Seattle in 1999 the need for a link between trade and labour was once again raised with some suggesting the use of sanctions against those countries violating international labour standards. The EU strongly advocated the promotion of CLS in its trade policy while rejecting the use of labour rights for protectionist reasons.[7] In addition, it also favoured an increased cooperation between the WTO and the ILO and proposed in this context ILO observership at the WTO and the creation of a joint ILO-WTO standing working forum

---

4 Jeff Kenner, 'Economic Partnership Agreements: Enhancing the Labour Dimension of Global Governance?' in Bart Van Vooren, Steven Blockmans and Jan Wouters (eds), *The EU'S Role in Global Governance: The Legal Dimension* (OUP 2013).

5 Hepple (2005), above note 2, Chapter 10.

6 WT/MIN(96)/DEC/Ministerial Conference Singapore: Declaration, § 4, 13 December 1996.

7 Council Conclusions on the third Ministerial Conference of the WTO, 26 October 1999.

on trade, globalization and labour issues. The strong interventionist approach advocated at this conference led to its failure. At the 2001 Doha Ministerial Conference the trade–labour linkage had lost momentum and the Singapore Declaration was merely confirmed. Further, the Council and the Commission became increasingly reluctant to favour a 'social' clause at the WTO because of fears that such a position would hinder the Doha Development Round.

2.3 Labour Standards and Decent Work at the ILO

While the introduction of a 'social' clause in the WTO context failed, the ILO has proven to have further standard-setting powers to ensure compliance with its own conventions' obligations.[8] In particular, the ILO's constitution foresees the setting up of a Commission of Inquiry where an ILO Member State does not fulfil its obligations and in cases of continued non-compliance the ILO's governing body may recommend the imposition of sanctions against the state concerned under Article 33 of the ILO constitution. The procedure was invoked for the first time against Myanmar (formerly Burma) in 2000.[9]

Outside the WTO context, the prominence of the labour dimension to international trade received increased support.[10] This led to the adoption of the 1998 Declaration on Fundamental Principles and Rights at Work to which ILO Member States committed themselves in respect and promotion of four CLS embodied in eight ILO Conventions: (i) freedom of association and the right to collective bargaining (Conventions 87 and 98); (ii) the elimination of all forms of forced or compulsory labour (Conventions 29 and 105); (iii) the effective abolition of child labour (Conventions 138 and 182); and (iv) the elimination of discrimination in respect of employment and occupation (Conventions 100 and 111). Pursuant to Article 2 of the 1998 Declaration, all ILO members must respect these conventions, even when they have not actually ratified them, by virtue of their membership.[11]

---

[8] Francis Maupain, 'Revitalization Not Retreat: The Real Potential of the 1998 ILO Declaration for the Universal Protection of Workers' Rights' (2005) 16 *European Journal of International Law* 448.

[9] Francis Maupain, 'Is the ILO Effective in Upholding Workers' Rights? Reflections on the Myanmar Experience' in Philip Alston (ed.), *Labour Rights as Human Rights* (OUP 2005), 85.

[10] Organization for Economic Cooperation and Development (OECD), *Trade, Employment and Labour Standards: A Study of Core Workers' Rights and International Trade* OECD Publishing, 9 September 1996; OECD, *International Trade and Core Labour Standards* OECD Publishing, 10 October 2000.

[11] All EU Member States have ratified the relevant conventions.

The 1998 ILO Declaration was important in so far as it increased the visibility of CLS conceiving them as fundamental rights, thus providing a key point of reference for their action.[12] As stated by Kenner:

> the more distinguishing characteristic of the CLS is that they have come to be regarded, through a process of meta-institutional iteration, as an élite set of higher human rights norms to be applied under international law irrespective of the traditional method of ratification or an individual country's level of development. . . . The adoption of CLS has revived the notion that labour rights are capable of having a transformative emancipating effect on the lives of individuals and therefore should be promoted centre stage as freestanding universal and indivisible human rights.[13]

Furthermore, the adoption of the 1998 ILO Declaration also contributed to the idea that the implementation of WTO rules must be read in the light of public international law including human rights law.[14] In particular, it could be argued that Article XX GATT, which enumerates the general exceptions that a WTO member may invoke to restrict access to its market, should be interpreted as allowing the restriction of trading goods produced in a manner that violates human rights, including CLS, in order to protect the public morals applicable in the importing country.[15] At the same time, the 1998 ILO Declaration has been subject to criticism also owing to its 'promotional' character and its limited scope.[16] In particular, the CLS are narrower in scope than the labour rights of the EUCFR,[17] which explicitly recognizes freedom of association and collective bargaining,[18] the prohibition of child labour, forced labour and

---

[12] For further analysis, see Kenner (2013), above note 4, 309–310.

[13] Ibid., 310.

[14] Christine Breining-Kaufmann, 'The Legal Matrix of Human Rights and Trade Law: State Obligations Versus Private Rights and Obligations' in Thomas Cottier, Joost Pauwelyn and Elizabeth Bürgi (eds), *Human Rights and International Trade* (OUP 2005), 116.

[15] Lorand Bartels, 'Article XX of GATT and the Problem of Extraterritorial Jurisdiction: The Case of Trade Measures for the Protection of Human Rights' (2002) 36(2) *Journal of World Trade* 353; Carlos Manuel Vásquez, 'Trade Sanctions and Human Rights: Past, Present and Future' (2003) 6(4) *Journal of International Economic Law* 797.

[16] Christopher McCrudden and Anne Davies, 'A Perspective on Trade and Labour Rights' (2000) 3(1) *Journal of International Economic Law* 43, 51–52.

[17] Philip Alston, '"Core Labour Standards" and the Transformation of the International Labour Rights Regime' (2004) 15(3) *European Journal of International Law* 457; Philip Alston, 'Facing Up to the Complexities of the ILO's Core Labour Standards' (2005) 16(3) *European Journal of International Law* 467.

[18] Articles 12 and 28 EUCFR.

slavery,[19] and equality between women and men in all areas, including employment, work and pay.[20]

Soon after the ILO's 2000 Decent Work Agenda (DWA) was adopted, which is based on four pillars: employment creation and enterprise development; standards and rights at work; social protection and labour market governance; and social dialogue. Hence the DWA goes beyond the promotion of CLS. Further to the 2004 recommendation of the World Commission on the social dimension of globalization to make 'decent work for all' a global goal,[21] the agenda has spread to the main international and regional organizations such as the EU. The formation of a strategic partnership between the EU and the ILO in 2004[22] was a necessity not only as a form of defensive collaboration to prevent the retrogression of transnational labour standards but also as a positive engagement to promote an alternative approach to policies of deregulation and privatization that tended to dominate the discourse of globalization.[23] Since then, the ILO's twin agenda for the promotion of its core labour standards (CLS) and DWA has been entwined with the EU's approach to promoting labour rights and social dialogue with reference both to ILO standards and the European social model.[24] The EU's GSP+ special incentive arrangement, examined further below, is illustrative of this EU-ILO collaboration. Recent developments at EU level, such as the Europe 2020 Strategy on Smart, Inclusive and Sustainable Development

---

[19] Articles 5 and 32 EUCFR.

[20] Article 23 EUCFR.

[21] World Commission on the Social Dimension of Globalization, Report on *A Fair Globalization: Creating Opportunities for All*, www.ilo.org/public/english/wcsdg/ (accessed 24 July 2014).

[22] European Commission – ILO, Memorandum of Understanding concerning the establishment of a strategic partnership between the International Labour Organization and the Commission of the European Communities in the field of Development, 17 July 2004, Brussels and 16 July 2004, Geneva, https://ec.europa.eu/europeaid/sites/devco/files/memorandum-of-understanding-ec-ilo-2004_en.pdf (accessed 25 July 2014); ILO, *The ILO and the EU, Partners for Decent Work and Social Justice: Impact of Ten Years of Cooperation*, Brussels, November 2012, http://www.ilo.org/wcmsp5/groups/public/---europe/---ro-geneva/---ilo-brussels/documents/publication/wcms_195135.pdf (accessed 25 July 2014).

[23] Jeff Kenner, 'Shaping the Social Dimension of Globalization? An Analysis of the Strategic Partnership between the EU and the ILO' paper presented at the Labour Law Research Network Inaugural Conference, Barcelona, 14–15 June 2013.

[24] Interview with Marco Ferri, First Counsellor in Social Affairs of the Permanent Delegation to the United Nations Office and other International Organizations in Geneva, 24 May 2013, Geneva, Switzerland.

(*in tandem* with the ILO's 2009 Global Jobs Pact),[25] the 2012 EU Strategy on Promoting Human Rights and Democracy[26] and the 2011 EU Agenda for Change for Development Policy[27] are evidence of a growing support in the EU's internal and external policies and actions for ILO standards and reflect the increasing importance in the EU of decent job creation, social dialogue and social protection for ensuring inclusive growth and sustainable development in the broader context of the global economic crisis.[28]

3. THE EU CONTEXT – UNILATERAL REGULATORY GLOBALIZATION

3.1 The Generalized System of Preferences

In the 2006 Decent Work Communication[29] the Commission maintained that the EU implements the DWA both in its internal and external policies and suggested a number of strategies to ensure that the EU would play an active role in promoting the DWA. In addition, the Communication stated that the EU's GSP with its special incentive scheme for sustainable development (GSP+) was the EU's main instrument to promote CLS.[30] Furthermore, the Commission stated that social development issues would be taken into consideration in trade review exercises as well as

---

[25] Information on the Europe 2020 Strategy is available at: http://ec.europa eu/europe2020/index_en.htm (accessed 25 July 2014); for the ILO's Global Jobs Pact: http://www.ilo.org/jobspact/lang--en/index.htm (accessed 25 July 2014).

[26] Council of the European Union, EU Strategic Framework and Action Plan on Human Rights and Democracy, Luxembourg, 25 June 2012.

[27] European Commission Communication from the Commission to the European Parliament, the Council, the European Economic and Social Committee and the Committee of the Regions, *Increasing the Impact of EU Development Policy: An Agenda for Change* COM(2011) 637 final.

[28] ILO, *Towards a Greener Economy: The Social Dimensions*, International Institute for Labour Studies, Geneva, 2011; ILO, *Building a Sustainable Job-Rich Recovery*, Geneva, 2011.

[29] European Commission, 'Promoting Decent Work for All – the EU Contribution to the Implementation of the Decent Work Agenda in the World' COM(2006) 249 Final; Council Conclusions on 'Decent Work for All' of 30.11.2006–1.12.2006.

[30] This has certainly been the case until 2008 when the EU started adopting a new generation of trade agreements, containing a 'Trade and Sustainable Development Chapter'.

increasing the promotion of Decent Work objectives in the negotiations on bilateral and regional free trade agreements (FTAs).[31]

The EU's GSP is a trade arrangement first set up in 1971[32] (and since then subject to periodical revision) through which the EU provides preferential access to the EU market to a certain number of developing countries and territories, in the form of reduced tariffs for their goods when entering the EU market. To this end, it accords tariff preferences to countries, which fulfil certain economic criteria in terms of poverty and non-diversification of exports. Hence, the first objective pursued by the GSP is to contribute to the growth of developing countries' economies. Secondly, it also aims at improving their political and social situation. In 2005 the GSP+ incentive regime ('GSP+') was set up,[33] offering additional benefits under certain conditions to support vulnerable countries in their ratification and implementation of international conventions, including ILO Conventions. To qualify for GSP+, countries must ratify and effectively implement international standards in the field of human rights, CLS, sustainable development and good governance.[34] The preferences granted by the GSP+ may be withdrawn from the beneficiary if the latter fails to implement the necessary conventions. There is also the special EBA arrangement, pursuant to which the Least Developed Countries (LDCs) receive full duty and quota-free access to the EU market with the exception of arms and armaments. The EU, via these unilateral trade preference schemes, pursues a two-fold objective: on the one hand, it rewards countries that are vulnerable but willing to ratify and

---

[31] European Parliament (EP) Resolution on promoting decent work for all (P6_TA(2007)0206), 23 May 2007. Compared with the Communication the resolution advocates for the adoption of much stronger and concrete measures in order to implement decent work objectives.

[32] Social considerations in the scheme were inserted only in January 1995 when the new EC GSP scheme for industrial products entered into force. Subsequent GSP Regulations have increasingly included the requirement of complying with ILO labour standards and specifically with ILO Conventions No. 87, 9, 138, 29, 105, 100, 111 and 182.

[33] Council Regulation (EC) No 980/2005 of 27 June 2005 applying a scheme of generalized tariff preferences, OJ L169/1. One of the reasons to reform the EU's GSP scheme was the decision handed down by the WTO Appellate body in January 2004 which upheld (albeit for different reasons) the previously established findings of the WTO adjudicating panel concluding the WTO-inconsistency of the EC's GSP scheme. DS246 *EC- Tariff Preferences*.

[34] For a list of the 27 core conventions, see Annex VIII of Regulation (EU) No 978/2012 which has changed the list by removing the 1976 International Convention on the Suppression and Punishment of the Crime of Apartheid and adding the 1992 UN Framework Convention on Climate Change.

implement key international conventions on sustainable development, including human rights and CLS, with additional tariff reductions under GSP+; on the other hand, it will temporarily withdraw GSP preferences in case of serious and continued violations of these conventions. The EU has used its power to withdraw access from beneficiary countries very rarely, and only in response to grave violations of ILO labour standards rather than human rights more generally. In 1997 the Council withdrew GSP status from Myanmar for forced labour practices,[35] which was then reinstated in June 2012.[36] In addition the Council suspended Belarus' access to the EU GSP as of June 2007, further to ILO and European Commission investigations, which revealed serious and persistent violations of the rights of freedom of association and collective bargaining in Belarus.[37]

3.2 Evaluation

The EU has not always applied the GSP scheme consistently. Other countries, such as Uzbekistan[38] and Turkmenistan, which similarly breach labour rights, continue to have access to the EU's GSP scheme. This 'selective human rights conditionality' has led many to question the legitimacy of the EU's role in promoting human rights and ILO labour standards. Many observers argue that the EU not only applies the GSP scheme at its own discretion but also that it uses it instrumentally in order to pursue foreign policy objectives rather than for ensuring the protection of labour rights.[39] More generally, while it is not clear whether the EU's

---

[35] Council Regulation (EC) No 552/97 temporarily withdrawing access to the generalized tariff preferences from Myanmar/Burma, OJ L 85, 27.3.1997, 8.

[36] Regulation (EU) No 607/2013 of the European Parliament and of the Council of 12 June 2013 repealing Council Regulation (EC) No 552/97 temporarily withdrawing access to the generalized tariff preferences from Myanmar/Burma, OJ L 181/13.

[37] Council Regulation (EC) No 1933/2006 of 21 December 2006 temporarily withdrawing access to the generalized tariff preferences from the Republic of Belarus, OJ L 4056/2006, 35.

[38] Under the Uzbekistan Partnership and Cooperation Agreement technical meetings were suspended in response to the Andjan massacre. However, in the Council Common Position there was no reference to the human rights clause, see Council Common Position 2005/792/CFSP concerning restrictive measures against Uzbekistan [2005] OJ L 299/72; see further Lorand Bartels, 'Human Rights and Sustainable Development Obligations in EU Free Trade Agreements' (2013) 40(4) *Legal Issues of Economic Integration Law* 297, 304.

[39] For a discussion of these issues, see Jan Orbie and Ferdi De Ville, 'Core Labour Standards in the GSP Regime of the European Union: Overshadowed by

GSP+ scheme is fully WTO-compliant,[40] its implementation has been subject to criticism because of various GSP+ beneficiary countries having a particularly poor record as regards one or more CLS. In particular, infringements of CLS have often been reported and the EU Parliament has continuously called upon the Commission to monitor more strictly compliance with ILO labour standards and requests for the suspension of preferences in respect of countries that breach fundamental social rights.[41] The effects of withdrawal of GSP+ benefits have varied. For example, in 2009 the Commission opened an investigation into El Salvador, following a judgment of the El Salvador Supreme Court that El Salvador's ratification of ILO Convention No 87 on freedom of association and the right to organize was unconstitutional. The prospect of loss of access to GSP+ benefits appears to have been instrumental in persuading the El Salvadorian government to amend the Constitution so as to render ratification of the Convention constitutional.[42] However, a Commission proposal to withdraw access to the GSP+ from Sri Lanka, further to an investigation which found widespread violations of the 1966 International Covenant on Civil and Political Rights (ICCPR), the 1984 Convention against Torture (CAT) and the 1989 Convention on the Rights of the Child (CRC), was not sufficiently persuasive with the Sri Lankan government to take adequate measures to address the violations identified by the investigation. Sri Lanka was then temporarily suspended from the GSP+ scheme in August 2010.[43] However, the EU's subsidy cut seems to have had little impact on the garment sector of the country as the demand for and thus exports of Sri Lankan garments remain high.

With regard to the EBA, the case of Cambodia's sugar industry illustrates some of the problems associated with this scheme. In the absence of

---

Other Considerations' in Colin Fenwick and Tonia Novitz (eds), *Human Rights at Work: Perspectives on Law and Regulation* (Hart 2010), 487.

[40] In particular, with the Most-Favoured Nation (MFN) principle (Article I:1 GATT).

[41] EP Resolution on promoting decent work for all, adopted on 23 May 2007, Strasbourg (P6_TA(2007)0206, para. 8. EP Resolution on the EU's GSP, adopted on 15 November 2006, Strasbourg (P6_TA(2006)0489, para. 4.

[42] European Commission, Report of the Investigation pursuant to Article 18(2) of the Council Regulation (EC) No 980/2005 with respect to the protection of the freedom of association and the right to organize in El Salvador, C(2009) 7934 (2009).

[43] Implementing Regulation (EU) No 143/2010 of 15 February 2010 temporarily withdrawing the special incentive arrangement for sustainable development and good governance provided under the Regulation (EC) No 732/2008 with respect to the Democratic Socialist Republic of Sri Lanka, OJ L 45/2010, 1.

effective human rights safeguards, Cambodia's policy of granting large-scale land concessions to private investors for agro-industrial development and the EU's policy of granting preferential tariffs to facilitate such investment in LDCs have both had quite a devastating human rights impact: forced evictions and land seizures have been part of the development of Cambodia's sugar industry.[44] The application of the scheme to Cambodia has had adverse effects on the population. An EU Parliament resolution adopted in January 2014 called for the Commission 'to act, as a matter of urgency, on the findings of the recent human rights impact assessment of the functioning of the EU's EBA initiative in Cambodia' and to require exporters seeking to take advantage of EBA privileges 'to testify that they have not evicted people from their land and homes without adequate compensation'.[45] The question is whether this unexpected and unwanted 'side-effect' of the implementation of the EBA in Cambodia would be a violation of an EU obligation. Probably the answer is no given that the EU is only obliged to pursue or promote the objective of, *inter alia*, reducing poverty.

Articles 3(5) and 21(3)(1) TEU require the EU to respect human rights in relation to its external policies and internal policies with external effects. However, it is not clear whether these provisions require the EU also to protect human rights extraterritorially or to fulfil human rights other than in general terms.[46] In these undesirable situations the EU would have to withdraw its preferential treatment to adhere to its ethical normative role, which would be highly unlikely in practice nor could it take coercive steps with a view to enforcing the other country's own obligations in this regard.[47]

The foregoing provides a mixed picture of the GSP scheme. While a mid-term review shows that the GSP has increased LDCs' exports and

---

[44] Inclusive Development International (IDI), 'Bittersweet – Harvest: A Human Rights Impact Assessment of the EU's Everything But Arms Initiative in Cambodia', http://www.inclusivedevelopment.net/wp-content/uploads/2013/10/Bittersweet_Harvest_web-version.pdf (accessed 24 July 2014); International Federation for Human Rights (FIDH), 'Cambodia: Deteriorating Human Rights Situation Calls for Urgent EU Action. A briefing paper prepared for the EU's human rights dialogue with Cambodia, Brussels, March 12, 2014', 5–6, http://www.fidh.org/IMG/pdf/cambodia_deteriorating_human_rights_situation_calls_for_urgent_eu_action.pdf (accessed 24 July 2014).

[45] EP Resolution on the situation of rights defenders and opposition activists in Cambodia and Laos, 16 January 2014, Strasbourg, P7_TA(2014)0044.

[46] Lorand Bartels, 'The EU's Human Rights Obligations in Relation to Policies with Extraterritorial Effects' (2014) 25(4) *European Journal of International Law* 1071.

[47] Ibid.

welfare, that a significant share of the gain accrues to the exporting country, and that countries seeking to benefit from the GSP+ attempt to ratify various conventions,[48] its impact has been limited. Stevens and Kennan argue that this is partially due to the fact that most of the exports from GSP beneficiaries are goods which would not pay any tariff even if there were no GSP since the EU's MFN tariff is zero and it is thus difficult to have an effective preference for these goods.[49] However, in this regard it should also be pointed out that MFN tariffs faced by exporters differ depending on the particular composition of their exports to the EU under a given GSP scheme. For some exported goods, therefore, particularly those products from GSP+ or EBA beneficiaries, the preferential treatment under the scheme does provide a certain level of economic benefit.[50] Another reason is that the GSP arrangements do not provide preferences on all of the remainder, with the exception of the EBA.[51] Added to this, export-led growth strategies might encourage developing countries to curb the process of standard improvement.[52] For these reasons, and because many beneficiaries also have access to other EU trade regimes such as for example FTAs, the GSP is best seen as a 'development safety net'[53] and, in more general terms, the causality between improved labour standards and economic growth remains controversial and difficult to establish.

In 2012 the EU adopted a reformed GSP law with the aim of strengthening the impact of the GSP scheme,[54] which is consistent with the new EU external trade strategy envisioned in the 2010 Communication on *Trade, Growth and World Affairs*.[55] The reform tackles some of the above problems. It reduces the number of beneficiaries to those developing countries

---

48 CARIS, 'Mid-term Evaluation of the EU's Generalized System of Preferences', Report commissioned by the EC, Brighton: Centre for the Analysis of Regional Integration at Sussex, University of Sussex, 2010, http://trade.ec.europa.eu/doclib/docs/2010/may/tradoc_146196.pdf (accessed 25 July 2014).

49 Christopher Stevens and Jane Kennan, *Reform of the Generalized System of Preferences*, Study, Directorate-General for External Policies of the Union, Policy Department, INTA, PE 433. 858, Brussels, April 2011.

50 I would like to thank Lorand Bartels for this counter-point.

51 Stevens and Kennan (2011), above note 49.

52 Jean-Marc Siroën, 'Core Labour Standards, Bilateral Relations and International Trade' (2013), http://www.etsg.org/ETSG2013/Papers/083.pdf (accessed 25 July 2014).

53 Ibid.

54 Regulation (EU) No 978/2012 of the European Parliament and of the Council of 25 October 2012 applying a scheme of generalized tariff preferences and repealing Council Regulation (EC) No 732/2008 OJ L 303/1, 31.10.2012; the revised scheme is in place as of 1 January 2014.

55 COM(2010)612.

most in need[56] and reinforces the incentives in respect of core human and labour rights, and environmental and good governance standards. In addition, the co-existence of different parallel preferential regimes for imports into the EU from the same developing country will no longer be possible. It also reverses the burden of proof on the beneficiary country, which is now under an obligation to demonstrate its compliance with its binding undertakings, and makes the withdrawal mechanism faster and more efficient.

4. THE EU CONTEXT – BILATERAL AND REGIONAL TRADE AGREEMENTS

4.1 A Shift in Focus

Following the failure of including a 'social' clause within the WTO legal framework, the EU has been increasingly relying on bilateral and regional trade agreements to strengthen the social dimension of its external trade relations. The EU made a clear commitment to the promotion of social norms with the 2001 Communication on *Promoting Core Labour Standards and Improving Social Governance in the Context of Globalization*,[57] which also signalled a renewed cooperation between the EU and the ILO to promote CLS internationally through the EU's external relations policies and development cooperation.[58]

Research conducted to date seems to indicate a rather mixed picture and the level of commitment to social norms differs between trade agreements.[59] Van den Putte et al. have identified three main categories of social norms in the EU's international trade agreements: (i) *general social norms* aimed at social cooperation which are for the most part not legally enforceable; (ii) *human rights based norms* such as ILO's four CLS,[60] for which the level of commitment is high; and (iii) *social governance norms*,

---

[56] The number of beneficiaries has been reduced from 176 to 90.

[57] European Commission, 'Promoting Core Labour Standards and Improving Social Governance in the Context of Globalization' COM (2001) 416.

[58] Kenner (2013), above note 4, 312.

[59] E.g. Bartels (2013), above note 38; Lore Van den Putte, Jan Orbie, Fabienne Bossuyt and Ferdi De Ville, 'Social Norms in EU Bilateral Trade Agreements: A Comparative Overview' in Tamara Takács, Andrea Ott and Angelos Dimopoulos (eds), *Linking Trade and Non-Commercial Interests: The EU as a Global Role Model?* CLEER Working Paper 2013/4, 35.

[60] For a list of CLS, see above.

including social dialogue and social protection.[61] The findings of the study suggest that enforceability of social norms, even where the level of commitment is higher, remains weak, although, at the same time, there seems to be an increased reliance on the use of dispute settlement and neutral experts. The analysis that follows uses the above research findings as preliminary points for discussion and evaluation.

Already since the 1990s it has been a policy of the EU that all framework agreements concluded with third countries, such as Association Agreements, Partnership Agreements and Cooperation Agreements, should include a 'human rights' clause [62] which provides that the respect for human rights, democracy and the rule of law constitutes the basis for the agreement and represents the 'essential element' of the agreement.[63] According to the Commission, sanctions under the clause should be reserved only for the most extreme and flagrant violations of human rights.[64] In addition, there is also a 'non-execution' clause stating that in the event that one party fails to comply with its obligations, the other party is able to adopt 'appropriate measures'. This form of unilateral enforcement is well illustrated by Article 8(3) of the 2012 EU-Colombia and Peru Trade Agreement,[65] which provides that 'any Party may immediately adopt appropriate measures in accordance with international law in case of violation by another Party of the essential elements referred to in Articles 1 and 2 of this Agreement'. Specifically in relation to labour issues the agreement requires the effective implementation in law and practice of CLS. One of the main objectives of the agreement was to maintain the provisions contained in the GSP Regulation while making access of

---

61 Van den Putte, Orbic, Bossuyt and De Ville (2013), above note 59, 37 et seq.

62 European Commission, *Communication on the Inclusion of Respect for Democratic Principles and Human Rights in Agreements*, COM(95) 216. One of the first agreements to include such a clause was the 1990 Argentina-EU Framework Trade and Economic Cooperation Agreement.

63 E.g. Article 1 of the 2012 EU-Central America Association Agreement; a database with a list of all the agreements can be found at: http://ec.europa.eu/world/agreements/default.home.do (accessed 25 July 2014).

64 Toby King, 'The European Union as a Human Rights Actor' in Michael O'Flaherty, George Ulrich, Zdzislaw Kedzia and Amrei Müller (eds), *Human Rights Diplomacy* (Martinus Nijhoff 2011) 77, 91.

65 This is the first time that the simplified title of 'trade agreement' has been employed omitting the reference to 'free', which has been used previously in similar agreements such as the one with South Korea. According to the Commission the decision to proceed with a simplified commercial deal was prompted by the decision of two out of four members of the Andean Community, namely Ecuador and Bolivia, to oppose the signature of a traditional FTA (these two countries subsequently withdrew from the negotiations of this agreement).

Colombian and Peruvian products to the EU market easier.[66] According to the Commission, the objective has been met since the agreement has GSP+ equivalent content or above, depending on the specific issue concerning labour and the environment. Arguably, the sustainable development chapter of the agreement goes beyond the GSP+ in some respects.[67] For example, it contains obligations on the effective implementation of, and non-derogation from, domestic labour laws, recognition of the ILO decent work principles and their relevance for trade and labour. It also includes a provision on equality of treatment as regards working conditions, with a focus on migrant workers legally employed in the Parties' respective territories.[68] There is also an 'implementation' clause such as the one contained in the 2012 EU-Central America Agreement providing that 'the Parties shall adopt any general or specific measures required for them to fulfil their obligations under this Agreement'. The exact meaning of this clause is unclear. According to Bartels, 'it could have the effect of imposing on the parties not only a negative duty to ensure that human rights and democratic principles are *respected* but also a positive duty to ensure that these norms are *ensured* and *fulfilled*'.[69]

4.2 Labour Provisions in EU Agreements

Since the mid-1990s, the majority of EU preferential agreements contain provisions on labour standards and cooperation in social affairs.[70] For example, the Preambles of the 1997 EU's Cooperation Agreements with Cambodia and Laos, Yemen and the Former Yugoslav Republic of Macedonia refer to the need to complement economic with social development as well as the respect for basic social rights. The 1999 EU-South Africa Trade, Development and Cooperation Agreement and the 2005 EU-Algeria Association Agreement also refer to the need to respect

---

[66] Roberto Bendini and Dominique Delaunay, *The EU Trade Agreement with Colombia and Peru*, Internal Study, Directorate-General for External Policies of the Union, Policy Department, DG EXPO/B/PolDep/Note/2011_145, Brussels, May 2011, 12.

[67] Ibid.

[68] E.g. Article 276.

[69] Bartels (2013), above note 38, 301(original emphasis). Cf. Article 8(1) of the EU-Colombia and Peru Agreement which makes explicit reference to all authorities and government levels of the Parties.

[70] Full text access to European FTAs and their labour provisions can be found at http://ilo.org/global/standards/information-resources-and-publications/free-trade-agreements-and-labour-rights/WCMS_115822/lang--en/index.htm#P4_728 (accessed 10 December 2014).

fundamental social rights and provide for dialogue and cooperation in social matters. The 2000 Cotonou Partnership Agreement (CPA)[71] occupies a particularly prominent position as both the EU and the African, Caribbean and Pacific (ACP) countries have equally committed themselves to respect CLS and to enhance cooperation in this area, for example through the adoption and enforcement of legislation, while, at the same time, rejecting the use of labour standards for protectionist purposes, as provided in Article 50, the key labour clause of the agreement. Alston criticizes the clause as being merely promotional in nature, reaffirming standards that do not create binding obligations and which may undermine ILO's supervision.[72] According to Kenner, Article 50 should not be viewed in isolation but within the broader context of the agreement's trade and development regime.[73] In particular, the clause 'entrenches the CLS within the partnership as recommended by the World Commission on the Social Dimension of Globalization (WCSDG)' and specifically states that the objectives of the ILO can be best achieved with the cooperation of certain regional actors and through transposition into the CPA of those obligations stemming from the 1998 ILO's Declaration, which in turn are 'subject to the oversight of the parties and coordinated action under the EU-ILO strategic partnership'.[74] In addition, the CPA provides for the use of dispute settlement in relation to the interpretation and application of their human rights clauses, including appropriate measures adopted under these clauses.[75] However, with the exception of Article 50 of the CPA, social norms in EU agreements seem to be included as objectives to be achieved rather than enforceable legal commitments as they do not provide for genuine enforcement mechanisms.

The principle of sustainable development is a case in point. As Bartels points out 'it is notable that the principle of sustainable development has never been treated as a concrete obligation in itself: none of the agreements admit the possibility of violating the principle of sustainable development'.[76] The agreements contain provisions on cooperation and obligations to respect and 'strive' to improve multilateral and domestic

---

71 The CPA has been revised twice: in 2006 and 2010.

72 Alston (2004), above note 17, 511.

73 Kenner (2013), above note 4, 316.

74 Ibid.

75 Cf. the EU-Central America Association Agreement, which provides that an affected party can request that an urgent meeting be called to bring the Parties together within 15 days for a thorough examination of the situation with a view to seeking a solution acceptable to the Parties, see Article 355(5).

76 Bartels (2013), above note 38, 306.

labour and environmental standards.[77] In particular, a first set of obligations contain minimum obligations to implement certain multilateral obligations and other obligations which require the parties to the agreement not to reduce their levels of protection and encouraging them to raise their levels of protection, subject to a proviso that this is not done for protectionist purposes.[78] Since the mid-1990s, sustainable development has become increasingly important in the EU's trade policy,[79] and the TL has elevated it to one of the key principles underlying EU external action.[80]

This overarching legal commitment has been given further effect with the adoption of a so-called 'new generation' of FTAs containing a 'trade and sustainable development' chapter, which includes provisions for the respect of labour and environmental standards. Examples of such agreements are the 2010 EU-Korea FTA,[81] the 2012 EU-Central America Agreement and the 2012 EU-Colombia/Peru Agreement. The 2013 EU-Singapore FTA (which is awaiting ratification) also contains such a chapter.[82] The 2008 EU-CARIFORUM agreement is worthy of mention as it is the first economic partnership agreement (EPA) concluded with a regional group.[83] It refers to the DWA and CLS and the clauses are worded in such a manner as to suggest that there is also reference to labour rights rather than merely standards or principles. It also contains a commitment by the signatory parties that they will not lower their domestic

---

[77] For further analysis, see Lorand Bartels, 'Social Issues: Labour, Environment and Human Rights' in Simon Lester and Bryan Mercurio (eds), *Bilateral and Regional Trade Agreements* (CUP 2009), 342.

[78] Bartels (2013), above note 38, 307–309.

[79] The first of the EU's agreements to make reference to the principle of sustainable development was the 1993 EU-Hungary Europe Agreement, Bartels (2013), above note 38, 306.

[80] Article 21(2)d and (3) TEU.

[81] It entered into force in July 2011 and it is the EU's first trade agreement with an Asian country. It is also the first completed agreement in a new generation of FTAs launched by the EU in 2007 as part of its strategy to create 'deep and comprehensive' free trade agreements (DCFTA) with selective partners following the Doha round stand-still at the WTO. On this point see, Frank Hoffmeister, 'The European Union as an International Trade Negotiator' in Joachim Koops and Gjovalin Macaj (eds), *The European Union as a Diplomatic Actor* (Palgrave Macmillan 2014), Chapter 9.

[82] It is the first bilateral agreement concluded by the EU with an ASEAN (Association of Southeast Asian Nations) country, and it will probably provide the blueprint for future bilateral agreements with other ASEAN countries.

[83] The regional group comprises 15 Caribbean countries: Antigua and Barbuda, Bahamas, Barbados, Belize, Dominica, Dominican Republic, Grenada, Guyana, Haiti, Jamaica, St Lucia, St Vincent and the Grenadines, St Kitts and Nevis, Suriname, Trinidad and Tobago.

labour standards to attract foreign direct investment (FDI),[84] and it has a separate chapter on the social aspects of trade.[85] Another innovative feature of this EPA is, firstly, the setting up of the Joint Council, which has 'the power to take decisions in respect of all matters covered by the Agreement'.[86] Secondly, the EPA provides for a consultation and monitoring process, under which each party may request consultations on the interpretation and application of the social clauses in the agreement, with an advisory role for the ILO.[87] The agreement also envisages that in the event of continued disagreement a Committee of Experts may be convened.[88] In general terms, while there is some variation between the provisions contained in the different agreements, there seems to be some level of commonality as to the substantive standards and the institutional set-up envisaged. The increased involvement and influence of the EU Parliament in the conclusion of trade treaties further to the changes introduced by the TL is pivotal to this development, and for a number of years it has been calling for the practice and policy developed in the context of cooperation and association agreements containing chapters on human rights to be extended to 'pure' trade agreements.[89]

While these are significant features of the 'new generation' of trade agreements, which contribute to injecting a social dimension in the EU's trade policy, it remains to be seen – in the absence of actions resulting in sanctions against the other party – whether they entail an improvement of the implementation capacity of developing countries to respect and protect labour standards and thus lead to an effective improvement of labour standards internationally. Some proposals to improve the effectiveness of labour provisions in trade agreements have been put forward. For example, developing and adding time-bound labour-related objectives to trade agreements has been suggested, to involve greater consultation of social partners and civil society in the negotiations and implementation of labour provisions, to ensure better coherence in the way ILO instruments are included in the various trade agreements,[90] and to provide for

---

84 Article 72.

85 Articles 191–196.

86 Article 229(1) of the EU-Cariforum EPA.

87 Article 195.

88 Ibid.

89 EP Resolution of 25 November 2010 on human rights and social and environmental standards in international trade agreements, P7_TA(2010)0434, § 12; EP Resolution of 27 September 2011 on a new trade policy for Europe under the EU 2020 strategy, P7_TA(2011)0412, § 6.

90 ILO (2013), above note 3, Chapter 4; see also Lorand Bartels, 'A Model Human Rights Clause for the EU's International Trade Agreements' German

a mechanism for reviewing the implementation of agreements in accordance with human rights norms, on the basis of a human rights impact assessment.[91] The US-Cambodia Textile Agreement[92] is often mentioned as an effective model for including labour provisions in FTAs and, in particular, as providing an incentive mechanism for so-called 'positive sanctions'. The agreement established that US import quotas would be increased on an annual basis in relation to progress on improving labour practices, and thus companies that fulfilled their undertakings would be rewarded fairly quickly. This provided incentives for the private sector and the Cambodian authorities to make an effort to improve labour standards in the textile sector. Siroën argues that such a system of positive sanctions could be introduced and applied more generally in trade agreements targeting companies, rather than the industry or country concerned as a whole. Incentive mechanisms in the form of additional preferences should promote improved practices and prevent undesirable effects, such as companies or workers moving into the informal economy.[93]

5. CONCLUSION

With the TL, human rights, labour standards, the environment, and corporate and global governance have become sources of normative negotiations and legal transplants that aim at changing the normative paradigm in international economic law.[94]

However, questions of coherence in the EU's external action remain, which are a reflection of the internal landscape of the EU where Member States do not offer a uniform socio-economic and political context for the trade–labour linkage. For instance, no Member State has acceded to the 1990 UN Convention on the Rights of All Migrant Workers and some Member States do not fully comply with ILO Conventions. This buttresses the legitimacy concerns voiced by many commentators as

---

Institute for Human Rights, Misereor, February 2014, http://www.institut-fuer-menschenrechte.de/uploads/tx_commerce/Studie_A_Model_Human_Rights_Clause.pdf (accessed 10 December 2014).

[91] James Harrison and Alessa Goller, 'Trade and Human Rights: What Does 'Impact Assessment' Have to Offer?' (2008) 8 *Human Rights Law Review* 587.

[92] Signed in January 1999 for a three-year period, and then extended for a further three years, the textile agreement between the US and Cambodia expired in January 2005.

[93] Jean-Marc Siroën, 'Labour Provisions in Preferential Trade Agreements: Current Practice and Outlook' (2013) 152(1) *International Labour Review* 85, 98.

[94] Voiculescu (2013), above note 1, 50–51.

well as developing countries in relation to the EU's purported role as a global human rights actor, indicating that these concerns are not without foundation.[95]

In addition, the reliance on a hybrid combination of tools strongly affects the actual effects of the EU's external action. As noted by King, 'human rights diplomacy is an inherently paradoxical concept, mixing together the absolutes of legal claims to rights with the nuances and ambiguities of diplomacy'.[96] Bartels also questions the desirability of the existing distinction between the human rights clauses found in cooperation and association agreements and the obligations stemming from the sustainability chapter in the new generation of trade agreements, particularly in light of the fact that ILO CLS are considered fundamental human rights and are covered by the human rights clauses.[97] The inevitable overlap between these different sets of provisions has negative repercussions in terms of countries' (non-)compliance and for identifying the appropriate measure to be applied.

The foregoing calls for a more comprehensive and coherent approach to linking trade and human rights.[98] Since the TL, the 'duty of consistency' features prominently in the Union's constitutional texts[99] and it can be conceived as a general principle of EU law applicable to all areas of EU external action.[100] However, translating the concept of coherence 'into *specific legal obligations* is not straightforward [also because] the case law of the Court of Justice (CJEU) is scarce and lacks concretization'.[101]

---

[95] For discussion, see Grainne de Búrca, 'The Road Not Taken: The EU as a Global Human Rights Actor' (2011) 105 *American Journal of International Law* 649.

[96] King (2011), above note 64, 100.

[97] Bartels (2013), above note 38.

[98] Leonhard den Hertog and Simon Stroβ, 'Coherence in EU External Relations: Concepts and Legal Rooting of an Ambiguous Term' (2013) 18(3) *European Foreign Affairs Review* 373, 376; Christophe Hillion, '*Tous pour un, un pour tous!* Coherence in the External Relations of the European Union' in Marise Cremona (ed.), *Developments in EU External Relations Law* (OUP 2008), 10.

[99] Article 21(3), second subpara. TEU; see also Article 13(1), 16(6), second and third subparas, Article 18(4), 26(2), second subpara. TEU and Article 7 TFEU.

[100] Federico Casolari, 'The Principle of Loyal Co-operation: A "Master Key" for EU External Representation?' in Steven Blockmans and Ramses A. Wessel (eds) *Principles and Practices of EU External Representation* CLEER Working Papers 5/2012 11, 13.

[101] Den Hertog and Stroβ (2013), above note 98, 378.

King has put forward a series of concrete proposals,[102] such as extending the condition of a partner country ratifying and implementing core human rights conventions to all EU trade agreements (and not only GSP+), developing new human rights impact assessment methodologies, establishing a policy to regulate the export of goods which can be used for repressive purposes from the EU to authoritarian countries, as well as adopting a coherent approach to the regulation of the import of goods made by prison, slave or child labour or from conflict zones. The underlying assumption on which these proposals are based is that they presume or require the existence of a single voice in the EU, which still remains an aspiration rather than an achieved goal.[103] While the TL has provided the framework and the legal tools to achieve coherence,[104] the latter is and remains essentially a policy imperative, which largely depends on the political will of the Member States and the EU Institutions. As Muižnieks pithily puts it, 'despite the new legal and political framework . . . human rights in the EU remain more often than not an issue "for export" than for domestic consumption'.[105] Hence, in terms of EU practice much remains to be done.[106]

---

[102] King (2011), above note 64, 93–94.

[103] The case of trade agreements being a case in point. Interview with Frank Hoffmeister, Deputy Head of Cabinet in Commissioner Karel De Gucht's Cabinet (International Trade) of 5 June 2013, Brussels, Belgium.

[104] Jan Wouters and Thomas Ramopoulos, 'Revisiting the Lisbon Treaty's Constitutional Design of EU External Relations', Leuven Centre for Global Governance Studies, Working Paper No. 119, September 2013.

[105] Nils Muižnieks, 'Talk about Human Rights in the EU', *European Voice*, 5 December 2013, 15.

[106] EP Report on Human Rights and Social and Environmental Standards in International Trade Agreements, Committee on International Trade, Rapporteur: Tokia Saïfi (2009/2219(INI)).

4. Divided we stand: the European Parliament's position on social trade in the post-Lisbon era

Lore Van den Putte

1. INTRODUCTION

Linking trade to social norms was a very controversial issue, especially in the 1990s (Waer, 1996, p. 25) and it remains so today. Also within the EU, linking social norms to trade (which we call 'social trade') has long been contested. Since the end of the 1990s, however, the EU has increasingly been seen as an international promoter of social norms, and the importance of the European Parliament (EP) in pushing this process forward has often been stressed (Orbie, Vos, & Taverniers, 2005; Waer, 1996). Already since the 1970s the EP has stood on the barricades for social trade (Orbie et al., 2005). It was even the driving force for taking up social norms in the World Trade Organization (WTO) (Waer, 1996), with resolutions in 1983 and 1986 asking for a provision in the GATT for members to expect the other three Core Labour Standards (CLS)[1] (Charnovitz, 1987). Unilaterally it has also included social norms as part of the eligibility criteria for the Generalized System of Preferences Plus (GSP+). The fact that the EU eventually reached a common position on the inclusion of social norms in its trade policy is, among other things,[2] the result of the 'Sainjion report' in 1994, which was requested by the EP and on the basis of which it called for a social clause in both the GATT/WTO context and in unilateral trade policies (Burgoon, 2004; European Parliament, 1994a, 1994b). Also the change of governments in Germany and the UK from centre-right to centre-left, contributed to

[1] Prison labour was already included in the GATT as a possible ground to discriminate against a trade partner, thereby closing one's market for goods produced by such labour.

[2] Another reason was a general fear in Europe about a deterioration of social protection (Hafner-Burton, 2009, p. 74).

a more favourable position in the EU towards social trade (Orbie et al., 2005, p. 173).

The high number of EP resolutions (partly) dealing with this topic show that Members of the European Parliament (MEPs) have continuously attached a great deal of importance to the promotion of social trade.[3] Since 1 December 2009, the influence of the EP on trade policy has been enhanced with the entry into force of the Lisbon Treaty, which has considerably changed the environment in which the EP works on trade. Not only do Free Trade Agreements (FTAs) now require the consent of the EP (art. 218(6)(a) TFEU), but the EP is now also a co-legislator together with the Council on EU trade policy (art. 207(2) TFEU). Furthermore, the Lisbon Treaty brought trade policy under the umbrella of external policy (art. 207 (1) TFEU), which in practice means that EU trade should be consistent with values such as sustainable development, human rights and fair trade. Based on these two Treaty changes, scholars have expected the EP to push even more[4] for social trade (Bungenberg, 2010; Devuyst, 2013; Hillman & Kleimann, 2010; Meunier & Nicolaïdis, 2011; Richardson, 2012).

Several of these scholarly expectations and assumptions seem to have materialized in practice, as can be derived from some concrete examples. In the trade agreement with Colombia, a country in which trade union rights are gravely violated, the EP demanded a road map to accompany the agreement in order to safeguard these rights and human rights in general (European Parliament, 2012b). With regard to the trade negotiations with India, the EP is pressing for legally binding clauses on human rights, social and environmental standards and for enforceable mechanisms (European Parliament, 2011) even though it is very well aware of India's reluctance to include social norms in a bilateral trade agreement (given their strong opposition in the WTO). While these are just illustrative examples, they seem to confirm the expectations raised in the literature and thus it seems justified to depart from the assumption that the EP devotes a lot of attention to social norms in its trade policy.

However, the question why the EP is such a strong supporter of linking social norms to EU trade policy has so far not been examined. While some studies dealing with social trade within the EU also touch upon the EP's stance (see, among others, Waer, 1996), these largely regard the EP as a monolithic actor.[5] Orbie et al. (2005) are an exception in the

---

3 An overview of these resolutions can be obtained from the author.

4 Note that we do not compare the position of the EP before and after Lisbon.

5 With the exception of Hafner-Burton (2009), but since her book focuses on the link between human rights and trade, we cannot assume that the same holds for social norms (with the CLS as a specific kind of human rights) and trade.

sense that they argue that while the EP has favoured a social clause since the 1970s, this support diminished with the European People's Party (EPP) ending the centre-left dominance in 1999. However, this argument has never been investigated more thoroughly. In contrast, it has often been highlighted that before the end of the 1990s a large discrepancy existed between centre-left governments in favour of a social clause and centre-right governments opposed to it. It is even argued that the coming into power of Labour in the UK and the SPD and the Greens in Germany were of crucial importance for a common EU position on the issue (Orbie et al., 2005, p. 173). While more conservative governments have in general not been very supportive of the inclusion of workers' rights in EU trade agreements, socialist and labour governments have been in favour of linking both (Hafner-Burton, 2009, pp. 70–83). There are no compelling reasons to expect a different pattern in the EP. On the contrary, one would expect views in the EP to differ even more than in the Council given that the EP is composed of political groups with very diverse ideologies.[6]

Interestingly, our research shows that debate in the EP has focused more on how social norms should be included in trade agreements, rather than on why. Indeed, little to no debate in the EP has been devoted to why social norms as such should be included in EU trade agreements.[7] Social trade seems to be a taken-for-granted issue among a large majority within the EP. This chapter therefore takes up the task of exploring the following question: How can we explain the broad consensus in the EP to include social norms in trade policy? We argue that while it is indeed true that the EP as a whole is strongly in favour of a social clause, different ideas lie beneath this policy consensus. And it is exactly these different interpretations which explain the current success of the concept of social trade within the EP. The notion of social trade is a storyline around which coalitions in the EP unite (Hajer, 1995, pp. 8–41). While at first sight these coalitions might share the same thoughts about the 'problem', a closer look reveals that they have different interpretations of it, which also connects to their respective social and cognitive commitment to it. On a

---

[6] Given that the EP is seen as a hatchery for a whole range of frames, we believe that the frames identified in the EP debates could also be present in discussions in other organizations such as the US Congress or lobby groups. At the same time, however, this does not preclude that other frames could exist within these institutions. In this regard this study could be the starting point for frame detection in other contexts.

[7] Surprisingly there also seems to be no debate as such about the (non-) enforceability of social trade and what should be done in case of a violation.

deeper level, the discourse on social trade reveals even more contradictory interpretations. We explicitly argue that the coalition of social trade is only kept together because its storylines are vague. People taking part in the storyline assume that there is some mutual understanding, while in reality this might not be the case (Hajer, 2006). This kind of situation can be very useful for building a political coalition, as Mathieu and Weinblum (2013) have already convincingly shown in their work on trade-defence instruments in the EP.

This research, therefore, aims to unveil the different conceptions behind the social emphasis of the EP. Since the EP functions along political lines, and views are expected to differ between the political groups, our analysis will consist of a stocktaking of the positions of the different political groups on this topic. First, it could explain why European centre-right political actors, who used to be very reluctant to include social norms in trade policy, are now in favour. While it is true that a consensus on this issue was facilitated by the coming into power of centre-left governments in Germany and the United Kingdom (Orbie et al., 2005, p. 165), this cannot explain why the consensus still exists in a constellation with a centre-right majority, both in most European countries and in the EP. By unveiling the frames used by centre-right politicians, this could also explain why there seems to be currently no opposition from this political spectrum to the inclusion of social norms. Secondly, given that the EP is a forum for the wide range of ideologies that exist in Europe, the analysis could also shed light on the discourse in the whole EU. Thirdly, the external legitimacy of the EP is at stake. If the protectionist frame is often used within the EP, it might undermine the European Commission's efforts to include social norms in an agreement with a country like India. Fourthly, in light of the 2014 EP elections, our analysis could also shed light on the general faith of social norms in the new EP and in particular on discussions on the labour part in a possible trade deal with the United States. Filling this void in the literature is even more compelling now because the EP is only now becoming a fully-fledged actor in EU trade policy.

This chapter consists of four further sections. In section 2 we review the literature on the different frames used in the discussion on social trade. In section 3 we explain our choice of Critical Frame Analysis (CFA) and justify why we have selected certain resolutions and legislative files and not others. In section 4 we then analyse the position of the political groups on these issues by connecting them to a certain frame. Section 5 discusses the results.

2. DIFFERENT JUSTIFICATIONS FOR SOCIAL TRADE

Ahead of the analysis, we should clarify what we understand by the term 'social norms', which we have defined in a previous paper (Van den Putte, Bossuyt, Orbie, & De Ville, 2013). Social norms are understood as comprising the four Core Labour Standards (CLS) as put forward by the International Labour Organization (ILO), and the so-called 'social governance norms', which consist of social dialogue and social protection.[8]

In exploring the frames the political groups in the EP use to justify the (non-)inclusion of social norms in trade, we follow the definition of Verloo, who defines a frame as an 'organising principle that transforms fragmentary or incidental information into a structured and meaningful problem, in which a solution is implicitly or explicitly included' (Verloo in Meier, 2008, p. 155). For the purpose of our chapter, we make a distinction between one group of major frames and two groups of minor frames. The group of major frames concern whether there should be a link between trade and social norms or not. This group is termed major because it concerns the fundamental question of whether EU trade policy should be concerned about social norms at all. The first group of minor frames concerns whether social norms are human rights or an element of economic competitiveness. The second group of minor frames relates to the question of whether economic development leads to social improvement or whether both should be advanced in harmony.

2.1 Is the Link between Social Norms and Trade Necessary and Desirable?

This research assumes that there is a broad majority within the EP in favour of social trade, given that it is often reflected in parliamentary resolutions and legislative files. However, the link between (EU) trade and social norms cannot be taken for granted. On this link, two major diverging frames concerning the link between both can be found in the literature. On the one hand, social norms can be regarded as an issue which should be dealt with in trade policy (being a **trade issue**). Proponents of this view also adhere to the universality of core labour rights/standards (Brown, 2001). On the other hand, social norms can be seen as a **non-trade issue**, something which should not be part of a trade agreement because it has nothing to do with trade liberalization. Those arguing against a social clause also deny the

---

[8] However, most efforts of MEPs focus on the CLS.

universality of those labour standards included in a social clause because of their biased nature. Critics such as Bhagwati argue that child labour is often proposed to be included (an issue which only affects developing countries), while union rights (where some developed countries also might have problems) are not included (Bhagwati, 1995, p. 756).[9] This sharp distinction has always underpinned the discussion on social norms at the multilateral level and is now also echoed at the bilateral level. As explained earlier, most of the opponents' reactions stem from the fear that a social clause could be used for protectionist actions against goods produced in developing countries. Others opposing the inclusion of a social clause in trade argue that it is a matter of domestic sovereignty (Brown, 2001, p. 103).

2.2 Social Norms as Process Standards or as Human Rights?

The first group of minor frames concern the nature of social norms themselves. In general, two views on this topic can be distinguished (Bhagwati, 1995), one being what we call the process standard or **competitiveness frame**, and the other being the **human rights frame**. According to the first, labour *standards* (note that we call it 'standards') need to be included in trade agreements because otherwise less developed countries could produce goods at lower costs so that they have a competitive advantage. Actors using this frame might fuel developing countries' suspicion of protectionist motivations by the developed countries. According to the second more value-related argument, labour *rights* (!) are universal and they need to be respected in the production process, otherwise this is immoral and illegitimate (an argument set out but not supported by Bhagwati (1995, p. 754)).

Note that their mere description as 'labour standards' or 'labour rights' is not innocent or just descriptive, as Diez rightly pointed out with regard to words used in EU discourse in general (Diez, 1999, p. 602). By describing them as standards they are put on the same level as standards common in trade agreements, such as, for example, Sanitary and Phytosanitary (SPS) Measures. When described as rights they seem a part of human rights, being their social component.

In practice it is often difficult to delineate between both frames. However, we believe we can distinguish both by looking at their primary motivation as expressed in the written or speech acts. If the primary reason

---

[9] Note that this article by Bhagwati was written before the 1998 Declaration on Fundamental Principles and Rights at Work which privileged the four CLS. On the question of whether this declaration of 'core' standards is a positive development, opinions differ widely (see Alston, 2004; Langille, 2005).

to include social norms is justified from an inward-looking perspective, to ensure a level playing field with European producers, then we detect a competitiveness frame. In the other case, if the inclusion is merely justified out of concern for the human rights situation in the third country (thus having an outward-looking perspective), then we detect a human rights frame.

2.3 Economic Development Leading to Social Development or Going Hand in Hand?

The last two frames concern the relationship between economic development on the one hand and social development on the other hand. On one end of the spectrum, one finds actors who argue that social development is a consequence of economic development. On the other end, some argue that social and economic development should go hand in hand. We call the former the **economic development frame** and the latter the **social development frame**. For adherents of the former frame, labour abuses are seen as a side-effect of underdevelopment (Lee, 1997, p. 177). If countries are granted better access to the European market, this negative side-effect will disappear after some time. According to this frame, trade liberalization is seen as beneficial for the long-term social development of the trade partner. According to the social development frame, trade liberalization should only be supported if a minimum level of social norms is respected.

3. A POST-LISBON CRITICAL FRAME ANALYSIS OF RELEVANT EP RESOLUTIONS AND LEGISLATIVE FILES

We are interested in the different ways in which the EP looks at the notion of social trade. We focus on political groups because we have noticed in the literature on this issue within the EU that views differ more when comparing ideology than when comparing nationality. So, the political conviction of the MEP concerned is seen as being interwoven with its position on social trade. Also on other issues the political group affiliation of an MEP matters more than his or her nationality (see, for example, Hix, Noury, & Roland, 2007). Another indicator why we look at political groups is the group cohesion on international trade issues (Van den Putte, De Ville, & Orbie, 2015) which is larger than on general issues.[10] We have included

---

[10] The data used in this chapter are based on information from the website http://www.votewatch.eu/ and concern votes from 14 July 2009 to 4 July 2013.

all political groups in our analysis, being the European Peoples' Party (EPP), the Group of the Progressive Alliance of Socialists and Democrats (S&D), the Group of the Alliance of Liberals and Democrats for Europe (ALDE), the Group of the European Greens/European Free Alliance (Greens/EFA), the European Conservatives and Reformists (ECR), the Europe of Freedom and Democracy Group (EFD) and the Confederal Group of the European United Left – Nordic Green Left (GUE).

That there are different views on social trade, is already evident in the final resolutions on the topic, which are a compromise text among the majority of the EP. If we would descend to a lower level, namely the discussion on this final text, we can expect even more different views on social trade. An evident way to elucidate these different notions on social norms in trade, would be discourse analysis. Indeed, recently this method has proved popular in analysing EU trade policy (see, among others, De Ville & Orbie, 2011; Mathieu & Weinblum, 2013; Siles-Brügge, 2011), with successful results. However, our research goal is different in the sense that we do not want to identify the dominant discourse surrounding a particular issue but rather we want to unveil the different meanings bestowed on the concept of social trade, independently of whether these interpretations are shared by a majority or by only a marginal group of MEPs.

Therefore we apply CFA, a tool developed in gender studies to investigate the different dimensions of a contested concept like gender equality, thereby building further on theoretical insights of social movement theory (Verloo & Lombardo, 2007). CFA is both a methodological and theoretical tool that is suited to unveiling the underlying interpretations of social trade, which serves as an empty signifier[11] to which everyone seems to adhere, albeit for different reasons. To unpack the different meanings bestowed on the concept of social trade, we (just like discourse analysis) look at language, because the set of language that is used to talk or write about a specific object constructs the world in a particular way (Diez, 1999, p. 603). However, we want to come to a deeper level of ideas. The focus is on what the problem is and how it can be solved.

Applying CFA requires looking for two aspects of the framing: the detection of the problem ('diagnosis') and the proposed solution ('prognosis') (Meier, 2008; Verloo & Lombardo, 2007). The researcher typically tries to detect how the problem and the proposed solution is framed by

[11] An empty signifier refers to a verbal term under which heading precise contents are interchangeable. It becomes very popular because a fixed meaning is absent. Another example is for example the term governance or the term social market economy (Offe, 2009, p. 561).

asking questions such as 'who caused the problem', 'for whom is it a problem' and 'who should solve it', etc.

The period under study includes the most recent legislature (2009–2014) for two main reasons. Firstly, the literature expects that the EP will use its recently acquired competences to support a more social agenda. Secondly, the EU is now negotiating trade agreements with partners of a very diverse social nature. As such, we expect this period to have a wide array of frames on social trade.

Regarding data, we have selected those documents which we believe should reveal most about the position of the EP with regard to the link between social norms and trade. The main locus of our attention was not on the resolution or legislative act as such (which is the end result of a struggle among different frames), but on the amendments tabled by members of the political groups,[12] the plenary debates and the explanation of votes. To disclose these underlying frames we have read and coded our data again and again (Rapley, 2007, 2011).[13]

Some of the selected files cover trade with countries having a rather high social score (Canada and Korea), while others concern countries with a more disputed social reputation (Colombia, Peru and the Central-American countries). While other resolutions could have been included,[14] we have in many resolutions found similar results. So we believe that our selected data are representative of the views of each political group on the issue in general.

4. SOCIAL TRADE IS NECESSARY TO ENSURE A LEVEL PLAYING FIELD AND ECONOMIC LIBERALIZATION WILL BRING SOCIAL PROGRESS

How do the political groups in the EP connect to the above-mentioned frames? While the operationalization of the different frames is not

---

12 Amendments tabled by committees were thus not taken up in the analysis. However, it would be interesting to contrast the amendments of different committees, since one could expect, for example, the committee on international trade (INTA) to emphasize more liberal ideas than the committee of development (DEVE).

13 A list of the analysed documents can be obtained from the author. Rapley does not offer a specific amount of times a researcher should go through his or her original data. However, he argues that qualitative data analysis requires a researcher to continuously evaluate and modify their labels and labelling practices.

14 Examples could be the resolution on an EU-India FTA (European Parliament, 2011) or the resolution on negotiations with Japan (European Parliament, 2012a).

included in this chapter,[15] we give some illustrations for why we put a political group on one or the other end of the spectrum. For every two opposing frames we make a qualitative assessment of the position of each of the groups.

4.1 Is the Link between Social Norms and Trade Necessary and Desirable?

In general, almost all political groups are in favour of including social norms in the EU's trade policy. The coherence of different policies (for example trade and foreign policy) is often a motivation. Some refer even to the Lisbon Treaty as a legal obligation to strive for policy coherence. A good example in this regard is the statement by Miroslav Mikolasik from the EPP:

> Mr President, the opportunities afforded by the adoption of the Treaty of Lisbon make possible the long-awaited establishment of a balance between commercial law and human rights. I firmly believe that the European Union, in the interests of upholding its credibility and integrity, must make active use of this opportunity, and start to act consistently over human rights, both in its internal and its external policies.

For other MEPs it is a matter of European values, which should also be upheld in its external policies, as witnessed for example by the statement by Mitro Repo (S&D):

> The European Union is a community of values, based on a respect for the principles of human rights and democracy. This obligation also extends to the Union's trade policy. It is vitally important that the EU implements its foreign and trade policy with reference to its values. Business is not just about business . . .

Marielle De Sarnez (ALDE) also makes this clear when explaining why she voted on the resolution on Trade, Growth & Development: 'Finally, if the European Union wants to preserve its key role in the world trade arena, all ongoing and future trade negotiations must be instruments for promoting European standards in social and environmental matters.'

Others want to use trade policy as an instrument to further social norms. Carl Schlyter (Greens/EFA), when referring to the reports on social standards in international trade agreements and Corporate Social

---

[15] More information on the operationalization of the six frames can be obtained from the author.

Responsibility (CSR), says: 'Mr President, I think that we can summarise these three reports by saying that we are moving from viewing people as tools to be used for trade to viewing trade as a tool to be used for people.' An ECR member speaking on India in the debate on social standards in international trade agreements also argues that 'Europe should not give in to pressure by India to leave non-trade issues out of the new trade agreement. Human rights and child labour cannot be regarded separately from trade and investment.' Also GUE is in favour of taking up social criteria in free trade agreements. Jacky Hénin argues in the debate on social standards in international trade agreements: 'Indeed, if competition is free then all forms of dumping are possible, starting with tax, social, monetary and environmental dumping. Competition is necessarily distorted. . . . environmental and social criteria guaranteeing equality in commercial activity and the rights of employees must be defined and enforced.'

While the EU in general has pressed for social norms in trade since the end of the 1990s (and as such supporting a link), not everyone in the EU sees this practice of linking as a positive development. Especially the EPP and ECR have an ambivalent position on this. The EPP seems to regard social norms as a trade issue, but they clearly do not want to overemphasize its importance in trade agreements. Daniel Caspary puts it the following way:

> . . . I often wonder what these individual areas of policy themselves achieve. Are we imposing a sufficiently strong obligation on the environmental and social policymakers and on policymakers in other areas to do their homework on their own subjects? . . . I should say that I think we all agree on the objectives. However sometimes I am concerned that we are overloading trade policy, when other areas of policy increasingly often do not do their homework.

An ECR member comments on the resolution on the trade agreement with Colombia and Peru that '. . . this is to confuse political agreements about political measures with trade agreements, which should be about jobs and market access. Trade agreements are not trade agreements when they become weighed down with non-trade issues.' Also the view of ALDE and the Greens/EFA seems inconsistent on this (albeit that they mostly apply the frame of social norms as a trade issue). ALDE seems conscious of the need to find a balance and to make sure that trade policy is trade policy. They argue that while trade policy should not be overburdened with issues not directly related to international trade, it cannot be dealt with in a vacuum and it needs to find a balance with other aspects of its external policy. Jadot from the Greens/EFA is in favour of incorporating values in EU trade policy, but warns against an overburdening with issues not directly related to international trade.

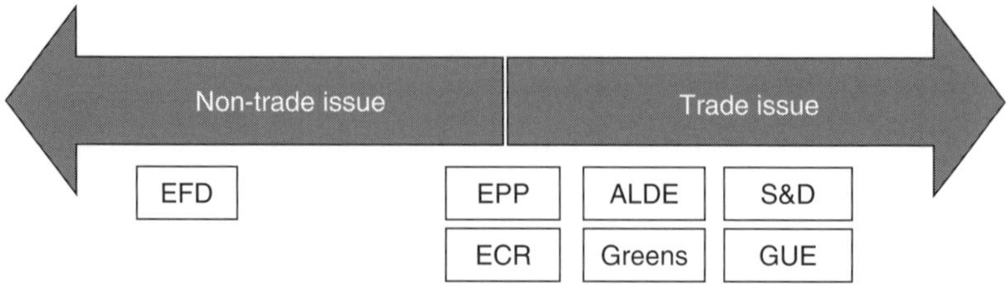

Figure 4.1 Qualitative assessment of the political groups on the non-trade issue vs. trade issue distinction

The only political group clearly opposing the incorporation of social norms in trade policy is the EFD. The Earl of Dartmouth (EFD) argues that trade policy shouldn't be burdened with a political agenda. He says: 'What we are seeing is an attempt to manipulate the trade policy of the European Union – which, unfortunately, the UK is bound by for the moment – in order to implement by stealth a largely Socialist agenda that has been consistently rejected.' However, there are also other views on the issue within the ECR. Another member argues that '[p]urely commercial interests must never be at the expense of concern for our fellow human beings in other countries, particularly in developing countries . . . Human rights and child labour cannot be regarded separately from trade and investment.'

Qualitatively assessing the position of the political groups with regard to these frames, results in the situation illustrated in Figure 4.1.

4.2 Social Norms as Process Standards or as Human Rights?

As set out earlier, we distinguish the competitiveness frame and the human rights frame by looking at their main motivation as having an inward- or outward-looking perspective. Tracing these frames throughout the documents we are mainly questioning 'for whom is it a problem if social norms are not respected?'

EPP members often apply the competitiveness frame. In a debate on the Korea safeguard regulation an EPP member wants all trade partners to abide by environmental and occupational standards so that 'trade is based on the principles of full competitiveness'. The EPP rapporteur on the 2010 resolution on social standards in international trade agreements wants to unite developing and developed countries in their stance on labour standards by referring to a level playing field. So while for the EPP there are also references to human rights and ethical standards, the main motivation to include social norms seems to be the comparative advantage third countries would otherwise have, which would lead to decreased competitiveness for

EU producers. This frame is also commonly used by S&D members. In the resolution on social standards in international trade agreements, an S&D-member wants it to be explicitly added that undertakings and workers in Europe have to comply with very stringent social standards. He also speaks about *defending* these objectives (i.e. human rights, social and environmental standards) as a priority in bilateral negotiations, instead of *pursuing* them (as mentioned in the draft resolution), thereby showing that he sees the issue as a matter of competition. Somewhere else it is argued that trade should be an additional means to promote European values and interests, and the inclusion of labour standards contributes to regulating globalization. If they are not taken up they not only go against the principles which should guide the EU's external action (thereby reflecting a 'trade frame'), but also undermine the European social model. So while in the S&D discourse there are often references to social norms as 'European values' (thus pointing to a possible human rights frame) the motivation is mostly inward-looking. Also ALDE often engages in the competitiveness frame as witnessed by a member who argues that 'Current free trade agreement negotiations should include clauses on human rights but also on economic, social and environmental standards. If this is not done, the unfair competitive advantage will mean that the EU is no longer able to compete with low cost and low quality imports.' An EFD member voices this quite explicitly by saying '. . . third countries that do not respect workers' rights and refuse to play an active part in fighting climate change all too often compete unfairly with EU companies'.

GUE is the most ardent user of the human rights frame. Its members are strongly opposed to the trade agreement with Colombia and Peru because it proves the hypocrisy of the EU concerning human rights issues. They do not want the EU to trade with a country where basic trade union rights are not respected. Their view becomes very clear in their analysis of the Rana Plaza accident in Bangladesh. While most other groups point primarily to the fact that these factories did not comply with safety standards, GUE goes one step further in analysing the causal mechanisms leading to the collapse of the building. For them the core problem is the lack of social and workers' rights which hampers the existence of democratic trade union structures to struggle for better health and safety standards and working conditions. These are also explicitly stated as basic human rights which have to be guaranteed before anything else.

With respect to the Greens/EFA it is not easy to discern their position on this issue. They often speak about social issues or social standards and less about social rights. In general they focus more efforts on environmental issues and they even seem to think that too much of the EP's efforts are focused on labour rights. However, they have also not connected the issue

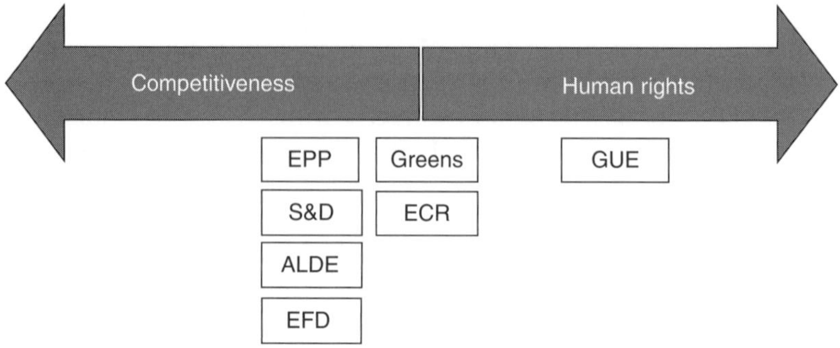

Figure 4.2 Qualitative assessment of the political groups on the competitiveness frame vs. human rights frame distinction

of low labour standards to competitiveness. Therefore, we argue that they take a middle position. The same goes for the ECR that sees social norms more as standards. However, they do not need to be included to ensure competitiveness of European producers.

These findings are visualized in Figure 4.2.

4.3 Economic Development Leading to Social Development or Going Hand in Hand?

Some political groups see the lack of social norms as a normal stage in the development of a country. For others this is not a normal or good evolution. For them labour issues cannot be temporarily put aside for economic reasons.

Most political groups apply the economic development frame, as is evident on the discussions on the trade agreement with Colombia and Peru. For the EPP the FTA merely serves as a reward for Colombian and Peruvian efforts in recent years to improve their democratic and human rights record, and many members also believe that economic integration in the EU will improve such conditions such as the protection of labour rights and the environment. For ALDE the agreement is also a reward for efforts undertaken by the Colombian government. The ECR also shares the view that the trade agreement can serve as an instrument to fight against remaining problems, while it has already made significant efforts to deal with these problems. Increased trade is also intended to result in the reduction of poverty. In addition, S&D also believes that the design of the trade agreement with Colombia and Peru works in favour of far-reaching social protection and sustainable development.

GUE argues against the view that economic development will result in more respect for human rights by noting that the Colombia/Peru FTA has only the 'declared' objective of reducing poverty. They doubt whether the consequences of the trade agreement will be positive and deny that the trade agreement will guarantee far-reaching social protection and sustainable development. Remarkably another GUE member argues that ILO CLS can have a beneficial role in promoting economic efficiency and productivity, so the competitiveness frame is reversed here. For the GUE, respecting social norms is an issue which also has to be brought up in negotiations with so-called 'developed' countries. The Greens/EFA seem to support GUE on the request for a minimum respect of CLS before the EU can offer trade liberalization. They support the road map for the Colombia/Peru trade agreement and want strong conditionality in the sense that they argue for some targets to come into effect before the EP votes on the ratification of the FTA. As such, it can be regarded as a minimum.

The position of S&D on this issue is somewhat ambiguous. David Martin argues that trade is not an end in itself and that it can be

> a driver for growth, which in turn, fuels prosperity and rising living standards, but trade is also influenced by, and can influence, human rights standards, labour standards, environmental standards, and they must be a key components of our trade policy, not as an alternative to trade liberalization, but as a key component of it.

Another member of the S&D group argues the following:

> Mr President, the EU should only conclude free trade agreements with countries which show full respect for human rights. It seems fundamental to me that the core labour standards of the International Labour Organization should be implemented and, above all, complied with. The labour clauses in the contract are good, but they do not go far enough.

Bernd Lange (S&D), in the debate on the EU-Korea FTA, mentions that in Korean law strikes are prevented and the rights of trade unions are limited. He then continues:

> I would also like to know why we are concluding free trade agreements with countries such as South Korea and Colombia which have the most problems with the standards of the International Labour Organisation. Therefore, my first question is this: How do you propose to use the free trade agreement to ensure that there are no unfair competition conditions in South Korea caused by restrictions on employees' rights?

A part of the EFD is in favour of the Colombia/Peru trade agreement because it aims to lead to comprehensive economic development, which

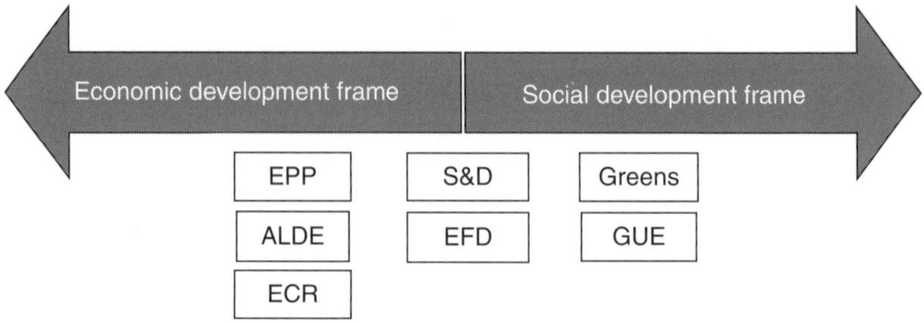

Figure 4.3 Qualitative assessment of the political groups on the economic development frame vs. social development frame distinction

can then improve working conditions. Another EFD member is against the trade agreement because it makes concessions to countries that blatantly violate human rights. So also on this issue, not only between the political groups but also within them, there is some ambiguity.

By assessing the positions of the different political groups in a qualitative way, the image as shown in Figure 4.3 emerges.

5. DISCUSSION

Our chapter has shown that there is a broad consensus in the EP on linking trade with social norms (except for the EFD). As such, on the level of specific policy ideas (see Mehta in Schmidt, 2008, pp. 306–307) they all agree. However, descending one level to the level of ideas or ways in which problems and solutions are defined, we learn that large differences of opinion exist between the groups. Within this shared storyline of 'social trade', views diverge between the political groups. Most of the groups want to see social norms included so that European producers are not disadvantaged by non-European producers with lower labour standards. Their main motivation stems thus from concern about European employment. Whether this is a result of the crisis or whether these political groups have employed this frame also in economically prosperous times, would be an interesting avenue for further research. Only GUE is a strong user of the human rights frame. Together with the MEPs from the Greens/EFA, they put social development before economic development. EPP, ALDE and ECR largely regard trade and liberalization as being beneficial to social development. S&D and EFD do not have a clear position on this issue. As such, we can conclude that social trade is indeed a storyline gluing almost all groups together.

In contributing to the literature, this is the first study digging deeper into the role of the EP in social trade, which has so far been assumed to be a monolithic social actor. We have shown that within this ideologically diverse setting, groups apply different (and sometimes even opposing) frames to argue for the inclusion of social norms. We can even argue that the frames used in the global context of the WTO (especially in the 1990s) are also reflected within the EP. An exception is the frame disqualifying the universality of the four CLS (Bhagwati, 1995). Indeed, all groups agree that these four social norms should be prioritized.[16] This chapter has also shown why centre-right actors within the EU are no longer opposed to social trade (as they were from the 1970s until the middle of the 1990s). Their motivation stems largely from the belief that economic development can lead to social development and from the need to protect domestic industries. But also the S&D applies the competitiveness frame. Given the context of the current EU trade policy of increasing liberalization focusing on competitive markets, combined with the economic crisis,[17] this might not come as a surprise. It also explains why the Committee on International Trade (INTA) within the EP proposed to include the monitoring of social norms in the safeguarding regulation with Korea. Given this focus on competitiveness, Hafner-Burton (2009) could be right when she argues that as with the US, the EU will be more prone to labour unions than in the past. Indeed, while the design of trade policy was previously almost exclusively the domain of the European Commission, those sectors fearing competition and their trade unions are likely to lobby the EP too now.[18]

Which implications do these findings have for EU trade policy? The first concerns the external legitimacy of the EP (and the EU in general) in bilateral and multilateral trade negotiations. Thinking about a case such as India, how can the European Commission explain that the Indian fears for disguised protectionism are unfounded? Is the EU concerned about the problem of child labour in India or does it want to prevent the European market from being further flooded by cheap Indian goods? This relates

[16] Only Laurence J.A.J. Stassen from the independent MEPs speaks about 'European social standards' in the explanation of votes on trade, growth and development.

[17] Sapir already argued that the issue of social trade comes up mostly when the world economy is globalizing (1995, p. 791).

[18] It would be interesting to investigate whether the political groups applying different frames are also lobbied by other interests. From our findings one could hypothesize that GUE and the Greens/EFA are more lobbied by NGOs, while other groups are more likely to be lobbied by trade unions.

also to the second implication for policy. If the underlying interpretations of, in our case, social trade are too different, this might pose a danger for concrete policy-making.[19] The more floating a signifier is (in other words, the broader the different meanings bestowed on it), the more difficult it becomes to derive concrete policy from it (Kögl & Kurze, 2013). While one group can push for inclusion to improve the human rights situation in the trade partner's country, another group can only emphasize social norms in those production sectors where it expects a comparative advantage compared to EU producers. If trade agreements lack concrete strategic goals, it becomes hard to design concrete policy.

All in all, it seems that social trade is likely to stay on the agenda of the EP, and given its increased formal powers, also on the agenda of the EU.

REFERENCES

Alston, P. (2004). 'Core Labour Standards' and the Transformation of the International Labour Rights Regime. *European Journal of International Law*, 15(3), 457–521.

Bhagwati, J. (1995). Trade Liberalisation and 'Fair Trade' Demands: Addressing the Environmental and Labour Standards Issues. *The World Economy*, 18(6), 745–759.

Brown, D.K. (2001). Labor Standards: Where Do They Belong on the International Trade Agenda? *Journal of Economic Perspectives*, 15(3), 89–112.

Bungenberg, M. (2010). Going Global? The EU Common Commercial Policy After Lisbon. In C. Herrmann, M. Krajewski & J.P. Terhechte (eds), *European Yearbook of International Economic Law* (pp. 123–151). Berlin: Springer.

Burgoon, B. (2004). The Rise and Stall of Labor Linkage in Globalization Politics. *International Politics*, 41, 196–220.

Charnovitz, S. (1987). The Influence of International Labour Standards on the World Trading Regime. *International Labour Review*, 126(5), 565–584.

De Ville, F. & Orbie, J. (2011). The European Union's Trade Policy Response to the Crisis: Paradigm Lost or Reinforced? *EIoP*, 15(2), http://eiop.or.at/eiop/texte/2011-002a.htm

Devuyst, Y. (2013). European Union Law and Practice in the Negotiation and Conclusion of International Trade Agreements. *Journal of International Business & Law*, 12(2), 259–316.

Diez, T. (1999). Speaking 'Europe': The Politics of Integration Discourse. *Journal of European Public Policy*, 6(4), 598–613.

European Parliament. (1994a). *Report of the Committee on External Economic Relations on the Introduction of a Social Clause in the Unilateral and Multilateral Trading System.*

[19] A similar remark is made in Van den Putte & Orbie (2015) on the concept of sustainable development in EU trade agreements.

European Parliament. (1994b). *Resolution on the Introduction of a Social Clause in the Unilateral and Multilateral Trading System.*
European Parliament. (2011). *Free Trade Agreement with India.*
European Parliament. (2012a). *EU Trade Negotiations with Japan.*
European Parliament. (2012b). *European Parliament Resolution on the EU Trade Agreement with Colombia and Peru.*
Hafner-Burton, E.M. (2009). *Forced to Be Good: Why Trade Agreements Boost Human Rights.* Ithaca: Cornell University Press.
Hajer, M.A. (1995). *The Politics of Environmental Discourse: Ecological Modernization and the Policy Process.* Oxford: Clarendon Press.
Hajer, M.A. (2006). Doing Discourse Analysis: Coalitions, Practices, Meaning. In M. van den Brink & T. Metze (eds), *Words Matter in Policy and Planning: Discourse Theory and Method in the Social Sciences* (pp. 65–74). Utrecht: Koninklijk Nederlands Aardrijkskundig Genootschap.
Hillman, J. & Kleimann, D. (2010). Trading Places: The New Dynamics of EU Trade Policy Under the Treaty of Lisbon. *Economic Policy Paper Series*: The German Marshall Fund of the United States.
Hix, S., Noury, A., & Roland, G. (2007). *Democratic Politics in the European Parliament.* Cambridge: Cambridge University Press.
Kögl, I. & Kurze, K. (2013). Sustainable Development: A Floating Signifier in the EU's Energy Policy Discourse? In P.M. Barnes & T.C. Hoerber (eds), *Sustainable Development and Governance in Europe: The Evolution of the Discourse on Sustainability* (pp. 61–74). London: Routledge.
Langille, B.A. (2005). Core Labour Rights – The True Story (Reply to Alston). *European Journal of International Law*, 16(3), 409–437. doi: 10.1093/ejil/chi124
Lee, E. (1997). Globalization and Labour Standards: A Review of Issues. *International Labour Review*, 136(2), 173–189.
Mathieu, J.F. & Weinblum, S. (2013). The Battle Against Unfair Trade in the EU Trade Policy: A Discourse Analysis of Trade Protection. *Perspectives on European Politics and Society*, 14(2), 185–202.
Meier, P. (2008). Critical Frame Analysis of EU Gender Equality Policies: New Perspectives on the Substantive Representation of Women. *Representation*, 44(2), 155–167.
Meunier, S. & Nicolaïdis, K. (2011). The European Union as a Trade Power. In C. Hill & M. Smith (eds), *International Relations and the European Union* (2nd edn, pp. 275–298). Oxford: Oxford University Press.
Offe, C. (2009). Governance: An 'Empty Signifier'? *Constellations*, 16(4), 550–562.
Orbie, J., Vos, H., & Taverniers, L. (2005). EU Trade Policy and a Social Clause: A Question of Competences? *Politique européenne*, 3(17), 159–187.
Rapley, T. (2007). *Doing Conversation, Discourse and Document Analysis.* Thousand Oaks, CA: Sage Publications.
Rapley, T. (2011). Some Pragmatics of Qualitative Data Analysis. In D. Silverman (ed.), *Qualitative Research* (3rd edn, pp. 273–290). London: Sage Publications.
Richardson, L. (2012). The post-Lisbon Role of the European Parliament in the EU's Common Commercial Policy: Implications for Bilateral Trade Negotiations. *EU Diplomacy Papers* (Vol. 5): College of Europe.
Sapir, A. (1995). The Interaction Between Labour Standards and International Trade Policy. *The World Economy*, 18, 791–803.
Schmidt, V.A. (2008). Discursive Institutionalism: The Explanatory Power of Ideas and Discourse. *Annual Review of Political Science*, 11, 303–326.

Siles-Brügge, G. (2011). Resisting Protectionism after the Crisis: Strategic Economic Discourse and the EU-Korea Free Trade Agreement. *New Political Economy*, 16(5), 627–653.
Van den Putte, L., Bossuyt, F., Orbie, J., & De Ville, F. (2013). Social Norms in EU Bilateral Trade Agreements: A Comparative Overview. In T. Takacs, A. Ott & A. Dimopoulos (eds), *Linking Trade and Non-commercial Interests: The EU as a Global Role Model*. Den Haag: TMC Asser Institute.
Van den Putte, L., De Ville, F., & Orbie, J. (2015). The European Parliament as an International Actor in Trade: From Power to Impact. In S. Stavridis & D. Irrera (eds), *The European Parliament and its International Relations* (pp. 52–69). Abingdon: Routledge.
Van den Putte, L. & Orbie, J. (2015). EU Bilateral Trade Agreements and the Surprising Rise of Labour Provisions. *International Journal of Comparative Labour Law and Industrial Relations*, 31(3), 263–282.
Verloo, M. & Lombardo, E. (2007). Contested Gender Equality and Policy Variety in Europe: Introducing a Critical Frame Analysis Approach. In M. Verloo (ed.), *Multiple Meanings of Gender Equality: A Critical Frame Analysis of Gender Policies in Europe* (pp. 21–46). Budapest: Central European University Press.
Waer, P. (1996). Social Clauses in International Trade: The Debate in the European Union. *Journal of World Trade*, 30(4), 25–42.

5. Asian and US perspectives on labor rights under international trade agreements compared

Ronald C. Brown

1. INTRODUCTION

Free Trade Agreements (FTAs) and Bilateral Investment Treaties (BITs) are evolving and growing in number,[1] though commitments to labor protections under social dimension provisions (SD), while also growing, may tend to be static from a particular country's perspective, whether it be a 'US perspective', an 'EU perspective', or an 'Asian perspective'. And, there is a question of whether there is such a thing as an 'Asian perspective', or whether that is as elusive a concept as 'Asian human rights?'[2] However, as will be argued in this chapter, there is one constant throughout the many different FTAs and BITs – the central role of the International Labour Organization (ILO)'s core labor standards. The ILO has categorized the approaches utilized by SD labor provisions as *conditional* or *promotional*, and researchers can seek to assess the degree of adherence by countries in meeting and maintaining those standards, not only in international trade and investment commitments, but more importantly as translated into domestic legislation that is meaningfully enforced.

'Asia', of course, is a big word and encompasses the many parts of Asia: Northeast Asia, Southeast Asia, Central Asia, South Asia, East Asia, etc.[3] Even Australia, a different continent, makes claims it is

[1] Int'l Labour Org (ILO), Int'l. Inst. for Labour Stud., *Social Dimensions of Free Trade Agreements*, ILO 2013, available at http://www.ilo.org/wcmsp5/groups/public/---dgreports/---inst/documents/publication/wcms_228965.pdf [hereinafter *ILO Report*].

[2] C. Raj Kamur, *Corruption, Development and Good Governance: Challenges for Promoting Access to Justice in Asia*, 16 Mich. St. J. Int'l. L. 475, 510 (2008).

[3] See *How is Asia Defined?*, www.smith.edu/artmuseum/content/. . ./1/. . ./How+is+Asia+Defined.pdf (last visited Aug. 15, 2014).

'Asian'.[4] Therefore, within the limits of recent FTA and BIT negotiations by the US, the US-Korea (KORUS) FTA is used as an illustration of the nature and parameters of the new US model of social dimension provisions being negotiated with labor protections. This, it is submitted, is the *US perspective* on FTAs.

'Asia' encompasses such a large number of countries and in varied stages of economic development, reaching a consensus on whether there is an 'Asian perspective' may well be premature and only a generalization. However, it can perhaps be useful in creating expectations in countries negotiating FTAs and BITs in Asia and certainly of interest to the Asian laborers and labor groups who might expect to benefit from labor protections in social dimension provisions. Leading experts proclaim: 'Trade and regional integration are likely to influence Asia's future growth, with some predicting that the region will account for over half of world GDP by 2050'.[5] This raises the question discussed in this chapter, whether any 'Asian perspective' will include meaningful social dimension provisions with labor obligations?

One of the variables in identifying an *Asian perspective* is when an Asian country is negotiating an FTA with the US, Canada, the EU, or Australia – one might assume the more economically dominant Western partner might guide the terms of the final agreement. Thus, comparisons are made from those, but also from inter-Asian FTAs and BITs to see to what extent social dimension provisions promoting and protecting labor are primarily a product of Western initiatives or a shared value.

This chapter discusses and analyzes international trade agreements' treatment of labor rights under ILO, US, and Asian perspectives, and concludes with a comparison of the Asian and US perspectives.

---

[4] Usha Mahajani, *Is Australia a Part of Asia?*, 36(2) The Australian Quarterly 25–34 (June 1964), available at http://www.jstor.org/stable/20633957?seq=1#page_scan_tab_contents

[5] Richard Baldwin, Masahiro Kawai, and Ganeshan Wignaraja, *Future of the World Trading System: Asian Perspectives*, Vox (June 12, 2013), available at http://www.voxeu.org/article/future-world-trading-system-asian-perspectives

2. ILO FRAMEWORK AND PERSPECTIVE

2.1 Evolution of Labor Rights in Social Dimension Provisions of Free Trade Agreements

The ILO has stated:

> Since the beginning of the 1990's, the need to create a minimum social foundation for the development of trade – one that guarantees certain safeguards against social dumping – has resulted in the signing of an increasing number of Free Trade Agreements (FTAs) which include a labor dimension, either in the agreement itself or in a parallel agreement.[6]

In recent years, the significance of labor provisions in trade agreements has risen significantly in relative terms. While only 4 percent of trade agreements that entered into force between 1995 and 1999 included labor provisions, this rose to 11 percent between 2000 and 2004. Between 2005 and 2013 about one third of all trade agreements that came into force included labor provisions, and by June 2013, of the 248 trade agreements that were in force and notified to the World Trade Organization (WTO), 58 contained labor provisions.[7]

Out of the 185 ILO member countries with trade agreements notified to the WTO, about 60 percent are covered by at least one trade agreement with labor provisions. In the Americas, almost all countries are covered by at least one trade agreement with labor provisions, while in the Asian Pacific region, roughly half of the countries have one or more trade agreements with labor provisions.[8]

2.2 Characterization of Social Dimension Provisions: Conditionality, Promotional, Enforcement and Cooperative Activities

The ILO, in a Report released in 2013, stated that labor provisions in trade arrangements are often distinguished between those containing *conditional*

---

[6] *Free Trade Agreements and Labor Rights*, INT'L. LABOUR ORG. (ILO), available at http://www.ilo.org/global/standards/information-resources-and-publications/free-trade-agreements-and-labour-rights/lang--en/index.htm (last visited Aug. 15, 2014).

[7] *ILO Report*, *supra* note 1, at 19–20. 'Of the 185 ILO member countries with trade agreements notified to the WTO, about 60 percent are covered by at least one trade agreement with labor provisions. For example, in the Americas, almost all countries are covered by at least one trade agreement with labor provisions, while in the Asian Pacific region, roughly half of the countries have one or more trade agreements with labor provisions' (ibid. at 20).

[8] Ibid., at 20.

and *promotional* elements.[9] According to the ILO, in the case of conditional elements, labor standards requirements are linked to economic consequences, in the form of sanctions or, less frequently, incentives, which concern trade or other benefits, including technical cooperation. Promotional elements combine (binding or non-binding) commitments relating to labor standards with cooperative activities, dialogue, and monitoring. A labor provision is considered to be of promotional character if it does not include economic sanctions or incentives as an implementation mechanism, but instead relies on cooperative activities, dialogue, and monitoring.

Promotional labor provisions can contain legally binding obligations and, as in the case of recent EU agreements, can contain a comprehensive institutional and procedural framework to ensure implementation. Promotional provisions are common in North-South agreements; for example, the EU-Republic of Korea Trade Agreement, the Chile-Colombia Trade Agreement and the Memorandum of Understanding on Labour Cooperation attached to the New Zealand-Hong Kong, China Trade Agreements.[10] In 34 out of the 58 existing trade agreements with labor provisions, the provisions are exclusively promotional – i.e. they do not entail any direct economic consequences in case of non-respect of the labor provisions. In most cases, promotional provisions take the form of cooperative activities between partner countries.[11]

Conditionality has been the primary feature of labor provisions in trade agreements. There are two main aspects of conditionality: the first, *pre-ratification conditionality*, addresses deficiencies in domestic labor standards prior to the ratification of the agreement; while the second is a *mechanism for complaints and dispute settlement after ratification*, which in the event of non-compliance can lead to the withdrawal of trade benefits or to monetary sanctions.[12]

Pre-ratification conditionality has been a characteristic of US trade agreements, and, according to the ILO, the US seems to be the only country officially to require the improvement of labor standards prior to ratification. While pre-ratification conditionality concerns legislative

---

[9] Ibid., at 21. See illustrative treaties collected on various trade agreements. *International Institute for Labour Studies*, INT'L LABOUR ORG. (2014), available at http://www.ilo.org/inst/lang--en/index.htm (hereinafter *IILS*), ibid.; *ILO Report*, *supra* note 1, at 33.

[10] *ILO Report*, *supra* note 1, at 67.

[11] Ibid.

[12] Ibid., at 30.

issues, post-ratification complaints deal primarily with the application of existing domestic labor law.[13]

Enforcement Mechanisms and Cooperative Activities:[14] Trade agreements using a conditional approach usually link commitments on labor standards to a sanction-based enforcement mechanism and provide for cooperative activities.[15] As the ILO has observed:

> This approach, employed notably by the United States and Canada . . . aims to increase the countries' capacity, while also providing economic disincentives for breaches of labor standards.[16] A common feature of this dual approach has been the obligation to effectively enforce national labor law in specific areas. Furthermore, such provisions also include standards with which the domestic labor law itself must comply.[17]
>
> The implementation of the above commitments is facilitated through an institutional framework of a joint cooperative body and national contact points, which rests on two main pillars [enforcement mechanisms and cooperative activities].[18]

Complaints filed under trade agreements (other than NAFTA/NAALC) have only been activated since 2008, leading to six cases filed up to June 2012; notwithstanding the existence of dispute settlement provisions, the reality is they are reported to be infrequently used in practice and almost never taken to final resolution, though arguably they may have some positive effect.[19]

---

[13] The *ILO Report* formed an assessment on trade agreements that are made conditional on certain labor standards – so-called '*pre-ratification conditionality*'; and where the trade agreement has already been concluded and includes conditional labor provisions – so-called '*post-ratification conditionality*'. Among the key findings was that '. . . pre-ratification conditionality has often led to significant changes in labor legislation . . . leading to improvements in workers' rights or the adoption of new legal protections, especially in the area of freedom of association' (ibid., at 29).

[14] Ibid., at 31–32.

[15] Ibid., at 31–32. Only a few trade agreements provide for conditional labor provisions without any promotional dimension. See, e.g., the Japan-Philippines Trade Agreement, ibid., at 24.

[16] See, e.g., Canada's trade agreements with Chile, Costa Rica, Peru, and Colombia, *Trade Agreements in Force*, SICE, Foreign Trade Information System (2014), available at http://www.sice.oas.org/agreements_e.asp. On the US and Canada's approach, see Cleopatra Doumbia-Henry and Eric Gravel, *Free Trade Agreements and Labour Rights: Recent Developments*, 145 Int'l. Lab. Rev. 185–206 (2006).

[17] *ILO Report*, *supra* note 1, at 33.

[18] Ibid., at 31.

[19] See also, *ILO Report*, *supra* note 1, at 40 and 51.

3. US PERSPECTIVE

3.1 Evolution and Spread of Free Trade Agreements

Free Trade Agreements (FTAs) have proved to be one of the best ways to open up foreign markets to US exporters.[20] Scholars note that the 'US has led the way in consistently attempting to make bilateral trade liberalization subject to the observance of labor standards'.[21] The social dimension provisions of US trade agreements use a conditional approach and usually link commitments on labor standards to a sanction-based enforcement mechanism and provide for cooperative activities. Additionally, there are obligations to effectively enforce national labor laws in specific areas and also include standards with which the domestic labor law itself must comply.[22]

As of 1 January 2014, the United States had 14 FTAs in force with 20 countries. The United States is negotiating a regional FTA, the Trans-Pacific Partnership, with Australia, Brunei Darussalam, Canada, Chile, Japan, Malaysia, Mexico, New Zealand, Peru, Singapore and Vietnam. The United States and the European Union launched negotiations on the Transatlantic Trade and Investment Partnership in June 2013.[23]

---

[20] Historically the United States first implemented labor standards in establishing trade agreements in 1890. The United States heightened this standard in 1984 to include penalties for violations of labor standards by withdrawing trade preferences. The idea behind implementing and enforcing a standardization of labor practice and including a social dimension to a country's trade agreement was to avoid globalization at the expense of the rights of workers, while aiding in the enforcement of international labor standards. Ibid., at 17–18; *Free Trade Agreements*, US Dept. of Commerce, Int'l Trade Administration, available at http://trade.gov/fta/ (last visited Aug. 15, 2014).

[21] Ludo Cuyvers and Tim De Meyer, *Chapter 5: Market-driven Promotion of International Labour Standards in Southeast-Asia – the Corporatization of Social Justice*, in Private Standards and Global Governance, Economic, Legal and Political Perspectives 141 (Alex Marx, Miet Maertens, Johan Swinne, and Jan Wouters, eds, 2012). See also, *United States Free Trade Agreements (FTAs)*, Int'l Labour Org. (Oct. 19, 2009), available at http://www.ilo.org/global/standards/information-resources-and-publications/free-trade-agreements-and-labour-rights/WCMS_115531/lang--en/index.htm#P0_0

[22] See, e.g., the US-Peru Trade Agreement; the US-Republic of Korea Trade Agreement; the US-Colombia Trade Agreement; the Canada-Peru Trade Agreement; and the Canada-Colombia Trade Agreement. Under many earlier United States trade agreements this commitment was not subject to sanctions (see Table 2.1 in *ILO Report*, *supra* note 1, at 33).

[23] *Free Trade Agreements*, U.S. Dept. of Commerce, Int'l Trade Administration, available at http://trade.gov/fta/ (last visited Aug. 15, 2014).

The US government in its negotiations in the Trans-Pacific Partnership Agreement stated its objectives in the area of labor, within the social dimension provision, as follows:[24]

> Ensuring respect for worker rights is a core value. That is why in TPP the United States is seeking to build on the strong labor provisions in the most recent US trade agreements by seeking enforceable rules that protect the rights of freedom of association and collective bargaining; discourage trade in goods produced by forced labor, including forced child labor; and establish mechanisms to monitor and address labor concerns.[25]

3.2 Model Provisions

To perhaps identify a 'US perspective' on labor rights and trade agreements, one must begin with the emergent US bilateral trade and investment frameworks, specifically the Model Free Trade Agreement and Model Bilateral Investment Treaty, with respect to labor provisions and relative enforcement mechanisms used in advancing international labor standards.[26] The 'US perspective' might be said to be one that seeks to embrace and promote commitments to the four ILO core labor standards as embodied in the 1998 ILO Declaration on Fundamental Principles and

---

[24] *Trans-Pacific Partnership: Summary of US Objectives*, Office of the US Trade Rep., available at http://www.ustr.gov/tpp/Summary-of-US-objectives (last visited Aug. 15, 2014).

[25] Further, the TPP seeks: '• Requirements to adhere to fundamental labor rights as recognized by the International Labor Organization, as well as acceptable conditions of work, subject to the same dispute settlement mechanism as other obligations in TPP; • Rules that will ensure that TPP countries do not waive or derogate from labor laws in a manner that affects trade or investment, including in free trade zones, and that they take initiatives to discourage trade in goods produced by forced labor; • Formation of a consultative mechanism to develop specific steps to address labor concerns when they arise; and, • Establishment of a means for the public to raise concerns directly with TPP governments if they believe a TPP country is not meeting its labor commitments, and requirements that governments consider and respond to those concerns' (ibid.).

[26] As will be seen, these US frameworks are not fully efficacious to do so, and recommendations to bolster them are provided, including comments on incorporation or utilization of Corporate Social Responsibility (CSR) and International Framework Agreements (IFA) provisions. Portions of this section were originally presented by Ronald C. Brown, 'The Efficacy of the Emergent US Model Trade and Investment Frameworks to Advance International Labor Standards in Bangladesh' at the *International Workshop on Fostering Labor Rights in the Global Economy*, Leuven University and the Leuven Centre for Global Governance Studies (Feb. 20–21, 2014) Int'l. Labour Rev. (ILR) at __ILR__ (forthcoming 2015).

Rights at Work,[27] not its individual conventions, and provide enforcement mechanisms and sanctions for states and investors for alleged trade or labor violations.[28] These frameworks will be contrasted to what may be called the 'Asian perspective'.

The US has only adopted two of the core International Labor Organization Conventions,[29] although it has approved the ILO Constitution vis-à-vis its membership in the ILO,[30] which explicitly references the freedom of association, a core labor standard, and the ILO Declaration.

To understand the US perspective and what parties can anticipate when entering into a US FTA or BIT standard trade and investment framework, it is useful to begin with the terms of adopting international labor norms and how the respective obligations of each will be enforced. As noted, the US is currently employing both a Model FTA and a Model BIT, discussed below.[31] While the US model bilateral trade and investment frameworks that emerged from these processes are in many ways similar to previous FTAs and BITs, they are vastly and significantly different in

---

27 *ILO Declaration on Fundamental Principles and Rights at Work*, ILO, available at http://www.ilo.org/declaration/lang--en/index.htm (last visited Dec. 2, 2014).

28 The 'EU perspective' may provide insights about the relative strengths and weaknesses of US FTAs. See generally, *Dispute Settlement*, European Comm'n – Trade, available at http://ec.europa.eu/trade/policy/accessing-markets/dispute-settlement/ (last visited Aug. 15, 2014).

29 *Ratifications for United States*, ILO, available at http://www.ilo.org/dyn/normlex/en/f?p=1000:11200:0::NO:11200:P11200_COUNTRY_ID:102871 (last updated 2012). The US has ratified two out of eight Fundamental Conventions, i.e. (1) Abolition of Forced Labor Convention (1957 [No. 105]) (Sept. 25, 1991) and (2) Convention Concerning the Prohibition and Immediate Action for the Elimination of the Worst Forms of Child Labor (1999 [No. 182]) (Dec. 02, 1999).

30 *ILO Country Profile: United States*, ILO, available at http://www.ilo.org/dyn/normlex/en/f?p=1000:11110:0::NO:11110:P11110_COUNTRY_ID:102871 (last updated 2012). The US has been an ILO member since 1980 and has ratified the ILO Constitution and Declaration (ibid.).

31 President Obama created the Model BIT for US-Chinese BIT negotiations in an effort to ensure bilateral investment promotes basic labor standards. At the US-China Strategic and Economic Dialogue (SED) in July 2013, representatives from the US, using the Model BIT as a framework, and the Chinese government announced that the two countries had entered into sustained BIT negotiations, moving from its technical framework to talks on the actual text. Ronald C. Brown, 'China: U.S. Implementation of ILO Standards by BITs and Pieces (FTAs)' in Fundamental Labour Rights in China: Legal Implementation and Cultural Logic, eds. Ulla Liukkunen and Chen Yifeng, pp. 199–232 (The Netherlands: Springer, forthcoming, 2015).

two important ways. First, alongside trade obligations, the FTA and BIT include labor obligations that incorporate the ILO *Declaration*. Second, the *FTA*, though not the BIT, weds bilateral trade with these labor obligations under a new substantive legal procedure and provides an unprecedented unitary enforcement mechanism for both sets of obligations, whereby trade sanctions may be brought for labor violations.

3.2.1 Model frameworks' integrated international labor norms

While similar to previous US FTAs, in that, under the US' new emergent Model FTA's labor chapter[32] both parties are obligated to 'not fail to effectively enforce its labor laws . . . in a manner affecting trade or investment between Parties', it also differs by requiring that both parties 'adopt and maintain its statutes and regulations, and practice' with enumerated fundamental labor rights 'as stated in' the 1998 ILO Declaration of Fundamental Principles and Rights at Work and its Follow-Up.[33] As such, according to the text of the Declaration, the US and its partner would seemingly be obligated to respect a whole array of new labor rights, including: (1) freedom of association; (2) the effective recognition of the right to collective bargaining; (3) the elimination of all forms of compulsory or forced labor; (4) the effective abolition of child labor; and (5) the elimination of discrimination in respect of employment and occupation.[34]

However, under the Model FTA, the US and its partner's labor obligations regarding these rights are sharply curtailed by a crudely placed exculpatory footnote that provides that 'the obligations set out in [the chapter], as they relate to the ILO, refer only to the ILO Declaration'.[35]

Likewise, under the 2012 US Model BIT, the US and its BIT partner commit to their respective obligations as ILO members and to their commitment to the ILO Declaration on Fundamental Principles and Rights of

---

32 Examples of contrasting earlier FTA provisions may be found in the DR-CAFTA at Articles 16.6.7, 17.10.7, and 20.17.1; see *Central American-Dominican Republic-US FTA (DR-CAFTA)*, US Office of Trade Rep., available at http://www.ustr.gov/trade-agreements/free-trade-agreements/cafta-dr-dominican-republic-central-america-fta/final-text (last visited Aug. 15, 2014). See also David A. Gantz, *Settlement of Disputes Under the Central America-Dominican Republic-United States Free Trade Agreement*, 30 B.C. Int'l & Comp. L. Rev. 331 (2007), available at http://lawdigitalcommons.bc.edu/iclr/vol30/iss2/3 (contrasting the Model FTA with differences in DR-CAFTA in terms of social dimensions).

33 US-Korea Free Trade Agreement, US-S. Kor., art. 19.3.1, Mar. 15, 2012, 125 Stat. 428, available at https://ustr.gov/trade-agreements/free-trade-agreements/korus-fta/final-text (hereinafter *KORUS FTA*).

34 Ibid.

35 Ibid., art. 19.2.1, n.1.

Work and its Follow-up.[36] However, as with the Model FTA, the Model BIT does not bind either country to specific ILO Core Conventions.[37] The 2012 US Model BIT further provides that when there is a dispute that falls under it, one should notify the other by writing a request for *consultations* with the other responding within thirty days, and with both agreeing to work towards a mutually satisfying resolution.[38]

Therefore to understand what the US and its trading or investment partner might be obligated to in terms of advancing international labor norms in an FTA or BIT, it is useful to understand the nature of the obligations flowing from the ILO *Declaration* versus the ILO *Conventions*.

In the ILO Declaration on Fundamental Principles and Rights at Work 1998, the ILO governing body declares that:

> all Members, even if they have not ratified the Conventions in question, have an obligation arising from the very fact of membership in the Organization, to respect, to promote and to realize, in good faith and in accordance with the

---

[36] Ibid., art. 13.1. The US Model Bilateral Inv. Treaty provides the following obligations regarding labor: '1. The Parties reaffirm their respective obligations as members of the ILO their commitments under the ILO Declaration on Fundamental Principles and Rights at Work and its Follow-Up. 2. The Parties recognize that it is inappropriate to encourage investment by weakening or reducing the protections afforded in domestic labor laws. Accordingly, each Party shall ensure that it does not waive or otherwise derogate from or offer to waive or otherwise derogate from its labor laws where the waiver or derogation would be inconsistent with the labor rights referred to in subparagraphs (a) through (e) of paragraph 3, or fail to effectively enforce its labor laws through a sustained or recurring course of action or inaction, as an encouragement for the establishment, acquisition, expansion, or retention of an investment in its territory. 3. For the purposes of this Article, "labor laws" means each Party's statutes or regulations, or provisions thereof, that are directly related to the following: (a) freedom of association; (b) the effective recognition of the right to collective bargaining; (c) the elimination of all forms of forced or compulsory labor; (d) the effective abolition of child labor and a prohibition on the worst forms of child labor; (e) the elimination of discrimination in respect of employment and occupation; and (f) acceptable conditions of work with respect to minimum wages, hours of work, and occupational safety and health. 4. A Party may make a written request for consultations with the other Party regarding any matter arising under this Article. The other Party shall respond to a request for consultations within thirty days of receipt of such request. Thereafter, the Parties shall consult and endeavor to reach a mutually satisfactory resolution. The Parties confirm that each Party may, as appropriate, provide opportunities for public participation regarding any matter arising under this Article' (note omitted), *KORUS FTA*, *supra* note 33, art. 13.2.

[37] *KORUS FTA*, *supra* note 33, art. 13.3 (a)–(f).

[38] Ibid., at art. 13.4.

> Constitution, the principles concerning the fundamental rights which are the subject of those Conventions.[39]

As the ILO Declaration applies universally, but the underlying ILO Conventions do not, both may be integral or both may be separate, depending on individual signatories. As to the US, the ILO Declaration then may be bifurcated from the ILO conventions, because while both countries have ratified the ILO Declaration, they may not have ratified the entire battery of Conventions.[40] To this end, the ILO Constitution seems to be enshrouded by the Declaration, but both clearly serve as the basis for the Conventions.[41]

The legal implication of obligations emanating from an ILO Declaration versus the Conventions is in the specificity contained in the latter and accompanying guides as to its proper application and interpretation, such as those in the US Model FTA and Model BIT.

---

[39] Int'l Labour Org., 'ILO Declaration on Fundamental Principles and Rights at Work', *International Labour Conference*, 86th Sess. (June 1998, Annex revised Jun. 15, 2010), available at http://www.ilo.org/public/english/standards/relm/ilc/ilc86/com-dtxt.htm2

[40] See, Emily A. Spieler, *Chapter 4. Risks and Rights: The Case for Occupational Safety and Health as a Core Worker Right*, in WORKERS' RIGHTS AS HUMAN RIGHTS 78, 99 n. 197 (James A. Gross, ed., 2003). The ILO Declaration was radical in that it utilized an international set of core labor rights to be universally adopted regardless of whether individual signatories had endorsed the corresponding ILO conventions, apoliticizing specific labor rights; but in promoting the universal adoption of the Declaration, its drafters simply alluded to aspirational labor rights in vague language rather than institutionalizing substantive ones. Philip Alston, *Core Labor Standards & the Transformation of the Int'l Labor Rights Regime*, 15 EUR. J. INT'L LAW 457 (2004).

[41] Brian Langille, *Core Labor Rights: True Story*, EUR. J. INT'L LAW 409, 424–425 (2005), available at http://www.ejil.org/pdfs/16/3/302.pdf. See also, Pablo Rangel, University of Tromsø, *The Unfinished History: The History of the ILO Declaration* (2013), 392, available at http://munin.uit.no/bitstream/handle/10037/3230/article.pdf?sequence=1. And see, Christopher McCrudden and Anne Davis, *A Perspective on Trade and Labor Rights*, 3 J. INT'L ECON. L. 43, 51 (2000). Reflecting this point, the ILO legal advisor remarked, 'The Declaration contemplated the implementation, not of specific provisions of Conventions, but rather of the principles of those Conventions'. Francis Maupain, *Revitalization Not Retreat: The Real Potential of the 1998 ILO Declaration for the Universal Protection of Workers' Rights*, 16 EUR. J. INT'L LAW 439, 448 n. 44 (2005). According to an AFL-CIO policy statement, the ILO Declaration's 'core labor standards are based on international human rights law' and the relevant ILO conventions 'give content to these core standards' *Voice@Work: The ILO Declaration of Fundamental Principles & Rights at Work*, AFL-CIO (Aug. 2, 2000), available at http://www.aflcio.org/About/Exec-Council/EC-Statements/Voice-Work-The-ILO-Declaration-on-Fundamental-Principles-and-Rights-at-Work

3.2.2 Model frameworks' enforcement mechanisms

The US Model FTA framework is unique in that it weds trade obligations with these integrated labor obligations, providing mutual sanctions. Under these FTAs, a panel would limit a prevailing party challenging another party in a labor matter – typically pursuant to labor right obligations – to an annual monetary payment. Since trade and labor regimes are wedded, a party can pursue the general dispute settlement procedures that apply to trade, to the same extent in labor disputes.

Adhering strictly to US FTA practice, the emergent model framework provides for two types of dispute settlement procedures, albeit uniformly encompassing disputes of either trade and/or labor matters: (1) State-State, applicable to the agreement's signatories; and (2) Investor-State, applicable to either state's investors who have investment obligations.[42]

Under the model framework, the scope of the agreement's obligations limits the parties' obligations, and subsequently how the parties may pursue a claim is restricted to delegated dispute settlement procedures; the scope of these obligations is important to consider when pursuing possible avenues of enforcement.[43] Disputes arise over: (1) the other party is undertaking a measure inconsistent with the framework's obligations; (2) the other party is failing to adhere to its obligations; or (3) the other party is acting to nullify or impair normally enumerated benefits that would accrue to it, such as a tariff reduction.

Like previous US FTAs, the model framework's investment chapter provides for what the US and its partners are obliged to provide for its nationals who invest in each other's countries, with investors' rights clearly identified as such. Under the model framework, a delegated investor-state dispute mechanism empowers investors to be able to resolve disputes by arbitration.[44]

---

[42] *Contra*, *North American FTA*, US Office of Trade Rep., available at https://www.nafta-sec-alena.org/Default.aspx?tabid=97&language=en-US (last visited Aug. 15, 2014). The North American Free Trade Agreement (NAFTA) is unique in containing a third type of dispute settlement, applicable where one NAFTA Party, that is, the US, Canada, or Mexico, undertakes an antidumping or countervailing duty investigation involving the goods of another NAFTA Party. Chapter 19 of the NAFTA permits a Party, either on its own accord or at the request of a private party entitled to domestic judicial review of a final agency determination in a domestic antidumping or countervailing duty proceeding, to request that a final agency determination be reviewed by a bi-national arbitral panel instead of by a court in the country in which the determination is rendered.

[43] *KORUS FTA*, *supra* note 33, art. 23.1.

[44] Mark E. Manyin, Cong. Research Serv., RL30566, South Korea-US Economic Relations: Cooperation, Friction, and Future Prospects 20 (2004),

3.3 NAALC under NAFTA

The North American Agreement on Labor Cooperation (NAALC) is a supplementary agreement to the North America Free Trade Agreement (NAFTA) signed on 13 September 1993 that includes the US, Canada, and Mexico. It is the first labor-related international agreement that originates from an international trade agreement and it seeks to improve many facets of labor standards, including working conditions and living standards, to 'encourage cooperation, and promote compliance with and effective enforcement of each state's labor laws for the mutual benefit of all parties to the treaty'.[45]

In order to implement the NAALC, the Commission for Labor Cooperation (CLC) was created. It is constituted by a Council of Ministers and a tri-national Secretariat that supports the Council and other bodies instituted by the NAALC.[46] Apart from the ILO, the CLC is the only other international body that is solely focused on labor rights and labor-related matters.[47]

NAFTA Party States commit themselves to enacting labor laws and regulations that would serve to increase labor standards, although the language of the NAALC is described as 'vague'. Article 42 specifically states

---

available at http://fpc.state.gov/documents/organization/34347.pdf; see also, *Model BIT Review Delayed Indefinitely; Korean BIT Still Pending*, INSIDE US TRADE (2000). 2012 Model BIT provides for 'court' enforcement of that which preserves the use of the arbitration process. 2012 U.S. Model Bilateral Investment Treaty, art. 26, sect. 3, US OFFICE OF TRADE REP., available at http://www.ustr.gov/sites/default/files/BIT%20text%20for%20ACIEP%20Meeting.pdf (last visited Aug. 16, 2014) (hereinafter *U.S. Model BIT*). 'Notwithstanding paragraph 2(b), the claimant (for claims brought under Article 24(1)(a)) and the claimant or the enterprise (for claims brought under Article 24(1)(b)) may initiate or continue an action that seeks interim injunctive relief and does not involve the payment of monetary damages before a judicial or administrative tribunal of the respondent, provided that the action is brought for the sole purpose of preserving the claimant's or the enterprise's rights and interests during the pendency of the arbitration' (ibid).

45 Frank H. Bieszcat, *Labor Provisions in Trade Agreements: From NAALC to Now*, 83 CHI.-KENT L. REV. 1387, 1388 (2008), available at http://scholarship.kentlaw.iit.edu/cgi/viewcontent.cgi?article=3695&context=cklawreview. President Clinton's support for NAFTA was contingent on the presence of an agreement protecting workers' rights and the environment. See, North American Agreement of Labor Cooperation, US-Can.-Mex., art. 1, Sept 14, 1993, 32 I.L.M. 1499, available at http://www.worldtradelaw.net/nafta/naalc.pdf.download (hereinafter *NAALC*).

46 *About the Commission*, SECRETARIAT FOR THE COMM'N FOR LAB. COOPERATION, http://www.naalc.org/commission.htm (last visited Aug. 16, 2014).

47 SECRETARIAT FOR THE COMM'N FOR LAB. COOPERATION, ibid.

that neither Party to the agreement is imbued with the power to 'undertake labor law enforcement activities in the territory of another Party'. It is important to note that Labor laws, as according to the NAALC, are defined as occupational health and safety, employment standards, industrial relations and migrant workers and collective agreements.[48]

The 'functionality' of the NAALC resides in its petition system, created to deal with affronts to labor standards in any of the NAFTA countries. Each country has established a National Administrative Office (NAO) and has designated a Secretary responsible for its administration and management.

The NAALC has received generally negative evaluations.[49] Many analysts and labor groups are of the opinion that it did not live up to expectations, contained certain fatal flaws in its system, and was poorly implemented.[50]

4. ASIAN PERSPECTIVE

4.1 Evolution

'Asia', of course, is a big word and encompasses the many parts of Asia, Northeast Asia, Southeast Asia, Central Asia, South Asia, East Asia,

---

[48] *NAALC*, US-Can.-Mex., art. 4, Sept 14, 1993, 32 I.L.M. 1499, available at http://www.worldtradelaw.net/nafta/naalc.pdf.download. See also Bieszcat, *supra* note 45, 1389. For an excellent review of NAFTA/NALLC, see Mary Jane Bolle, CONG. RESEARCH SERV., 97-861 E, NAFTA LABOR SIDE AGREEMENT: LESSONS FOR THE WORKER RIGHTS AND FAST-TRACK DEBATE (updated October 9, 2001), available at http://fpc.state.gov/documents/organization/6211.pdf

[49] For a partial summary of the past 20 years of NAALC from the point of view of the US Labor Education in the Americas Project (USLEAP), a worker-based NGO arguing its ineffectiveness; see, Rebecca Van Horn, *NAFTA, Labor, and Immigration: A Package Deal*, LABORRIGHTSBLOG.COM (Apr. 19, 2011), http://laborrightsblog.typepad.com/international_labor_right/2011/04/nafta-labor-and-immigration-a-packagedeal.html?utm_source=feedburner&utm_medium=feed&utm_campaign=Feed%3A+typepad%2FILRF%2Finternational_labor_right+%28Labor+Is+Not+A+Commodity+Blog%29%20NAFTA,%20Labor,%20and%20Immigration:%20A%20Package%20Deal

[50] It is argued that the system is flawed due to the fact that it follows an adversarial and litigious approach towards solving labor issues. Isabel Studer, *The NAFTA Side Agreements: Toward a More Cooperative Approach?*, 45 WAKE FOREST L. REV. 469–490 (2010); see also, Tamara Kay, Univ. of Cal. Berkeley, *Analysis of the Labour Aspects of NAFTA: Preliminary Document for Commentaries of Work Group I of the Inter-American Conference of Ministers of Labour*, INT'L. LAB. ORGANIZATION (June 2003).

etc. – even Australia, a different continent, claims it is 'Asian'.[51] So, to define an 'Asian perspective' is a big task, involving generalizations.

Across Asia and the Pacific, trade liberalization and economic integration in the region have proliferated.[52] A recent ADB-sponsored study stated '[F]our main factors underlie the recent spread of FTA initiatives in Asia: (i) deepening market-driven economic integration in Asia, (ii) European and North American economic integration, (iii) the 1997–1998 Asian financial crisis, and (iv) slow progress in the WTO Doha negotiations'.[53] The authors provide a critical analysis of the emerging trend of FTAs in Asia based on three developing issues: (1) Asia's growth and development in production across regional borders; (2) Asia's growing number of FTAs, with ASEAN emerging as the hub of policy development in international and inter-regional trade; and (3) emerging literature on the economic effects of Asian FTAs show that the use of FTAs, a newer phenomenon to the region, is distorted, with excessive exclusions and deferential treatment to certain countries and partners.[54] The study concludes that 'the Asian FTAs have maintained a strong cross-regional orientation, the trade coverage of FTAs has increased, and issues other than trade liberalization – such as investment, intellectual property rights, and labor standards or mobility – have been included'.[55]

---

[51] *How is Asia Defined?*, *supra* note 3.

[52] See discussion in Asian Dev. Bank, *Regional Cooperation and Integration in a Changing World*, 17–26 (2013), available at http://www10.iadb.org/intal/intalcdi/PE/2013/11842.pdf (hereinafter *RCICW*). And see ibid. at 21. See also, Bilateral FTAs by Geographic Area, WTO Notification and Status 2000 and 2014, ASIA REG'L INTEGRATION CTR., available at http://aric.adb.org/fta (last visited Aug. 16, 2014).

[53] Masahiro Kawai and Ganeshan Wignaraja, *Asian FTAs: Trends, Prospects, and Challenges*, 4 (ADB Economics Working Paper Series No. 226, 2010), available at http://www un.org/esa/ffd/msc/regionalcooperation/ADB_WPs.pdf

[54] Ibid., at 1. Asian FTAs are under scrutiny for their scope, such as their inclusion of new issues that go beyond the World Trade Organization framework. Ibid., at 17. 'Two leading participants in Asian FTAs – Japan and Singapore – strongly favor a WTO-plus approach to FTAs. All of Japan's agreements and most of Singapore's are WTO-plus. Likewise, Brunei Darussalam, Indonesia, the Republic of Korea, Malaysia, the Philippines, and Viet Nam largely follow a WTO-plus format' (ibid., at 19). Singapore's primary issues were found to be newer additions to the scope of an FTA agreement, and included investment, competition, intellectual property, and public procurement ('the four Singapore issues') (ibid., at 2). These go beyond the scope of the WTO requirements and thus are sometimes incorporated to FTAs and characterized as 'WTO-plus'. These newer issues were economically focused, without inclusion of a social dimension.

[55] Kawai and Wignaraja, *supra* note 53, at 30. 'Asia began emphasizing FTAs as a trade policy instrument in the later 1990s and the region is today at the forefront of world FTA activity' (ibid.).

In another ADB report, it is stated that not only has there been a blossoming of trade liberalization initiatives in the last decade, but also a resulting 'convoluted "noodle bowl" of overlapping free trade agreements'.[56] As of January 2013, the number of ratified FTAs involving at least one country from the region was 109. This is more than triple the number in 2002. There are another 148 FTAs at various stages of development, bringing the total to 257.[57] Nearly three-quarters of the FTAs, or 189 out of a total of 257, were bilateral (i.e., involving two countries); only 68 were multi-lateral.[58]

Leading the way in numbers are the FTAs involving the ten members of the Association of Southeast Asian Nations (ASEAN) and their trade partners Australia, the People's Republic of China, India, Japan, the Republic of Korea, and New Zealand, which together have increased from 27 in 2002 to 179 by January 2013, a 600 percent increase.[59] The ADB Report states that ASEAN is leading negotiations with its six partners to establish the Regional Comprehensive Economic Partnership (RCEP) by 2015, the deadline ASEAN set to achieve the ASEAN Economic Community, which envisages a highly competitive single market and production base that is fully integrated into the global economy.[60] This will have a market size of 3.4 billion people and a combined GDP of $21.4 trillion or about 30 percent of world GDP.[61]

---

56 *RCICW*, *supra* note 52, at 16. The potential for negative effects of FTAs because of the complexity and inconsistency of some regulations, has been described as the 'noodle bowl' (or 'spaghetti bowl') effect arising from different rules of origin (ROOs). Yunling Zhang and Minghui Shen, *The Status of East Asian Free Trade Agreements* 3 (ADBI Working Paper Series No. 282, 2011), available at http://www.econstor.eu/handle/10419/53698. See summary at *Asian Free Trade Agreements: Untangling the Noodle Bowl*, Asian Development Bank (Aug. 8, 2013), available at http://www.adb.org/features/free-trade-untangling-asia-s-noodle-bowl. Two proposals have been advanced to disentangle the Asian free trade noodle bowl: consolidation – which creates a regional FTA to harmonize bilateral FTAs; and multi-lateralization – which grants non-discriminatory preferences to nonmembers, eliminating preference discrepancies. *Asian Economic Integration Monitor – March 2013*, Asian Development Bank, http://www.adb.org/publications/asian-economic-integration-monitor-march-2013 (last visited Aug. 16, 2014).

57 *RCICW*, *supra* note 52, at 17.

58 Ibid., at 18.

59 Ibid.

60 Asian Dev. Bank, *Asian Development Outlook 2013 Asia's Energy Challenge*, at 13 (2013), available at http://www.adb.org/sites/default/files/pub/2013/aem-201303.pdf (hereinafter *ADO*).

61 Ibid., at 14.

Currently, the ASEAN+6 countries account for 70 percent of the total FTAs in Asia.[62]

Mega-regional trade deals have come into vogue.[63] Asia's own mega-regional trade deal – the Regional Comprehensive Economic Partnership (RCEP) – was launched in 2012 and could create the world's largest trading bloc and have significant implications for the world economy.[64] The objective is to 'achieve a modern, comprehensive, high-quality and mutually beneficial economic partnership agreement among the ASEAN Member States and ASEAN's FTA Partners'.[65] At the same time,

> [a] key purpose is to reconcile two long-standing proposals into a large region-wide trade agreement: the East Asian Free Trade Agreement, which included ASEAN, China, Japan and South Korea, and the Comprehensive Economic Partnership, which added Australia, India and New Zealand. The RCEP bridges the two proposals by adopting an open accession scheme. Negotiations among the 16 parties began in early 2013 and are scheduled to conclude by the end of 2015.[66]

---

62 *RCICW*, *supra* note 52, at 18.

63 Ganeshan Wignaraja, *Why the RCEP Matters for Asia and the World*, East Asia Forum (May 15, 2013), available at http://www.eastasiaforum.org/2013/05/15/why-the-rcep-matters-for-asia-and-the-world/

64 *ASEAN Regional Comprehensive Economic Partnership*, Ass'n of Se. Asian Nations, http://www.asean.org/news/item/asean-framework-for-regional-comprehensive-economic-partnership (last visited Aug. 16, 2014). James Wallar, *Achieving the Promise of the ASEAN Economic Community: Less Than You Imagine, More Than You Know*, Nat'l Bureau of Asian Research, 20 (2014), available at http://www.nbr.org/downloads/pdfs/ETA/wallar_paper_072814.pdf

65 *Guiding Principles and Objectives for Negotiating the Regional Comprehensive Economic Partnership*, ASEAN.org (August 30, 2012), available at http://www.asean.org/images/2012/documents/Guiding%20Principles%20and%20Objectives%20for%20Negotiating%20the%20Regional%20Comprehensive%20Economic%20Partnership.pdf; Wallar, *supra* note 64, at 20 n. 43.

66 Wignaraja, *supra* note 63. 'Because the RCEP will contain three of the largest economies in the world – China, India and Japan – it is globally important. The bloc represents 49 per cent of the world's population and accounts for 30 per cent of world GDP. It also makes up 29 per cent of world trade and 26 per cent of world FDI inflows. Conservative estimates using various computable general equilibrium models suggest that if the RCEP were implemented it would bring large income gains to the world economy of between US$260–644 billion in a decade or so' (ibid.). A critique on the trajectory of the RCEP and its relationship with regional FTAs in East Asia is found in a recent ADB report. See generally, Yoshifumi Fukunaga and Ikumo Isono, *Taking ASEAN+1 FTAs Towards the RCEP: A Mapping Study* (ERIA Discussion Paper Series, ERIA-DP-2013-02, 2013), available at http://www.eria.org/ERIA-DP-2013-02.pdf

Other regional developments are also moving forward. In March 2014, China, Japan, and South Korea held their fourth round of negotiations over a trilateral free trade agreement (China-Japan-South Korea FTA).[67]

The relatively recent evolution of FTAs emanating from the East Asia Region and the significance of ASEAN in that growth is described below in a recent ADB-issued Report.[68]

> ASEAN's role is unique in East Asia. On one hand, ASEAN seeks to benefit from FTAs with itself as the hub, creating a hub-spoke structure with its ASEAN+1 FTAs. On the other hand, as an integrated regional market, ASEAN is attractive to other regional groups, leading the latter to seek FTAs with ASEAN. . . . The PRC's first FTA initiative was with ASEAN, and was aimed at establishing ASEAN as both a regional market and a close geographic partner.
>
> The PRC's FTA with ASEAN aroused quick responses from other countries, particularly Japan and Korea, leading to several parallel ASEAN+1FTAs in East Asia.
>
> Few economies restricted the pursuit of FTAs to East Asia as the search for FTA partners assumed a global reach. For East Asian economies, however, FTAs had clearly become a significant new strategy . . . and part of a strategy against globalization and regionalism in other regions.[69]

Some FTAs, notably those of Japan in East Asia, resemble the EU experience of developing a hybrid form of an FTA, called an Economic Partnership Agreement (EPA or CEPA for Comprehensive EPA).[70] EPAs

---

67 Shannon Tiezzi, *China-Japan-South Korea Hold FTA Talks Despite Political Tension*, The Diplomat (Mar. 5, 2014), available at http://thediplomat.com/2014/03/china-japan-south-korea-hold-fta-talks-despite-political-tension/

68 Yunling Zhang and Minghui Shen, *The Status of East Asian Free Trade Agreements* 3 (ADBI Working Paper Series No. 282, 2011), available at http://www.econstor.eu/handle/10419/53698. It is argued that from a regional perspective, east Asian economies have been encouraged to turn to practicable bilateral or sub-regional approaches by the failure of Asia-Pacific Economic Cooperation (APEC) to realize its Bogor Goal – i.e., free trade and investment in Asia and the Pacific by 2010 for developed members and by 2020 for developing members. In 1997, APEC initiated an Early Voluntary Sector Liberalization program by selecting 15 sectors for liberalization. The program, however, failed due to its voluntary approach and the subsequent Asian financial crisis (ibid., at 4) (citing T. Feridhanusetyawan, *Preferential Trade Agreements in the Asia-Pacific Region* (Wash., DC: Int'l Monetary Fund, Int'l Monetary Fund Working Paper 05149, 2005)). The slow progress of APEC after the 1997 financial crisis encouraged its members to turn to other strategies centering on FTAs (ibid., at 4).

69 Zhang and Shen, *supra* note 68, at 4.

70 *FTA vs. CEPA*: FTA and CEPA are terms used to describe economic pacts between countries that are aimed at reducing tariffs and improving bilateral trade. Whereas FTA stands for Free Trade Agreement, CEPA stands for Comprehensive Economic Partnership Agreement. Though both are economic pacts, there are

are a scheme to create a *free trade area* to promote trade and development. Japan has concluded EPAs with 12 countries and ASEAN.[71]

The first non-ASEAN FTA proposal in East Asia, for a Japan-Korea FTA, was put forward in 1998.[72] That proposal remains stalled, but more FTA initiatives were subsequently proposed between East Asian countries as well as some between East Asian countries and countries in other regions (see Tables 5.1 and 5.2).[73]

---

differences between the two which will be highlighted in this article. Unlike FTA, which is a free trade agreement, CEPA aims at lowering trade barriers instead of complete elimination. CEPA is said to be a diluted version of FTA. Olivia, *Difference Between FTA and CEPA*, DIFFERENCE BETWEEN. Also see, CUSTOMS & TARIFF BUREAU MOF JAPAN, JAPAN'S ECONOMIC PARTNERSHIP AGREEMENT (EPA) 3 (2008), available at http://www.customs.go.jp/english/epa/files/japans_epa.pdf. com (April 16, 2011).

[71] Japan has concluded EPAs with Singapore, Mexico, Malaysia, Chile, Thailand, Indonesia, Brunei, ASEAN, Philippines, Switzerland, Viet Nam, India, and Peru. *Free Trade Agreement (FTA) and Economic Partnership Agreement (EPA)*, MINISTRY OF FOREIGN AFF. OF JAPAN (April 2014), http://www.mofa.go.jp/policy/economy/fta/

[72] See, Zhang and Shen, *supra* note 68, at 5–6.

[73] 'The Japan-Singapore Economic Partnership Agreement (JSEPA) was considered an innovative FTA in the region when it was concluded in 2002 because it covers more than the conventional areas of liberalization. Trade, investment, and services are covered, as are a mechanism for dispute settlement, and economic and technical cooperation at various functional levels. The PRC took the lead in concluding a large-scale FTA with ASEAN. In 2003, Japan signed the ASEAN-Japan Comprehensive Economic Partnership framework agreement with ASEAN and concluded six bilateral FTAs with individual ASEAN countries (Brunei Darussalam, Indonesia, Malaysia, the Philippines, Singapore, and Thailand). Negotiation of the ASEAN-Japan Comprehensive Economic Partnership (AJCEP) was concluded in 2008. Korea accelerated negotiations with ASEAN and the ASEAN-Korea Comprehensive Economic Cooperation Agreement (AKCEC), covering both goods and services, was concluded in November 2007. Including FTAs with economies in other regions, east Asian economies had concluded 50 FTAs by July 2010, with 43 more under negotiation and an additional 32 proposed . . . [see Tables 5.1 and 5.2]. Singapore had concluded the most FTAs (35), with 10 under negotiation and 4 proposed. Korea, the PRC, and Thailand followed with 26, 25, and 24 FTA initiatives, respectively. Of these, 6 were being implemented by Korea, 10 by the PRC, and 11 by Thailand. In general, the more developed economies were more active in negotiating FTAs because they often possess stronger negotiating capacities. The less developed economies (e.g., Cambodia, the Lao People's Democratic Republic, and Myanmar) tended to rely more heavily on FTAs based on AFTA and ASEAN+1. Most (102) of the125 FTAs concluded or initiated by East Asian economies were with countries outside of east Asia' (Zhang and Shen, *supra* note 68, at 5–8).

Table 5.1 East Asian Free Trade Agreements (ASEAN + 3 countries)

Negotiating body	Under Implementation	Signed	Under Negotiation	Proposed	Total	Partners	
						Inside EA	Outside EA
ASEAN	6	0	1	2	9	5	4
Brunei Darussalam	8	0	2	4	14	6	8
Cambodia	6	0	1	2	9	5	4
China, People's Republic of	10	1	6	8	25	9	16
Indonesia	7	1	2	7	17	6	11
Japan	11	0	5	6	21	11	10
Korea, Republic of	6	1	9	10	26	8	18
Lao People's Dem Rep.	8	0	1	2	11	6	5
Malaysia	8	2	6	3	19	7	12
Myanmar	6	1	2	2	10	5	5
Philippines	7	0	1	4	12	6	6
Singapore	18	3	10	4	35	8	27
Thailand	11	0	7	6	24	9	15
Viet Nam	7	0	3	3	13	6	7
Total	40	10	43	32	125	23	102
Under Implementation						16	24
Signed						1	9
Under Negotiation						1	42
Proposed						5	27

Notes:

1. ASEAN = Association of Southeast Asian Nations: Brunei Darussalam, Cambodia, Indonesia, Lao People's Democratic Republic, Malaysia, Myanmar, Philippines, Singapore, Thailand, Viet Nam. EA = East Asia (ASEAN + 3).
2. The total avoids double counting and does not correspond to the vertical sum of agreements by status.
3. Status of free trade agreements: (i) under negotiation = under negotiation with or without a signed framework agreement; (ii) proposed = involved parties are considering creating an agreement, establishing joint study groups or joint task forces, and/or conducting feasibility studies for an agreement; and (iii) concluded = negotiations are completed and parties have signed an agreement and/or begun to implement provisions of an FTA (for example, tariff cuts have begun).

Source: Asia Regional Integration. *FTA Database*, Asia Reg'l. Integration Ctr. (2014), http://www.aric.adb.org

Table 5.2 Free Trade Agreements involving countries in East Asia (ASEAN + 6 countries)

	Japan	Rep. of Korea	PRC	ASEAN	India	Australia	New Zealand
Japan		⊙		☑	⊙	⊙	⊘
Rep. of Korea	⊙		⊘	☑	☑	⊙	⊙
PRC		⊘		☑	⊘	⊙	☑
ASEAN	☑	☑	☑	☑	☑	☑	☑
India	⊙	☑	⊘	☑			
Australia	⊙	⊙	⊙	☑			☑
New Zealand	⊘	⊙	☑	☑		☑	

Notes:
1. ASEAN = Association of Southeast Asian Nations: Brunei Darussalam, Cambodia, Indonesia, Lao People's Democratic Republic, Malaysia, Myanmar, Philippines, Singapore, Thailand, Viet Nam. PRC = People's Republic of China.
2. ☑ = concluded, ⊙ = under negotiation, and ⊘ = under consideration.

Source: *FTA Database,* Asia Reg'l. Integration Ctr. (2014), http://www.aric.adb.org

While there is much growth in FTAs in Asia, Asian FTAs generally do not include *social dimension provisions*, as discussed below. However, of current interest in the discussion of labor protections from an 'Asian perspective' of FTAs are the Economic Partnership Agreements generally,[74] and the still unsigned Trans-Pacific Economic Partnership Agreement specifically,[75] both of which reference some labor protection provisions, unlike most of the inter-Asian FTAs. These are discussed below, along with BITs in Asia.

---

[74] These are familiar to the European Union (EU) which has been using them for some time, particularly with the less developed countries; however in Asia, Japan in particular also has negotiated a number of EPAs. *Economic Partnerships*, European Comm'n, available at http://ec.europa.eu/trade/policy/countries-and-regions/development/economic partnerships/ (last visited Aug. 16, 2014); see also, *Free Trade Agreements (FTAs) and Economic Partnership Agreements (EPA)*, Ministry of Foreign Aff. of Japan (April 2014), available at http://www.mofa.go.jp/policy/economy/fta/

[75] *Trans-Pacific Strategic Economic Partnership Agreement*, N.Z. Ministry of Foreign Aff. & Trade, http://www.mfat.govt.nz/Trade-and-Economic-Relations/2-Trade-Relationships-and-Agreements/Trans-Pacific/0-P4-Text-of-Agreement.php (last visited Aug. 16, 2014).

4.1.1 Asian Bilateral Investment Treaties (BITs)[76]

Asian countries, particularly those in ASEAN, also conclude Bilateral Investment Treaties (BITs), though none have social dimension provisions covering labor standards.[77] The US is currently in negotiations with China, which does contain a social dimension provision on labor, which if concluded will be a first for China.[78]

4.2 Asia-US Social Dimension Provisions

The United States has signed 20 FTAs with various countries, two of these being East Asian countries, notably Korea and Singapore.[79] One of the variables in identifying an 'Asian perspective' is that when an Asian country is negotiating an FTA with the US, Canada, the EU, or Australia, one might assume the more economically powerful Western countries would dominate and might guide the terms of the final agreement,[80] which is often the

---

[76] See discussion in, Jun Xiao, *The ASEAN Investment Agreement: A Regionalization of Chinese BITs*, 6 FRONTIERS OF LAW IN CHINA 241 (2011), available at http://link.springer.com/article/10.1007%2Fs11463-011-0127-3#page-1. China also has concluded a free trade agreement with ASEAN and one ASEAN nation, Singapore. *The ASEAN-China Free Trade Agreement*, MINISTRY OF FOREIGN AFF. & TRADE BRUNEI, available at http://www.mofat.gov.bn/index.php/free-trade-agreements-ftas/agreements-in-force/asean-china-free-trade-area-acfta (last visited Aug. 16, 2014).

[77] ASEAN countries have BITs with ASEAN and a number of Asian countries. *Bilateral Investment Treaties signed by Brunei Darussalam*, U.N. CONF. ON TRADE AND DEVELOPMENT (Jun. 1, 2010), available at http://unctad.org/Sections/dite_pcbb/docs/bits_Brunei_darussalam.PDF

[78] See the discussion in a paper presented by Ronald C. Brown, 'China: Implementing ILO Standards by BITS and Pieces (within FTAs)' at the Seminar on ILO Labor Rights in China: *Legal Implementation and Cultural Logic*, University of Helsinki Finnish Center of Chinese Law and Chinese Culture, ILO Labor Rights in China: Legal Implementation and Cultural Logic (forthcoming, Wolters Kluwer 2015). See also Xiao, *supra* note 76.

[79] *Free Trade Agreements*, OFFICE OF THE US TRADE REP., http://www.ustr.gov/trade-agreements/free-trade-agreements (last accessed June 18, 2014).

[80] For example, in the recently concluded Australian-Korea FTA, there is a chapter 17 on labor provisions. Australia-Korea Free Trade Agreement, Austl.-S. Kor., ch. 17, Apr. 8, 2014, available at, http://www.dfat.gov.au/fta/kafta/downloads/KAFTA-chapter-17.pdf (hereinafter *Austl-S.Kor. FTA*). In the recent Canada-Korea FTA there is a detailed labor section, see, Canada-Korea Free Trade Agreement, Can.-S.Kor., ch. 18, Mar. 11, 2014, available at http://www.international.gc.ca/trade-agreements-accords-commerciaux/agr-acc/korea-coree/toc-tdm.aspx?lang=eng. The EU-Korea FTA also includes some labor provisions; Chapter 13 is titled Trade and Sustainable Development and is mainly aspirational, reaffirming the ILO principles and calling for a domestic advisory group.

case, but not always.[81] Thus, the typical labor provisions are highlighted below to identify the US approach that appears in its FTAs with Asian nations. Comparisons are made subsequently regarding inter-Asian FTAs and BITs to see whether the social dimension provisions protecting labor indicated below are only a product of Western initiatives.[82]

Within the limits of recent FTA and BIT negotiations by the US, discussed above, the US-Korea (KORUS) FTA is used as an illustration of the nature and parameters of the new US model of social dimension provisions being negotiated with labor protections. This, it is submitted, is the 'US perspective' on FTAs, *particularly arising in FTAs with Asian partners.*

The US-Korean FTA came into effect on 15 March 2012 and does have certain provisions with social dimensions.[83] The US-Korea FTA, for instance, states in its preamble that both countries desire 'to raise living standards, promote economic growth and stability, create new employment opportunities, and improve the general welfare in their territories by liberalizing and expanding trade and investment between their territories'.

See EU-Korea Free Trade Agreement, EU-S.Kor., ch. 13, July, 2011, available at http://eurlex.europa.eu/legalcontent/EN/TXT/HTML/?uri=OJ:L:2011:127:FULL&from=en.

[81] Interestingly, in the Australia-Malaysia FTA, there is a negative covenant in two side letters, which stipulate it will not include labor provisions; however, they agreed to revisit that decision in two years after the FTA comes into force. See, http://www.dfat.gov.au/fta/mafta/documents/Side-Letter-Labour-Australia-to-Malaysia.pdf (last visited Aug. 17, 2014); and a side letter, available at http://www.dfat.gov.au/fta/mafta/documents/Side-Letter-Labour-Malaysian-confirmation-to-Australia.pdf (last visited Aug. 17, 2014). Likewise, there are no labor provisions in Australia's FTAs with Singapore or Thailand.

[82] With respect to the EU, Canada, and other Western developed countries' FTAs and BITs being negotiated, it is submitted that their inclusion of labor protections within social dimension provisions varies primarily in the degree of commitment and level of enforcement. However, at a minimum they, like the provisions in the US FTAs, are designed to promote labor protections. One of the variables in identifying an 'Asian perspective' is when an Asian country is negotiating an FTA with the US, Canada, the EU, or Australia – one might assume the more economically-dominant Western partner might guide the terms of the final agreement. Thus, comparisons are made subsequently regarding inter-Asian FTAs and BITs to see whether social dimension provisions protecting labor are only a product of Western initiatives.

[83] *KORUS FTA*, *supra* note 33. This approach of including social dimension provisions in FTAs is consistent with the 'EU perspective'. The EU-Korea FTA includes provisions on social dimensions, found in the chapter on trade and sustainable development, with firm commitments on both sides to labor standards. Kawai and Wignaraja, *supra* note 53, at 28. See also, *EU-South Korea Free Trade Agreement: A Quick Reading Guide*, Eur. Comm'n (Oct. 2010), http://trade.ec.europa.eu/doclib/docs/2009/october/tradoc_145203.pdf

KORUS obliges both countries to uphold the fundamental ILO labor rights in their laws.[84] Furthermore, the Agreement institutes a Labor Affairs Council,[85] and a Labor Cooperation Mechanism.[86]

The US-Singapore FTA has been in effect since 1 January 2004 and has already been through its fifth annual review in 2009.[87] The purpose of the review is to evaluate the implementation of the FTA and also provide an 'opportunity for labor officials from both governments to discuss labor issues and potential areas for labor cooperation'.[88] However, unlike the US-Korea FTA, there is no creation of a Labor Affairs Council. The task of supervising the Labor Cooperation Mechanism falls to the Joint Committee instituted in Chapter 20, which then has the option of creating a subcommittee on Labor Affairs consisting of officials of the labor ministry and other appropriate agencies or ministries of each Party.[89]

The United States is also in negotiations for a regional, Asia-Pacific trade agreement, known as the Trans-Pacific Partnership (TPP) Agreement, with the objective of shaping a high-standard, broad-based regional pact.[90] The agreement is currently being negotiated by the US and 11 other countries: Australia, Brunei Darussalam, Canada, Chile, Japan, Malaysia,

---

[84] *KORUS FTA*, *supra* note 33, arts 19.2, 19.3, and 19.4.

[85] Ibid. art. 19.5.

[86] This is further outlined in Annex 19-A as a detailed initiative of labor priorities implemented via cooperative activities. *KORUS FTA*, *supra* note 33, art. 19.6. In sum, KORUS commits the US to the obligations of the Declaration and not the specific ILO conventions, establishes a collaborative body, provides for state-state or state-investor disputes, weds trade/labor sanctions, and authorizes an expert panel to grant trade sanctions or monetary awards.

[87] In 2006, a Trade and Investment Framework between the United States and the Association of South East Asian Nations (TIFA) was signed which in general terms outlined the goals of future negotiations of FTAs with ASEAN countries, see, Trade and Investment Framework between the United States and the Association of South East Asian Nations, US-ASEAN, Aug. 25, 2006, available at http://www.bilaterals.org/IMG/pdf/US-ASEAN_TIFA_2006.pdf (hereinafter *US-ASEAN Framework*). Singapore FTA, Office of the US Trade Rep., available at http://www.ustr.gov/trade-agreements/free-trade-agreements/singapore-fta (last visited Aug. 17, 2014). US-Singapore Free Trade Agreement, US-Sing., art. 17.1 (2) and 17.5, May 6, 2003, available at http://www.ustr.gov/trade-agreements/free-trade-agreements/singapore-fta (hereinafter *US-Sing. FTA*).

[88] *US-Sing. FTA, supra* note 87, art. 17.1.

[89] Ibid., art. 17.4.

[90] The TPP will be stemming from the four-nation Trans Pacific Strategic Economic Partnership or more commonly referred to as the Pacific Four ('P4') that is a plurilateral agreement among Brunei Darussalam, Chile, New Zealand, and Singapore.

Mexico, New Zealand, Peru, Singapore, and Vietnam.[91] An outline of the TPP was established during a meeting in Honolulu in 2011. Within this outline is a section on labor which states that:

> TPP countries are discussing elements for a labor chapter that include commitments on labor rights protection and mechanisms to ensure cooperation, coordination, and dialogue on labor issues of mutual concern. They agree on the importance of coordination to address the challenges of the 21st-century workforce through bilateral and regional cooperation on workplace practices to enhance workers' well-being and employability, and to promote human capital development and high-performance workplaces.[92]

Their most recent round of negotiations was held in Ottawa during July 2014.[93]

The United States also has a Trade and Investment Framework Arrangement with ASEAN. It says in its preamble that the parties recognize the ILO Declaration's core labor standards and the importance of adequate and effective protection of workers' rights in accordance with each participant's 'own law'.[94]

Bilateral Investment Treaties (BITs) are present in Asia, as discussed above. Today, the US has investment treaties with South Asian nations Bangladesh and Sri Lanka[95] and, in East Asia, with Korea and Mongolia.[96] Currently the US is in negotiations with China for a BIT which includes a social dimension provision on labor protections (discussed above). If concluded, it would be the first such social dimension provision agreed to by China.[97]

---

91 *Trans-Pacific Partnership (TPP)*, Office of the US Trade Rep., http://www.ustr.gov/tpp (last visited June 19, 2013).

92 *Outlines of TPP*, Office of the US Trade Rep., http://www.ustr.gov/tpp/outlines-of-TPP (last visited June 19, 2013).

93 Chief negotiators discussed labor, state-owned enterprises, services, investment, and all areas of market access, among other topics. *Trans-Pacific Partnership (TPP) Free Trade Negotiations*, Foreign Aff., Trade, & Dev. Can. (July 12, 2014), http://www.international.gc.ca/trade-agreements-accords-commerciaux/agr-acc/tpp-ptp/rounds-series.aspx?lang=eng

94 *See US-ASEAN Framework*, *supra* note 87, Preamble.

95 Ben Leo, *US Treaties Are Missing in Asia Too*, Ctr. for Global Dev. (Apr. 11, 2014), http://www.cgdev.org/blog/us-investment-treaties-are-missing-asia-too

96 'Granted, the regional GDP coverage rates are largely driven by the absence of BITs with China and India. But, there are many other major Asian economies without a US investment agreement, such as Indonesia, Malaysia, Pakistan, Philippines, Thailand, and Vietnam. If the Trans-Pacific Partnership negotiations are ultimately successful, then US BIT coverage would extend to Malaysia and Vietnam' (ibid.).

97 See discussion *supra* note 31. While China and ASEAN have a bilateral free trade and investment agreement, it does not touch upon social dimensions. *China*

4.3 Inter-Asian Social Dimension Provisions

The ILO states that trade agreements incorporating *labor provisions* have steadily increased, with '[f]ifty-eight trade agreements includ[ing] labor provisions in June 2013, up from 21 in 2005 and 4 in 1995'.[98] Of the nearly 190 countries with trade agreements, about 120 are partners to trade agreements that include labor provisions.[99] However, in inter-Asian FTAs, social dimension (SD) provisions on labor protections are much scarcer and are not a usual protocol.[100] For example, the ASEAN FTA

FTA Network, China Ministry of Commerce, available at http://fta.mofcom.gov.cn/english/fta_qianshu.shtml (last visited Aug. 17, 2014); *China-ASEAN FTA*, China Ministry of Commerce, http://fta.mofcom.gov.cn/dongmeng/annex/xiey-i2004en.pdf (last visited Aug. 17, 2014). In addition, China has concluded a free trade agreement with one ASEAN nation, Singapore. However, like the China-ASEAN FTA, the China-Singapore FTA deals mostly with trade and tariffs and does not envelop social dimensions such as employment and labor provisions and so does not touch social security regimes. *China-Singapore FTA*, China Ministry of Commerce, available at http://fta.mofcom.gov.cn/topic/ensingapore.shtml (last visited Aug. 17, 2014). China is working with both Japan and South Korea on a joint study concerning the feasibility of pursuing such an FTA agreement. *China FTA Network*, China Ministry of Commerce, available at http://fta.mofcom.gov.cn/english/fta_qianshu.shtml (last visited Aug. 17, 2014).

[98] See *ILO Report*, *supra* note 1, at 1. About 40 percent of trade agreements include a conditional dimension, compromising trade agreements for lack of cooperation by one party or the other, while the remaining 60 percent are purely promotional provisions in nature (found mainly in the EU, New Zealand, and South-South trade agreements). Ibid., at 1–2.

[99] *ILO Report*, *supra* note 1, at 5. Exports under bilateral free trade agreements executed by Asian countries 'by 1995 were less than one per cent of GDP in East Asia and the Pacific, but reached over 3.25 per cent of GDP by 2011' (ibid. at 9). Additionally, export volume between economies with bilateral free trade agreements in 2012 was highest in Asian economies, and eight of the ten bilateral trade partners with the highest volume in exports in 2012 included at least one Asian economy (ibid.). Six of the ten agreements were between two exclusively Asian parties (ibid., at 9–10).

[100] There is a China-Singapore FTA that, like the China-ASEAN FTA, deals mostly with trade and tariffs and does not envelop social dimensions such as employment and labor provisions. *China-Singapore FTA*, China Ministry of Commerce, available at http://fta.mofcom.gov.cn/topic/ensingapore.shtml (last visited Aug. 17, 2014). There is a side-letter to the China-Singapore FTA. The Singapore letter to the Chinese letter is not available, but the responding Chinese letter to Singapore confirmed that Singaporean workers transferred to China would continue 'to meet certain salary criteria', perhaps suggesting that the Singaporean Government wanted such assurance (ibid.). China is working with both Japan and South Korea on a joint study concerning the feasibility of pursuing such an FTA agreement. *China FTA Network*, China Ministry of Commerce,

has no SD provision, though it does have a labor mobility provision covering certain categories of workers, as does the ASEAN-Australian/New Zealand FTA.[101] While China and ASEAN have a bilateral free trade and investment agreement,[102] the FTA deals with trade and tariffs and does not touch upon social dimensions of trade so as to include employment and labor provisions.[103]

Of interest are the Korean FTAs with other Asian countries; whereas Korea has SD provisions with the US, EU, Australia, and Canada, it has no such labor provisions in its FTAs with Singapore or India.[104] By contrast, Japan's EPAs with Singapore, Malaysia, Thailand, Indonesia, Brunei, ASEAN, the Philippines, Viet Nam and India,[105] contain a labor provision entitled 'Investment and Labour'[106] that generally reiterates the

---

available at http://fta.mofcom.gov.cn/english/fta_qianshu.shtml (last visited Aug. 17, 2014); see also, Wallar, *supra* note 64, at 20.

[101] ASEAN-Australia-New Zealand Free Trade Area (AANZFTA), ch. 9 – Movement of Natural Persons, available at http://www.asean.fta.govt.nz/chapter-9-movement-of-natural-persons/ (last visited Aug. 17, 2014). The ASEAN-India FTA, ASEAN-Japan FTA, ASEAN-Korea FTA: all have nothing regarding labor or movement of natural persons. See *Free Trade Agreement*, available at http://www.miti.gov.my/ (Apr. 18, 2014, 12:28 PM), available at http://www.miti.gov.my/cms/content.jsp?id=com.tms.cms.section.Section_8ab55693-7f000010-72f772f7-46d4f042&curpage=tt

[102] *China FTA Network*, China Ministry of Commerce, http://fta.mofcom.gov.cn/english/fta_qianshu.shtml (last visited Aug. 17, 2014) ['Agreement on Trade in Goods of the Framework Agreement on Comprehensive Economic Co-operation between China and ASEAN'].

[103] China-ASEAN Free Trade Agreement, China-ASEAN, Nov. 2004, available at http://fta.mofcom.gov.cn/dongmeng/annex/xieyi2004en.pdf (hereinafter *ASEAN-China FTA*). ASEAN-China FTA: There is a mention that 'human resources development' is an area of cooperation between the two parties. However, nothing else is said (*ASEAN-China FTA*, art. 7.1(c)). ASEAN has negotiated FTAs with its major regional dialogue partners: China, South Korea, Japan, New Zealand and Australia (jointly), and India. These agreements vary in quality, with recent agreements, particularly the FTA with Australia and New Zealand (AANZ), offering greater levels of market access, broader coverage, and more rigorous obligations. Wallar, *supra* note 64, at 20.

[104] *FTA Status of ROK*, Ministry of Foreign Aff. Republic of Korea, http://www.mofa.go.kr/ENG/policy/fta/status/overview/index.jsp?menu=m_20_80_10 (last visited Aug. 17, 2014). Ministry of Foreign Aff. Republic of Korea, *supra* note 103.

[105] See discussion *supra* note 87.

[106] See, e.g., *Free Trade Agreements (FTAs) and Economic Partnership Agreements (EPA)*, Ministry of Foreign Aff. Japan (April 2014), available at http://www.mofa.go.jp/policy/economy/fta/. The Japan-Philippines Economic Partnership Agreements (EPAs) is the exception and has no investment and

ILO core labor rights and states that investment cannot be encouraged at the expense of weaker labor laws and their enforcement.[107]

The Trans Pacific Strategic Economic Partnership, more commonly referred to as the Pacific Four (P-4), is also in effect. It is a plurilateral agreement among Brunei Darussalam, Chile, New Zealand, and Singapore.[108] It also includes mechanisms for on-going cooperation and dialogue on labor and environment issues. The P-4 partners are currently negotiating with Australia, Malaysia, Peru, the US and Viet Nam, to expand the P-4, and upon its conclusion it will be referred to as the Trans-Pacific Partnership (TPP).[109]

The P-4 has an important side agreement on labor presently in effect, namely the Labour Cooperation Memorandum of Understanding (MOU) that reflects a shared desire to encourage and promote sound labor practices.[110] This MOU has the *promise* of improved labor provisions,

---

Labour provision. Japan-Philippines Free Trade Agreement, Japan-Phil., art. 103, Sept. 9, 2006, available at http://www.mofa.go.jp/region/asia-paci/philippine/epa0609/main.pdf

[107] Indonesia has an EPA with Japan that has no labor standards but does have chapter 7 that deals with the movement of natural persons pertaining only to visas. Japan-Indonesia Free Trade Agreement, Japan-Indon., ch.7, Aug. 20, 2007, available at http://www.mofa.go.jp/region/asia-paci/indonesia/epa0708/agreement.pdf

[108] *Brunei Darussalam's FTA Policy*, MINISTRY OF FOREIGN AFF. TRADE BRUNEI, available at http://www.mofat.gov.bn/index.php/free-trade-agreements-ftas/brunei-darussalam-s-fta-policy (last visited Aug. 17, 2014).

[109] The Trans-Pacific Partnership (TPP) is a proposed regional free trade agreement that is currently being negotiated by 12 countries throughout the Asia-Pacific region (Australia, Brunei Darussalam, Canada, Chile, Japan, Malaysia, Mexico, New Zealand, Peru, Singapore, the United States, and Vietnam). The agreement began in 2005 as the Trans-Pacific Strategic Partnership Agreement (TPSEP or P4). Trans-Pacific Strategic Economic Partnership Agreement, Brunei-Chile-N.Z.-Sing., May, 28, 2006, available at http://www.mfat.govt.nz/Trade-and-Economic-Relations/2-Trade-Relationships-and-Agreements/Trans-Pacific/0-P4-Text-of-Agreement.php (hereinafter *P4*). The Memorandum aims to improve understanding and encourage dialogue on labor matters, as well as promoting sound labor policies and practices. According to the text of the TPP, article 20.4 states that the TPP amongst the original four members would come into effect on 1 January 2006, once the signatories have deposited 'instruments of ratification'. See Memorandum of Understanding on Labour Cooperation Among the Parties to the Trans-Pacific Strategic Economic Partnership Agreement, Brunei-Chile-N.Z.-Sing. Jun 19, 1998, available at http://www.fta.gov.sg/tpfta/p3_authentic_labour_mou_text_english_v1.pdf (hereinafter *MOU*).

[110] *MOU, supra* note 109; see also *Trans-Pacific Strategic Economic Partnership Agreement (P4) Chile-Brunei Darussalam-New Zealand-Singapore*, FOREIGN TRADE INFO. SYS. OAS SEDI DESD, http://www.sice.oas.org/TPD/CHL_Asia/CHL_Asia_e.asp (last visited Aug. 17, 2014). Article 6 of the MOU states that the

placing some obligations on the parties, as described in the labor section below.[111]

> *Memorandum of Understanding on Labour Cooperation among the Parties to the Trans-Pacific Strategic Economic Partnership Agreement*
>
> Article 2: Key Elements/Commitments
>
> 1. Parties that are members of the ILO reaffirm their obligations as such.
> 2. The Parties affirm their commitment to the principles of the ILO Declaration on Fundamental Principles and Rights at Work and its Follow-up (1998).
> 3. Each Party shall work to ensure that its labor laws, regulations, policies and practices are in harmony with their international labor commitments.
> 4. The Parties respect their sovereign rights to set their own policies and national priorities and to set, administer and enforce their own labor laws and regulations.
> 5. The Parties recognize that it is inappropriate to set or use their labor laws, regulations, policies and practices for trade protectionist purposes.
> 6. The Parties recognize that it is inappropriate to encourage trade or investment by weakening or reducing the protections afforded in domestic labor laws.
> 7. Each Party shall promote public awareness of its labor laws and regulations domestically.

4.4 EPAs

Under Economic Partnership Agreements (EPAs) in effect in Asia, mostly with Japan (which has concluded EPAs with 12 countries and ASEAN),[112] there do not appear to be any social dimension provisions for labor. However, Japan does have a policy initiative relating to one aspect of labor – movement of natural persons.[113]

MOU is in effect between those countries that have ratified. See *MOU, supra* note 109, art. 6. The parties are engaged in labor educational and training activities under the MOU. See generally, Int'l Lab. Office, Skills and Employability Dept., *Report on the Training and Up-skilling of Vulnerable Groups in TPSEP Countries: Brunei Darussalam, Chile, and Singapore*, ILO EMP/SKILLS Rep. No. 2 (2009), available at http://www.ilo.org/wcmsp5/groups/public/@ed_emp/@ifp_skills/documents/publication/wcms_104623.pdf

111 *MOU, supra* note 109, arts 2–3.

112 See text *supra* note 70.

113 Ministerial Comm. on Comprehensive Econ. P'ships., *Basic Policy on Comprehensive Economic Partnerships*, MINISTRY OF FOREIGN AFF. OF JAPAN

> *Movement of Natural Persons*. The Government of Japan will consider measures to address the issues relating to the movement of natural persons from abroad, such as nurses and certified care workers, on the basis of its efforts to promote the 'employment and human resources strategies' described in its New Growth Strategy, and it will do so with due attention to future domestic demographic trends, the possible effect of such movement on employment in Japan, requests from other countries, as well as securing Japan's economic growth and social stabilization.[114]

5. COMPARATIVE DIFFERENCES: ASIAN AND US PERSPECTIVES ON SOCIAL DIMENSION PROVISIONS IN TRADE AGREEMENTS

5.1 The 'US Perspective'

Social dimension provisions in FTAs and BITs are part of the 2012 Model Provisions and are included in recent and all prospective FTAs, with a limit on commitment to only the ILO Declaration. The dispute settlement provisions wed trade and labor violations, but there is no easy access by interested third parties. Written obligations are primarily conditional, not promotional, yet the actual implementation, to some, may appear in practice to be more promissory. The use of related side agreements and its institutions for settlement of disputes, such as NAALC under NAFTA, to many appear to be ineffectual and are not currently raised in negotiations.

Even though most would agree that the US is ahead of Asia in implementing labor protections in trade agreements through the social dimension provisions, the current US Model still has shortcomings in terms of furthering ILO Standards. Without question, the US model

---

(November 6, 2010), available at http://www.mofa.go.jp/policy/economy/fta/policy20101106.html

[114] An illustrative provision can be found in the Japan-Singapore Economic Partnership Agreement, Japan-Sing., Annex VI, Jan. 2007, available at http://www.mofa.go.jp/region/asia-paci/singapore/jsepa-7.pdf. There is no labor provision, but there is a 'human resources development' provision in the agreement. See the joint coordinating team report for details. Full text available at *Japan-Philippine Economic Partnership Agreement: Joint Coordinating Team Report*, Ministry of Foreign Aff. of Japan (Dec. 2003), available at http://www.mofa.go.jp/region/asia-paci/philippine/joint0312.pdf (hereinafter *JPEPA*). See also, Erlinda M. Medalla and Melalyn C. Mantaring, *On Free Trade Agreements (FTAs): The Philippine Perspective* (Phil. Institute for Dev. Studies, Discussion Paper Series No. 2009-35, 2009), available at http://dirp3.pids.gov.ph/ris/dps/pidsdps0935.pdf

bilateral trade and investment frameworks are an improvement in that they attempt to wed free trade with international labor norms in an effort to halt the race to the bottom. But, the efficacy of the US model frameworks to advance international labor standards is inadequate for several reasons. First, while the US model frameworks integrate international labor norms, it is clear that the ILO commitments are to the ILO Declaration and not the ILO Conventions, and are likely not sufficiently substantive to be enforceable. Second, given the frameworks' dubious dispute settlement mechanisms for enforcing the labor obligations, it is unclear how they would likely be enforced. Third, while the Model FTA's dispute settlement mechanisms allow for wedded enforcement of trade and labor obligations, only states and individual investors may bring claims; third parties such as non-governmental organizations, unions, and labor groups, and/or workers, cannot bring similar challenges, limiting enforcement. As for BITs, there is only consultation. And, fourth, while the model frameworks place an onus on the states to enforce labor standards, they do not provide such an onus to companies to adhere to basic corporate social responsibility (CSR) norms in their operations, which means they can easily evade compliance, through such activities as subcontracting.[115]

Recommendations have been made to improve the US model frameworks that currently place the onus squarely on the parties to advance international labor norms within their domestic laws, which limits effectiveness, given that those entities actually transacting across borders are companies, like US retailers and local employers, who are not obliged to ensure similar standards are adopted in practice.[116] Under the US model frameworks as they are, US companies would be able to continue to flaunt international standards by subcontracting with companies in the country to run factories, without any obligation to avoid substandard practices.[117]

---

115 For more detailed discussion, see Ronald C. Brown, 'The Efficacy of the Emergent US Model Trade and Investment Frameworks to Advance International Labor Standards in Bangladesh' at the *International Workshop on Fostering Labor Rights in the Global Economy*, Leuven University and the Leuven Centre for Global Governance Studies (Feb. 20–21, 2014) Int'l Labour Rev. (ILR) at __ILR__ (forthcoming 2015).

116 Ibid.

117 *Corporate Social Responsibility: Disaster at Rana Plaza*, ECONOMIST, May 4, 2013, available at http://www.economist.com/news/leaders/21577067-gruesome-accident-should-make-all-bosses-think-harder-about-what-behaving-responsibly

5.2 The 'Asian Perspective'

While inter-Asian business grows and FTAs flourish in and with Asia, the inclusion of social dimension provisions in FTAs or BITs is practically non-existent except where Western influence appears to dominate and social dimension provisions are included, such as in FTAs with South Korea and with Singapore.[118]

Within the Asian Region, there is the Trans Pacific Strategic Economic Partnership Agreement (Pacific Four or P-4) involving a plurilateral agreement among Brunei Darussalam, Chile, New Zealand and Singapore. There is also a side agreement of the parties referred to as the 'Labour Cooperation Memorandum of Understanding' (MOU) that provides promises of labor protections by committing to the ILO Declaration, agreeing to improve labor legislation and conditions, and undertaking cooperative activities and institutional contacts to achieve improved labor rights and protections.[119]

There is also the promise of potential inclusion of labor protection provisions in new trade agreements being negotiated inter-Asia, some of which also will include the US and other Western partners. For example, the currently negotiated TPP includes the US, Australia, Brunei Darussalam, Canada, Chile, Japan, Malaysia, Mexico, New Zealand, Peru, Singapore, and Vietnam. In that negotiation, some of the provisions under discussion are said to include a section on a labor chapter that includes commitments on labor rights protection and mechanisms to ensure cooperation, coordination, and dialogue on labor issues of mutual concern.[120] This likely will build upon and further develop the beginnings of the P-4's MOU on labor cooperation.

Finally, in Asia there are Economic Partnership Agreements (EPAs) which include FTAs. While these do not normally include social dimension provisions, they do often include a provision dealing with the movement of natural persons. This is needed to facilitate the trade aspects of the EPA. Though perhaps it is better related to immigration issues than to labor protections, it may be a small step toward recognizing the significance of labor rights in trade agreements.[121]

---

[118] 'Western' particularly includes the EU, Canada, and Australia, all of which typically include social dimension provisions in their FTAs with Asian countries.

[119] *MOU*, *supra* note 109.

[120] *Outlines of TPP*, Office of the U.S. Trade Rep., http://www.ustr.gov/tpp/outlines-of-TPP (last visited June 19, 2013).

[121] Japan's EPAs contain a labor provision entitled 'Investment and Labour' that generally reiterates the ILO core labor rights and states that investment

There is another possible variable to consider, and that is the *accretion factor*. That possible factor would suggest that the Western FTAs with social dimension provisions seeking to improve labor protections will not only do so with the FTA Asian partner, but also possibly with those third-party countries that deal with the Asian partner.

6. OBSERVATIONS, REFLECTIONS AND CONCLUSION

6.1 Observations

Why the dichotomy in trade agreements between US-Asia and inter-Asia in seeking to include labor protections within social dimension provisions?

The expected answers (not without dispute) might be:

1. More-developed countries tend to place greater value in FTAs on labor rights.
2. More-developed countries impose these values on their partners in trade agreements.
3. Labor unions in Asia do not yet have the strength of voice that exists in Western countries.[122]
4. Surplus labor in many Asian countries allows a lesser value on labor protections.
5. Asian countries see social dimension provisions as a disguised form of protectionism.
6. Developing Asian countries see social dimension provisions as a way to limit their economic advantages of cheaper labor and its attraction to foreign investors.

---

cannot be encouraged at the expense of weaker labor laws and their enforcement. *Free Trade Agreements (FTAs) and Economic Partnership Agreements (EPA)*, MINISTRY OF FOREIGN AFF. OF JAPAN (April 2014), available at http://www.mofa.go.jp/policy/economy/fta/

[122] Even in Japan, a developed country, the union voice of RENGO does not seem to find its way into FTA provisions protecting labor. Japan's recent FTAs are said to have 'neglected social aspects both in the negotiation procedures and in the content of their agreements'. ANOTHER JAPAN IS POSSIBLE: NEW SOCIAL MOVEMENTS AND GLOBAL CITIZENSHIP EDUCATION, 93 (Jennifer Chan ed., Stanford University Press 2008).

7. Some Asian countries believe or at least state that labor provisions do not belong in trade talks, much like the original discussions under WTO.

6.2 Reflections

Why is it that Asian countries may agree to social dimension provisions on labor in trade agreements with Western countries while at the same time not including them in inter-Asian trade agreements?

The expected answers (not without dispute) might be:

1. The benefits of Western trade are so great.
2. Asians do not share the same values on labor protections as Western countries.
3. Asian countries lack the political or labor union pressures to include such provisions in inter-Asian trade agreements.
4. Asian countries understand the vagaries of meaningful enforcement.

6.3 Conclusion: 'Pivoting towards Asia'[123]

The expected protocols and dichotomies for social dimension provisions in trade agreements with Asia and within Asia may tend to blend in future years as there seems to be a 'global pivot' towards Asia, and in doing so, the West is entering into more multiplural FTAs which are likely to include social dimension provisions on labor. The 'US perspective' does not automatically advance international labor rights 'on the ground', but it does enhance their visibility and presumably their eventual advancement. The 'Asian perspective' would seem to be evolutionary and anachronistic in the face of arguable advancement in the global quest for social dialogue and decent work environments. And, proponents of the *accretion theory*

---

[123] William S. Cohen, *The Pivot to Asia and Obama's Second Term*, HINDUSTAN TIMES, Nov. 11, 2012, available at http://www.cohengroup.net/news/op_ed/op_ed11112012.cfm. At the very outset of his Administration, the President made a strategic decision to increase the United States' focus on the Asia-Pacific region by rebalancing US engagements, activities, and resources toward this vital region. The President made this plain in his speech before the Australian parliament in 2011: 'the United States will play a larger and long-term role in shaping this region and its future, by upholding core principles and in close partnership with our allies and friends', *The White House Blog*, WHITEHOUSE.GOV (Apr. 12, 2013, 12:52 PM), available at http://www.whitehouse.gov/blog/2013/04/12/resourcing-rebalance-toward-asia-pacific-region

would find solace in the argument that as Western economies join Asian economies it seems unlikely the 'US perspective' on labor rights under trade agreements will succumb to the 'Asian perspective', thus providing an optimistic but probably long-range prediction for those supporting increased labor rights protections.

6. EU economic governance and labour rights: diversity and coherence in the EU, the Council of Europe and ILO instruments

Frank Hendrickx and Pieter Pecinovsky

1. INTRODUCTION

Since the beginning of the financial crisis in 2008, the European Union has been in search of effective policy responses to overcome the crisis and to rescue the Economic and Monetary Union (EMU). This went hand in hand with a strong emphasis on 'fiscal' consolidation, stricter economic and budgetary surveillance and new enforcement mechanisms. Through the 'Six Pack' legislation and the European semester new legal and governance techniques have been introduced to keep convergence and reform agendas in place. In addition, specific measures were made for member states in budgetary difficulties with a strong emphasis on austerity. In this framework, the question is how this 'economic governance' can go together with 'social governance', having in mind that both economic and social progress are central aims of European integration. It has become clear that social challenges are either at the origin or at the outcome of economic governance mechanisms.

Labour law is only one, though highly relevant, component in this economic governance context, as it includes 'sensitive' matters, such as wage setting, collective bargaining and retirement schemes. These issues are subject to monitoring through recommendations by the EU institutions and are part of national reform programmes. The question of this contribution is how economic governance methods relate to more traditional understandings of (transnational) labour standard setting to which European Union member states have contributed and to which they need to show respect in the international arena. The three main international institutions that are considered to be relevant in this contribution are the European Union (EU), the Council of Europe (CoE) and the International Labour Organization (ILO).

It is suggested that EU economic governance stands in a difficult and problematic relationship with fundamental and internationally recognized labour standards, set in a 'triangle' made up by the Council of Europe, the ILO and the EU. It is proposed that, although there are divergent approaches of labour standard setting and monitoring in this international context, problems of coherence in labour rights protection arise.

This contribution starts by setting the scene of EU economic governance and the connected potential criticism that may be formulated in light of (its relation with) fundamental labour rights protection. It will then look at the two major perspectives of coherence, that is, internal and external coherence. In the first place, the issue of internal coherence relates to the difficult relationship between economic and social policies at the level of the European Union. As the tension between economic and social progress pre-exists the EU economic governance debate and touches EU governance more broadly, it is considered to be a necessary perspective to understanding the problems and criticism surrounding EU economic governance and the coherence issue. It will be made clear that it does not necessarily concern an exclusive problem of EU economic governance, and relevant parallels will be made with the debate following the *Viking*[1] and *Laval*[2] cases of the Court of Justice of the European Union. In the second place, external coherence will be discussed. This relates to the relationship between EU (economic) governance and international labour standards, such as those promoted by the Council of Europe and the International Labour Organisation.

In using the term coherence as a criterion, it is understood to mean the absence of contradiction between fundamental labour rights involved or protected in various international legal orders, allowing a situation in which states and international bodies can respect and promote fundamental labour rights in their own legal order without contradicting the other legal orders. In defining coherence, or the lack thereof, as a problem, the viewpoint is taken that member states should be able to deal with both a European and international legal order compatible with regard to the state's obligations to respect fundamental rights protection. This contribution, however, does not claim to have a preference towards complete uniformity of international labour standards approaches, and diversity may well be a desired situation. This nuance will be further

---

1 CJEU 11 December 2007, C-438/05, *ITF and FSU v. Viking Line E.C.R.* 2007, I-10779.

2 CJEU 18 December 2007, C-341/05, *Laval un Partneri v. Svenska Byggnadsarbetareförbundet a.o., E.C.R.* 2007, I-11767.

discussed in the concluding section of this contribution where coherence and diversity issues are elaborated and related to the analysis made in this contribution. Furthermore, the term coherence is preferred over the term consistency. In our view, something can be consistent but nevertheless lead to incoherence.[3] In light of this, it is relevant to note that the Treaty on the Functioning of the European Union Treaty (TFEU) aims 'to ensure consistency between its policies and activities, taking all of its objectives into account' (article 7 TFEU). In other language versions of the Treaty (e.g. French or German), the term coherence (*coherence*, *Kohärenz*) is used. The reference in the TFEU promotes coherence between policy areas in the EU as well as between EU policy areas and member states' policies.[4] This is, however, also seen as contributing to more coherence vis-à-vis fundamental labour rights protection in the 'triangular' relationship between the EU, the Council of Europe and the ILO.

2. SETTING THE SCENE OF EU ECONOMIC GOVERNANCE

2.1 EU Economic Governance and the European Semester

The EU economic governance mechanism is connected with the EU's strategic objectives, currently defined under the heading of 'Europe 2020', which succeeded the Lisbon agenda (2000–2010). The ultimate goal of 'Europe 2020' is to go for 'a smart, sustainable and inclusive economy' with 'high levels of employment, productivity and social cohesion'.[5] To attain this goal, five targets for 2020 were set out regarding employment (75 per cent of the 20–65-year-olds should be employed), research and development, climate, education, and social inclusion, accompanied by ten integrated guidelines for the economic and employment policies of the member states.[6]

---

[3] Cf. S. Pethick, 'Solving the Impossible: The Puzzle of Coherence, Consistency and Law', *N.I.L.Q.* 2008, vol. 59, no. 4, 400.

[4] L. den Hertog and S. Stroβ, 'Coherence in EU External Relations: Concepts and Legal. Rooting of an Ambiguous Term', *E.F.A.Rev* 2013, vol. 18, no. 3, 377.

[5] *Europe 2020: A strategy for sustainable growth and jobs: Contribution from the President of the European Commission to the informal meeting of Heads of State and Government of 11 February 2010*, http://ec.europa.eu/commission_2010-2014/president/news/statements/pdf/20100210_en.pdf

[6] Europe 2020: integrated guidelines for the economic and employment policies of the Member States, European Commission, Recommendation for a

Against this progression of EU member states towards the targets of Europe 2020 various policy measures, including economic and employment policies, have come into existence, one of which is 'economic governance'. The EU itself describes economic governance as follows: 'The EU and its Member States have taken a series of important decisions that will strengthen economic and budgetary coordination for the EU as a whole and for the euro area in particular. As a result, the EU's interdependent economies will be better placed to chart a path to growth and job creation.'[7]

This makes clear what the central aspect of economic governance is: economic and budgetary coordination alongside growth and job creation. In order to achieve this, since 2010 the EU economic governance has been installed in a system generally called 'the European semester'.[8] This European semester functions as an integrated tool to control (monitor) and coordinate the economic policies of the member states. It is a rather complicated system, but it can be seen as a monitoring calendar which is comprised of many different mechanisms and processes.

The European semester entails:[9]

(a) the formulation, and the surveillance of the implementation, of the broad guidelines of the economic policies of the member states and of the Union (broad economic policy guidelines) in accordance with article 121(2) TFEU;
(b) the formulation, and the examination of the implementation, of the employment guidelines that must be taken into account by member states in accordance with article 148(2) TFEU (employment guidelines);
(c) the submission and assessment of member states' stability or convergence programmes under this Regulation;
(d) the submission and assessment of member states' national reform programmes supporting the Union's strategy for growth and jobs

---

Council recommendation 27 April 2010 on broad guidelines for the economic policies of the Member States and of the Union, Part I of the Europe 2020 Integrated Guidelines, COM(2010)193 final, http://ec.europa.eu/eu2020/pdf/Brochure%20Integrated%20Guidelines.pdf

[7] See: http://ec.europa.eu/economy_finance/economic_governance/index_en.htm (consulted on 19 February 2014).

[8] Cf. article 2-bis Regulation 1466/07, modified by Regulation 1175/11; European Commission, *The European Union explained: Europe 2020: Europe's growth strategy, growing to a job-rich and sustainable future*, 2013, 6, http://ec.europa.eu/europe2020/pdf/europe_2020_explained.pdf

[9] Cf. article 2-bis Regulation 1466/07, modified by Regulation 1175/11.

and established in line with the guidelines set out in points (a) and (b) and with the general guidance to member states issued by the Commission and the European Council at the beginning of the annual cycle of surveillance;

(e) the surveillance to prevent and correct macroeconomic imbalances under Regulation (EU) No 1176/2011 of the European Parliament and of the Council of 16 November 2011 on the prevention and correction of macroeconomic imbalances.

By the start of each new calendar year, the 'Annual Growth Survey' is launched by the Commission, containing an overview of the economic situation of the union. This document marks the start of the European semester and is studied and discussed by the European parliament and the Council. It is used by the Council as the main basis to set out the economic priorities of the Union in light of which the member states are expected to act. In spring, the member states publish their 'National Reform Programmes', in which they explain which measures they have taken to make progress towards the Europe 2020 targets. The European Commission examines these national reform programmes and consequently sets up 'Country Specific Recommendations' (CSRs) in May for each member state, to provide guidelines about the actions that member states should take or to point out whether taken measures can be considered to be sufficient or not. These CSRs are normally adopted by the Council in June and July. The monitoring cycle of the European semester starts over again by the beginning of the following year.

2.2 Instruments and Frameworks for Economic Governance

The EU's economic governance, including the European semester as part of its mechanism, uses various important frameworks and instruments, such as the 'SGP', the 'Six Pack', the 'Two Pack', the 'Fiscal Compact' and the 'Macroeconomic Imbalance Procedure' (MIP).

The origin and basis for the economic governance of the EU is to be found in the establishment of the 'Economic and Monetary Union' (EMU) by the Treaty of Maastricht (in force since 1993)[10] and the subsequent introduction of the euro (1990–2002).[11] In preparation for the realization

[10] Treaty on the European Union of 7 June 1992, *O.J.C.* 29 July 1992, no. 191.

[11] F. Snyder, 'EMU – Integration and Differentiation: Metaphor for European Union' in P. Craig and G. De Burca (eds), *The Evolution of EU Law*, Oxford, Oxford University Press, 2011, 697–700; Committee for the study of economic and monetary union (Jacques Delors (EU Commission)), Report

of the EMU, the 'Stability and Growth Pact' (SGP) was introduced in 1997, which nowadays finds its legal basis in articles 112 and 126 TFEU.[12] This instrument is one of the oldest and most important parts of the EU economic governance and is set up to guarantee the stability of the EMU and of the euro. The two main rules of the SGP, which are also enshrined in primary EU law,[13] provide that a member state cannot have a budgetary deficit higher than 3 per cent of the GDP and that the national debt should stay under 60 per cent of the GDP (with certain exceptions). These two rules are part of the 'Maastricht Criteria' or 'euro convergence criteria', laid down in art. 140 TFEU.[14] The SGP has two arms, a 'preventive' and a 'corrective' one. If a member state fails to comply with the 'preventive' arm, showing an excessive deficit, an 'Excessive Deficit Procedure' (EDP) could be launched, which ultimately could lead to sanctions under the 'corrective' arm if the member state fails to give an adequate follow-up to the recommendations they are given under the EDP. Sanctions could, theoretically, take the form of enormous fines (up to 0.5 per cent of GDP) although they have never been applied.

The original SGP was amended in 2005, since important countries like France and Germany demanded more flexibility after they were placed under an Excessive Deficit Procedure.[15] However, the European member states opted for a stricter budgetary monitoring, since the economic and financial crisis (which started around 2007–2008) showed the problematic

on economic and monetary union in the European Community, 17 April 1989, *Archive of European Integration*, http://aei.pitt.edu/1007/1/monetary_delors.pdf

[12] Amsterdam Council Resolution (EU), 17 June 1997 on the Stability and Growth Pact, *O.J.C.* 2 August 1997, no. 236; Council Regulation (EC) no 1466/97, 7 July 1997 on the strengthening of the surveillance of budgetary positions and the surveillance and coordination of economic policies, *O.J.L.* 2 August 1997, no. 209, 1–5; Council Regulation (EC) no. 1467/97, 7 July 1997 on speeding up and clarifying the implementation of the excessive deficit procedure, *O.J.L.* 2 August 1997, no. 209, 6–11.

[13] Art. 140 TFEU; Protocol no. 12, 13 December 2007 on the excessive deficit procedure, *O.J.C.* 9 May 2008, no. 115; Protocol no. 13, 13 December 2007 on the convergence criteria, *O.J.C.* 9 May 2008, no. 115.

[14] The five Maastricht Criteria are those which European Union member states are required to meet to enter the third stage of the Economic and Monetary Union (EMU) and adopt the euro as their currency.

[15] A. De Streel, 'The Evolution of the EU Economic Governance Since the Treaty of Maastricht: An Unfinished Task', *MJ* 2013, no. 3, 340–342; L. Schulknecht, P. Moutot, P. Rother and J. Stark, 'The Stability and Growth Pact: Crisis and Reform', *DICE Report* 2011, nr. 9.3, (10–17), 11–12; M. Vuta, 'From the Rules of Stability and Growth Pact at Six-pack: Financial Certainty', *CrossCultural Management Journal* 2013, no. 27, 230–235, 232.

consequences of an out of control budget and growing national debt, not only for the national economies but also for the stability of the EMU.[16] In this context, the 'Six Pack' legislation (a package of five regulations and one directive) was adopted to improve the enforceability of the SGP.[17] A 'Two Pack' in 2013 introduced further additional surveillance and monitoring procedures for members of the euro area, including harmonized frameworks for draft budgetary plans.[18]

Additional measures were taken in 2013 under the so-called 'Fiscal Compact' (installed by the Treaty on Stability, Coordination and Governance in the Economic and Monetary Union), the 'fiscal' counterpart of the Monetary Union.[19] It concerns an inter-governmental treaty

---

[16] N. de Sadeleer, 'The New Architecture of the European Economic Governance: A Leviathan or a Flat-footed Colossus?', *MJ* 2012, no. 3, 358–360; A. De Streel, 'The Evolution of the EU Economic Governance Since the Treaty of Maastricht: An Unfinished Task' *MJ* 2013, no. 3, 342–343.

[17] Regulation (EU) of the European Parliament and of the Council no. 1175/2011, 16 November 2011 amending Council Regulation (EC) no. 1466/97 on the strengthening of the surveillance of budgetary positions and the surveillance and coordination of economic policies, *O.J.L.* 23 November 2011, no. 306; Council Regulation (EU) no. 1177/2011, 8 November 2011 amending Regulation (EC) no. 1467/97 on speeding up and clarifying the implementation of the excessive deficit procedure, *O.J.L.* 23 November 2011, no. 306; Regulation (EU) of the European Parliament and of the Council no. 1173/2011, 16 November 2011 on the effective enforcement of budgetary surveillance in the euro area, *O.J.L.* 23 November 2011, no. 306; Council Directive no. 2011/85/EU, 8 November 2011 on requirements for budgetary frameworks of the Member States, *O.J.L.* 23 November 2011, no. 306; Regulation (EU) of the European Parliament and of the Council no. 1176/2011, 16 November 2011 on the prevention and correction of macroeconomic imbalances, *O.J.L.* 23 November 2011, no. 306; Regulation (EU) of the European Parliament and of the Council no. 1174/2011, 16 November 2011 on enforcement measures to correct excessive macroeconomic imbalances in the euro area, *O.J.L.* 23 November 2011, no. 306.

[18] Regulation (EU) of the European Parliament and of the Council no. 473/2013, 21 May 2013 on common provisions for monitoring and assessing draft budgetary plans and ensuring the correction of excessive deficit of the Member States in the euro area, *O.J.L.* 140, 27 May 2013; Regulation (EU) of the European Parliament and of the Council no. 472/2013, 21 May 2013 on the strengthening of economic and budgetary surveillance of Member States in the euro area experiencing or threatened with serious difficulties with respect to their financial stability, *O.J.L.* 27 May 2013, no. 140; N. de Sadeleer, 'The New Architecture of the European Economic Governance: A Leviathan or a Flat-footed Colossus?', *MJ* 2012, no. 3, 368.

[19] Treaty on Stability, Coordination, Governance in the Economic and Monetary Union of 2 March 2012, http://european-council.europa.eu/media/639235/st00tscg26_en12.pdf; LB and JHR, 'The Fiscal Compact and the European Constitutions: "Europe Speaking German"', *EuConst* 2012, no. 8,

in which the member states promise to keep their budget and debt in line with the 'Maastricht criteria' of the SGP (max. deficit of 3 per cent GDP, max. debt of 60 per cent GDP), in an even stricter way than the SGP, especially due to its balanced budget rule providing that the budget must be in surplus or in balance and due to the fact that countries can make complaints against other member states before the Court of Justice of the EU if they see that a country does not comply. All EU member states signed up, except for the UK, the Czech Republic and (for now) Croatia.[20]

Next to the SGP the other important economic governance instrument which plays a big role in the European semester is the 'Macroeconomic Imbalance Procedure' (MIP), introduced by the Six Pack in 2011.[21] The crisis made clear to the member states that a solely budgetary monitoring would not suffice to keep the economies under control. The MIP was henceforth installed as an instrument to monitor the macroeconomic situation of the member states, taking into account many more criteria than just the budget and national debt.[22] Like the SGP, the MIP works with a preventive and corrective arm. Under the preventive arm, the Commission will present around November an 'Alert Mechanism Report' (AMR) based on (economical and financial) scoreboard indicators[23] and an economic reading thereof. With this AMR it will identify the member

---

2–5; M.D. Bordo, L. Jonung and A. Markiewicz, 'A Fiscal Union for the Euro: Some Lessons from History', *CESifo Economic Studies* 2013, vol. 59, no. 3, 449–452 and 456–457; A. Gostynska, 'The Fiscal Compact and European Union Economic Governance: An Institutional and Legal Assessment', *The Polish Quarterly of International Affairs* 2012, no. 2, 28–45.

[20] The Fiscal Compact is only binding for euro area member states after they ratified it. Non-euro-area member states will be bound once they adopt the euro or signal it.

[21] Regulation (EU) of the European Parliament and of the Council, no. 1176/2011, 16 November 2011 on the prevention and correction of macroeconomic imbalances, *O.J.L.* 23 November 2011, no. 306, 25–32; Regulation (EU) of the European Parliament and of the Council no. 1174/2011, 16 November 2011 on enforcement measures to correct excessive macroeconomic imbalances in the euro area, *O.J.L.* 23 November 2011, no. 306.

[22] M. Buti and N. Cardot, 'The EMU Debt Crisis: Early Lessons and Reforms', *Journal of Common Market Studies* 2012, vol. 50, no. 6, 906–909; S. Essl and S. Stiglbauer, 'Prevention and Correction of Macroeconomic Imbalances: The Excessive Imbalances Procedure', *Monetary Policy & the Economy* 2011, vol. 4, no. 11, 99–112.

[23] See for example: Eurostat, 'Macroeconomic Imbalances Procedure Scoreboard: Eurostat Publishes Latest Indicators for Early Detection of Macroeconomic Imbalances', 13 November 2013, press release 116/2013, http://epp.eurostat.ec.europa.eu/cache/ITY_PUBLIC/2-13112013-BP/EN/2-13112013-BP-EN.PDF

states which feature possible macroeconomic imbalances. For those countries the Commission can opt to do an in-depth review, resulting in three possible decisions: (1) that there is no problem; (2) that an imbalance exists, in which case the Council can recommend the member state to take appropriate measures according to art. 121, §2 TFEU; (3) that an excessive imbalance exists, in which case there is an 'Excessive Imbalance Procedure' (EIP) and the Council can ask the member state to make a 'Corrective Action Plan' (CAP) according to art. 121, §4 TFEU, which it is obliged to follow. If a member state of the Euro Area does not comply with the recommendations of the Council or with its CAP, this can lead to a sanction: a fine of up to 0.1 per cent of its GDP.

2.3 EU Economic Governance and Member States in Crisis

Besides the standard EU economic governance mechanisms of the European semester, there is also a complex series of hard-core economic governance instruments for member states that had to ask enormous financial support of the EU (and the IMF) in order to prevent bankruptcy following the consequences of the crisis.[24] Greece was first bailed out by the *ad hoc* Greek Loan Facility in 2010.[25] Consequently, the EU Commission installed in the same year a temporary loan facility called the European Financial Stabilisation Mechanism (EFSM).[26] From their side, the member states of the Eurogroup established the European Financial Stability Facility (EFSF).[27] The EFSM and/or the EFSF bailed out Ireland (2010), Greece for a second time (2011) and Portugal (2011). The temporary loan facilities EFSF and EFSM were replaced, starting from 2013, by the permanent European Stability Mechanism (ESM), which finds its legal base in art. 136, §3 TFEU.[28] Cyprus is thus far the

---

[24] Only the financial support mechanisms for members of the Eurogroup are discussed; see E. Balamoti, 'Evaluating the New Rules of EU Economic Governance in Times of Crisis', *ELLJ* 2014, vol. 5, no. 1, 98–99.

[25] Website of the EU Commission, 'Financial Assistance to Greece', http://ec.europa.eu/economy_finance/assistance_eu_ms/greek_loan_facility/index_en.htm

[26] Regulation (EU) of the Council no. 407/2010, 11 May 2010 establishing a European financial stabilization mechanism, *O.J.L.* 12 May 2010, no. 118.

[27] Extraordinary ECOFIN Council of 9 and 10 May 2010, 9596/10 (Presse 108), http://www.consilium.europa.eu/uedocs/cms_data/docs/pressdata/en/ecofin/114324.pdf

[28] Treaty establishing the European Stability Mechanism of 2 February 2012, http://www.esm.europa.eu/pdf/ESM%20Treaty%20consolidated%2013-03-2014.pdf; European Parliament resolution of 23 March 2011 on the draft European

only country which was bailed out by the ESM (in 2013), the other loans remain under the responsibility of the temporary mechanisms.

There are severe conditions for bail out. When a member state asks for financial assistance, a Troika of the EU Commission, the European Central Bank (ECB) and the International Monetary Fund (IMF) investigates whether financial aid is necessary or not. If the support mechanism decides (on the basis of the Troika's research) to grant a bail-out, it will order the Troika to negotiate a 'Memorandum of Understanding' with the member state concerned. This memorandum contains the conditions of the financial support, and indicates the weak points of the member state (taking into account the SGP, MIP and former CSRs) as well as the chosen support instrument (which are mostly loans). If the parties agree on the Memorandum of Understanding, a first partial bail-out follows. The Troika sets up a macroeconomic 'Economic Adjustment Programme' (EAP) for the member state. This is a sort of extremely detailed and long Country Specific Recommendation(s), which indicates the measures a country can or should take in order to return to economic and financial stability. The Troika then closely and regularly supervises the implementation of the EAP, and if the state fails to comply, it can be denied a further part of the financial support. The imposed recommendations contain budgetary measures like tax increases and cost reductions, but also other structural measures, including the reform of pensions or labour law systems.[29] Obviously, countries in such severe need of money rarely have other choices but to take the recommended actions.[30]

2.4 Possible Criticism from a Labour Rights Perspective

Looking into the substance of economic governance, it is clear that, notwithstanding the terminology, it goes beyond pure economic policy aspects. It concerns and affects employment policies, the functioning of the labour market, and recommendations and national reform programmes

---

Council decision amending Article 136 of the Treaty on the Functioning of the European Union with regard to a stability mechanism for Member States whose currency is the euro, OJ CE 247, 17 Aug 2012; I. Schömann, 'Changes in the General European Legal Framework' in N. Bruun, K. Lörcher and I. Schömann, *The Economic and Financial Crisis and Collective Labour Law in Europe*, Oxford and Portland, OR, Hart Publishing, 2014, 15–24.

[29] V. De Stefano, 'A Tale of Oversimplification and Deregulation: The Mainstream Approach to Labour Market Segmentation and Recent Responses to the Crisis in European Countries', *Ind. L.J.* 2014, vol. 43, 264–266.

[30] E. Balamoti, 'Evaluating the New Rules of EU Economic Governance in Times of Crisis', *ELLJ* 2014, vol. 5, no. 1, 107.

cut deep into (national) labour law and welfare systems. For example, recommendations require reforms of national policy with regard to minimum wages (e.g. France 2011, 2012, 2013), dismissal law (Italy 2011, 2014; Spain 2014), wage setting frameworks (Italy 2011, 2013; Belgium 2014; Spain 2014) and employment contract types (Spain 2014).[31] Furthermore, specific crisis measures, in particular for member states in difficulties, have been shown to lead to severe impacts on labour systems.[32] At this substantial level, the question arises how these economic programmes are related to the EU's main objectives laid down in the EU Treaty, such as the aim to work towards a 'social market economy, aiming at full employment and social progress', to 'combat social exclusion and discrimination' and to 'promote social justice and protection'.[33] It can also be questioned what this means with regard to the social ambitions of the EU.

Looking into economic governance from a more procedural point of view, questions arise with regard to the role of the (European) social partners. The 'Six Pack' provisions which regulate the European semester mention the social partners (trade union and employers' representatives), but their role is not elaborated and is left unclear. It is provided that 'relevant stakeholders, in particular the social partners, shall be involved within the framework of the European Semester, on the main policy issues where appropriate, in accordance with the provisions of the TFEU and national legal and political arrangements'.[34]

This stands in contrast with the role that the social partners enjoy under the social policy title of the TFEU, where they have a right to be consulted in the case of the legislative social policy initiative by the European

---

[31] The country specific recommendations can be found at: http://ec.europa.eu/europe2020/making-it-happen/country-specific-recommendations/index_en.htm

[32] E. Balamoti, 'Evaluating the New Rules of EU Economic Governance in Times of Crisis', *ELLJ* 2014, vol. 5, no. 1, 95–109; S. Clauwaert and I. Schömann, 'The Crisis and National Labour Law Reforms, a Mapping Exercise', *ELLJ* 2014, vol. 5, no. 1, 57–69; M. Doherty, 'Can the Patient Survive the Cure? Irish Labour Law in the Austerity Era', *ELLJ* 2014, vol. 5, no. 1, 86–87; A. Monteiro Fernandes, 'Regressive Labor Legislation – the Magic Potion for all Crises: The Case of Portugal', *Comp. Lab. L. & Pol'y J.* 2014, vol. 35, no. 3, 397–411; J. Pagones, 'The European Union's Response to the Sovereign Debt Crisis: Its Effect on Labor Relations in Greece', *Fordham International Law Journal* 2013, vol. 36, 1517–1553; J. Prassl, 'Contingent Crises, Permanent Reforms: Rationalising Labour Market Reforms in the European Union', *ELLJ* 2014, vol. 5, no. 3, 215; M. Yannakourou and C. Tsimpoukis, 'Flexibility without Security and Deconstruction of Collective Bargaining: The New Paradigm of Labor Law in Greece', *Comp. Lab. L. & Pol'y J.* 2014, vol. 35, 331–369.

[33] Cf. article 3 TEU.

[34] Article 2a Regulation 1466/97, 7 July 1997, *O.J.L.* 2 August 1997, no. 209.

Commission, and under which they can take over the initiative or initiate negotiations autonomously when they are ready to do so (cf. arts 154–155 TFEU). Furthermore, art. 154, §1 TFEU provides that 'the Commission shall have the task of promoting the consultation of management and labour at Union level'. This provision requires the European Commission to positively involve social partners in all relevant fields. In the Charter of Fundamental Rights of the EU, 'solidarity' is the heading under which fundamental social rights are included. Solidarity is arguably an element of legitimacy for public policy and social partner involvement in European labour markets and industrial relations.[35]

The European social partners[36] have themselves raised the issue of a lack of social dialogue and involvement in the creation of EU economic governance. In a Declaration of 24 October 2013 they highlighted the principle that the EU should facilitate social dialogue, respecting the autonomy of the social partners.[37] Moreover, they stress the fact that the decision on how to organize wage bargaining is a national competence. Indeed art. 153, §5 TFEU excludes wage bargaining from the EU's competence, yet CSRs, for example, often give specific guidelines for dismantling certain index mechanisms. The overall feeling is that the social partners are left out, although it would be coherent with the EU's own rules if they were sufficiently involved in the economic governance process. Finally, the social partners indicate in the 2013 Declaration in which specific steps of the different economic governance instruments they would like to be involved.

3. INTERNAL COHERENCE PROBLEMS IN THE EU

3.1 Social and Economic Europe

The criticism concerning economic governance, from the angle of labour law and social policy, must be understood against the wider perspective of an internal coherence problem in the EU. It runs parallel with the debate about the tension between economic and social policies.

In the EU, the question of how economic and social integration should be balanced, has been a matter of (high) debate for a long time. The

---

35 Cf. S. Sciarra, 'Notions of Solidarity in Times of Economic Uncertainty', *Ind. L.J.* 2010, vol. 39, no. 3, 223–243.

36 Business Europe, UEAPME, CEEP and ETUC.

37 Declaration by the European Social Partners of 24 October 2013, 'Social Partner Involvement in European Economic Governance', http://ec.europa.eu/europe2020/pdf/2014/socjointcontrib_ags2014.pdf

tension, some have called it a schism,[38] between the 'economic' and the 'social' dimension, ultimately affects the role and understanding of labour law at the level of the European Union. Furthermore, in terms of regulatory approaches, labour law at the European Union level receives attention in many diverse ways. Labour law can have a plurality of positions in the European Union legal order. Different policy areas related with European integration law involve or affect labour law. These policy areas, such as social policy, internal market policy and employment policy, would seem to become less distinctive areas.[39] But still, they have their own dynamics and the question remains whether they have a common thread. In the light of its own dynamics, social policy is supported by partial or incomplete strategies of (positive) labour regulation and minimum harmonization. Internal market policy, on the other hand, is strongly driven by a de-regulation agenda. Furthermore, employment policy follows a less strict regulatory pathway and includes governance mechanisms such as the 'open method of coordination', focusing on economic growth, a better functioning of the labour market, promoting adaptability and economic competitiveness.

Social policy, including the protection of workers as an explicit objective of the European Union, has been controversial from the very beginning of the European project. It is well known that the original Treaties only aimed at the creation of an economic community of states. The other policy areas would only come from the *spill-over* effect of economic integration. Little by little, ways were paved for social policy. An important landmark was the Social Action Programme (SAP), which was adopted by the Council in a resolution of 21 January 1974.[40] It underlined the necessity to take measures towards realizing priorities such as full and better employment, the improvement and harmonization of living and working conditions, and increased involvement of management and labour in the economic and social decision-making process, both at the European level and in undertakings. The document reflected high and broad ambitions and the SAP was seen as announcing a 'golden period of harmonisation'.[41]

---

[38] E. Szyzsczak, 'The Evolving European Employment Strategy' in J. Shaw (ed.), *Social Law and Policy in an Evolving European Union*, Oxford and Portland, OR, Hart Publishing, 2000, 199.

[39] C. Barnard, 'Internal Market v. Labour Market: A Brief History' in M. De Vos (ed.), *European Union Internal Market and Labour Law: Friends or Foes?* in *Social Europe Series*, nr. 19, Antwerp, Intersentia, 2009, 19–43.

[40] 'Social Action Programme. Resolution of the Council of 21 January 1974', *BCLR* 1974, no. 5, 135–187.

[41] R. Blanpain, *European Labour Law*, The Hague, Kluwer Law International, 2008, 208.

However, the labour law legislation that followed was important but stayed limited to well-defined and specific areas.[42] Many legislative proposals failed to obtain approval in the Council.

While there remained a gap between ambition and reality, it is striking that the 1974 Social Action Programme already contained the important consideration that 'it is essential to ensure the coherence of social and other Community policies so that measures taken will achieve the objectives of social and other policies simultaneously'. The necessity of coherence between the original economic purposes of European integration and the spill-over fields was thus already seen.

The adoption of the 1989 Charter of Fundamental Rights and the introduction of the Maastricht Protocol on Social Policy in 1991, undoubtedly marked a major development for European labour law and social policy. It laid the basis for a social chapter, which became fully integrated by the 1997 Amsterdam Treaty[43] and which is now incorporated in articles 151 and following of the TFEU. Initiatives based on the social chapter have been significant, and have produced a large variety of European labour law legislation, including subjects such as, for example, equal treatment, health and safety, working time, working conditions, European works councils, information and consultation. Nevertheless, essential aspects of labour law (such as pay, freedom of association and the right to strike) are excluded from the TFEU's social chapter,[44] meaning that the European Union addresses labour law only partially. The question of the relationship between the economic and social dimension thus remained.

3.2 Viking and Laval

The discussion reached a peak with the *Viking*[45] and *Laval*[46] case law of the Court of Justice of the EU. Both cases concern the conflict between 'market rights' and 'labour rights' and have sharpened the tension. The

---

42 Cf. equal treatment, collective dismissal, transfer of undertakings, employer insolvency, health and safety.

43 Treaty of Amsterdam, amending the Treaty on European Union, the Treaties establishing the European Communities and certain related acts, signed at Amsterdam, 2 October 1997, *O.J.C.* 10 November 1997, no. 340.

44 Cf. article 153, para. 5 TFEU.

45 CJEU 11 December 2007, *ITF and FSU v. Viking Line* C-438/05, *E.C.R.* 2007, I-10779.

46 CJEU 18 December 2007, C-341/05, *Laval un Partneri v. Svenska Byggnadsarbetareförbundet a.o.*, *E.C.R.* 2007, I-11767.

case law is seen as creating an imbalance between the economic and social aspects of the European Union.[47]

The *Viking*[48] case concerned a Finnish company, Viking, which sought to reflag its ship to Estonia or Norway in order to be able to enter into a new collective agreement with a trade union established in one of those countries, the point being to lower the labour costs and stay economically viable. The unions who wanted to avoid the reflagging were found to be in violation of Viking's freedom of establishment. In *Laval*,[49] a Latvian company sent workers from Latvia to Sweden to work on school premises in the town of Vaxholm. The Swedish construction industry trade union engaged in industrial action including blockades in order to push Laval into negotiations with a view to establishing (Swedish) rates of pay for the Latvian workers and in order to include Laval in the collective agreement of the building sector. The Court found an infringement of European Union law on free movement of services, protecting Laval's interests.

Both cases deal with the right to take collective action, a matter which is not only strongly related to national tradition but is also a matter excluded from the European Treaty's social chapter.[50] In this area, member states are guided by the principles of the International Labour Organization and the Council of Europe, two frameworks that recognize the fundamental right to strike vested under the supervision of authoritative expert bodies[51] or a European Human Rights Court. The European Court's assessment and decision provoked a great deal of

---

47 D. Ashiagbor, 'Unraveling the Embedded Liberal Bargain: Labour and Social Welfare Law in the Context of EU Market Integration', *E.L.J.* 2013, vol. 19, no. 3, 303–324; C. Barnard, 'Internal market v. labour market: a brief history' in M. De Vos (ed.), *European Union Internal Market and Labour Law: Friends or Foes?*, Antwerp, Intersentia, 2009, 19–43; N. Hos, 'The Principle of Proportionality in Viking and Laval: An Appropriate Standard of Judicial Review?', *ELLJ* 2010, vol. 1, no. 2, 236–253; P. Syrpis and T. Novitz, 'Economic and Social Rights in Conflict: Political and Judicial Approaches to their Reconciliation', *E.L. Rev.* 2008, vol. 33, no. 3, 411–426; U. Wendeling-Schröder, 'Fundamental Freedoms of the EC Treaty Versus the Fundamental Social Right to take Collective Action' in E. Ales, T. Jaspers, P. Lorber, C. Sachs-Durand and U. Wendeling-Schröder (eds), *Fundamental Social Rights in Europe: Challenges and Opportunities*, Antwerp, Intersentia, 2009, 25–35.

48 CJEU 11 December 2007, C-438/05, *E.C.R.* 2007, I-10779.

49 CJEU 18 December 2007, C-341/05, *E.C.R.* 2007, I-11767.

50 Cf. article 153, 5 TFEU.

51 Cf. The ILO's Committee on Freedom of Association and the Council of Europe's European Committee of Social Rights.

criticism.[52] Applying the *Schmidberger*[53] doctrine, the Court did not give immunity to the right to strike, meaning that the collective action was tested against the fundamental Treaty freedoms reflecting the internal market objectives. The 'immunity' argument would, however, have been possible if borrowed from the area of European competition law. A form of immunity of labour law from market principles has been granted by the European Court in what can be called the *Albany* approach.[54] In this case, the Court found that, although certain restrictions of competition are inherent in collective agreements between organizations representing employers and workers, the social policy objectives pursued by such agreements would be seriously undermined if management and labour were subject to Article 105 of the Treaty[55] when seeking jointly to adopt measures to improve conditions of work and employment. According to the Court it therefore follows from an interpretation of the provisions of the Treaty as a whole that is both effective and consistent that agreements concluded in the context of collective negotiations between management and labour in pursuit of such objectives must, by virtue of their nature and purpose, be regarded as falling outside the scope of Article 105 of the Treaty.[56] For a similar idea, reference can also be made to the language used in the *Monti* Regulation on the free circulation of goods in the EU,[57] which provides that this legal instrument 'may not be interpreted as affecting in any way the exercise of fundamental rights as recognised in Member States, including the right or freedom to strike'.[58] A comparable concept underlies the European Services Directive,[59] providing that it 'does not affect labour law'.[60] It seems quite obvious that, if the Court

---

52 Cf. A. Davies, 'One Step Forward, Two Steps Back? The *Viking* and *Laval* Cases in the ECJ', *ILJ* 2008, vol. 37, no. 2, 147: 'The decisions in *Viking* and *Laval* are not surprising, but they are disappointing. Although the ECJ has recognized the existence of a right to strike in EU law, it has subordinated that right to the free movement rights contained in Articles 43 and 49 EC. This reflects the fact that the ECJ regards its own role as one of protecting and promoting the fundamental principles of Community law.'

53 CJEU 12 June 2003, C-112/00, *Eugen Schmidberger*, *E.C.R.* 2003, I-5659.

54 CJEU 21 September 1999, C-67/96, *Albany*, *E.C.R.* 1999, I-5751, para. 59.

55 That is, the provisions on competition law, at the time of the case: Article 85(1) of the EC Treaty.

56 Ibid., para. 60.

57 Council Regulation (EC) no. 2679/98, 7 December 1998 on the functioning of the internal market in relation to the free movement of goods among the Member States, *O.J.L.* 12 December 1998, no. 337.

58 Cf. article 2.

59 Directive 2006/123, *O.J.L.* 27 December 2006, no. 376.

60 Cf. article 6.

had used an 'immunity approach' in *Viking* and *Laval*, the criticism would have been much different or even absent. It is very likely that most social policy commentators would have seen this as a form of coherence between the implied (social and economic) policy areas.

The matter raises questions about the internal coherence of the European Union policy framework, not only taking into account the social policy ambitions in the Treaty's social chapter that leave member states autonomous in regulating collective action,[61] but certainly since the adoption of the Charter of Fundamental Rights of the European Union, which became binding since the entry into force of the Lisbon Treaty on 1 December 2009. The Court has confirmed in other cases that fundamental rights have primacy in the hierarchy of norms of European Union law, since they are enshrined in the EU Treaty as 'a foundation of the Union'.[62] Fundamental rights have thus privileged status over other rights and principles of European Union law.[63] It would logically follow that constitutional approaches are to be applied in social rights discourses.[64] This may change the nature of the European Court's judgments.[65] As the right to take collective action is safeguarded by article 28 of the EU Charter, the CJEU might take up the role of a human rights court and attribute a higher value to fundamental (social) rights than it has done in *Viking* and *Laval*.[66] It is, at least, legitimate to expect this from the perspective of coherence between the economic and internal market policies, the social policies and the fundamental rights aspirations of the EU.

---

[61] It is an excluded matter on the basis of art. 153, §5 TFEU.

[62] CJEU 3 September 2008, C-402/05 P and C-415/05 P, *Kadi and Al Barakaat International Foundation v. Council and Commission*, *E.C.R.* 2008, I-635, para. 303.

[63] S. PEERS, 'Supremacy, Equality and Human Rights: Comment on Kucukdeveci (C-555/07)', *E.L.R.* 2010, vol. 35, no. 6, 856.

[64] D. SCHIEK, 'Constitutional Principles and Horizontal Effect: Kücükdeveci Revisited', *ELLJ* 2010, vol. 1/3, 368–379.

[65] A.T. WILLIAMS, 'Promoting Justice after Lisbon: Groundwork for a New Philosophy of EU Law', *OJLS* 2010, vol. 30, 678.

[66] G. DE BÚRCA, 'After the EU Charter of Fundamental Rights: The Court of Justice as a Human Rights Adjudicator?', *MJ* 2013, vol. 20, no. 2, 168–184; S. CARRERA, M. DE SOMER and B. PETKOVA, 'The Court of Justice of the European Union as a Fundamental Rights Tribunal: Challenges for the Effective Delivery of Fundamental Rights in the Area of Freedom, Security and Justice', *Liberty and Security in Europe* 2012, no. 49, 5-8; F. HENDRICKX, *Labour Law for the United States of Europe*, Tilburg, Tilburg University, 2011, 37–38.

3.3 Employment Policy and Flexicurity

A similar debate on the relationship between Europe's economic and social dimension has been triggered in the EU's employment policy context. When the Employment Title, adopted in the 1997 Amsterdam Treaty, conferred employment policy competences at the European level, it did not change the basic starting point that the member states would have the sole competence for employment policies, leaving a more coordinated role for EU institutions. It concerned an 'open method of coordination': the Union would formulate guidelines while member states would remain full actors, subject to reporting and evaluation, in a system of mutual learning and peer review.

It was described as a 'new mode of governance'[67] but its ambiguity was observed from the start:

> if we were to describe this new Title on employment as yet another example of proceduralisation in the field of social policies, we would say too little and too much at the same time: too little, because this matter goes beyond the domain of social policies, too much because procedures, as they are known in European labour law tradition, must disclose a legally meaningful outcome.[68]

The EU strategy with regard to employment policies thus brought the issue of Europe's regulatory approach in the field of social policy to the forefront. From a traditional labour law point of view, modes of governance with degressive (hard law) intervention[69] were rather new. For some it concerned something 'meaningful',[70] while for others it was a 'weak

---

[67] According to Caroline de la Porte and Philippe Pochet: 'New modes of governance can be referred to as "the range of innovation and transformation that has been and continues to occur in the instruments, methods, modes and systems of governance in contemporary polities and economies, and especially within the European Union (EU) and its member states (both current and prospective)"', C. DE LA PORTE and P. POCHET, 'The European Employment Strategy: Existing Research and Remaining Questions', *Journal of European Social Policy* 2004, vol. 14, no. 1, 71.

[68] S. SCIARRA, 'The Employment Title in the Amsterdam Treaty: A Multi-language Legal Discourse' in D. O'KEEFFE and P. TWOMEY (eds), *Legal Issues of the Amsterdam Treaty*, Oxford and Portland, OR, Hart Publishing, 1999, 169.

[69] Cf. B.K. KELLER, 'The Employment Chapter of the Amsterdam Treaty: Towards a New European Employment Policy?' in R. BLANPAIN and M. WEISS (eds), *Changing Industrial Relations and Modernisation of Labour Law. Liber Amicorum in honour of Professor Marco Biagi*, The Hague, Kluwer Law International, 2003, 234–235.

[70] M. BIAGI, 'The Impact of European Employment Strategy on the Role of Labour Law and Industrial Relations', *Int. J. Comp. L.L.I.R.* 2000, 173.

institutional set-up'.[71] In general, the European employment strategy was perceived as a soft law mechanism. This may have made it acceptable, but the diversity and innovation in approaches that it portrayed, did not seem to be unproblematic.[72]

It is clear that through employment policy, EU social and economic policies became more and more blurred. This may be evident, but it is also a sign of the problematic relationship between economic and social policies in the EU, as the logics of dynamics of economic policy strongly influence social objectives. The connection, or interaction, between economic and social policies becomes clear from the aims of employment policy laid down in article 145 TFEU, stating that it is about 'developing a coordinated strategy for employment and particularly for promoting a skilled, trained and adaptable workforce and labour markets responsive to economic change'.

With its connection between economic and social policies, the EU's employment policy also imported, to a certain extent, the tension or contradiction between the economic and social dimension. Looking at its origins, the economic traces of employment policy are apparent. The strongest impulse for EU employment policy was given in the 1990s on the initiative of the European Commission of Jacques Delors. Under Delors' direction, the European Commission issued the *White Paper on Growth, Competitiveness and Employment (1993)*.[73] It concluded that the economic and social problems faced by the Community at that time were a result of some fundamental inefficiencies, like the under-use of the quality and quantity of the labour force.[74] This document produced broad and intense discussion from 1993 onwards on how the EU could ensure sustainable jobs and better opportunities for disadvantaged jobseekers. At the same time, the *White Paper* made clear that employment policies were seen to imply a strong, and perhaps inevitable, relationship between economic and social policy. But this was not 'tension free' as has become clearer in

---

[71] S. Sciarra, 'The Employment Title in the Amsterdam Treaty: A Multi-language Legal Discourse' in D. O'Keeffe and P. Twomey (eds), *Legal Issues of the Amsterdam Treaty*, Oxford, Hart Publishing, 1999, 169.

[72] See for a further discussion: C. Barnard, 'EU "Social" Policy: From Employment Law to Labour Market Reform' in P. Craig and G. de Burca (eds.), *The Evolution of EU Law*, Oxford, Oxford University Press, 2011, 658–659; C. De la Porte, 'Is the Open Method of Coordination Appropriate for Organizing Activities at European Level in Sensitive Policy Areas?', *E.L.J.* 2002, vol. 8, no. 1, 38–41.

[73] White Paper on growth, competitiveness, and employment: The challenges and ways forward into the 21st century, COM(93)700final, Brussels, 5.12.1993.

[74] Conclusion 1, Chapter 10.3, COM(93)700final.

later stages. The soft policy methods of coordination helped the EU institutions to develop policy initiatives beyond the limited concept of 'hard' European legal competence in the area of social policy. It put reform and modernization of labour law on the agenda and, nourished by the European policy ideas of the nineties, it delivered a roadmap for the much criticized concept of 'flexicurity' (flexibility and security on the labour market).[75] Nevertheless, the fact that issues such as flexibility on the labour market, labour cost, flexible work and employment security have come under the heading of employment policy, ultimately raised questions about how employment policy is exactly related to the hard competences in the area of social policy, where pay is an excluded area and job security is subject to unanimous voting in the Council and thus left to member state control (cf. art. 153 TFEU).

3.4 Reflections on Economic Governance

The tensions between the economic and social dimension of European integration are similarly reflected in EU economic governance. Moreover, employment policies, part of the EU's social governance framework, are strongly implied in the EU economic governance system. The further blurring of economic and social policy areas is quite clear. As the employment policy framework developed over the years, it made use of various monitoring instruments, such as the 'Joint Employment Report' (JER), the 'Joint Assessment Framework' (JAF), the 'Employment Performance Monitor' (EPM) and the 'Social Protection Performance Monitor' (SPPM).[76] These instruments are not discussed here, but it is relevant

---

[75] P. Auer, 'What's in a name? The rise and fall of flexicurity', *J.I.R.* 2010, vol. 52, no. 3, 371–386; L. Burroni and M. Keune, 'Flexicurity: A Conceptual Critique', *European Journal of Industrial Relations* 2011, vol. 17, no. 1, 75–91; European Trade Union Confederation (ETUC), 'Flexicurity Will Get Nowhere without Reinforcing Rights for Workers, says the ETUC', https://www.etuc.org/press/flexicurity-will-get-nowhere-without-reinforcing-rights-workers-says-etuc#.VaN7bP5RFMs (30 January 2015).

[76] European Commission and Council of the EU, Foundations and structures for a Joint Assessment Framework (JAF), including an Employment Performance Monitor (EPM) to monitor the Employment Guidelines under Europe 2020 – COM-EMCO-SPC report, 26 November 2010; Joint EMCO-SPC opinion on The Joint Assessment Framework and the Employment Performance Monitor, 26 November 2010, nr. 16984/10; Council of the EU, Conclusions of 9 December 2011, 25 January 2012, EUCO 139/1/11, 2, http://www.consilium.europa.eu/uedocs/cms_data/docs/pressdata/en/ec/126714.pdf; European Commission, Strengthening the Social Dimension of the Economic and Monetary Union, 2 October 2013, COM(2013) 690, 6, http://ec.europa.eu/commission_2010-

to point out that they deliver crucial information to the Commission and the Council to assess member state performance and convergence in the EU.[77] As employment policy is so much connected to both social as well as economic policy and since employment policy developed into a governance system which is an important part of the European semester, it is clear that the generic terminology of the EU 'economic' governance does not really cover all its aspects. It probably deserves a broader name, such as 'economic and social governance', although that may imply different accents in the assessment of member states' reform agendas. Furthermore, this broader terminology might be unrealistic, as the question of how employment, social and economic policies are related still stands and is under-developed in terms of coherence. Critics of economic governance claim that the EU demands its member states to dismantle acquired social rights in a one-sided crusade for austerity and economic growth.[78]

Furthermore, in comparison with employment policies, there are reasons why one can hesitate to simply label EU economic governance as soft law. The Six Pack legislation of 2011 introduced serious changes to the enforceability of EU economic governance.[79] For example, the SGP is monitored through reporting by the member states about their mid-term goals and planned structural programmes and the subsequent assessment

---

2014/president/news/archives/2013/10/pdf/20131002_1-emu_en.pdf; Council of the EU, Conclusions of 24 and 25 October 2013, 25 October 2013, EUCO 169/13, 14, http://www.consilium.europa.eu/uedocs/cms_data/docs/pressdata/en/ec/139197.pdf

[77] Cf. art. 5, §1, 9 Reg. 1466/97 as amended by Reg. 1175/11: 'The Council and the Commission shall also examine whether the stability programme facilitates the achievement of sustained and real convergence within the euro area and the closer coordination of economic policies, and whether the economic policies of the Member State concerned are consistent with the broad economic policy guidelines and the employment guidelines of the Member States and of the Union.'

[78] C. Barnard, 'The Social Partners and the Governance Agenda', *E.L.J.* 2002 vol. 8, no. 1, 86; C. Crouch, 'Entrenching Neo-liberalism' in N. Contouris and M. Freedland (eds), *Resocialising Europe*, Cambridge, Cambridge University Press, 2013, 43–44; M. De Vos, 'Interne Markt en eurocrisis: arbeidsrecht in de tang van de Europese Unie', *TSR* 2013, no. 3, 694–697; J. Fudge, 'The Way Forward for Social Europe: How Do We Get There From Here?', book review of N. Contouris and M. Freedland (eds), *Resocialising Europe*, Cambridge, Cambridge University Press, 2013 in *M.L.R.* 2014, vol. 77, no. 5, 811.

[79] S. Bekker and S. Klöse, 'The Changing Legal Context of Employment Policy Coordination: How Do Social Policy Issues Fare After the Crisis?', *ELLJ* 2014, vol. 5, no. 1, 8; S. Deakin, 'Social Policy, Economic Governance and EMU: Alternatives to Austerity' in N. Bruun, K. Lörcher and I. Schömann, *The Economic and Financial Crisis and Collective Labour Law in Europe*, Oxford, Hart Publishing, 2014, 92–96.

by the European Commission.[80] However, the Council, on a recommendation from the Commission, can invite the member state concerned to adjust its programme,[81] and if that does not take place in a satisfactory manner, an interest-bearing deposit of up to 0.2 per cent of GDP can be imposed.[82] When the Council decides that there is an excessive deficit, a non-interest-bearing deposit of 0.2 per cent of GDP can be imposed,[83] and this can be converted into a fine.[84] Soft law employment policy instruments form part of the assessment criteria of member states performance, and this may ultimately have hard law effects. Similar remarks can be made with regard to EU economic governance for member states in crisis that have to deal with a Memorandum of Understanding, which is difficult to bypass if a country wants to receive the next phase of financial support.[85]

4. EXTERNAL COHERENCE PROBLEMS IN THE EU

4.1 Lessons from the Viking and Laval Experience

The earlier mentioned *Viking* and *Laval* cases of the Court of Justice of the European Union have not only brought up questions about coherence within the EU legal order itself, they also raise questions on how they are related with international labour standards set at the level of the Council of Europe and the International Labour Organization. The cases are good examples of an emerging 'triangular' relationship between the EU, the Council of Europe and the ILO.

In this context, reference should be made to the protection of the right to take collective action under article 11 of the European Convention of Human Rights (ECHR). The relevance of the ECHR increased with the *Energi Yapi Yol Sen* case of 21 April 2009,[86] in which the European Court of Human Rights (ECtHR) explicitly recognized the right to strike under

---

80 Art. 5, §1 Reg. 1466/97 as amended by Reg. 1175/11.

81 Art. 5, §2 Reg. 1466/97 as amended by Reg. 1175/11.

82 Art. 4, §1 Reg. 1173/11.

83 Art. 5, §1 Reg. 1173/11.

84 Art. 6, §1 Reg. 1173/11.

85 See for examples: M. Doherty, 'Can the Patient Survive the Cure? Irish Labour Law in the Austerity Era', *ELLJ* 2014, vol. 5, no. 1, 86–87; E. Balamoti, 'Evaluating the New Rules of EU Economic Governance in Times of Crisis', *ELLJ* 2014, vol. 5, no. 1, 106–108.

86 ECtHR 21 April 2009, 68959/01, *Enerji Yapi-Yol Sen v. Turkey*.

article 11 ECHR. Under that protection, the right to strike is considered fundamental, though not absolute and is thus subject to limitations, but any interference with this right is subject to a test of legality, legitimacy and necessity in a democratic society. The link with this *Energi* case and *Viking* and *Laval* has emerged from the Charter on Fundamental Rights of the EU providing that 'in so far as this Charter contains rights which correspond to rights guaranteed by the ECHR, the meaning and scope of those rights shall be the same'.[87] The interpretation of the European Court of Human Rights can thus hardly be neglected by the European Court of Justice.[88]

The link with the ECHR becomes even more interesting when account is taken of the integrated approach of the European Court on Human Rights with regard to referencing international labour standards. In the case of *Demir and Baykara*, the ECtHR used for the first time a remarkable method of interpretation of the ECHR and cross-referred to international human rights treaties (ILO conventions, the EU Charter of Fundamental Rights and the European Social Charter) as well as to the practices of the member states, in order to strengthen and broaden the protection of the right to collective bargaining and the right to strike under article 11 ECHR.[89] This cross-referencing also took place in the *Viking* and *Laval* judgments, where the Court of Justice of the European Union referred to the European Social Charter (Council of Europe) and Convention No 87 (ILO).[90] However, the approach of the EU case law sits very uncomfortably with the ILO's approach on the right to strike.[91]

In the so-called *BALPA* case, the ILO's Committee of Experts explicitly addressed the *Viking* and *Laval* case law.[92] The British Airline Pilots'

---

[87] Article 52 of the Charter of Fundamental Rights of the European Union of 7 December 2000.

[88] W. Weiss, 'Human Rights and EU Anti-trust Enforcement: News from Lisbon', *Eur. Comp. Law Rev.* 2011, vol. 32, no. 4, 190.

[89] ECtHR 12 November 2008, 34503/97, *Demir and Baykara/Turkey*; A. Jacobs, 'Article 11 ECHR: The Right to Bargain Collectively under Article 11 ECHR' in F. Dorssemont, K. Lörcher and I. Schömann (eds), *The European Convention on Human Rights and the Employment Relation*, Oxford, Hart Publishing, 2013, 311–314.

[90] *Viking*, para. 43; *Laval*, para. 90.

[91] See for an overview of principles on the right to strike: ILO, General Survey, 1994, Freedom of association and collective bargaining: the right to strike, Report III, part 4B, http://www.ilo.org/ilolex; B. Gernigon, A. Odero and H. Guido, 'ILO Principles on the Right to Strike', *International Labour Review* 1998, vol. 137, no. 4, 441–443.

[92] ILO Report of the Committee of Experts on the Application of Conventions and Recommendations, 2010, 99th session of the International Labour

Association (BALPA) wished to undertake strike action after British Airways (BA) decided to establish a subsidiary company in another EU country, and after unsuccessful attempts to start up negotiations on the impact of this on the terms and conditions of employment in the group. BA, however, requested an injunction against the strike action before a UK Court, as it believed that a strike would violate the fundamental freedom of establishment under EU law, as established in the *Viking* and *Laval* case law. BA sought damages of £100 million per day of work stoppage. Fearing enormous damages, BALPA did not proceed with strike action, yet it expressed its deep concern about the UK court's adoption of the *Viking* and *Laval* approach.[93] The ILO Committee of Experts, subsequently examining the case, was of the opinion that it was not competent to assess the correctness of the *Viking* and *Laval* cases to the extent that they gave an interpretation of European Union law. However, it examined whether the consequences of these cases on a national level would violate the rights following from ILO Convention no. 87. First, the ILO Committee rejected the CJEU's proportionality test, based on the view that it never felt the need to assess the proportionality of interests, bearing in mind a notion of freedom of establishment or freedom to provide services. Second, the ILO Committee held that the threat of damages that could bankrupt the trade union, rendered the exercise of the rights under Convention no. 87 impossible. The ILO Committee was of the opinion that 'the doctrine that is being articulated in these ECJ judgments is likely to have a significant restrictive effect on the exercise of the right to strike in practice in a manner contrary to the Convention'.

It is thus clear that various international legal orders come into play when a strike issue is dealt with under EU law. It is also apparent that this may lead, as the *Viking* and *Laval* experience shows, to incompatibility and contradiction.

4.2 Lessons from the Austerity Experience

Similar relational issues arise between the EU, the Council of Europe and the ILO where their respective (legal) approaches to austerity measures are concerned. As described above, the EU has a (soft/hard) power through

---

Conference, Report III (Part 1A), 208–209, http://www.ilo.org/public/libdoc/ilo/P/09661/09661(2010-99-1A).pdf; A. Seifert, 'The Still Complex Relationship between the ILO and the EU: The Example of Anti-Discrimination Law', *Int. J. Comp. L.L.I.R.* 2013, vol. 29, no. 1, 55–56.

[93] K.D. Ewing and J. Hendy, 'The Dramatic Implications of Demir and Baykara', *Ind. L.J.* 2010, vol. 39, no. 1, 44–45.

its economic governance mechanisms in order to force member states to take austerity measures in view of the Maastricht criteria and budget control, or, in certain particular cases, in order to avoid bankruptcy. The most severe austerity programmes in southern European Countries, like Portugal, Spain, Cyprus and Greece (but also Ireland), have caused social unrest and despair.[94] Although set up under an EU initiative and mainly to settle EU problems, both the Council of Europe and the ILO have addressed austerity measures and identified legal problems. Before these institutions, a number of Greek austerity measures had been under debate.

The first case concerns a collective complaint before the European Committee of Social Rights (ECSR), which supervises the European Social Charter, from the General Federation of Employees of the National Electric Power Corporation (GENOP-DEI) and the Confederation of Greek Civil Servants' Trade Unions (ADEDY).[95] The Greek unions argued that certain austerity measures of the Greek government, which were introduced in the context of the Troika's Economic Adjustment Programmes, were in violation of the European Social Charter (ESC). The complaint was restricted to the Greek Act No. 3863 of 15 July 2010, introducing 'special apprenticeship contracts' between employers and individuals aged 15 to 18, which was created with the intention of reducing youth unemployment.

In its conclusion, the ECSR, referring to earlier opinions[96] held that the Greek Act No. 3863 violated the European Social Charter, as it did not provide for the necessary three weeks of annual leave and since it excludes apprentices from the scope of labour legislation.[97] Another violation was seen in the fact that the Greek legislator left too many issues open to the

---

[94] E. Balamoti, 'Evaluating the New Rules of EU Economic Governance in Times of Crisis', *ELLJ* 2014, vol. 5, no. 1, 95–109; C. Crouch, 'Entrenching Neo-liberalism', in N. Contouris and M. Freedland (eds), *Resocialising Europe*, Cambridge, Cambridge University Press, 2013, 36–60; A. Monteiro Fernandes, 'Regressive Labor Legislation – the Magic Potion for all Crises: The Case of Portugal', *Comp. Lab. L. & Pol'y J.* 2014, vol. 35, no. 3, 397–411; J. Pagones, 'The European Union's Response to the Sovereign Debt Crisis: its Effect on Labor Relations in Greece', *Fordham International Law Journal* 2013, vol. 36, 1517–1553; M. Yannakourou and C. Tsimpoukis, 'Flexibility Without Security and Deconstruction of Collective Bargaining: The New Paradigm of Labor Law in Greece', *Comp. Lab. L. & Pol'y J.* 2014, vol. 35, 331–369.

[95] ECSR 23 May 2012, 66/2011, *General Federation of Employees of the National Electric Power Corporation (GENOP-DEI) and the Confederation of Greek Civil Servants' Trade Unions (ADEDY) v. Greece.*

[96] ECSR, Conclusions XIX-2 (2009), General Introduction, no. 15.

[97] ECSR, *GENOP-DEI and ADEDY v. Greece*, nos. 25–32.

agreement of the contracting parties, thus paving the way for abuse by the employer.[98] It was, furthermore, considered that:

> the highly limited protection against social and economic risks afforded to minors engaged in 'special apprenticeship contracts' has the practical effect of establishing a distinct category of workers who are effectively excluded from the general range of protection offered by the social security system at large and that this represents a deterioration of the social security scheme which does not fulfil the criteria to be compatible with article 12 §3 of the 1961 Charter.[99]

Finally, the ECSR held that Act No. 3863 constituted a violation of article 4 §1 of the 1961 Charter in so far as it provided for the payment of a minimum wage to all workers below the age of 25 which is below the poverty level.[100]

The second case concerns *Koufaki and Adedy v. Greece*, a decision of the European Court of Human Rights of 7 May 2013.[101] The case revolved around two consecutive acts, adopted in light of the austerity measures, providing for a 20 per cent reduction in the salaries and pensions, as well as reductions in other allowances and benefits, of all Greek public servants. Miss Koufaki, a civil servant, and her union (ADEDY) filed complaints against these measures, believing that they could be considered as an interference with the legal right to the peaceful enjoyment of possessions under art. 1 of Protocol No. 1 to the ECHR. The Court, however, did not follow the complainants, considering that the reduction of the first applicant's salary from EUR 2,435.83 to EUR 1,885.79 was not such that it risked exposing her to substantial difficulties incompatible with article 1 of Protocol No. 1. The Court also took into account the particular climate of economic hardship in which it occurred. The Court, furthermore, judged that the legislature did not overstep the limits of its margin of appreciation when it compensated the removal of the 13th and 14th months' pensions by a one-off bonus. Conclusively, the Court dismissed the application.

It is striking that, even within the Council of Europe's supervising mechanism, there may be different outcomes depending on the body dealing with a case, even if it concerns measures taken under a similar austerity programme. This does not necessarily mean that there is a dichotomy between the 'case law' within the Council of Europe system. It

---

98 ECSR, *GENOP-DEI and ADEDY v. Greece*, nos. 36–41.

99 ECSR, *GENOP-DEI and ADEDY v. Greece*, nos. 45–49.

100 ECSR, *GENOP-DEI and ADEDY v. Greece*, nos. 57–65.

101 ECtHR 7 May 2013, 57665/12 and 57657/12, *Koufaki and Adedy v. Greece*, http://hudoc.echr.coe.int/sites/eng/pages/search.aspx?i=002-7627

is more realistic to conclude that the outcome will probably depend on the austerity measures under scrutiny.

Moreover, in the *GENOP-DEI and ADEDY v. Greece* case, the ECSR also held that 'states enjoy a wide margin of appreciation when it comes to the design and implementation of national employment policies'.[102]

A third case concerns the ILO instruments on the basis of which Greek and international trade unions filed a complaint, against Greece, before the Committee of Freedom of Association (CFA). The complaint mainly referred to numerous violations of trade union and collective bargaining rights within the framework of austerity measures, implemented in the context of the international loan mechanism of the Greek economy.[103] The unions referred to the abolition of the 'favourability principle' that ensured the prevalence of terms in collective agreements which are more favourable for workers, the nullification and banning of any future extension of collective agreements, the reduction of the negotiated national minimum wage by 22 per cent and its further freeze until the end of the programme period, the suspension of clauses providing for wage increases or relating to seniority, the enforcement of a maximum duration for collective agreements of three years and the mandatory expiration of collective agreements in place for 24 months or more or with a residual duration of one year. The ILO Committee observed 'that the long list of issues raised by the complainants demonstrate important and significant interventions in the voluntary nature of collective bargaining and in the principle of the inviolability of freely concluded collective agreements'.[104] Although the exceptional circumstances – the Greek financial crisis – were recognized, the Committee considered that 'such repeated and extensive intervention in collective bargaining can destabilize the overall framework for labour relations in the country if the measures are not consistent with the principles of freedom of association and collective bargaining'. It continued by stating that repeatedly resorting to statutory limitations on collective bargaining would, in the long run, 'only prove harmful and destabilize labour relations, as it deprived workers of a fundamental right and means of furthering and defending their economic and social interests'.[105]

The conclusions of the CFA clearly make the Greek austerity measures, in furtherance of the recommendations of the Troika's Economic

---

[102] ECSR, *GENOP-DEI and ADEDY v. Greece*, no. 20.

[103] CFA, Report no. 365, Case no. 2820, *GSEE, ADEDY, GENOP–DEI–KIE, OIYE and ITUC v. Greece*.

[104] CFA, Report no. 365, Case no. 2820, 995.

[105] Ibid.

Adjustment Programme, problematic in light of the fundamental right to collective bargaining, enshrined in ILO Convention no. 98.

5. DISCUSSION AND CONCLUSIONS

It is clear that the current economic governance of the EU runs into conflict with fundamental labour rights. This is not only seen within the EU's own legal system, taking into account the growing tension between economic governance, social policies and the EU Charter of Fundamental Rights, it is also visible in the light of long-established fundamental labour rights protection and promotion by various European and international instruments, such as those of the Council of Europe and the ILO. This can be seen from the discussions that have already taken place before the various bodies of these intergovernmental organizations. Coherence problems, therefore, exist both within the EU's legal and governance system and in relation to international instruments. In terms of finding answers or remedies for the signalled problems, different fields or pathways could be envisaged. The first field of improvement seems to lie in the internal governance or legal system of the EU itself, while the second pathway would be directly connected to the relationship between the EU, the Council of Europe and the ILO.

A first area of concern relates to the fact that, within the EU, the relationship between the economic and the social dimension should be further clarified. As long as there is an imbalance between economic and social policies in the EU, there will remain good reasons for criticism towards economically motivated EU measures which are designed to have a (potentially negative) impact on labour rights and welfare systems. Looking at the EU internally, the relationship between market objectives, social policy ambitions and employment policy, all representing various titles and provisions in the legal framework of the European treaties, need a stronger link. This link is not only required because of article 7 TEU requiring the Union 'to ensure consistency between its policies and activities, taking all of its objectives into account'. The need for linkage may also be found in the general provisions of the EU Treaty, referring to the social market economy, mentioned in article 3, §3 TEU, although a stronger basis for more legal balance is the Charter of Fundamental Rights of the EU. With the adoption of the Lisbon Treaty on 13 December 2007 and its entry into force on 1 December 2009, the EU Charter of Fundamental Rights received 'the same legal value as the Treaties' (art. 6, §1 TEU). The protection of fundamental labour rights in the EU becomes connected with protecting those of the Council of Europe, through article

52, §3 of the Charter of Fundamental Rights of the EU, which provides that, in so far as the EU Charter contains rights which correspond to rights guaranteed by the ECHR, 'the meaning and scope of those rights shall be the same'. It has been pointed out above that it is difficult for the Court of Justice of the EU to neglect these provisions. It would imply that, with regard to the interpretation of the Charter, the Court of Justice of the EU will be somehow 'bound' by the case law of the European Court of Human Rights. However, there will remain room for discussion, taking into account the fact that the ECtHR's judgments do not constitute generally applicable rulings.[106] There will also remain room for autonomy in the EU Court, and the relevant provisions of EU law do not really set up a hierarchy between the two European courts.

Another aspect, internally related with the EU set-up, concerns the role of the social partners in EU economic governance. It has been pointed out that the 'Six Pack' provisions make reference to the social partners, but their role remains unclear and rather limited. This stands in contrast with the more (pro-)active role that the European social partners are given under articles 154–155 TFEU. It also has been the subject of criticism from the social partners themselves. A cautious sign of improvement is the European Commission's communication on 'strengthening the social dimension of the Economic and Monetary Union',[107] which follows its earlier 'blueprint for a deep and genuine economic and monetary union'.[108] The Commission Communication emphasizes the role of collective bargaining and social dialogue. It provides that 'the EU-level social dialogue plays an essential role in advancing our social market economy, producing benefits for employers, workers, and for the economy and society as a whole', and continues by stating that, 'when strengthening economic governance, it is critical to involve the social partners in policy debates and decision-making processes' and 'to timely and efficiently consult the social partners at key steps of the decision-making process at European level'.[109] The Communication can be seen as a positive step towards more internal coherence within the EU framework.[110]

---

[106] P. Lemmens, 'The Relation between the Charter of Fundamental Rights of the European Union and the European Convention on Human Rights', *MJ* 2001, vol. 8, no. 1, 51–52.

[107] Brussels, 2.10.2013, COM(2013)690.

[108] Brussels, 28.10.2012, COM(2012)777.

[109] COM(2013)690, 12.

[110] B. Veneziani, 'Austerity Measures, Democracy and Social Policy in the EU' in N. Bruun, K. Lörcher and I. Schömann, *The Economic and Financial*

A second field of concern is more directly connected with the relationship between the EU, the Council of Europe and the ILO. The question is how this relationship should be conceived. If different legal orders, all responsible for labour rights protection, contradict each other, or if their enforcement mechanisms lead to conflicting conclusions, the question remains which order has the authority to make the other correct its views or approaches. In the current situation, it seems that neither the ILO, nor the Council of Europe is really capable of imposing their views on the EU. The Union's member states are bound by the ILO's conventions, the European Social Charter and the ECHR, but the EU is not bound by the instruments directly.

In light of this, the possible accession of the EU to the ECHR can be mentioned as a step that will improve the connection between the two institutions and their instruments.[111] It will, however, not necessarily lead to full uniformity in the case law of the Court of Justice of the European Union and the European Court of Human Rights. In its Opinion 2/13 of 18 December 2014 concerning the draft accession agreement, the Court of Justice of the EU stressed the fact that 'the autonomy enjoyed by EU law in relation to the laws of the Member States and in relation to international law requires that the interpretation of those fundamental rights be ensured within the framework of the structure and objectives of the EU'.[112] The Court of Justice of the EU held the view that, after accession, 'the EU and its institutions, including the Court of Justice, would be subject to the control mechanisms provided for by the ECHR and, in particular, to the decisions and the judgments of the ECtHR', but it also referred to 'the need to preserve the autonomy of the EU legal order'.[113] Nevertheless, these steps may well work towards more coherence with regard to fundamental labour rights protection.

Besides this strict legal approach, it may be proper to leave the idea of hierarchy between different legal orders. A network governance approach may deliver more useful perspectives and allow the EU, the Council of

Crisis and Collective Labour Law in Europe, Oxford, Hart Publishing, 2014, 149–150.

111 Draft accession agreement, fifth negotiation meeting between the CDDH Ad Hoc Negotiation Group and the European Commission on the accession of the European Union to the ECHR – final report to the CDDH, 10 June 2013, no. 47+1(2013)008rev2, http://www.coe.int/t/dghl/standardsetting/hrpolicy/Accession/Meeting_reports/47_1(2013)008rev2_EN.pdf

112 Opinion 2/13 of 18 December 2014, para. 170, not yet published (http://curia.europa.eu/).

113 Opinion 2/13 of 18 December 2014 paras 181–182, not yet published (http://curia.europa.eu/).

Europe and the ILO (and their labour standard instruments) to be seen as autonomous actors standing in a more horizontal instead of a vertical relationship, where diversity of approaches may be inherent. Conflicts between horizontal network actors may involve 'power struggles', but also allow for 'bargaining' and 'deliberation'.[114] In this way, interaction between the network actors can deliver mutually agreeable and beneficial outcomes.[115]

This alternative view is perhaps already visible in practice. For example, the ILO is represented at the level of the Council of Europe. On the basis of an Agreement between the ILO and the Council of Europe, established on 23 November 1951, the two institutions have committed themselves to consulting regularly on matters of common interest for the purpose of realizing their objectives and of coordinating their actions.[116] Furthermore, through the European Commission, the EU has the status of observer in the ILO. In this way, dialogue between the institutions can grow and influence can be exercised, also by the EU in the activities and policies of the ILO. The various forms of cooperation between the ILO and the EU have made scholars conclude that the 'multilateral coherence of both institutions has grown in the past decade'.[117] The network governance model seen here is probably close to what is described as 'participant governance', where various entities govern the (perhaps loose) structure themselves with no separate and unique governance entity.[118]

Relative autonomy combined with cooperation may stimulate cross-referencing and allow voluntary paths to reach coherence. An example may be the European Parliament's resolution of 2014 addressing 'euro area programme countries', inviting 'the Commission to ask the ILO and the Council of Europe to draft reports on possible corrective measures and incentives needed to improve the social situation in these countries' and 'to ensure full compliance with the European Social Charter, with the Protocol

---

[114] E. Sorensen and J. Torfing, 'The Democratic Anchorage of Governance Networks', *Scandinavian Political Studies* 2005, vol. 28, no. 3, 197.

[115] P. Kenis and K. Provan, 'Models of Network Governance', *J. Public Adm. Res. Theory* 2008, vol. 18, no. 2, 231; R.A.W. Rhodes, *Understanding Governance: Policy Networks, Governance, Reflexivity and Accountability*, Buckingham, Open University Press, 1997; R.A.W. Rhodes, 'Understanding Governance: Ten Years On', *Organization Studies* 2007, vol. 28, no. 8, 1243–1246.

[116] *Official Bulletin* of the ILO, Vol. XXXV, 1952, No. 4.

[117] G. Casale, 'International Labour Standards and EU Labour Law', in N. Contouris and M. Freedland (eds), *Resocialising Europe*, Cambridge, Cambridge University Press, 2013, 93.

[118] P. Kenis and K. Provan, 'Models of Network Governance', *J. Public Adm. Res. Theory* 2008, vol. 18, no. 2, 234–236.

thereto and with the ILO's Core Conventions and its Convention 94, since the obligations deriving from these instruments have been affected by the economic and financial crisis and by the budgetary adjustment measures and the structural reforms requested by the Troika'.[119]

In conclusion, as far as the protection of fundamental labour rights is concerned, there is a clear tension but also a growing need for coherence between the EU, the Council of Europe and the ILO. Their reciprocal relationship has its own dynamics, but between these institutions, forms of dialogue, cross-referencing and mutual participation and influence may further grow and contribute to more coherence. Nevertheless, full convergence of labour standards and approaches between the EU, the Council of Europe and the ILO may not be realistic or desirable, as each of the institutions produces a legal order with its own internal logic. This, however, does not alter the fact that, as the discussed 'case law' shows, it is currently possible for the ILO, or the Council of Europe, through their various bodies, to monitor the legitimacy of EU or member state action if issues concerning fundamental labour rights arise in the light of economic governance. The follow-up of this remains a question which increases the need for further clarification of the relationship between the EU, the ILO and the Council of Europe. However, it is also clear from the EU economic governance discussion that the most urgent and evident path for improvement is delivering more (internal) coherence between economic and social policies in the EU.

---

[119] European Parliament Resolution, 13 March 2014 on Employment and social aspects of the role and operations of the Troika (ECB, Commission and IMF), 2013/2277(INI).

7. Trade unions and collective bargaining power in global labor governance

Sigrid Koch-Baumgarten and Melanie Kryst

1. INTRODUCTION

In the days of the national welfare state, which were also the days of a 'national unionism' (van der Linden 2000), trade unions were the driving force in governing working conditions and defending labor rights around the world. Regulations within the frontiers of the nation state were set up by means of legal enactment and collective bargaining. From the outset, trade unions also sought to establish international regulations, which ranged from minimum standards in the International Labour Organization (ILO) and social clauses in foreign trade agreements (Scherrer and Greven 2001) to transnational cooperation in collective bargaining (Koch-Baumgarten 1998a, 2006a). Governance research has recently begun to focus on how labor governance is shifting from the national to the global level. The debate focuses on a number of issues, such as how to govern the global economy, which has long been considered 'ungovernable' (Habermas 1998), the reasons and mechanisms of the emerging global governance scheme (Bartley 2007; Vogel 2008), and how to incorporate democracy and the efficiency of global norms (Benz and Papadopoulos 2006; Stevis and Boswell 2008). Researchers are also discussing new forms of private governance and public-private initiatives involving the state and networks of non-state actors. In this context, the debate focuses on the performance of *new* actors and *new* ways of enforcing and monitoring labor rights, such as labelling initiatives and codes of conduct. These are introduced by private actors like companies and employers, and also by NGOs and civil society actors, and are based on consumer power, democratic participation and corporate social responsibility. Apart from trade union researchers, national and global trade unions are hardly noticed as relevant players in regulating labor at a global level (O'Brien et al. 2000: 75; Koch-Baumgarten 2006b).

Our chapter examines the importance of trade unions and how their corporate and economic power in collective bargaining helps regulate, implement and monitor labor rights and labor protection in a global economy. We begin by setting out some conceptual observations concerning the basic assumptions behind our approach. Next, we examine the role that trade unions play in, and how they actually contribute to, the emerging global labor governance. In doing so, we assume that different forms of governance – by government, with government, and without government (Benz and Papadopoulos 2006; Benz and Dose 2010; Koch-Baumgarten 2011) – overlap. We focus on specific actions, resources and the potential power that trade unions can bring to state and networked approaches to drawing up regulations. In addition, we address the parts of private governance that can be managed by trade unions, either alone or in a bipartite system. We then argue that even though national and international trade unions have lost their long-standing monopoly in the field of labor regulation, they still have a major and dynamic role to play in developing global labor governance. Trade unions articulate social questions in international policy-making and organizations, and bring self-regulatory components to the fragmented patchwork of transnational labor regulation, such as International Framework Agreements (IFAs) and a unique global collective bargaining system in the maritime sector. They also enhance the new policy instruments of advocacy coalitions by providing them with traditional collective bargaining power and a transnational network (Pries 2010: 15, 22; Koch-Baumgarten 2011).

Our analysis is based on the literature on industrial relations and international trade unions, and on our research findings on the International Transport Workers' Federation (ITF), the trade union regulation of the maritime industry, and an analysis of the Clean Clothes Campaign (CCC), an example of NGOs cooperating with trade unions to defend labor rights transnationally. These qualitative case studies are based on a historic-genetic organizational study, document analysis and expert interviews.

2. LABOR GOVERNANCE AS A SPARSE PATCHWORK OF GLOBAL REGULATIONS

Our conceptual starting point is the governance approach as understood in international relations (Benz and Dose 2010). For a long time, governance was almost entirely absent from research into trade unions and industrial relations. Only recently has it started to be a subject of investigation (Koch-Baumgarten 2006a, 2006b, 2011; Platzer and Müller 2009/I: 63ff.; Pries 2010). By the same token, governance research was in the beginning only interested in executive policymaking and paid little attention to social issues and labor regulation. These days – and especially in approaches based on 'complex multilateralism' (O'Brien et al. 2000) – the importance of non-state actors in global governance has become more pronounced. By following a transformative perspective, the governance approach pulls back from the arguments of 'ungovernable' and 'powerless' (Habermas 1998: 95; Beck 2002: 99) which derive from a prominent section of the political economy and from globalization and trade-union research. We are hearing that institutionalized industrial relations are breaking down, that the economic and political power trade unions once held in their traditional strongholds in Europe is disintegrating, and that working standards are suffering from a global race to the bottom (Bieler and Lindberg 2011: 8). This revives the traditional research paradigm that pits the infinite powerlessness of the trade unions against the power without boundaries of capital (Tudyka et al. 1978). With the focus now shifted to businesses and NGOs, global and national trade unions are no longer considered to be among the most relevant players in the global economy (Beck 2002; Hassel 2008).

Given the many initiatives that exist to regulate labor standards, we can assume that a diverse 'landscape of labour regulations across national boundaries' (Pries 2010: 22, 15; see also Koch-Baumgarten 2011) is developing in the global economy. Certainly, labor standards are among the most difficult to create and enforce internationally (DeSombre 2006: 135). International regulations (their level and degree, the quality of standards, etc.) are not comparable to national standards for labor regulation in institutionalized industrial relations that exist within coordinated capitalism or even within certain sectors of liberal capitalism. The emerging labor governance exists in a specifically international and therefore highly complex context (Benz and Papadopoulos 2006: 2f.), which affects its capacities.

No central state, no global authority or state hierarchy exists. At the same time, there is no institutional framework comparable to national systems of industrial relations or institutionalized forms of cooperation and of conflict resolution outside of the EU (Koch-Baumgarten 1998a, 1999; Colucci 2004). Instead, we have a plurality of decision-making centers. This makes it just as hard to reach decisions and agree compromises on diverging interests – often by climbing down to the lowest level of compliance – as it does to implement and monitor international rules (O'Brien et al. 2000; Scherrer and Greven 2001). There is an 'interplay of formal and informal patterns' (Benz and Papadopoulos 2006: 2f.), a situation where private and public-private regulations interact.

There is a plurality of non-state actors, all of whom represent different interests, normative orientations, resources and tools. The tripartite alliance has lost its monopoly over labor regulation. Employers are taking up action through their individual companies, sometimes only following specific PR interests. Beside trade unions, as *past* and *present* civil society actors, advocacy coalitions and social movements are entering the arena of labor regulation with new approaches (consumer power, protests and mass-media support) (O'Brien et al. 2000; Walk et al. 2001). They are also standing as representatives of democratic, participatory ideals and as a mouthpiece for underprivileged social groups. This includes regional and global trade unions, which, depending on the industry and sphere of activity, can vary widely in terms of their scope for action and the tasks assigned to them by national unions (for types of functional profiles of global unions, see Platzer and Müller 2009/I: 49).

When it comes to non-state actors, trade unions are the only representatives of economically founded and institutionally networked power. If we look at the traditional trade-union strongholds – Europe, North America, Japan and Australia – of course the foundations of the political and economic union power have been challenged by socio-economic structural changes and by globalization for decades. Trade unions are facing serious problems: declining membership numbers; an ageing membership; unemployment; a lack of representation (beyond traditional industry strongholds) in key economic sectors and employee groups; deregulation of systems of industrial relations; competition with newcomers to the now pluralized union territory; erosion of traditional links to socialist and social democratic parties; and the end of corporatist arrangements. Overall, we are seeing a diminishing capacity of trade unions in the global north to mobilize resources, political support and economic power to influence international politics and global labor regulation. In addition, in countries of the global south independent trade unions often do not exist under authoritarian regimes, and employee organizations in developing and newly industrialized countries are, bar a few exceptions, still quite weak. However, to speak of a pervasive sense of powerlessness would be an overstatement. There still exist substantial national, regional and sectoral differences in the political influence and economic negotiating power of individual unions, and in the regulatory capacities of systems of industrial relations (Koch-Baumgarten 1998a, 1999; Frege and Kelly 2003; Avdagić and Crouch 2006; Ehmke et al. 2009; Keune and Schmidt 2009).

Furthermore, unions (and their members) in the Northern countries with high labor standards, wages and high social protection often are not deeply interested in being involved in global advocacy policies for the poor labor force in Asia and Africa. In the past US and European unions as well as global union federations (GUFs) have held a protectionist position in international labor policies, as product and labor markets globalized and triggered global market competition. Thus, conflicting interests between trade unions in countries with high standards and in those with low standards and in states that export work or capital have been an important obstacle to international union engagement and decision-making. Contrary to assumptions within Marxist trade union studies, global union policies are not guaranteed either by normative orientations (solidarity) or by shared material interests of global workers arising from an international conflict between capital and labor. It is the conflict between the unions of labor exporting and low standard countries of the South and interest groups of the capital exporting and high standard countries of the North which deeply influences global union policies. This has given rise to cross-class coalitions or to cooperation between unions and (even authoritarian) states (Koch-Baumgarten 1998a: 393–402; 1999: 346–55, 464–76).

With that in mind, we suggest that labor governance should also have its conceptual basis in a model built of poly-centric trade union power and of multiple (even conflicting) trade union interests. We see global labor governance as a fragmented and diverse patchwork of multilateral rules, guidelines and types of regulation on labor and employment. They cover a variety of policy areas, exist on different (multiple) regulatory levels – the subnational, national, regional and international – and are set up and put into practice by a plurality of actors. (In this chapter we do not address the EU which is an exceptional case, although it should, however, be included in a systematic examination.) As is often the case with governance structures, the patchwork contains regulations that are limited in scope, thus creating serious problems for implementation and monitoring, and it exhibits a 'networked minimalism' (Nye and Keohane 2000 cited in Koch-Baumgarten 2011: 65). This includes any kind of regulatory intervention in the market economy and financial industry that is designed to minimize social and employment-related risks. It also includes all efforts to enforce democratic rights by having civil society actors participate in drawing up universally applicable regulations within international organizations, in establishing transnational regimes, and in the economy or individual companies. Labor governance is a kind of hybrid: it combines state and non-state actors, draws up rules in both top-down and bottom-up processes, and forms a complex patchwork of different forms of governance – with and without governments – that overlap and intertwine (Djelic and Quack 2010: 394f.).

3. TRADE UNIONS IN A COMPLEX, HYBRID-LIKE GLOBAL LABOR GOVERNANCE

3.1 Institutional Factors of Trade Unions in Global Labor Governance

Trade unions bring a multi-faceted institutional factor to a complex global labor governance picture. Trade unions have an essential role to play in establishing and monitoring existing intergovernmental regulations and private governance initiatives and in expanding them in the future. In doing so, the main contribution of trade unions lies in a number of *institutional factors*.

Firstly, national and international trade unions engage in forms of traditional and 'silent' lobbying through direct channels in state and intergovernmental decision-making centers. Despite the structural problems of trade unions mentioned above, to this day trade unions still have formal and informal access to national governments in key developed countries (Anner 2006: 77). Because they have direct access to state actors, trade unions can exert pressure and their representatives are sometimes included in national delegations to international conferences. They may influence the agenda setting within international organizations or intergovernmental regimes. In addition the GUFs have direct contacts to key members of the secretariats of important IGOs, and in some cases even expert, observer or advisory status. Trade unions can thus create a key channel for exerting influence on labor governance – or, at the very least, they can use their privileged access to information to support their networks (Koch-Baumgarten 1999: 378–83; O'Brien et al. 2000: 84; Lillie 2006: 103; Javed and Ganter 2009). Of course, we have to keep in mind that diverging national or regional union interests have often been an obstacle to finding a compromise or a common union global policy. Conflicting interests between interest groups of the global North and South might hamper union lobbying in international organizations and politics.

Nevertheless, the contact between the unions and the executive can, in certain cases, be used to mobilize state support and create a shadow of hierarchy. At the same time, institutional access opens up the potential for pursuing formal procedures, for instance in the ILO. If we were to include the EU, we could mention the unique tool of social dialogue and the possibility of incorporating it directly into an EU legislative procedure (Smismans 2008; Platzer and Müller 2009). That does not mean trade unions avoid using direct mobilization by organizing demonstrations or campaigns. The so-called Social Movement Unionism stresses the bottom-up approach of trade unions through collective actions and social alliances

(Waterman 2001; Bronfenbrenner 2007; Fairbrother 2008; Bieler and Lindberg 2011).

This brings us to a second institutional factor: the existence of GUFs, which act as a forum for agreeing union interests, for coordinating strategies and, at the most basic level, for sharing information (Platzer and Müller 2009/I: 49). GUFs have representative decision-making institutions and formal decision-making processes that exist centrally and at the sectoral and regional level. They have networks of contacts that cover every region of the world and extend right down to the local level. They manage extensive contact files and collect data on labor, employment and social standards and problems in countries and companies all over the world, and on collective bargaining systems, social systems and labor law. This puts them in possession of considerable practical and contextual knowledge about local areas (Curbach 2003: 183). This expertise can be of benefit to alliances with other NGOs, and is fundamental to influence (inter)governmental work on drawing up regulations. Additionally, trade union activities almost naturally include capacity- and institution-building: GUFs in Asia, Africa and South America have traditionally aimed at establishing local and regional union organizations and collective bargaining structures (Koch-Baumgarten 1999: 346–54, 386–97).

Thirdly, it is worth noting that, along with other NGOs, trade unions can help to reduce the lack of democracy in international politics – although trade unions and GUFs do have their own democratic problems (see Koch-Baumgarten 1999: 327ff.). Even today, they continue to represent more men than women, more skilled workers than underprivileged employees, more traditional industries than new service sectors (and certainly not the informal sector), and more associations from the North than from the South. Trade unions bear responsibility for 'the damages of their Cold War legacy' (O'Brien et al. 2000: 86). They have supported authoritarian regimes, pursued protectionist policies and exhibit serious shortcomings in their internal democracies (Koch-Baumgarten 1999: 349–53). Nonetheless, trade unions generally have a higher degree of representativeness than NGOs do. They have millions of members all over the world and are accountable to them (O'Brien et al. 2000: 67, 76; Koch-Baumgarten 2006b). They represent a long-standing (European) tradition and experience in 'participatory democracy and social justice' (Phelan 2006: 11).

The fourth institutional factor concerns the key role that collective bargaining plays in public-private and private governance. Here, again, we find structural problems in trade unions: a lack of autonomous industrial relations and independent unions in developing countries and authoritarian regimes and the declining bargaining power of unions in Europe and the US. But up to now trade unions have maintained long-standing strongholds in certain sectors and multinational companies. The 'global shadow of domestic industrial relations systems' (Stevis 2011: 139) thus appears to be a key determining factor in successful examples of good governance. We highlight the importance of *employee networks* that begin in local subsidiaries and go right up to company headquarters in developed countries (Fichter and Helfen 2011: 111; Papadakis 2011: 4). Local trade union committees, active local union members, and employee representatives play an important role in articulating problems and in the implementation and monitoring of minimum social and environmental standards and of efforts to enforce human and union rights in developing countries and in subsidiaries or suppliers used by multinational corporations. They provide advocacy coalitions and the components of governance handled by unions with crucial knowledge of the local context and with different ways to take action. The networks of actors within the GUFs and their regional organizations are useful, as they can provide direct access to local employees and associations. From a centralized point of view, direct access to the headquarters of multinationals via shop stewards and trade unions is the single most important ingredient in successfully enforcing and monitoring union components in private labor governance, as will be shown below. Furthermore, we will see that union activities are structurally designed to expand organizations and negotiating systems that, historically, were the prerequisites for sustainable improvements in labor regulation: 'Real success was achieved by labor when it was able to move beyond moral appeals and protest actions by institutionalising collective bargaining structures' (Crouch 2009: 58).

3.2 Trade Unions' Influence, Components and Networks to Establish Global Labor Governance

Global intergovernmental labor regulation is, at best, still in its infancy. The state has so far failed to cast an effective shadow of state hierarchy across global labor governance, which seems crucial to securing further successes for the governance of labor (DeSombre 2006: 53ff., 205; Dunn 2006: 46f.). Trade unions are involved in different intergovernmental attempts of labor regulation. To start with, union lobbying has been successful in getting social clauses included in regional and national trade agreements in the US and Europe (O'Brien et al. 2000: 89f., 100, 219; Anner 2006: 75ff.; Stevis and Boswell 2008: 90–98). Social issues are also on the agenda of major intergovernmental organizations, such as the World Bank, the OECD and the IMF. However, their efforts rarely deliver tangible results (O'Brien et al. 2000; Scherrer and Greven 2001).

It would make sense to examine, at least at the sectoral level, whether further-reaching intergovernmental regulations or regimes exist that affect (indirectly) matters of labor regulation, as will be shown below in the case of the maritime sector.

Furthermore, public actors engage in private labor governance schemes and thus combine traditional and new governance elements. The increasing presence of private governance instruments does not necessarily lead to less state regulation. Instead, public and private governance are seen as complementary efforts which can have a common effect on working conditions (Amengual 2010; King and Pearce 2010: 257f.). The state can serve as public monitor, influential buyer, legitimizer or even initiator and financier with regard to private standard-setting attempts (Weil and Mallo 2007; Vogel 2008: 275f.; Overdevest 2010). IGOs provide informal guidelines for voluntary company commitments, such as the UN's Global Compact and the OECD's Guidelines for Multinational Enterprises. These must be implemented, developed and monitored by private actors – either through networks of civil society actors, unilaterally through companies, or through trade unions (Scherrer et al. 1998: 76–123; Pries 2010: 164–70, 251–9).

The role of trade unions as co-decision-makers and a driving force within the tripartite ILO needs to be highlighted. The ILO core labor rights and a comprehensive portfolio of ILO conventions and recommendations together form a scaffold of minimum standards that can be implemented by states (through labor law), by social partners (through industrial relations) or by other civil society actors (through a variety of activities). The ILO regulations would very likely not exist had the unions not been involved (Koch-Baumgarten 1999: 374–79). Although the ILO's labor standards suffer from sluggish, controversial decision-making and from structural deficits in implementation, they still act as a point of reference to any actor who aims to defend labor rights and set up transnational labor regulation. At the same time, institutional access opens up the potential for pursuing formal procedures, for instance in the ILO, in cases where union rights are breached (see Reutter 1994) or when implementing ILO recommendations via collective agreements.

When it comes to private governance, trade unions can make an independent contribution at a variety of levels – under their own steam, as part of new coalitions with other civil society actors and as a supplement to the tools and resources available to those actors. One of the trade-union specific components in private global labor governance are *IFAs*. IFAs take their cue from ILO standards and the codes of conduct in the Global Compact. They set out union rights and rights for collective agreements. They also establish minimum social standards for subsidiaries and suppliers that multinational corporations use in developing and newly industrialized countries. IFAs are negotiated by transnational networks made up of employee representatives that cover the company level right the way up to the global unions and the management – in particular corporate headquarters. The differences between IFAs and the unilateral codes of conduct for companies in the Global Compact lie in the scope of the regulations and in the formalized implementation and monitoring processes that involve company and union representatives. So far, about 160 IFAs (Papadakis 2011: 5) have been realized – mostly in *European* multinationals that operate in industries that are particularly keen to avoid negative publicity, or that have a tradition of co-determination through employee representatives. Researchers have identified showcase approaches as well as cases of successful application. Certain factors play a key role in enterprises adopting and implementing IFAs:

(a) Strong unions and strong employee representatives with direct access to company headquarters are necessary.
(b) A culture of social dialogue and trust between management and labor representatives is important. It is a goal of IFAs to spread the idea and institutions of social dialogue and to build up new channels of labor-management negotiations.
(c) Employee networks are needed that extend from local subsidiaries up to company headquarters in developed countries (Riisgaard 2005; Schömann et al. 2008; Telljohann 2009; Fichter and Helfen 2011).

Another component that trade unions bring to global labor governance is the *ITF's unique collective bargaining system for maritime shipping*. The global shadow of domestic industrial relations is one of the main pillars of this system. The system is part of a governance structure that covers the whole of the fully globalized sector of maritime transport – a sector that, with its global, not unionized, labor market and unregulated international (open) registries, has grown since the 1970s to become an 'archetype of unbridled free-market capitalism' (Lillie 2006: 1; see also Koch-Baumgarten 1998a: 374ff.; DeSombre 2006). In the space of several decades, maritime transport has produced a unique and complex international system of coordinated international collective bargaining. What we are talking about is a subsidiary, multi-level system of collective bargaining and agreements that builds on minimum global standards for wages and various conditions of employment (holiday, crew, getting sailors home, etc.) and sets out compensatory social security allowances. Originally, these standards were specified by the trade unions alone. In highly unionized countries, pressure from the port unions saw to it that the standards were implemented by individual companies. A system of port union controls was responsible for the monitoring and comprised a network of union inspectors operating in numerous major ports, particularly those in traditional maritime states. Since then, multilateral negotiations between the ITF and employer associations have taken root and have turned a union-driven regulatory system into a bipartite set-up. Collective agreements now cover about a third of what was previously an entirely unregulated employment sector. Despite some issues with implementation (fraud through double-entry bookkeeping is the biggest problem), this has managed to put a stop to the downward spiral in labor conditions and wages (Lillie 2006: 2).

This type of bipartite governance demonstrates that unions can bring some major strengths to regulating the global economy:

(a) The institutional context of a long-standing, international trade union made it possible to establish a private union-driven regime which has laid the foundation for global cooperation between unions. This involved: reaching agreements on how to divide competences between national and international actors involved in collective bargaining; establishing decision-making procedures and committees to set out minimum global standards and draw up collective agreements; and developing the cross-border monitoring systems for the port union controls. As a consequence, institution building was stipulated in several ways: The international collective bargaining system supported unionization processes in some labor exporting countries; maritime trade unions in Asia founded regional organizations in order to increase their influence in decision-making within the ITF (Koch-Baumgarten 1999: 393ff., 467ff.). And in the end bipartite negotiation committees came into being. The ITF's initial pressure on individual shipowners to sign a collective agreement for a particular vessel has in the end led to institution building, since a multi-employers' collective bargaining system in maritime shipping has been introduced (DeSombre 2006: 141–3).

(b) The global network of port trade unions acts as the backbone of enforcement and monitoring (Koch-Baumgarten 1998a: 394f., 401; Lillie 2006: 53; Turnbull 2007; Dimitrova 2010: 45f.). Those in port union strongholds (e.g. Scandinavia) create an effective shadow of domestic industrial relations and generate the remaining, fragmented economic bargaining power that forces employers to enter into collective agreements and imposes penalties on those who fail to comply with minimum global standards. It is also an effective shadow of trade union hierarchy that incorporates reluctant, oppositional unions into the ITF and forces unions to apply international standards to their own field of domestic activity (Koch-Baumgarten 1998a: 395f.; 1999: 457f.).

(c) We have already mentioned the fundamental importance of the shadow of state hierarchy over various intergovernmental regulations. In the sector of maritime shipping, intergovernmental regimes on port state controls were introduced to help the port authorities of maritime states monitor global safety and environmental standards on all ships, irrespective of their nationality. Despite decades of union pressure the port state controls do not actually require the monitoring of social standards. However, port unions in traditional maritime regions with strong trade unions use the port state controls as a framework for their own (private) regulations on social standards (port union controls). These kinds of controls are the foundation of the international collective bargaining system within shipping, i.e. the unilateral or bipartite establishment of international labor and wage standards (Koch-Baumgarten 1998a, 1998b; 2006a; DeSombre 2006: 136, 145, 222f; Lillie 2006: 70ff.; Dimitrova 2010: 43–7). Furthermore, a look at individual ports reveals (under-researched) links between the port state controls and the port union controls, e.g. in cases when union and state monitoring staff work together (Lillie 2006: 103). The union regime within maritime transport should thus be understood as forming part of an overarching public-private system of governance, in which the unions have to take control of labor regulation after its neglect by the state.

Even though trade unions are traditionally assigned to processes of collective bargaining, they are involved in coalitions of non-state actors where they negotiate, codify, certify and monitor labor rights based on private mechanisms. Trade union/NGO coalitions point on the one side to differences between the actors, e.g. when it comes to organizational structures or the orientation towards the political or economic sphere. On the other side they show how to overcome conflicts, e.g. by building mutual trust, by finding a common ideology or by reacting to external events (e.g. Anner and Evans 2004; Braun and Gearhart 2004; Compa 2004; Egels-Zandén and Hyllman 2006, 2011). Assumed characteristics and roles of trade unions and NGOs in common coalitions should not be regarded as rigid. Nevertheless, the importance of trade unions' abilities within those networks is evident. The insights of the CCC highlight the role of trade unions within this patchwork of multi-faceted and interwoven activities of private labor governance.

The CCC was founded in 1990 to strive for better working conditions in the textile industry. Global value chains, low incomes and vulnerable (women) workers, which are especially difficult to organize, are central characteristics of the textile sector. The coalition of trade unions and NGOs responds to those challenges by building a transnational network including member organizations from Europe and production countries. National textile unions and diverse NGOs with a focus on labor rights, women's rights, development politics, consumer rights or a church background form the CCC network. In addition, GUFs, namely the International Trade Union Confederation (ITUC) and the International Textile, Garment and Leather Workers' Federation (ITGLWF), now part of IndustriALL, cooperate with the CCC (Zajak 2012: 263ff.).

The CCC developed a model code of conduct to which companies are held accountable, defined according to the core labor standards of the ILO, including the right to collective bargaining and freedom of association. However, this code of conduct is explicitly not regarded as a replacement for independent trade unions or collective bargaining (CCC 1998). The coalition functions through the use of media and public pressure, but also through negotiations behind closed doors and common pilot projects with single companies (Krüger 2002: 139ff.; Merk 2009; Kryst 2012). The CCC wants to get transnational corporations with headquarters in consumer countries to the table with the aim of negotiating about specific cases of labor rights violations or codes of conduct. Therefore, the coalition tries to put public pressure on the companies through protest activities and campaigns focusing on leading sportswear companies or other well-known brands. Later on, big retailers are chosen as a new target group of the CCC, and a sector-wide approach, as has been used for the so-called Asian Floor Wage Campaign, becomes apparent.

One of the tools of the CCC are so-called Urgent Appeals, which appeal to consumers to complain to companies about specific cases of labor rights violations, often dealing with trade union rights violations (Merk 2009: 608; Kryst 2012: 111f.). Trade unions are likewise taking up those public or consumer-based instruments within the coalition, and their role as local actors is particularly crucial to connect the campaigning organizations from consumers' countries with production countries. In several examples where the CCC is involved, local actors, 'notably unions' (Merk 2009: 605), which can act independently (Zajak 2012: 279) are detected as an important link for success. Even though the problems of those consumer-based instruments are well known, e.g. green washing, they can lead to improvements with regard to specific cases of labor rights violations or reactions at a later point in time – which might of course also be short-lived – as well as to the institutionalization of a niche market through political consumerism (Balsiger 2010, 2011).

Since the beginning of the 2000s, codes of conduct and similar voluntary non-binding instruments have increasingly come into question throughout the CCC network due to problems in the implementation process. Furthermore, those campaigns are often based on visible brands and the pressure of consumers, and not necessarily on that of workers. That is why they are often criticized by trade unions. Some discussions within national CCCs show how trade unions take a very critical stance towards codes of conduct in favor of binding global collective agreements, social clauses in trade agreements, legislations or negotiations on the ground through local and national unions in the global south (Egels-Zandén and Hyllman 2006: 307; Kryst 2012: 118f.). Hence, new strategies of the CCC, beginning in the early 2000s, are pointing towards a stronger involvement of state actors and binding agreements.

Not only are parts of the CCC network pushing for state regulation by laws, but they also target state actors as consumers. The EU regulation on public procurement becomes a stimulus for the coalition. Public procurement shows a hybrid strategy between public and private governance, which might serve as a more effective approach for trade unions and NGOs in the textile sector (Kryst 2012: 116ff.). Additionally, members of the CCC regard the newly established Accord of Fire and Building Safety in Bangladesh as a possible turning point towards more binding regulations. After the collapse of the Rana Plaza factory in April 2013 the CCC and global and local unions successfully fought for an agreement with international brands and retailers to establish a safety program in Bangladeshi factories. The agreement was signed by leading textile and garment retailers and by IndustriALL, UNI Global Union and several local unions. It is regarded by the CCC as unique in its legal enforcement (CCC 2013) and demonstrates from a trade union's perspective, unlike NGOs, their specific legitimacy and capability to sign legally effective contracts (Kryst 2012: 118f.).

Several lessons can be learned from these coalitions, which are active in private labor governance:

(a) Trade unions are involved in so-called consumer-driven approaches of labor governance, which are typically assigned to NGOs (Egels-Zandén 2009: 179). Initial approaches and changing strategies of the union/NGO coalition supply evidence of its interaction with consumer initiatives, labor policies and sectoral specifics of the textile industry.

(b) The shadow of state hierarchy becomes apparent in private labor governance: the coalitions' code of conduct uses the legitimacy of the public-private ILO standards. Even more far-reaching, state authorities are addressed by the CCC to become involved in private governance schemes by public procurement.

(c) The role of trade unions within these coalitions should not be limited to the traditional identity of defining itself with regard to the industrial relations system (Egels-Zandén and Hyllman 2011: 254). But, in fact, unions can contribute to the common coalition by using traditional channels towards state authorities, for example in cases of labor rights violation in production countries. Furthermore, their expertise and bargaining power should not be underestimated when it comes to negotiations with companies. Trade unions can serve as legitimized representatives of workers and work towards the establishment of a long-term bargaining system.

(d) The global network of trade unions, as well as the transnational contacts of NGOs, serve as a crucial factor of the coalitions' effectiveness. In particular, trade unions in production countries are extremely relevant at the local level: advocating for a code of conduct by reporting to consumers about labor abuses is only possible through direct contacts with the manufacturing base. Reports of workers are important in bringing up initiatives in specific cases of labor rights violations to the transnational level, in investigating and negotiation with companies or state authorities as well as in the certification and monitoring process of codes of conducts or other voluntary agreements of private actors.

(e) Finally, these networks and private consumer-driven initiatives can help trade unions to strengthen their role within the labor governance architecture. First of all, the coalition permanently includes trade union rights in their demands. Even though trade union rights remain among the most problematic cases to win (Merk 2009: 603ff.), this can have either a direct effect on specific cases or might lead in the long term to the global capacity-building of trade unions. In return, trade unions can expand their arenas and instruments within the new private governance schemes and thus broaden their room for maneuver (Kryst 2012).

4. CONCLUSION

Even after the traditional system of national labor regulation has come to an end, trade unions are a considerable force in the new global labor governance architecture. Having in mind the changing appearance of nation states, a missing global state authority or institutional framework for labor regulation and a plurality of old and new non-state actors that engage in public and private labor governance, we define global governance of labor as a diverse and fragmented patchwork of rules, frameworks and governance forms in different policy areas and on different levels, established and implemented by a variety of actors. The global governance of labor is characterized by intertwined and hybrid forms of governance and through complex linkages of state actors and non-state actors.

Among these diverse actors, trade unions have, despite their well-known structural problems, a basis of fragmented and poly-centric power. Trade unions play a role in different elements of the complex and hybrid architecture of global labor governance. They are involved in the development of intergovernmental regulation, for instance through the ILO, in labor-driven modules of transnational self-regulation by IFAs and by a unique transnational collective bargaining system, as well as in so-called consumer-driven private governance instruments through networks with NGOs.

As shown in the examples discussed, trade unions bring a specific, multifaceted factor to global labor governance which is based on institutional influence. On the one side, we develop the argument for how a shadow of state hierarchy functions in public and public-private labor regulation with the participation of trade unions. Through traditional lobbying and through informal or institutional channels to international organizations they put pressure on agenda-setting and get access to formal procedures. Additionally, GUFs serve as highly important networks for decision-making, strategic coordination and exchange of information. Thus, trade unions have worldwide contacts, expertise and experience, which they make use of to influence global regulations. Furthermore, trade unions, although having problems of democratic representation themselves, help to diminish the lack of democracy and legitimacy within international rule-setting. On the other side, with regard to private labor governance forms, we stress the importance of a shadow of industrial relation systems: trade unions offer direct access to transnational or local corporate actors; they profit from their worldwide network in terms of transnational mobilizing tools, and especially when it comes to initiating, implementing and monitoring private governance instruments at the local level. Finally, trade unions particularly aim for organizations and collective bargaining structures within the complex labor governance patchwork of public and private regulation.

We argue that for a more complete and better understanding of the evolving labor governance schemes on a global level, trade unions need to be considered as an important force with regard to all interlinked elements of public, public-private and private governance. Literature on industrial relations can profit from governance research which reflects this complexity of governance. While literature on governance has so far mainly concentrated on business and NGOs as non-state actors, trade unions should be systematically integrated into observations on business self-regulation and labor or trade policies in a globalized economy.

REFERENCES

Amengual, M. (2010): 'Complementary Labor Regulation: The Uncoordinated Combination of State and Private Regulators in the Dominican Republic', in: *World Development*, 38: 405–14.

Anner, M. (2006): 'The Paradox of Labour Transnationalism: Trade Union Campaigns for Labour Standards in International Institutions', in: Phelan (2006): 63–90.

Anner, M. and Evans, P. (2004): 'Building Bridges Across a Double Divide: Alliances Between US and Latin American Labour and NGOs', in: *Development in Practice*, 14, 1&2: 34–47.

Avdagić, S. and Crouch, C. (2006): 'Organized Economic Interests: Diversity and Change in an Enlarged Europe', in: Heywood, P. M. et al. (eds): *Developments in European Politics*, Basingstoke: Palgrave Macmillan: 196–215.

Balsiger, P. (2010): 'Making Political Consumers: The Tactical Action Repertoire of a Campaign for Clean Clothes', in: *Social Movement Studies*, 9, 3: 311–29.

Balsiger, P. (2011): *Campaigning for Clean Clothes: The Origins and Strategic Interactions of a Social Movement Campaign Targeting Retailers in Switzerland and France*. Doctoral thesis, University of Lausanne, unpublished.

Bartley, T. (2007): 'Institutional Emergence in an Era of Globalization: The Rise of Transnational Private Regulation of Labor and Environmental Conditions', in: *American Journal of Sociology*, 113, 2: 297–351.

Beck, U. (2002): *Macht und Gegenmacht im Globalen Zeitalter. Neue Weltpolitische Ökonomie*, Frankfurt a.M.: Suhrkamp.

Benz, A. and Dose, N. (eds) (2010): *Governance – Regieren in komplexen Regelsystemen. Eine Einführung*, 2nd edn, Wiesbaden: VS-Verlag: 13–33.

Benz, A. and Papadopoulos, Y. (2006): 'Introduction: Governance and Democracy', in: Benz, A. and Papadopoulos, Y. (eds): *Governance and Democracy. Comparing National, European and International Experiments*, London: Routledge: 1–26.

Bieler, A. and Lindberg, I. (2011): *Global Restructuring, Labour and the Challenges for Transnational Solidarity*, London and New York: Routledge.

Braun, R. and Gearhart, J. (2004): 'Who Should Code Your Conduct? Trade Union and NGO Differences in the Fight for Workers' Rights', in: *Development in Practice*, 14, 1&2: 183–96.

Bronfenbrenner, K. (ed.) (2007): *Global Unions: Challenging Transnational Capital Through Cross-Border Campaigns*, Ithaca and London: ILR Press.

Clean Clothes Campaign (CCC) (1998): 'Code of Labour Practices for the Apparel Industry including Sportswear', in: https://www.cleanclothes.org/resources/publications/clean-clothes-campaign-model-code-of-conduct (accessed 2 February 2014).

Clean Clothes Campaign (CCC) (2013): 'Accord on Fire and Building Safety

in Bangladesh', in: http://www.cleanclothes.org/img/pdf/accord-on-fire-and-building-safety-in-bangladesh (accessed 2 February 2014).
Colucci, M. (2004): *The Globalisation of Labour Standards: The Soft Law Track*, The Hague: Kluwer Law International.
Compa, L. (2004): 'Trade Unions, NGOs, and Corporate Codes of Conducts', in: *Development in Practice*, 14, 1&2: 210–15.
Crouch, C. (2009): 'Collective Bargaining and Transnational Corporations in the Global Economy: Some Theoretical Considerations', in: *International Journal of Labour Research*, 1, 2: 43–60.
Curbach, J. (2003): *Global Governance und NGOs. Transnationale Zivilgesellschaft in internationalen Politiknetzwerken*, Opladen: Leske + Budrich.
DeSombre, E.R. (2006): *Flagging Standards: Globalization and Environmental, Safety and Labour Regulations at Sea*, Cambridge: MIT Press.
Dimitrova, D.N. (2010): *Seafarers' Rights in the Globalized Maritime Industry*, Alphen aan den Rijn: Kluwer Law International.
Djelic, M.-L. and Quack, S. (2010): 'Transnational Communities and their Impact on the Governance of Business and Economic Activity', in: Djelic, M.-L. and Quack, S. (eds): *Transnational Communities: Shaping Global Economic Governance*, Cambridge: Cambridge University Press: 377–413.
Dunn, B. (2006): 'Globalization, Labour and the State', in: Phelan (2006): 37–62.
Egels-Zandén, N. (2009): 'Transnational Governance of Workers' Rights: Outlining a Research Agenda', in: *Journal of Business Ethics*, 87, 2: 169–88.
Egels-Zandén, N. and Hyllman, P. (2006): 'Exploring the Effects of Union-NGO Relationships on Corporate Responsibility: The Case of the Swedish Clean Clothes Campaign', in: *Journal of Business Ethics*, 64: 303–16.
Egels-Zandén, N. and Hyllman, P. (2011): 'Differences in Organizing Between Unions and NGOs: Conflict and Cooperation Among Swedish Unions and NGOs', in: *Journal of Business Ethics*, 101: 249–61.
Ehmke, E., Simon, A. and Simon, J. (2009): 'Internationale Arbeitsstandards im globalen Kapitalismus', in: Ehmke, E. et al. (eds): *Internationale Arbeitsstandards in einer globalisierten Welt*, Wiesbaden: VS-Verlag: 12–42.
Fairbrother, P. (2008): 'Social Movement Unionism or Trade Unions as Social Movements', in: *Employee Responsibilities and Rights Journal*, 20: 213–220.
Fichter, M. and Helfen, M. (2011). 'Going Local with Global Policies: Implementing IFAs in Brazil and the US', in: Papadakis (2011): 85–115.
Frege, C. and Kelly, J. (2003): 'Union Revitalization Strategies in Comparative Perspective', in: *European Journal of Industrial Relations*, 9: 7–24.
Habermas, J. (1998): *Die postnationale Konstellation. Politische Essays*, Frankfurt a.M.: Suhrkamp.
Hassel, A. (2008): 'The Evolution of a Global Labor Governance Regime', in: *Governance: An International Journal of Policy, Administration and Institutions*, 21, 2: 231–51.
Javad, S. and Ganter, S. (2009): 'Kein Zurück zum (Doing) Business as Usual. Die neue Gewerkschaftsbewegung in der globalen Beschäftigungskrise', in: *Kurzberichte Internationale Gewerkschaftskooperation Friedrich-Ebert Stiftung*, 9.
Keune, M. and Schmidt, V. (2009): 'Global Capital Strategies and Trade Union Responses: Towards Transnational Collective Bargaining?' in: *International Journal of Labour Research*, 1, 2: 9–26.
King, B.G. and Pearce, N.A. (2010): 'The Contentiousness of Markets: Politics,

Social Movements, and Institutional Change in Markets', in: *Annual Review of Sociology*, 36, 1: 249–67.
Koch-Baumgarten, S. (1998a): 'Trade-Union Regime Formation under the Conditions of Globalization in the Transport Sector: Attempts at Transnational Trade Union Regulation of Flag-of-Convenience Shipping', in: *International Review of Social History*, 43, 3: 369–402.
Koch-Baumgarten, S. (1998b): 'Konflikt und Kooperation in internationalen Gewerkschaftsbeziehungen unter Bedingungen der Globalisierung. Multinationale Tarifpolitik in der Handelsschifffahrt', in: *Industrielle Beziehungen*, 5, 1: 413–37.
Koch-Baumgarten, S. (1999): *Gewerkschaftsinternationalismus und die Herausforderung der Globalisierung – Das Beispiel der Internationalen Transportarbeiterföderation (ITF)*, Frankfurt a.M. and New York: Campus Verlag.
Koch-Baumgarten, S. (2006a): 'Globale Gewerkschaften und industrielle Beziehungen in der Global Governance', in: *Industrielle Beziehungen*, 13, 3: 205–33.
Koch-Baumgarten, S. (2006b): 'Global Governance, internationale Zivilgesellschaft und Globale Gewerkschaften', in: Koch-Baumgarten, S. and Rütters, P. (eds): *Pluralismus und Demokratie. Interessenverbände – Länderparlamentarismus – Föderalismus– Widerstand. Festschrift für Siegfried Mielke*, Köln: Bund-Verlag: 161–97.
Koch-Baumgarten, S. (2011): 'Gewerkschaften und Global Governance: Grenzen und Möglichkeiten einer grenzüberschreitenden Regulierung von Erwerbsarbeit', in: *Internationale Politik und Gesellschaft*, 2: 51–68.
Krüger, S. (2002): *Nachhaltigkeit als Kooperationsimpuls. Sozial-ökologische Bündnisse zwischen NGOs und Gewerkschaften*, Münster: Westfälisches Dampfboot.
Kryst, M. (2012): 'Coalitions of Labor Unions and NGOs: The Room for Maneuver of the German Clean Clothes Campaign', in: *Interface: A Journal For and About Social Movements*, 4, 2: 101–29.
Lillie, N. (2006): *A Global Union for Global Workers: Collective Bargaining and Regulatory Politics in Maritime Shipping*, New York and London: Routledge.
Merk, J. (2009): 'Jumping Scale and Bridging Space in the Era of Corporate Social Responsibility: Cross-border Labour Struggles in the Global Garment Industry', in: *Third World Quaterly*, 30, 3: 599–615.
Nye, J.S. (Jr.) and Keohane, R.O. (2000): 'Introduction', in: Nye, J.S. (Jr.) and Donahue, J.D. (eds): *Governance in a Globalizing World*, Washington DC: The Brookings Institution: 1–44.
O'Brien, R. et al. (2000): *Contesting Global Governance: Multilateral Economic Institutions and Global Social Movements*, Cambridge: Cambridge University Press.
Overdevest, C. (2010): 'Comparing Forest Certification Schemes: The Case of Ratcheting Standards in the Forest Sector', in: *Socio-Economic Review*, 8: 47–76.
Papadakis, K. (ed.) (2011): *Shaping Global Industrial Relations: The Impact of International Framework Agreements*, Basingstoke: Palgrave Macmillan.
Phelan, C. (ed.) (2006): *The Future of Organised Labour: Global Perspectives*, Oxford: Peter Lang.
Platzer, H.-W. and Müller, T. (2009): *Die globalen und europäischen Gewerkschaftsverbände. Handbuch und Analysen zur transnationalen Gewerkschaftspolitik*, 2nd edn, Berlin: Edition Sigma.

Pries, L. (2010): *Erwerbsregulierung in einer globalisierten Welt*, Wiesbaden: VS-Verlag.
Reutter, W. (1994): 'Gewerkschaften und Menschenrechte. Der Beitrag der Internationalen Textil-, Bekleidungs- und Lederarbeitervereinigung zur Verteidigung von Gewerkschafts- und Menschenrechten', in: *WSI-Mitteilungen*, 8: 516–23.
Riisgaard, L. (2005): 'International Framework Agreements: A New Model for Securing Workers Rights?' in: *Industrial Relations*, 44, 4: 707–37.
Scherrer, C. and Greven, T. (2001): *Global Rules for Trade: Codes of Conduct, Social Labeling Workers' Rights Clauses*, Münster: Westfälisches Dampfboot.
Scherrer, C., Greven, T. and Frank, V. (1998): *Sozialklauseln – Arbeitsrechte im Welthandel*, Münster: Westfälisches Dampfboot.
Schömann, I. et al. (2008): 'International Framework Agreements: New Paths to Workers' Participation in Multinationals' governance?' in: *Transfer* 14, 1: 111–26.
Smismans, S. (2008): 'The European Social Dialogue in the Shadow of Hierarchy', in: *Journal of Public Policy*, 28, 1: 161–80.
Stevis, D. (2011): 'The Impacts of International Framework Agreements: Lessons from the Daimler Case', in: Papadakis (2011): 116–42.
Stevis, D. and Boswell, T. (2008): *Globalization and Labor: Democratizing Global Governance*, Lanham: Rowman & Littlefield.
Telljohann, V. et al. (2009): 'European and International Framework Agreements: New Tools of Transnational Relations', in: *Transfer* 15, 3/4: 505–25.
Tudyka, K.P., Etty, T. and Sucha, M. (1978): *Macht ohne Grenzen und grenzenlose Ohnmacht. Arbeitnehmerbewußtsein und die Bedingungen gewerkschaftlicher Gegenstrategien in multinationalen Konzernen*, Frankfurt a.M.: Campus Verlag.
Turnbull, P. (2007): 'Dockers Versus the Directives: Battling Port Policy on the European Waterfront', in: Bronfenbrenner (2007): 117–36.
van der Linden, M. (2000): 'Conclusion: The Past and Future of International Trade Unionism', in: Carew, A. et al. (eds): *The International Confederation of Free Trade Unions*, Bern: Peter Lang Verlag: 519–42.
Vogel, D. (2008): 'Private Global Business Regulation', in: *Annual Review of Political Science*, 11: 261–82.
Walk, H., Klein, A. and Brunnengräber, A. (2001): 'NGOs Die "Entschleuniger" der Globalisierung, Einleitung', in: Walk, H., Klein, A. and Brunnengräber, A. (eds): *NGOs als Legitimationsressource. Zivilgesellschaftliche Partizipationsformen im Globalisierungsprozess*, Opladen: Leske + Budrich: 9–22.
Waterman, P. (2001): *Globalization, Social Movements and the New Internationalisms*, London and New York: Continuum.
Weil, D. and Mallo, C. (2007): 'Regulating Labor Standards via Supply Chains: Combining Public/Private Interventions to Improve Workplace Compliance', in: *British Journal of Industrial Relations*, 45, 4: 791–814.
Zajak, S. (2012): *In the Shadow of the Dragon: Transnational Labor Activism between State and Private Politics: A Multilevel Analysis of Labor Activism Targeting China*. Doctoral thesis, University of Cologne, unpublished.

8. The rapprochement of ILO standards and CSR mechanisms: towards a positive understanding of the 'privatization' of international labour standards

Ruben Zandvliet and Paul van der Heijden

1. INTRODUCTION

According to *The Body Shop* founder Anita Roddick, 'The business of business should not just be about money, it should be about responsibility. It should be about public good, not private greed.'[1] One of the central questions in the debate about corporate social responsibility (CSR) is whether the 'public good' is defined by private or public actors and processes. Most definitions of CSR appear to support the former position. According to the International Labour Organization (ILO), 'CSR is a voluntary, enterprise-driven initiative and refers to activities that are considered to exceed compliance with the law'.[2] Still, private and public regulation intersect in various ways. Critics of CSR raise two concerns in this regard.

First, there is the 'displacement hypothesis', which holds that CSR crowds out public regulatory initiatives.[3] By taking the initiative to codify their social commitments companies pre-empt legislation. Although this

[1] The Body Shop, 'Our Company', available at: http://www.thebodyshop.com/services/aboutus_company.aspx (last visited 30 July 2013).

[2] International Labour Office, Governing Body 295th Session: Subcommittee on Multinational Enterprises, InFocus Initiative on Corporate Social Responsibility (CSR), GB.295/MNE/2/1, March 2006.

[3] Tim Bartley, 'Corporate Accountability and the Privatization of Labor Standards: Struggles over Codes of Conduct in the Apparel Industry', 14 *Research in Political Sociology* (2005), p. 212. See also: Susan Strange, *The Retreat of the State: The Diffusion of Power in the World Economy* (Cambridge: Cambridge University Press, 1996).

might be the motive behind some CSR policies, history also shows many examples of CSR initiatives that subsequently became hard law. Secondly, there is – what we call – a 'convenience hypothesis' with regard to the content of the normative commitments in CSR codes. Instead of private standards becoming public this point is concerned with the opposite situation. The convenience hypothesis holds that companies appropriate public norms in their CSR policies, but are subsequently free to define and interpret them as they please. An ILO study in 1998 concluded that in corporate codes of conduct '[s]elf-definition appeared to be the leading method of establishing labour practice goals . . .'.[4] Diller, when referring to this study, argued that: 'Most self-definitions differ from, and even contradict, international labour principles.'[5] But even with non-hostile references to freedom of association it is often unclear what the normative commitments of the company are. What does it mean when The Carlsberg Group states that it 'shall respect employees' rights to form, join or not join a labour union or other organisation of their choice, and to bargain collectively in support of their mutual interests . . .' without a reference to the ILO?[6] To what extent is this different from its competitor SABMiller, which states that the company 'is committed to conducting its business with due observation of the principles of . . . the ILO Tripartite Declaration of Principles concerning Multinational Enterprises and Social Policy, and ILO Core Conventions on Labour Standards'.[7] Should ethical consumers (assuming they are not influenced by taste, price, marketing or other superficial concerns) order a Carlsberg or a Peroni Nastro Azzurro?

The convenience hypothesis is not restricted to CSR. The inclusion of labour standards in human rights law, and more recently in reciprocal and unilateral trade arrangements, has led to parallel systems of international

---

[4] International Labour Organization, Governing Body: Working Party on the Social Dimensions of the Liberalization of International Trade, Overview of global developments and Office activities concerning codes of conduct, social labelling and other private sector initiatives addressing labour issues, G.273/WP/SDL/1 (Rev.1), November 1998.

[5] Janelle Diller, 'A Social Conscience in the Global Marketplace? Labour Dimensions of Codes of Conduct, Social Labeling and Investor Initiatives', 138(2) *International Labour Review* (1999), p. 116.

[6] The Group, Labour & Human Rights Policy (1 April 2009), p. 3. Available at: http://www.carlsberggroup.com/csr/ourfocusareas/LabourandHumanRights/Documents/Carlsberg_Policy_LHR_group.pdf (last visited 24 January 2014).

[7] SABMiller Position Paper – Human Rights, *Having Respect for Human Rights* (June 2012), p. 1. Available at: http://www.sabmiller.com/docs/default-source/sustainability-documents/position-paper-human-rights.pdf?sfvrsn=2 (last visited 24 January 2014).

rights enforcement. The ILO itself, as Philip Alston has argued, has enabled this process. The 1998 Declaration on Fundamental Principles and Rights at Work (1998 Declaration) has introduced a voluntarist system in the organization itself, and 'has laid the groundwork for a decentralized system of labour standards implementation which significantly reduces the emphasis on governmental responsibilities and encourages a diverse range of actors . . . to take the lead in defining, promoting, and even enforcing these standards'.[8] This process is commonly referred to as the 'decentralization' or 'privatization' of international labour standards, depending on whether the appropriator is a public or private actor respectively.[9] Amongst these actors, companies are certainly the most suspicious, as CSR is often perceived as merely an exercise in public relations, and no clear framework exists to determine the relationship between private and public regulation.

The purpose of this chapter is to examine the relevance of international labour law in the context of corporate social responsibility. Alston's trinity of 'defining, promoting and enforcing' implies that a plethora of (procedural) promotion and enforcement mechanisms leads to a plethora of (normatively convenient) interpretations and definitions. The central research question at hand is thus: to what extent do ILO standards mitigate self-definition and interpretation in CSR? Section 2 deals with the relationship between international labour law and CSR; section 3 turns to the perceived dichotomy between CSR and enforcement; and section 4, finally, highlights the main research findings and formulates some concluding remarks.

2. INTERNATIONAL LABOUR LAW AND CORPORATE SOCIAL RESPONSIBILITY

2.1 Fragmentation and Coherence in International Labour Law

The risk of normative convenience is not restricted to the relationship between international labour law and CSR instruments. Many of the

---

[8] Philip Alston, 'Core Labour Standards and the Transformation of the International Labour Rights Regime', 15(3) *European Journal of International Law* (2004), p. 460.

[9] Bob Hepple, *Labour Laws and Global Trade* (Oxford and Portland: Hart Publishing, 2005), p. 86. See also: Tony Royle, 'The ILO's Shift to Promotional Principles and the "Privatization" of Labour Rights: An Analysis of Labour Standards, Voluntary Self-regulation and Social Clauses', 26(3) *The International Journal of Comparative Labour Law and Industrial Relations* (2010) pp. 249–271.

international and regional human rights instruments that were adopted after World War II contain rights that could already be found in ILO Conventions. Jenks wrote as early as 1953 about the overlap between the detailed international labour code and the more broadly defined obligations in the drafts of the international covenants. Jenks argues: 'The difficulty of avoiding inconsistencies and conflict between statements of general principle which cannot, by their very nature, contain the qualifications and exceptions necessary to make them workable in practice and the detailed instruments on the subject which embody such reservations and exceptions is considerable.'[10] The committees and courts that are tasked with the interpretation of the international and regional human rights conventions have taken a different stance towards the legal framework of the ILO in recent years. The Human Rights Committee (HRC) has long been dismissive with regard to reading a right to strike in the International Covenant on Civil and Political Rights' (ICCPR) provision on freedom of association, mainly because this right was expressly provided in its sister Covenant, the International Covenant on Economic, Social and Cultural Rights (ICESCR). This has been described as a 'ceiling effect', which occurs when 'an institution . . . refers to human rights commitments found in a legal instrument other than its own to *limit* the meaning, and thus the scope of protection, given to a right in that institution's own instrument'.[11] In later cases the HRC abandoned the distinction between freedom of association as a civil right (ICCPR) and a social right (ICESCR).[12] In recent years therefore, the HRC seems to have accepted the right to strike.[13]

Similarly, the case-law of the European Court of Human Rights on freedom of association shows a wide range of references to ILO Conventions,[14] the factual determinations of its supervisory bodies,[15] as

---

[10] Wilfred Jenks, 'The Conflict of Law-Making Treaties', 30 *British Yearbook of International Law* 401, pp. 409–410.

[11] Craig Scott, 'Reaching Beyond (Without Abandoning) the Category of "Economic, Social and Cultural Rights"', 21 *Human Rights Quarterly* (1999) pp. 638–639.

[12] Sarah Joseph and Melissa Castan, *The International Covenant on Civil and Political Rights: Cases, Materials and Commentary*, 3rd edition (Oxford: Oxford University Press, 2013), p. 661.

[13] See e.g. Concluding Observations on Chile (1999) UN doc CCPR/C/79/Add.104, para. 25 and Concluding Observations on Estonia (2010) UN doc CCPR/C/EST/CO/3, para. 15.

[14] ECtHR, *Gustafsson v. Sweden* (Application No. 15573/89), Judgment of 30 June 1998.

[15] ECtHR, *Danilenkov and Others v. Russia* (Application no 8919/80), judgment of 23 November 1983, paras 108 and 130.

well as their legal interpretations by the supervisory bodies.[16] Here, as Ebert and Oelz note, the most profound development at the ECtHR has also been the acceptance of the right to collective bargaining and the right to strike under Article 11. Before 2008 the Court had never examined the ILO Conventions or the work of its supervisory bodies when a claimant argued (unsuccessfully) the existence of the right to strike.[17] However, in *Demir and Baykara v. Turkey* the ECtHR reversed its position, and stated that it 'can and must take into account elements of international law other than the Convention [and] the interpretation of such elements by competent organs . . .'.[18]

Fragmentation and coherence between different norms of public international law differ from the role that public international law plays in the formulation of CSR norms. First, the Vienna Convention on the Law of Treaties explicitly provides that in the interpretation of treaty provisions one should take into account '[any] relevant rules of international law applicable in the relationship between the parties'.[19] Such a formal requirement does not exist with regard to CSR. Second, both the ILO Conventions and the regional and international human rights treaties concern obligations of states. CSR, on the other hand, concerns the responsibility of private actors. Consequently, not all norms may be applicable, or have to be adjusted to regulate corporate conduct. Instead of a conceptual discussion on whether it is possible to 'transpose' international labour law into credible CSR norms, the subsequent paragraphs will take a more empirical approach and examine how ILO norms are used in CSR instruments.

2.2 From Voluntarism to the Voluntary Appropriation of Public Norms

CSR was put on the international agenda during the late 1960s, when newly independent developing states expressed their concerns about the influence of Western corporations. The UN, ILO and the Organisation for Economic Co-operation and Development (OECD) all embarked

---

[16] ECtHR, *Wilson, National Union of Journalists and Others* (Application nos. 30668/96, 30671/96 and 30678/96), judgment of 2 July 2002, para. 48.

[17] Franz Ebert and Martin Oelz, 'Bridging the Gap between Labour Rights and Human Rights: The Role of ILO Law in Regional Human Rights Courts', International Institute for Labour Studies Discussion Paper, DP/212/2012 (2012), pp. 9–10.

[18] European Court of Human Rights, Grand Chamber, *Demir and Baykara v. Turkey*, 12 November 2008, Application No. 34503/97, para. 85.

[19] Article 31.3(c) Vienna Convention on the Law of Treaties.

upon the quest to determine a set of guidelines on the relationship between multinational corporations and host states. In 1976, the OECD was the first to publish its Guidelines for Multinational Enterprises (OECD Guidelines).[20] The intention of the original OECD Guidelines was to grease the wheels of international investment. They were mainly intended to solve economic and social problems, such as concentrations of power and taxation, and to recognize the sovereign right to regulate of host states. The part on 'employment and industrial relations' was limited and mainly concerned trade union rights, reasonable notice dismissals and non-discrimination. No references to the ILO were made. Shortly after the OECD Guidelines were published, the ILO adopted its Tripartite Declaration of Principles concerning Multinational Enterprises and Social Policy (ILO MNE Declaration).[21] This document dealt with a much broader range of issues, such as employment promotion, non-discrimination, security of employment, training, wages, health and safety, trade union rights, collective bargaining, and grievance procedures. The OECD Guidelines and the ILO MNE Declaration have been amended several times. For the ILO this meant that more recent developments in the international labour code could be included in the Declaration. The OECD Guidelines gradually became more deferential to the ILO. The 2000 version, the first revision after the ILO's 1998 Declaration, states that '[the] provisions of the [OECD Guidelines] chapter echo the relevant provisions of the 1998 Declaration, as well as the [ILO MNE Declaration]'.[22] In its description of the core labour standards, the OECD commentary extensively refers to the underlying Conventions. The latest version, which was finalized in 2011, also contains direct references to ILO Conventions and Recommendations for definition and

---

[20] OECD Declaration on Decisions on International Investment and Multinational Enterprises, with the following annexes: (1) OECD Guidelines for Multinational Enterprises; Recommendations for Responsible Business Conduct in a Global Context; and (2) Decision of the Council on OECD Guidelines and Procedural Guidance, adopted by the 42 adhering governments at the OECD's 50th Anniversary Ministerial Meeting of 25 May 2011.

[21] ILO Tripartite Declaration of Principles Concerning Multinational Enterprises and Social Policy, adopted by the Governing Body of the International Labour Office at its 204th Session (Geneva, November 1977), as amended at its 279th (November 2000) and 295th Session (March 2006); including Procedure for the examination of disputes concerning the application of the Tripartite Declaration by means of interpretation of its Provisions, adopted by the Governing Body of the International Labour Office at its 232nd Session (Geneva, March 1986).

[22] OECD Guidelines for Multinational Enterprises, 2000 version, para. 20. Available at: http://www.oecd.org/investment/mne/1922428.pdf

interpretation purposes. Initially efforts by the United Nations were less fruitful. Several attempts to adopt binding codes of conduct foundered. In 1999, Kofi Annan announced the UN Global Compact, a set of business principles that companies can associate themselves with. It includes references to the four core labour standards, but does not provide guidance on what companies ought to do after they have signed up. The 2011 Guiding Principles on Business and Human Rights, which introduced the 'protect, respect and remedy' framework, gave a new impetus to the CSR debate within the UN Human Rights Council.[23] However, the main focus of the Guiding Principles is to clarify the respective responsibilities of states and business actors, and the rights of alleged corporate human rights violations. With regard to the substantive norms that corporations would have to respect, it notes that '[because] business enterprises can have an impact on virtually the entire spectrum of internationally recognized human rights, their responsibility to respect applies to all such rights'.[24] With regard to labour, the core labour standards embodied in the 1998 Declaration represent 'a minimum', but it does not elaborate on the role of the relevant ILO Conventions or the interpretative work of the ILO supervisory bodies in substantiating the scope of these normative commitments.

Also during the 1970s the first corporate codes of conduct emerged. Similar to the OECD and ILO instruments their content gradually shifted from the relationship of the company with the host state towards the relationship with a broader set of stakeholders. CSR codes thus evolved from proclamations not to interfere with domestic law in the host state, to commitments to complement that law. In other words: CSR fills the gap between the level of (enforcement of) labour standards in the host state, and what the company itself deems morally adequate and economically viable. This determination may be influenced by consumers, NGOs, trade unions, international organizations, home state governments and peer-pressure. Various studies have examined the content of private sector initiatives. Table 8.1 compares the results of five studies on the references to specific labour issues. The ILO study (1998) consisted of 215 codes of conduct,[25]

---

[23] Human Rights Council, Report of the Special Representative of the Secretary-General on the issue of human rights and transnational corporations and other business enterprises, John Ruggie; Guiding Principles on Business and Human Rights: Implementing the United Nations 'Protect, Respect and Remedy' Framework, A/HRC/17/31, 21 March 2011.

[24] Principle 12, Guiding Principles on Business and Human Rights, *supra* n. 23.

[25] International Labour Organization, Overview of global developments and Office activities concerning codes of conduct, social labelling and other

Table 8.1 Reference to labour practices in CSR codes (%)

	Health & Safety	Wages	Child Labour	Forced Labour	Discrimination	Freedom of Association
2006 – Ruggie	95.7	42.6	80.9	80.9*	100	87.2
2004 – Schömann	88	34	62	52	90	54
2001 – ILO	72	51	47	42	70	33
1999 – OECD	75.5	45.3	43.2	38.5	60.8	29.7
1998 – ILO	75	40	45	25	25	15

Note: * The study by John Ruggie did not distinguish between forced labour and child labour.

the OECD study (1999) collected 246 codes,[26] the most recent ILO study (2001) 258,[27] and Schömann (2004) 50.[28] They do not indicate which companies were investigated. The OECD study recognizes that 'the set of codes is not random, and may not be representative'.[29] It does, however, provide a breakdown of country of origin and sector. All studies coded the documents themselves. The results of Ruggie (2006), however, are based on online questionnaires to the 500 largest firms by revenue, from which he received 102 responses.[30] Schömann's study only included unilateral codes of conduct, and no sectoral or other broader initiatives. Despite their methodological differences and limited transparency about the data, a comparison of the various studies indicates that in recent years the core labour standards have received much broader recognition in CSR codes.

These numbers only indicate whether a specific issue is included in CSR policies. With regard to the commitments undertaken there is much divergence within codes of conduct, between codes of conduct, and between

private sector initiatives addressing labour issues, GB.273/WP/SDL/1 (Geneva: ILO, 1998).

26 Kathryn Gordon and Maiko Miyake, 'Deciphering Codes of Conduct: A Review of their Contents', OECD Working Papers on International Investment, No. 1992/2, 1999.

27 Michael Urminsky (ed.), 'Self-regulation in the Workplace: Codes of Conduct, Social Labeling and Socially Responsible Investment', MCC Working Paper No. 1 (Geneva: International Labour Office, 2001).

28 Isabelle Schömann (ed.), 'Corporate Social Responsibility: A Threat or an Opportunity for the Trade Union Movement in Europe?' *Transfer* 3/2004, Brussels, 2004.

29 Gordon and Miyake, *supra* n. 26, p. 8.

30 John G. Ruggie, 'Human Rights Policies and Management Practices of Fortune Global 500 Firms: Results of a Survey', Working Paper No. 28, October 2006.

unilateral codes and multi-stakeholder initiatives. The marked difference between wage policies and discrimination indicates that many companies are selective regarding the inclusion of certain issues. Even if a code of conduct covers a wide range of labour standards, the level of commitment often differs. In its 'Policy on Employees' & Human Rights' Heineken relies on the normative framework of the ILO in three different ways. On freedom of association it merely refers to the principles contained in the 1998 Declaration, on child labour it adheres to the limits set forth in the Minimum Age Convention No 138 and on working hours it relies on statements by the Committee of Experts.[31]

With respect to the differences between unilateral CSR instruments and multi-stakeholder initiatives, the study by Schömann found that 72 per cent of International Framework Agreements (IFAs) referred to wages and 60 per cent to working hours, while unilateral codes included these issues 34 per cent and 22 per cent of the time, respectively.[32] In addition to IFAs, which are concluded between a multinational enterprise and global trade union federation, there are various other examples of CSR codes and initiatives that are developed by, or in cooperation with, third parties. This category also includes diverse projects like the Ethical Trading Initiative, the Fair Labour Association, the Worker Rights Consortium, the Harkin-Engel Protocol[33] and the Rainforest Alliance. Also, the agreements that were adopted in the aftermath of the Rana Plaza disaster, the 'Accord on Fire and Building Safety' and the 'Alliance for Bangladesh Worker Safety', are examples of initiatives that transcend a single corporation.[34] Like the documents adopted by international organizations, these multi-stakeholder initiatives help to achieve consist-

[31] Heineken Policy on Employees' & Human Rights, available at: http://www.theheinekencompany.com/sustainability/governance/our-policies

[32] Isabelle Schömann et al., *Codes of Conduct and International Framework Agreements: New Forms of Governance at Company Level*, European Foundation for the Improvement of Living and Working Conditions, 2008, p. 22.

[33] Its official name is the 'Protocol for the Growing and Processing of Cocoa Beans and Their Derivative Products in a Manner that Complies with ILO Convention 182 Concerning the Prohibition and Immediate Action for the Elimination of the Worst Forms of Child Labor'. The protocol is available at: http://www.cocoainitiative.org/en/documents-manager/english/54-harkin-engel-protocol/file

[34] For an excellent legal analysis of the post-Rana Plaza CSR initiatives, see Beryl ter Haar and Maarten Keune, 'One Step Forward or More Window-Dressing? A Legal Analysis of Recent CSR Initiatives in the Garment Industry in Bangladesh', 30(1) *The International Journal of Comparative Labour Law and Industrial Relations* (2014) 5–26.

ency with the ILO framework. Compared to unilateral CSR policies they often rely explicitly on ILO norms. This sometimes includes very detailed provisions. The Alliance's Members Agreement, for example, includes a provision that workers may refuse work in the case where a safety situation presents an imminent and serious danger to their life or health. This is derived from the ILO's Occupational Health and Safety Convention No. 155, which Bangladesh has not ratified.

Deference to ILO norms can also be observed in various other CSR initiatives developed by organizations like Social Accountability International and the International Organization for Standardization (ISO). Before the ISO began the drafting of the ISO26000 standard, it signed a Memorandum of Understanding with the ILO stating, *inter alia*, that:

> The Parties agree . . . that any guidance or other ISO International Standard to be developed in the area of social responsibility, which implicates ILO issues[,] will be fully consistent with the object and purpose of the provisions of international labour standards incorporated in ILO instruments, and their interpretation by the competent bodies of the ILO[,] and in no way detract from the provisions of those standards . . .[35]

In addition to documents that prescribe the normative framework the company adheres to, reporting templates have become increasingly important. The Global Reporting Initiative (GRI) provides the most used standardized template to report on CSR issues. The use of the GRI template further adds to the internal coherence of CSR commitments, and consistency with the ILO framework. Reporting templates wield influence on the normative commitments, as they list specific categories and aspects that companies should report on when they seek GRI verification. These include a range of labour issues, from occupational safety and health to freedom of association. Companies that do not have a policy on freedom of association are thus nonetheless required to disclose information on it if they use the GRI template. The GRI Reporting Guidelines contain many references to legal standards as the source of inspiration for the CSR indicators. Table 8.2 summarizes the various ways in which ILO standards are used.

The GRI indicates that merely trying to deduce corporate obligations from ILO Conventions is too narrow. Instead, the ILO framework is used in a variety of ways. Of particular importance is the country risk analysis,

[35] Memorandum of Understanding between the International Labour Organization and the International Organization for Standardization in the Field of Social Responsibility, 4 March 2005, Article 2(1).

Table 8.2 Usage of ILO standards and concepts in the GRI Implementation Manual

Issue	GRI Mechanism	Use of ILO Standards and Concepts
Discrimination, forced labour	Definition – Obligation to identify incidents of discrimination 'as defined by the ILO'. Direct citation of forced labour definition in the glossary	Definition – ILO Convention 111 defines discrimination, ILO Convention 29 defines forced labour
Freedom of association, child labour, forced labour	Risk analysis – Report on operations in countries where labour rights may be at risk	State compliance – 'The process of identification can draw from recognized international data sources such as the ILO [CEACR reports and the CFA Digest]'
General implementation, health and safety	Social dialogue – 'Provide a list of stakeholder groups engaged by the organization'/'Report whether formal agreements (either local of global) with trade unions cover health and safety'	Tripartism – The ILO standard-setting system is based on tripartism and social dialogue
Various labour standards	Proxy compliance indicators – 'Ratio of basic salary and remuneration of women to men by employee category'/'Report the percentage of total employees covered by collective bargaining agreements'	Issues – The GRI has developed indicators on ILO Conventions and Recommendations that do not carry direct obligations for companies

Source: Global Reporting Intitiative, *Implementation Manual*. Available at: https://www.globalreporting.org/resourcelibrary/GRIG4-Part2-Implementation-Manual.pdf (last visited 15 December 2014).

which makes host country compliance part of the CSR framework. When a GRI-reporting company has 'operations or suppliers' in, for instance, Belarus, it should note that the freedom of association of the workers on site is at risk. ILO information thus triggers the due diligence obligation but it is up to the company to determine the subsequent actions, which could range from divesting to merely reporting that violations occur.

2.3 Use of ILO Standards and Concepts in the 2003 UN Draft Norms

In addition to normative documents and reporting templates, the efforts to impose direct international obligations upon corporations provide further examples of how ILO standards can be used in the CSR context. In 2003, a working group of the UN Sub-Commission on the Promotion and Protection of Human Rights, consisting of academics instead of diplomats, published their draft 'Norms on the Responsibilities of Transnational Corporations and Other Business Enterprises with regard to Human Rights' (Draft Norms).[36] The UN Commission on Human Rights, which was replaced in 2006 by the Human Rights Council, did not adopt the Draft Norms. Instead it was noted that they were not requested by the Commission and do not have legal status.[37] They nonetheless remain illustrative of the way in which ILO standards could be used to formulate binding or voluntary norms for private actors. The Draft Norms contain, *inter alia*, rules on freedom of association and collective bargaining, non-discrimination, forced labour, child labour, occupational health and safety and adequate remuneration.[38] According to Ruggie, the Draft Norms 'sought to impose on companies, directly under international law, essentially the same range of human rights duties that States have adopted for themselves . . .'.[39] Article 7, for example, provides that: 'Transnational corporations and other business enterprises shall provide a safe and healthy working environment as set forth in relevant international instruments and national legislation as well as international human rights and humanitarian law.' Although the material object of most ILO Conventions is to impose obligations on private actors,[40] this usually takes place through implementing legislation at the domestic level. For example, the main obligation when a state ratifies the ILO Occupational Safety and

---

[36] UN Sub-Commission on the Promotion and Protection of Human Rights, Fifty-fifth session, Norms on the responsibilities of transnational corporations and other business enterprises with regard to human rights, E/CN.4/Sub.2/2003/12/Rev.2, 26 August 2003.

[37] UN Commission on Human Rights, Dec. 2004/116, UN Doc. E/CN.4/DEC/2004/116 (22 April 2004).

[38] The provision on non-discrimination is not placed under Part D on 'Rights of Workers' as it has a more general application in the UN Draft Norms.

[39] John Ruggie, Remarks by SRSG John Ruggie, 'The Protect, Respect and Remedy Framework: Implications for the ILO', International Labour Conference, Geneva, 3 June 2010, p. 1.

[40] Olivier de Schutter, 'The Challenge of Imposing Human Rights Norms on Corporate Actors', in: O. de Schutter (ed.) *Transnational Corporations and Human Rights* (Portland: Hart Publishing, 2006) 1, p. 19.

Health Convention is to 'formulate, implement and periodically review a coherent national policy on occupational safety, occupational health and the working environment'.[41] It is impossible to simply transpose such broad obligations of conduct into corporate occupational health and safety standards. On a closer look at the text of the UN Draft Norms and its interpretative commentary, however,[42] we distinguish six ways in which ILO standards or concepts are appropriated to shape corporate obligations (shown in Table 8.3).

Again, the work of the ILO is used in a variety of ways. Where it is possible to transpose a state obligation into a corporate obligation, the Draft Norms do so. While some of the obligations are derived from ILO Conventions, the interpretative work of the ILO supervisory bodies is also relied upon. In other instances, the Draft Norms formulate novel corporate obligations based on analogy with existing state obligations, or merely make use of the definitions contained in ILO Conventions.

3. JUDICIAL AND NON-JUDICIAL ENFORCEMENT OF CSR COMMITMENTS

Writing in 2001, the European Commission found that: 'Most definitions of corporate social responsibility describe it as a concept whereby companies integrate social and environmental concerns in their business operations and in their interaction with their stakeholders on a voluntary basis'.[43] Also the ILO definition that was alluded to in the introduction supports this position. In recent years, however, the 'voluntary' versus 'mandatory' debate has lost its relevance.[44] This is especially visible with regard to the enforcement of CSR commitments. The original draft of the OECD Guidelines captured an important distinction where it stated that: 'Observance of the guidelines is voluntary *and* not legally enforceable.'[45]

---

[41] Article 4, ILO Convention No. 155.

[42] UN Sub-Commission on the Promotion and Protection of Human Rights, Fifty-fifth session, Commentary on the Norms on the responsibilities of transnational corporations and other business enterprises with regard to human rights, E/CN4./Sub.2/2003/38/Rev.2, 26 August 2003.

[43] Commission of the European Communities, Green Paper – Promoting a European Framework for Corporate Social Responsibility, Brussels, 18.7.2001, COM(2001) 366 final, para. 20.

[44] Jennifer A. Zerk, *Multinationals and Corporate Social Responsibility: Limitations and Opportunities in International Law* (Cambridge: Cambridge University Press, 2006), pp. 32–36.

[45] OECD Guidelines, 1976 version, para. 6 (emphasis added).

Table 8.3 Usage of ILO standards and concepts in the UN Draft Norms

Issue	Corporate Obligation	Use of ILO Standards and Concepts
Forced labour	'Transnational corporations and other business enterprises shall not engage in nor benefit from . . . forced or compulsory labour as defined by international law'	Definition – Definitions of forced labour are contained in the Forced Labour Convention (Art. 2) and the Abolition of Forced Labour Convention (Art.1).
Wages	'Wages are a contractual obligation of employers that are to be honoured even into insolvency, in accordance with the Protection of Workers' Claims (Employer's Insolvency) Convention, 1992 (No. 173)'	Rule – 'In the event of an employer's insolvency, workers' claims arising out of their employment shall be protected by a privilege so that they are paid out of the assets of the insolvent employer before non-privileged creditors can be paid their share' (Art. 5 Protection of Workers' Claims Convention)
Freedom of association & collective bargaining	'[Transnational corporations] shall respect the right of workers to strike'	ILO interpretation – 'The right to strike is an intrinsic corollary to the right to organize protected by Convention No. 87' (CFA Digest of Decisions, para. 523)
Child labour	'Transnational corporations and other business enterprises using child labour shall create and implement a plan to eliminate child labour'	Analogy – 'Each Member shall design and implement programmes of action to eliminate the worst forms of child labour' (Art. 6 Worst Forms of Child Labour Convention)
Child labour	'Transnational corporations and other business enterprises may employ persons aged 13 to 15 years in light work if national laws or regulations permit'	Confirmation – 'National laws or regulations may permit the employment or work of persons 13 to 15 years of age on light work' (Art. 7(1) Minimum Age Convention)

Table 8.3 (continued)

Issue	Corporate Obligation	Use of ILO Standards and Concepts
Occupational safety and health	'Transnational corporations and other business enterprises bear responsibility for the occupational health and safety of their workers and shall provide a working environment in accordance with . . . international standards . . .'*	General reference – Listed documents do not contain direct obligations for companies.

Note: * International Covenant on Economic, Social and Cultural Rights, the ILO Plantations Convention, 1958 (No. 110), the Radiation Protection Convention, 1950 (No. 115), the Guarding of Machinery Convention, 1963 (No. 119), the Hygiene (Commerce and Offices) Convention, 1964 (No. 120), the Maximum Weight Convention, 1967 (No. 127), the Benzene Convention, 1971 (No. 136), the Occupational Cancer Convention, 1974 (No. 139), the Merchant Shipping (Minimum Standards) Convention, 1976 (No. 147), the Working Environment (Air Pollution, Noise and Vibration) Convention, 1977 (No. 148), the Occupational Safety and Health Convention, 1981 (No. 155), the Occupational Health Services Convention, 1985 (No. 161), the Asbestos Convention, 1986 (No. 162), the Safety and Health in Construction Convention, 1988 (No. 167), the Chemicals Convention, 1990 (No. 170), the Prevention of Major Industrial Accidents Convention, 1993 (No. 174), the Safety and Health in Mines Convention, 1995 (No. 176), the Maternity Protection Convention, 2000 (No. 183) and relevant recommendations, as well as ensuring their application under the Labour Inspection Convention, 1947 (No. 81), the Labour Inspection (Agriculture) Convention, 1969 (No. 129), the Workers' Representatives Convention, 1971 (No. 135) and their successor conventions.

When a company makes a CSR commitment it is possible to distinguish between the pre-adoption and post-adoption phase. The former may be voluntary in the sense that no legal impetus exists that requires the company to adhere to a CSR policy in the first place. But once the decision has been made to adhere to one, there may be legal consequences when the policy is not observed in practice.

Enforcement covers a broad spectrum of procedural mechanisms, such as external verification, non-judicial grievance mechanisms, international arbitration and domestic legal procedures. There are many differences between these enforcement mechanisms, but what connects them is the fact that an external authority is called upon to assess compliance with CSR commitments. Here, the same logic applies as in the context of the ILO or the parallel systems of labour rights, namely that application inevitably involves interpretation. Various different actors can perform this role. It can even be the company itself, when it makes a determination whether a supplier has complied with a contractual CSR provision to respect the right to freedom of association. External verification is also done by independent auditors, and by governments that make observance of CSR policies – such as the OECD Guidelines – mandatory for companies in the context of public procurement, export finance, participation in trade missions, etc. The OECD Guidelines themselves are implemented through National Contact Points (NCPs),[46] which provide good offices and mediation services on alleged issues of non-compliance, called 'specific instances'. Questions of whether an NCP has correctly interpreted the Guidelines are considered by the OECD Investment Committee. A similar, but less popular grievance mechanism exists to deal with a disagreement on the 'meaning' of the 1977 ILO MNE Declaration, 'arising from an actual situation, between Parties to whom the Declaration is commended'.[47] Also NGO or multi-stakeholder initiatives are often complemented by grievance mechanisms.[48] The confidential nature of most of these procedures makes it difficult to ascertain the extent to which they rely on ILO standards, however.

At the other end of the spectrum, CSR commitments may be the object of judicial procedures before a court or arbitral tribunal. One early example of the use of codes of conduct in tort law is the decision in *Kasky v. Nike*. In this case it was argued that Nike had made 'false statements and/or material omissions of fact' regarding the labour conditions at its foreign suppliers. The Supreme Court of California held that CSR commitments should be regarded as commercial speech, which is subjected to an increased level of scrutiny.[49] Legislative efforts have centred mainly on transparency and due diligence requirements. Since 2003, large companies in the European Union have an obligation to report on 'non-financial key performance indicators relevant to the particular business, including information relating to environmental and employee matters'.[50] In 2013, the European Commission proposed amendments to substantiate this

---

[46] For a recent review of the role of NCPs in the implementation of the OECD Guidelines, see Juan Carlos Ochoa Sanchez, 'An Empirical Examination of the Function of the OECD National Contact Points to Handle Complaints on an Alleged Breach of the OECD Guidelines for Multinational Enterprises', 89 *Bulletin for Comparative Labour Relations* (2015), p. 159.

[47] ILO, *supra* n. 21.

[48] Erik V. Koppe, Corporate Social Responsibility and Labor Dispute Remedies: An overview of existing non-judicial and non-governmental grievance mechanisms in relation to labor standards, 28 December 2011.

[49] *Kasky v. Nike*, 45 P.3d 243 (Cal. 2002).

[50] Parliament and Council Directive L 178/16, Amending Directives 78/660/EEC, 83/349/EEC, 86/635/EEC and 91/674/EEC on the annual and consolidated

obligation. Under this new legislation, large companies will be required to include in their annual reports:

> . . . a non-financial statement containing information relating to at least environmental, social and employee matters, respect for human rights, anti-corruption and bribery matters, including: (i) a description of the policy pursued by the company in relation to these matters; (ii) the results of these policies; (iii) the risks related to these matters and how the company manages those risks. Where a company does not pursue policies in relation to one or more of these matters, it shall provide an explanation for not doing so.[51]

Also in the United States CSR transparency requirements have been enacted in recent years, both at the federal level and in the state of California.[52] Similar to deceptive advertisement, providing false information, or concealing information, may lead to legal actions. Dutch law, for instance, provides several possibilities for enforcing deceptive CSR claims contained in annual reports.[53] Although no cases have yet been reported that alleged misleading CSR claims in an annual report, Dutch courts have in the past interpreted broad standards of good employment practices in Dutch company law on the basis of voluntarily accepted CSR commitments.[54]

Lastly, the (indirect) horizontal application of international labour standards can also assist in determining the extent to which these standards can carry obligations for companies. The Netherlands has no domestic

---

accounts of certain types of companies, banks and other financial institutions and insurance undertakings, 2003 O.J. (L 178) 16 (EC).

[51] European Commission, Proposal for a Directive of the European Parliament and of the Council, amending Council Directives 78/660/EEC and 83/349/EEC as regards disclosure of nonfinancial and diversity information by certain large companies and groups, Strasbourg, 16.4.2013, COM(2013) 207 final, 2013/0110 (COD).

[52] The 2010 Dodd-Frank Act requires all companies that trade securities in the United States to perform due diligence and disclose information on the use of minerals from the Democratic Republic of Congo or an adjoining country, as well as disclosing payments made to foreign governments for the purpose of the commercial development of oil, natural gas, or minerals, a principle known as 'publish what you pay'. The 2010 California Transparency in Supply Chains Act requires publicly listed companies to disclose their efforts to eradicate slavery and human trafficking in their supply chains.

[53] Tineke Lambooy, *Corporate Social Responsibility: Legal and Semi-Legal Frameworks Supporting CSR* (Uitgaven vanwege het Instituut voor Ondernemingsrecht, Rijksuniversiteit Groningen en de Erasmus Universiteit, No.77, 2010), pp. 158–159.

[54] Liesbeth Enneking, *Foreign Direct Liability and Beyond* (The Hague: Eleven International Publishing, 2012) p. 227.

legislation on the right to strike. But because courts have recognized the direct effect of Article 6(4) of the European Social Charter, employees can rely on the protection offered therein. It is possible to imagine more fact-patterns in which rights can be derived from international obligations that have not yet been implemented, or are not enforced. The extent to which this is possible would depend upon the domestic legal system. This is also the case in the context of foreign direct liability claims against corporations. In the United States, however, the Alien Tort Statute grants jurisdiction for torts committed 'in violation of the law of nations',[55] which arguably covers customary rules of international labour law.

These judicial and non-judicial mechanisms assess compliance with a wide variety of norms. They range from unilateral CSR codes to customary international law. In all these situations, however, ILO standards can be used to interpret the 'primary' set of rules. This may be influenced by the extent to which these primary rules refer to the ILO, as well as the precision of the commitments and their internal coherence.[56] The fact that the commitments of SABMiller refer more directly to ILO standards than The Carlsberg Group's CSR code could be relevant if an external authority is called upon to assess compliance. Detailed CSR codes, on the other hand, could limit the need for consideration of ILO standards. Other factors include the international obligations of the host country (lack of ratification or lack of implementation; due to inability or unwillingness), the corporate structure (ownership of subsidiaries or contractual arrangements with suppliers), and the status of CSR statements (*ex ante* commitments or *ex post* reports). Regarding the ILO standards that are used to interpret the primary rules, there are also important distinctions to be made. These relate to the source of the norm (Convention, Recommendation or supervisory body interpretation) and the content of the norm (workers' rights suitable for direct application or broad obligations of conduct). Similar to the ILO Convention on Occupational Health and Safety that was cited above, the Discrimination Convention does not contain a right not to be discriminated against, but merely requires state parties to 'declare and pursue a national policy'.[57] The starting point of the Freedom of Association Convention, on the other hand, is to define a set of rights. Article 2, for example, provides that: 'Workers and

---

[55] 28 United States Code §1350.

[56] M. Antonio García-Muñoz, Beryl ter Haar and Attila Kun, 'Soft on the Inside: Hard on the Outside: An Analysis of the Legal Nature of New Forms of International Labour Law', 27(4) *The International Journal of Comparative Labour Law and Industrial Relations* (2011) 337, p. 343.

[57] Article 2, ILO Convention No. 111.

employers, without distinction whatsoever, shall have the right to establish and, subject only to the rules of the organisation concerned, to join organisations of their own choosing without previous authorisation.'[58] It is arguably more difficult to transform state obligations into corporate obligations than it is to derive corporate obligations from worker rights.

4. CONCLUSIONS

In this chapter we asked to what extent international labour law, including the work of the ILO supervisory bodies, is relevant in the context of corporate social responsibility. We first looked at the use of ILO standards by other fields of public international law. We noted that there is a trend towards more reliance on ILO standards in the interpretation of non-ILO labour standards. The recognition of the right to strike by the Human Rights Committee and the European Court of Human Rights is the clearest example thereof. Second, the work of the ILO is used in a variety of ways. Potential appellants rely on the ILO to assess whether their claim has merit. Once the adjudication phase is reached, the work of the ILO is used to provide definitions, interpretations and factual determinations.

We subsequently turned to the interaction between international labour law and CSR. This relationship is often perceived as binary. One can either support legal obligations, which can be copied and pasted from existing international agreements and subjected to judicial enforcement, or moral responsibilities, which can be shaped, interpreted and enforced (or violated) at the discretion of the company. Whereas Alston mourned the (potential) decline in the 'legalism of ILO Conventions' as the result of corporations taking the lead in defining their labour commitments, Ruggie warned that: 'Imposing on corporations the same range of duties as states for all rights they may affect conflates the two spheres and renders effective rule making itself highly problematic.'[59] We tried to demonstrate that without 'imposing' duties upon corporations, and relying on private initiatives to shape CSR, the normative framework of the ILO does not lose its relevance. The term 'privatization' of international labour law is often used in a pejorative sense. According to Hepple, we have 'witnessed the galloping privatization, and lowering of public

58 Article 2, ILO Convention No. 87.

59 John Ruggie, 'Business and Human Rights: The Evolving International Agenda', 101(4) *American Journal of International Law* (2007) 819, p. 827.

labour standards. This is a different kind of "race to the bottom", not a genuine "race to the top"'.[60]

Although we agree with some of his analysis, we propose an alternative understanding of the term privatization. First, privatization of public standards should not be equated with private standards that lack this public underpinning. Contemporary CSR practice shows a trend towards more complete and more specific references to international labour law. If there is any cause and effect relationship of the 1998 Declaration, it would be that most CSR initiatives do now recognize all core labour standards, often complemented by health and safety standards. Other factors that foster consistency with ILO norms are the use of international or multi-stakeholder codes, the work of the ISO, and the GRI reporting template. The enforcement of CSR commitments can also contribute, according to the same logic as in the public parallel systems, to a more important role for the ILO in interpreting non-ILO labour standards or open norms in domestic tort law. Secondly, while private standards are indeed undesirable, privatization of public norms is necessary. Although most ILO instruments are intended to regulate the relationship between employers and workers, it is the state that assumes international responsibilities. This is also what distinguishes CSR from the application of labour standards in public and state-oriented parallel systems as described in section 2. Often ILO Conventions and Recommendations have to be transposed into domestic law before the precise rights of workers and duties of employers become clear. This process may also lead to divergence between states, but if they deviate too far from the purpose of the Convention, the ILO supervisory bodies come into play. Similarly, if a state does not have international obligations but companies nonetheless maintain that as a matter of CSR they 'observe the principles of non-discrimination', they could have some leniency in substantiating their commitments, as long as this does not conflict with the benchmarks provided by international law. Thirdly, privatization is usually accompanied by public regulation. Privatized sectors like finance, telecommunications and utilities are still the most regulated ones. Similarly, states and international organizations can and should (remain to) play a role in the 'privatization' of international labour law, in order to shape, clarify and systemize the application of public labour standards in CSR. This will help to use CSR to close governance gaps that cannot be closed by public international law, without yielding to a form of normativity that is guided by public relations and economic efficacy.

---

[60] Hepple, *supra* n. 9, p. 86.

9. Between the dragon's gift and its claws: China in Africa and the (un)civil fostering of ILO's Decent Work Agenda[1]

Abdul-Gafar 'Tobi' Oshodi

> In Europe, a country of 14 million people is a big country. China has a population 100 times as large. Let me share with you an interesting statistic. Last fall, about 150,000 tourists flocked to the Fragrant Hill in Beijing every day to see the red maple leaves, but altogether there are only 70,000 trees, so it's one tree for two people. I'm afraid only in China can you find such things and it can be very difficult for foreigners to imagine this. Every year, China needs to create 25 million jobs, roughly five times the population of Denmark. As many as 6.8 million university graduates will enter the job market this year alone, and that's about the population of Switzerland. There are 83 million disabled people in China, the same as the population of Germany. The most important task for China is to make sure that the 1.3 billion people can lead a good life, and you can imagine how challenging this task is and what enormous pressure this puts on the government. I believe nothing is more important than this. Everything else must serve this central task (Yucheng, 2012).[2]

> We don't have a choice because we need to survive. But if it was possible to chase all the Chinese away, I would (Smith, 2012).[3]

> As Chinese companies invest across Africa, the question – a critical one – is on whose terms. Will the companies operate outside the law, or will governments protect their workers' rights, with benefits for the local population and the Chinese investors? (Wells, 2011)

[1] This research is supported by the Social Science Research Council's (SSRC) Next Generation Social Sciences in African Fellowship Program, with funds provided by the Carnegie Corporation of the New York.

[2] This statement is credited to China's Assistant Foreign Minister, Le Yucheng.

[3] This is a quote from a carpenter working on a Chinese construction site in Zimbabwe.

1. INTRODUCTION

The presence of China in Africa is no longer news, buttressed as it is by galloping Sino-Africa trade and the recent $200 million African Union (AU) secretariat gift by China to African countries. While this massively increasing presence has been described as the 'most momentous development' in Africa since the Cold War (Taylor, 2009: 1), specifically, not only has China increased its financial support to African states but the number of major Chinese companies on the continent has increased to about a thousand. But with Sino-Africa trade increasing from less than $10 billion in 1999 to over $200 billion in 2013 (Brautigam, 2009; Xinhua, 2014), China's increasing visibility in Africa has attracted pessimism, optimism and caution. At one extreme, China is on some sort of a colonial mission. At the other extreme, China is a partner and/or some sort of benevolent conqueror in the likeness of Zhuge Liang,[4] whose interest is to support Africa's development. Yet in reality, and as buttressed by Africa's historical relations with international powers, the fact that a country provides some kinds of 'gifts' does not necessarily mean that such gifts eventually improve the lives of the toiling masses of Africa. Thus, the much publicised 'Dragon's gift' (Brautigam, 2009) does not mean, and should in fact not be assumed to mean, that the Dragon does not have claws. Most importantly, while the simplicity of China's 'non-interference' approach endears it to democratic and rogue African leaders, the presence of Chinese companies has also generated civil and uncivil responses from ordinary Africans. Both responses, in themselves, speak to non-state fostering of the International Labour Organization's (ILO) Decent Work Agenda (hereafter referred to as DWA).

This chapter interrogates the contexts and manifestations of China's labour practices in Africa vis-à-vis struggles for the incorporation of the ILO's DWA across the continent. In situating its analysis within three interconnected realities of China's presence in Africa (represented by Chinese domestica, Chinese internationa and Chinese Africana), the chapter highlights the 'points of exit' of African governments and the 'points of engagement' of African non-state actors in the fostering of the

[4] See Chan's (2013) work on the morality of China in Africa for an interesting depiction of Africa as the 'barbarian' King Meng Huo and China as the tactical King Zhuge Liang. This depiction is based on the epic Chinese tale that portrayed Zhuge Liang as a leader who sought to win the hearts of Meng Huo and his people. This goal led the former to engage the latter in a battle seven times. On each occasion, Zhuge Liang won the battle and captured Meng Huo but released him each time because the latter had not conceded defeat until the seventh time.

DWA on China and its companies. With examples, the chapter not only identifies the civil contexts of non-state points of engagement but most importantly warns against the possibility of increased uncivil confrontations as a reaction to the exit of African governments in the prioritisation of the DWA. The rest of this chapter is divided into five parts that cover the DWA, the three realities of 'China in Africa', China's labour practices in Africa, and non-state fostering of the DWA on China and its companies. This is followed by a conclusion.

2. WHAT IS THE DECENT WORK AGENDA?

It is unarguable that work is central to a people's well-being owing to its role in societal development. Starting from this simple logic, the ILO has been at the forefront of promoting the best possible ways to go about work and continues to champion the course of labour as an element of global development. The DWA is just one of such strategies initiated to improve the lives of workers. As an ILO report puts it, the DWA 'evolved from an internal agreement within the ILO as to how best to express its role in the twenty-first century and reinvigorate its capacity to deliver the policy advice and technical service its constituents needed' (ILO, 2007a: 15). The report further states:

> Decent work sums up the aspirations of ordinary people in their working lives. It involves opportunities for work that is productive and delivers a fair income, security in the workplace and social protection for families, better prospects for personal development and social integration, freedom for people to express their concerns, organize and participate in the decisions that affect their lives, and equality of opportunity and treatment for all women and men. (Ibid.)

The DWA is itself predicated on the achievement of four 'strategic objectives': creating jobs, guaranteeing rights at work, extending social protection, and promoting social dialogue. The DWA is aimed at engendering an economy that generates opportunities for entrepreneurship, investment, job creation and sustainable livelihood. Second, it aims to guarantee the rights of workers through recognition, participation, representation and good laws. Third, it aims to promote social protection for workers against low and declining standards of living. This entails that workers have free time, rest and adequate healthcare, and compensation when required. Fourth, the DWA aims to promote social dialogue and negotiation between workers and other stakeholders as a means to resolving problems. This means that strong and independent workers' and employers' organisations are important actors in negotiations.

But though these objectives have found their way into national, continental and global legal documents, in Africa, while the ILO maintains that there has been some measure of success, work still remains to be done in implementing the DWA. It must, however, be stressed that, in a real sense, the meaning, benefits and challenges of decent work is not new to Africa. This explains why the DWA, even where it is not expressly labelled as such, remains a historical quest in Africa. While African governments, historically and up to now, claim to be aiming for a decent agenda for workers, non-state actors have also championed this cause, as will be highlighted in this chapter. Most importantly, because the DWA speaks to fairness and justice for workers, and to the extent that it relates to Africa's age-old quest for development, it can only gain deeper meaning in the historical struggles of the toiling masses of Africa whose governments have not translated the continent's potentialities into development. Africa's developmental trajectory – from the import substitution industrialisation (ISI) and export-led growth strategies of the 1960s, through the Lagos Plan of Action of the late 1970s and the Structural Adjustments of the 1980s and 1990s to the current New Partnership for Africa's Development (NEPAD) – has been largely chequered. There have been wars and violent conflicts, corruption, poor policies and a sheer lack of strategy, among other issues. It is this development challenge that has led some to hope for, or foresee, a 'third liberation' (Mills and Herbst, 2012) of the continent. If this quest for third liberation is to be realised, contemporary thinking in Africa suggests that Sino-Africa relations remain a factor that might hold one of the crucial keys.

3. THE THREE REALITIES OF CHINA IN AFRICA

Two caveats must be stated at this juncture. The first caveat is that there is a popular assumption of a monolithic 'China in Africa', where there is one China and one Africa. This simplistic narrative allows commentators to assume that China's behaviour in Africa is constant and uncomplicated. This is not always the case in reality. For instance, in terms of Chinese investment in Africa, not only is there the presence of state-owned companies, but there are private Chinese, Diaspora Chinese (such as American Chinese) and African Chinese businesses. Though it is accepted that the activities of the various *Chineses* largely differ in capital source, intensity and focus, Chinese businesses are here viewed in terms of those companies that are state owned or owned by Chinese citizens who had travelled from mainland China to Africa in recent times. The second caveat is that even where it is easy to assume that Africa and African governments relate to

Chinese presence in the same way, in reality, there are instances of difference. In contrasting Africa's governments 'points of exit' from civil society's 'points of engagement', this chapter contributes to this slowly but growing multi-context understanding of China in Africa.

Unquestionably, foreign policies and the behaviour of nation-states is shaped by realities within and outside them. The case of China is not different and it is the reality of this interconnectedness of national and international contexts – even in relation to Africa – that explains what has been termed the three interconnected realities of China in Africa: Chinese domestica, Chinese internationa and Chinese Africana (see for instance Oshodi, 2012a, 2012b, 2013). Chinese domestica represents the interplay among domestic propellants, hindrances, threats and the challenges of China's current rise. Propellants include, among other factors, China's currency manipulation, state capitalism, investment and exportation policies, visionary leadership, authoritarianism, gradualism, economic reforms, geographic location, decentralisation, saving culture, and education. Challenges include the hugeness of China's population, internal cohesion, unemployment, environmental disasters, terrorism, corruption, disparities and gaps among regions, rural poverty and fears of economic reversals.

However, in spite of the aforementioned challenges, Chinese domestica is popularly represented in terms of features of China's rise. In addition to removing over 600 million of its citizens from extreme poverty in less than 30 years (World Bank, 2011), China is currently the second largest economy in the world. While Western Europe took 100 years, China took 50 years to move life expectancy from 39.3 and 42.3 for males and females respectively between 1950 and 1955 to 71.3 and 74.8 respectively in 2005–2010 (BBC, 2009). Beyond improvement in the living standard of Chinese citizens, which might be considered as the ultimate gauge of measuring human development, China has produced some of the most successful multinationals in recent times. Its rail system, especially the high-speed trains, double the number of similar trains in the whole of Europe, and it remains the largest in the world. It is forecasted that in a few years, China will have developed more high-speed trains than the rest of the world put together (Robinson, 2010). China has the largest foreign reserves in the world. Since it began undertaking economic reforms in 1978, the Chinese economy has grown about 10 per cent every year, with a per capita Gross Domestic Product (GDP) that has increased 12 times from what it was three decades ago (Yao, 2010). This enormous growth has generated a number of forecasts. For instance, while the IMF and the World Bank, respectively, forecast that the Chinese economy will overtake that of the US in 2016 and 2030 (Hutchinson, 2011), Goldman Sachs suggests a later date of 2041 (*The Economist*, 2010). Even as the future would confirm or refute these forecasts, apart from being the second-largest consumer of energy (Angang, 2011), China's foreign exchange reserves amount to $3000 billion and could rise to $6000 billion in 2016 (Yang, 2011).

Logically, it follows that Chinese domestica will have an international manifestation. Chinese domestica speaks to the internal realities of contemporary China, and this reality connects with, and impacts, the international. This is not a new phenomenon in China or elsewhere. In the case of China, there has been a historical internal-external nexus for the stability or instability of the Chinese state (and its neighbours). Dynasties and rulers have collapsed through being incapable of ensuring the balance between the domestic and the international. For instance, the Ming Dynasty collapsed in 1644 following a rebellion by peasants, on the one hand, who took over Beijing, and Manchu and the Ming generals that invaded from the north (Jisi, 2011). In the same vein, just as it was three centuries later, when the Manchu's Qing dynasty collapsed after an internal revolt coincided with Japanese and Western invasion, the fall of Kuomintang rule (Chinese Nationalist Party) was essentially caused by internal revolt inspired by the Soviet Union (Jisi, 2011). Today, managers of the Chinese state still understand the need to ensure a balance between domestic and international policies, especially as there are now about 5.5 million Chinese citizens working abroad (Downs, 2011). Between 2005 and 2009, China spent $145 billion on overseas acquisitions, spending $50 billion in 2010 alone (Yang, 2011). The hugeness of China's foreign reserve suggests that overseas acquisition may become a norm rather than an aberration. This international dimension is what I referred to as 'Chinese internationa'.

Chinese internationa is represented by China's growing influence, massive volume of international trade and distrust. For sure, the attention being paid to China's rise follows as a result of the perceived implications or consequences of this rise for global peace and security, superpower relations, international energy politics and its consequences for the environment (Wang, 2010). What happens to a reigning hegemon when another hegemon emerges? Can these hegemons co-habit even when there are fault lines in their understanding – Washington/post-Washington consensus versus Beijing consensus – and pursuit of development? Thus, John Mearshimer contends that 'The rise of China will not be peaceful at all' (Mearshimer, 2005). Yet others have noted the need to avoid 'Thucydides' Trap' in US–China relations, maintaining that any serious collision between the two will lead to 'mutually assured destruction of economy' (MADE) and 'mutually assured destruction of society' (MAD) (Wilke, 2011). Nevertheless, one representation of Chinese internationa is the growing number of Chinese multinationals. These multinationals have continued to move into Western territories and some of the most successful are Huawei Technologies, ZTE, China Civil Engineering Construction Corporation (CCECC), Minmetals Resources, Chinese National Offshore Corporation (CNOOC), Chinese National Petroleum Corporation (CNPC), the Chinese Petroleum and Chemical Corporation (Sinopec), Citic Group, Aluminium of China (Chalco), Haier Group, Sinochem, Baosteel, BOE Technology Group, China World Best Group, Hisense, Holley Group, Jincheng Group, Lenovo Group, NFC, Shanghai Electric, Shougang Group, Shanghai Motors, the TCL Corporation and the Wanxiang Group. Some of these companies have acquired Western firms. The Swedish carmaker, Volvo, was acquired in 2010 by Chinese automobile manufacturer, Geely. The Italian concrete-pump maker, Cifa, was acquired by Zoomlion, the Chinese machinery group. Shanghai Motors bought Rover of the UK. The IBM PC business was taken over by Lenovo and China's Wanda Group acquired AMC Entertainment Holdings, Inc., the second largest movie theatre chain in the United States, with over 350 theatres, over 5000 screens and more than 20,000 employees.

Ultimately, Chinese internationa is driven by the need to ensure the continued rise of China. Through its soft power projections, China infiltrates Asia and Latin America. Through its currency devaluation, it out-competes the US. Through its burgeoning economy, military spending and capacity, its leadership profile in the Asian region continues to grow, amid Japanese suspicion, while the US continues to expect massive challenges from the Eastern dragon. These power projections speak to China's quest to become a major player in the emerging international configuration. This same quest guides China's behaviour in Africa. In other words, Chinese Africana is merely the African face of Chinese internationa.

Three broad arguments on the role of China in Africa have developed. The Sino-optimists view China as a helper and a partner in Africa's development project; one that gives loans unconditionally, transfers technology and provides an alternative development model (see, for instance, Wade, 2008; Wenping, 2007). This view considers most criticisms of China in Africa as 'Western inspired hypocrisy and arrogance' (Le Pere, 2007: 6). The pessimists argue that China's presence in Africa should not be celebrated as it represents a scramble for Africa, colonisation, re-colonisation, re-colonisation by invitation, dependence and de-industrialisation (Nwoke, 2007; Oshodi, 2012a). The third view attempts to moderate the positions of the pessimists and optimists to an extent that they argue that Africa could benefit from China if certain actions are taken. Suggested actions/conditions include, among others: a trilateral (US–EU–China) aid governance partnership; adoption of an agriculture-led growth model;

and good governance (Oshodi, 2013). Regardless of contestations over the usefulness of China's presence in Africa, China is currently Africa's largest trading partner (BBC, 2012).

At this juncture, three points must be made. First, Africa does not necessarily represent an exceptional region in China's surge for economic relevance and buoyancy. There are a lot of similarities between the way China deals with Africa and non-African entities. Second, the presence of China in Africa necessarily has implications for African and non-African entities owing to historical and contemporary structures and patterns of globalisation. These multiple implications range from economic to governance factors and explain reactions from individuals, groups, governments and institutions on the 'real' role(s) of China in Africa. Third, China's behaviour in Africa, regardless of the official utterances of public figures, is shaped by Jisi's (2011) three questions: 'What are China's core interests?', 'What external forces or principalities threaten them?' and 'What can the Chinese leadership do to safeguard those core interests?' Answers to these questions lie at the heart of China's behaviour. China, in this regard, relates to Africa as a reaction to its core national interest which is, first and foremost, to improve the lives of its citizens – as opposed to promoting the well-being of Africans – as noted in the opening quote of this chapter. China's Chinese-first policy is not new and state actors in most cases often (re)echo this point. But if China seeks to benefit the Chinese, shouldn't African states also seek to protect their own people first too?

4. UNDERSTANDING CHINA AND ITS LABOUR PRACTICES IN AFRICA

Three points must be stressed in understanding China's labour practices in Africa. First, just as it would be simplistic and reductionist to argue that there is a monolithic 'China in Africa', it is far from reality to contend that there is a single Chinese labour practice across all Chinese companies operating in Africa. Clearly, Chinese multinationals like Huawei will operate labour standards differently to the less well known Durapak, a Hong-Kong-owned nylon bag factory, where Kenneth Frederick, a Nigerian worker, died in May 2013 (Sun, 2013). However, even where some Chinese companies operate good global practices (Kabemba, 2012), and even as the challenge of having a universal measurement of the DWA (ILO, 2008) remains, some Chinese companies disregard the DWA, as represented in their anti-union posture, inhumane working hours, brutalisation and casualisation of the workforce, use of child labour, and poor health and safety standards and work environment (see for instance

Amnesty International, 2013; Falayi, 2014; Human Rights Watch, 2011; Smith, 2012; Sun, 2013). Reported cases of such incidences in Chinese companies abound in Africa. From Democratic Republic of Congo's Magma Mining, to Liberia's Lee Group, to Mozambique's China Henan International Cooperation Group Co. Ltd (CHICO), to Niger's SOMINA Uranium Mine, to Nigeria's Jivan Plastic Company, to Zambia's Chinese owned Chambishi Copper Mine (CCCM) and to Zimbabwe's Makwiro Platinum Concessions, among other companies, workers' rights have been an issue.

A second point is that it is not the case that all African governments always do nothing in the face of Chinese companies' disregard for the DWA. For instance, even in Zambia prior to the victory of Patriotic Front's Micheal Sata, who was very critical of Chinese labour practices, in the 2011 presidential election riding on the crest of growing anti-China sentiments, incumbent President Rupiah Banda's Movement for Multi-Party Democracy (MMD) administration had closed down a Chinese firm, Chinese Collum Coal Mine (CCCM), five times for poor standards. The point, however, is that non-state actors are increasingly becoming key figures in the fostering of the DWA with regard to Chinese companies operating in Africa. Even in the case of Zambia, the fundamental change in the state's engagement of Chinese firms was due to the voting out, by the people, of a government perceived to be too soft on Chinese firms. CCCM, in particular, was subject to strikes and arrests of workers by the government in 2008.

Third, China's negative labour practices in Africa do not exist in a vacuum. It is a reflection of the crises of development in most African countries. With high rates of poverty and unemployment, Chinese companies tend to find workers who will accept their work practices, good or bad! A commentator on China's labour practices in Nigeria bluntly notes that, 'the big challenge for Nigeria is the question of how to ensure worker's [sic] rights while also respecting their desire for employment' (Sun, 2013). In Nigeria, it is not uncommon for crowds of youths to assemble at the gates of factories in search of jobs. Not all these youths can be employed by these factories; hence, those that are selected count themselves lucky. So even where an individual worker or a group of workers elect to protest, they would easily be replaced by others waiting to fill their positions. This is not only a Nigerian challenge, it is an African challenge.

The challenge is made even more gargantuan with the increasing role of China as a major development financier in Africa. Between 2000 and 2011, China's development finance reached about 1700 projects in 50 African countries (Provost and Harris, 2013). China's thirst for Africa's natural resources has also generated renewed competitive interest in that sector.

Most importantly, the fact that China has the needed financial resources to continue to invest in Africa has endeared it to African governments. With billions of dollars to spend, African states have sought to be in the 'good books' of China while presenting themselves as the best place for Chinese investment. Thus, while Nigeria's former President Olusegun Obasanjo, at the visit of China's Hu Jintao in 2006, had told Hu that 'When you are going to the moon, we don't want to be left behind' (Nwoke, 2007: 46), Senegalese Abdullahi Wade was less diplomatic, noting that he achieved more in a one-hour meeting with China's Hu Jintao than in the 2007 G8 meeting with African leaders in Germany (Wade, 2008: 20). Yet, this narrative of look-East-where-good-things-come-from has not blinded some non-state actors to labour abuses by some Chinese firms.

5. FOSTERING THE DWA IN AFRICA: SOME INSTANCES

The discussion of non-state fostering of the ILO's DWA would be based on examples mainly from Nigeria. The selection of Nigeria is based on four main reasons: its relative population size, huge Chinese investment, Pax Nigeriana, and the sheer size of Africa. First, Nigeria's population is about 170 million which makes it the most populous in Africa, whose total population is slightly over a billion. Nigeria's population seems a microscopic representation of Africa's contradictions in terms of challenges such as epochal legacies of colonialism, corruption, maladministration, ethno-religious conflicts and rentierism. Second is the huge and increasing presence of Chinese interest in the areas of oil, infrastructure, agriculture, furniture and in other small businesses. An outgoing Chinese Ambassador to Nigeria, Deng Boqing, stated that Sino-Nigerian trade in 2013 rose to about $13 billion (Falayi, 2014), making it one of China's top three African trading partners. Third, Nigeria, especially within the context of Pax Nigeriana, holds a pivotal position on the continent. This makes Nigeria an interesting case in the analysing of China's presence in Africa. Fourth, it would be unnecessarily over-ambitious to carry out a country-by-country analysis of non-state actors' reactions to Chinese companies operating poor standards in a chapter. Yet, in spite of the foregoing, it is understood that Nigeria is not Africa. It is only a country within Africa. The history and political economy of African countries, even where similar, cannot be assumed to be the same. In appreciation of this reality, examples will also be drawn from a few other African countries.

The ILO's DWA has been endorsed in Africa – as it has in most continents. Specifically, the Tenth African Regional Meeting of ILO Member

States in Addis Ababa in 2003 and the African Union Extraordinary Summit of Heads of State and Government on Employment and Poverty Alleviation in Africa in Ouagadougou in 2004, endorsed the DWA (ILO, 2007b). Since Ouagadougou, the ILO for its part has continued to engage the African Union (AU), regional economic communities (RECs), United Nations specialised agencies, and national governments on the need to pursue the DWA as a development strategy within global, continental, regional and national contexts. In accepting this, Africa has resolved to pursue the four objectives of the DWA: creating jobs, guaranteeing rights at work, extending social protection, and promoting social dialogue. However, an implication of the fatalistic tactic of 'looking east' for support, and its attendant over-indulgence of Chinese labour practices, is that it expands Africa's governments' 'points of exit'. This usage of 'exit' is similar to Osaghae's (1999), where ordinary citizens gradually bypass the state and adopt self-help strategies in the provision of services that ought to have been provided by the state. Here, I locate my usage in terms of the reluctance of African states to frontally/aggressively question China's labour practices.

With the over-indulgent slant of African states, non-state actors have taken initiatives to foster the ILO's DWA on China and its firms. In this sense, the points of exit of African states have tended to create and widen the points of engagement between China and non-state actors in Africa. These points of engagement with regard to fostering the DWA have been both civil and uncivil. By being civil, there is the implied use of legal means. The uncivil means entail illegal or violent responses. The civil fostering of the DWA includes media and newspapers' reportage aimed at calling attention to poor practices. In carrying out their role of informing society, numerous African and non-African press reports have called attention to negative practices in Chinese companies. These calls range from the uncritical to the very critical. A few headlines suffice, for example: 'Chinese expats treat Nigerian employees as punching bags', whose first sentence reads: 'The Chinese kick Nigerian workers on the testicles when they are not submissive' (*Sahara Reporters*, 2011). Others are: 'Labour movements picket, install workers union in foreign companies that deny workers' welfare' (*Sahara Reporters*, 2013); 'Chinese Labour Practices Haunt Zim Factory Workers' (*Mail & Guardian*, 2012); 'China, Africa's new colonial masters?' (Baako, 2013); 'Man accuses Chinese boss of brutality' (Akinkuotu, 2014a); 'China in Zambia: trouble down in the mines' (Wells, 2011); and 'We're treated like slaves but we're afraid of losing our jobs – Nigerians in Chinese, Indian companies' (Falayi, 2014). While some of these reports highlight the working conditions in Chinese-owned firms, others note that Chinese companies 'appear to be exporting abuse along with investment' (Wells, 2011). This last report alludes to poor working conditions back home in China where cases have been reported such as that of Foxconn, where working conditions and workers' treatment were poor (see *The Punch*, 2012). *The Economist* describes Chinese expatriates as coming from China with 'rough-and-tumble, anything-goes business culture that cares little about rules and regulations' (*The Economist*, 2011).

Essentially, the narrative in these newspapers is similar and often speaks to five core issues. First, is the issue of poor working conditions, which some equate with 'slavery' (Falayi, 2014). These conditions are such that workers often work for long hours, usually for over 10 hours without health insurance. Second is the issue of poor salaries. Workers are reported to earn about ₦15,000 (about $92) per month. Third is casualisation. In employing casual workers, Chinese companies achieve two goals. One, they escape the demands of having a workers' union since their members of staff are largely temporary. Two, casualisation allows management to hire and fire at will. Workers are therefore reported as being at the mercy of their employers. A fourth issue is assault on workers. The story in *The Punch* on 30 January 2014 shows the blood covered head of a victim of such an assault, Adeleke Owolabi (Akinkuotu, 2014a). The story reported that Owolabi, who had started work as a marketer on 8 January 2014 with Jivan Plastic Company, a Chinese firm based in Sagamu, Ogun State in Nigeria, suffered head injuries and his testicles kicked following a disagreement with his Chinese boss, Mike Jackson and his boss's cousin, Tony Jackson. It was after *The Punch* publicised the case that the police decided to arrest the two Chinese nationals (Akinkuotu, 2014b). This case is similar to a story reported in *Sahara Reporters* (2011) entitled 'Chinese expats treat Nigerian employees as punching bags'. It was reported that Maaji Meriga, a casual worker of China Civil Engineering and Construction Company (CCECC), one of China's state-owned multinational construction companies operating in Nigeria, had been assaulted by his boss, Marcho Chin, in Abuja, Nigeria's capital city. It was reported that Meriga, a 62-year-old man, was 'kicked . . . on his testicles and punched . . . on the ear to prove who is boss' (*Sahara Reporters*, 2011). Again, just as in the case of Owolabi, Meriga and another victim, Michael Francis, who was similarly assaulted, took their cases to the media. A fifth point is that these reports often mention state failure in coming to the rescue of workers. For instance, in the case of Owolabi, *The Punch* reported the failure of the state to act after the victim reported the assault to the police. Such state failure is not peculiar to Nigeria; in Zambia, even where the law states that workers can only work for 48 hours per week, miners at Sino Metals operated 12-hour shifts per day, which translates to 60 hours in five days (Smith, 2011). In Zimbabwe, it is reported that construction workers work in 14-hour shifts (*Mail & Guardian*, 2012).

The fact that a good number of these newspapers in Africa and elsewhere have online versions also expands the points of engagement from the pages of newspapers to the world wide web. Stories become more visible across national boundaries, making it easy for such news reports to be read, and acted upon, by thousands. This could either promote actions or merely enhance stereotypes among readers about what goes on in Chinese companies. This stereotype was confirmed when Chinedu Bosah of the Campaign for Democratic Workers' Rights, who had never visited a Chinese factory before, reportedly described working conditions in Chinese companies thus: 'You can't ask questions, you can't make phone calls, you stand for twelve hours, you can't even talk to each other, you can't even talk to yourself' (Sun, 2013). The power of these media reports is further expanded through the instrumentality of new social media. In addition to numerous comments on online versions of stories, other online platforms such as blogs, Facebook and Twitter are used to call attention to poor working conditions. Pictures are often cross-posted and news reports are re-posted. For instance, following *The Punch*'s publicity of Owolabi's case, blogs such as Ajetun Blog, NGVibes, Just Pye's Blog and Citigist relayed the news, making it accessible to more people and generating more public comments.

Media aside, the DWA has been pushed by labour unions. For instance, just like their counterparts in Liberia, South Africa and Zambia, who have frequently clashed with Chinese management, the Nigerian Labour Congress (NLC) and its affiliates have picketed such firms (*Sahara Reporters*, 2013). In Abuja, in November 2013, growing worries over China's activities on the continent led three national labour groups from Nigeria, Ghana and South Africa to jointly urge African governments to review their relations with China. If the Chinese importation of textiles between 2003 and 2006 can lead to the loss of 62,000 jobs in South Africa (SABC, 2006), then what happens to the textile industries in less sophisticated economies like Nigeria or Ghana? Obviously, because Chinese importation deprives workers of their jobs and, as a result, the protection of the ILO's DWA, national labour unions are often critical of China.

Individuals, some of whom do not work in Chinese firms, have also supported workers against Chinese employers. Victims, having failed to get the police to come to their aid, have approached, or were approached by, lawyers and other human right activists offering to fight for their case. It is not uncommon for these individuals to operate within non-governmental organisations (NGOs), such as Human Rights Watch, Amnesty International and Joint Action Front (JAF), among others.

These NGOs have brought the actions of Chinese companies to the fore by attracting press coverage. For instance, the Human Rights Watch (2011) had not only conducted research on four subsidiaries of China's Non-Ferrous Metals Mining Corporation in Zambia and written a 122-page report, but most importantly, their actions forced Chinese companies to respond to criticisms, with some promising to improve standards. Beyond labour practices, Amnesty International in June 2013 called on Chinese companies to employ due diligence checks on firms that they do business with in Africa (Amnesty International, 2013). In its report, the group specifically called attention to the exploitative and degrading conditions under which small-scale miners in Katanga, Democratic Republic of Congo, work.

But while the foregoing speaks to civil fostering of the ILO's DWA, there are instances where non-state actors have deployed uncivil means to vent their dislike against poor practices in Chinese firms. These have included the use of violence or other illegal means. For instance, two Nigerian workers for the Chinese multinational telecommunications company, ZTE, Aduloju Taiwo and Ufot Akayiene, were reported to have kidnapped their Chinese boss, Kuang Vingjun, and extorted money from the company because they 'felt unfairly treated' (Ezeobi, 2013). Elsewhere, from the 2006 post-election gang attacks on Chinese shops in Zambia to hostilities against Chinese in Angola in 2010, Chinese businesses and workers have become targets rather than unintended victims. While Chinese workers and/or interests have been attacked by armed groups in Nigeria, Sudan, Niger and Angola, the poor labour practices by Chinese companies could, in future, mix with existing conflict narratives in some African countries. As such, in the face of points of exit by African governments, anti-Chinese sentiment, and lack of due diligence by Chinese companies, ideologues and/or unscrupulous non-state actors could use that guise to mobilise and attack Chinese interest. Angola provides an example: In 2010, Rodrigues Mingas, a factional spokesman for the armed group 'Front for the Liberation of the Enclave of Cabinda' (FLEC) noted thus: 'They [the foreigners attacked] were all Chinese. . . They are not our guests. They work for the Angolan government' (Faucon and Su, 2010). My point: the dangerous dimensions of uncivil fostering of the DWA could graduate from one of a seemingly exceptional criminal act by disgruntled African workers in Chinese companies to one that locates Chinese interests as targets in some of the continent's complex arms conflicts.

To be sure, China and Chinese firms have also been influenced by the actions of the aforementioned non-state actors. For instance, just as labour-picketed Chinese firms have agreed to allow for the establishment of unions in Nigeria, so too did the 122-page report of Human Rights Watch on poor practices in four subsidiaries of China Non-Ferrous Metals Mining Corporation (CNMC) elicit a positive response from some of the affected mines. The Chinese government too, while encouraging more people-to-people contact, has advocated better relations. Some officials, such as China's Ambassador to Namibia, Xin Shunkang, have even called for 'effective corrective measures' (*New Era*, 2012) in cases where Chinese companies do not abide by local labour laws. But what are the likely trajectories in the relationships between Chinese firms and non-state actors that champion the ILO's DWA?

6. CONCLUSION

The three opening quotes of this chapter, in a way, summarise the context, tragedy and challenges of Chinese investments and labour practices in Africa. China, like any state, aims to make the lives of its citizens better. To achieve this goal, Chinese products and citizens would have to move from the local (Chinese domestica) to the international (Chinese internationa). The movement of Chinese capital into Africa (Chinese Africana) has, however, been marked by instances of poor labour conditions, the antithesis of the ILO's DWA. With the increasing appeal of China to Africa's leaders, non-state actors have become active in forcing China and its companies to address labour issues. The danger lies in the possibility of linking China's presence in Africa and the maltreatment of African workers to the entrenched ethnic, class or conflict narratives. The emerging milieu will not only disrupt Chinese businesses, but it might provide justifications for groups and ideologues whose interest(s) might or might not be connected to the interests of African workers to attack Chinese interests and nationals. In assuming state responsibility as marked by regulating the actions of Chinese companies, some of Africa's non-state actors might thus be forced (or at least encouraged) to employ uncivil means to achieve their goals. In this case, utilisation of uncivil means, unfortunately, might eventually become the norm where African states blatantly fail in their core responsibility to their people. Ultimately, while Chinese presence provides much needed jobs for Africans, the real challenge is for China to understand that the African people, rather than governments, can guarantee the long-term presence and stability of Chinese businesses in Africa.

REFERENCES

Akinkuotu, E. (2014a). Man accuses Chinese boss of brutality. *The Punch*. 20 January. Available from: http://www.punchng.com/metro-plus/man-accuses-chinese-boss-of-brutality/ (accessed 2 February 2014).

Akinkuotu, E. (2014b). Police detain Chinese for assaulting employee in Ogun. *The Punch*. 31 January. Available from: http://www.punchng.com/metro-plus/police-detain-chinese-for-assaulting-employee-in-ogun/ (accessed 2 February 2014).

Amnesty International (2013). *Profit and loss: mining and human rights in Katanga, Democratic Republic of Congo*. London: Amnesty International.

Angang, H. (2011). *China in 2020: a new kind of superpower*. Washington, DC: Brookings Institution Press.

Armstrong, H. (2010). China mining company causes unrest in Niger. *The Christian Science Monitor*. 29 March. Available from: http://www.csmonitor.com/World/Africa/2010/0329/China-mining-company-causes-unrest-in-Niger (accessed 14 December 2013).

Baako, B. (2013). China, Africa's new colonial masters? *Sahara Reporters*. 20 March. Available from: http://saharareporters.com/article/china-africa%E2%80%99s-new-colonial-master-kwesi-baako (accessed 14 December 2013).

BBC (2009). China: 60 years in facts and figures. 2 October. Available from: http://news.bbc.co.uk/2/hi/asia-pacific/8285357.stm (accessed 18 April 2011).

BBC (2012). Viewpoint: Africa must do more to profit from China. 22 May. Available from: http://www.bbc.com/news/world-africa-18143515 (accessed 15 July 2014).

Brautigam, D. (2009). *The dragon's gift: the real story of China in Africa*. Oxford: Oxford University Press.

Chan, S. (2013). *The morality of China in Africa: the Middle Kingdom and the Dark Continent*. London and New York: Zed Books.

Downs, E. (2011). New interest groups in Chinese foreign policy. Testimony before the US-China Economic & Security Review Commission on China's Foreign Policy: Challenges and Players. 13 April. Available from: http://www.brookings.edu/research/testimony/2011/04/13-china-companies-downs (accessed 11 May 2013).

Ezeobi, C. (2013). We kidnapped our Chinese boss for unlawful dismissal, say suspects. *Thisday*. 16 July. Available from: http://www.thisdaylive.com/articles/we-kidnapped-our-chinese-boss-for-unlawful-dismissal-says-suspects/153465/ (accessed 12 June 2014).

Falayi, K. (2014). We're treated like slaves but we're afraid of losing our jobs – Nigerians in Chinese, Indian companies. *The Punch*. 8 February. Available from: http://www.punchng.com/news/nigerians-who-work-in-chinese-indian-lebanese-companies-were-treated-like-slaves-but-were-afraid-of-losing-our-jobs/ (accessed 9 February 2014).

Faucon, B. and Su, S. (2010). Hostility toward workers cools Angola–China relationship. *The Wall Street Journal*. 10 August. Available from: http://www.wsj.com/articles/SB10001424052748704388504575418990791137242 (accessed 11 August 2015).

Human Rights Watch (2011). *'You'll be fired if you refuse': labour abuses in Zambia's Chinese state-owned copper mines*. Washington, DC: Human Rights Watch.

Hutchinson, M. (2011). IMF forecast: can China really overtake the US economy by 2016?' *Money Morning*. 28 April. Available from: http://moneymorning.com/2011/04/28/imf-forecast-can-china-really-overtake-the-u-s-economy-by-2016/ (accessed 30 April 2011).
ILO (2007a). *Director-General's report on the Decent Work Agenda in Africa: 2007–2015*. Geneva: ILO. Available from: http://www.ilo.org/public/english/standards/relm/rgmeet/11afrm/dg-thematic.pdf (accessed 2 February 2014).
ILO (2007b). *Director-General's report on ILO activities in Africa: 2004–2006*. Geneva: ILO. Available from: http://www.ilo.org/wcmsp5/groups/public/---africa/documents/publication/wcms_166860.pdf (accessed 2 February 2014).
ILO (2008). *Sixth supplementary report: measuring decent work*. Geneva: ILO. Available from: http://www.ilo.org/wcmsp5/groups/public/---ed_norm/---relconf/documents/meetingdocument/wcms_091183.pdf (accessed 2 February 2014).
Jisi, W. (2011). China's search for a grand strategy: a rising great power finds its way. *Foreign Affairs*, 90(2): 68–79.
Kabemba, C. (2012). Balancing the books: Chinese companies' respect for worker rights. Open Society Initiative for South Africa (OSISA). 10 October. Available from: http://www.osisa.org/books/regional/balancing-books-chinese-companies%E2%80%99-respect-worker-rights (accessed 14 December 2013).
Le Pere, G. (2007). China in Africa. *Africa Review of Books*, 3(2): 6–7.
Mail & Guardian (2012). Chinese labour practices haunt Zim factory workers. 6 January. Available from: http://mg.co.za/article/2012-01-06-chinese-labour-practices-haunt-zim-factory-workers/ (accessed 14 December 2013).
Mearshimer, J. (2005). The rise of China will not be peaceful at all. *The Australian*, 18 November.
Mills, G. and Herbst, J. (2012). *Africa's third liberation*. Johannesburg: Penguin.
New Era (2012). Chinese businesses told to respect labour laws. 29 August. Available from: http://allafrica.com/stories/201208290892.html (accessed 14 December 2013).
Nwoke, C.N. (2007). The scramble for Africa: a strategic policy framework. *Nigerian Journal of International Affairs*, 33(2): 31–56.
Osaghae, E. (1999). Exiting from the state in Nigeria. *African Journal of Political Science*, 4(1): 83–98.
Oshodi, A.T. (2012a). Does China's activities in Africa mean colonisation? *The Constitution*, 12(3): 1–54.
Oshodi, A.T. (2012b). ECOWAS and the Chinese option. In: Koffi, S., Bamba, L. and Semedo, G. (eds), *Sortir Du Sous-Dèveloppement: Quelles Nouvelles Pistes Pour L'afrique De L'ouest? (Tome 2)*. Paris: L'Harmattan, pp. 71–96.
Oshodi, A.T. (2013). Chinese *Africana* versus Chinese *internationa*: Africanising the Chinese option. In: Adelaja Odukoya (ed.), *Alternative development strategies for Africa*. Lagos, Nigeria: CBAAC and Concepts Publications, pp. 217–242.
Provost, C. and Harris, R. (2013). China commits billions in aid to Africa as part of charm offensive. *The Guardian*, 29 April. Available from: http://www.theguardian.com/global-development/interactive/2013/apr/29/china-commits-billions-aid-africa-interactive (accessed 10 June 2014).
Robinson, M. (2010). China: shaking the world. BBC, 12 July. Available from: http://www.bbc.co.uk/worldservice/documentaries/2010/05/100513_china_shaking_the_world_part_one.shtml (accessed 13 April 2011).
SABC (2006). COSATU warns of job losses on SA-China trade deal. 13 April.

Available from: http://www.bilaterals.org/spip.php?page=print&id_article=4413 (accessed 14 December 2013).

Sahara Reporters (2011). Chinese expats treat Nigerian employees as punching bags. 18 October. Available from: http://saharareporters.com/report/chinese-expats-treat-nigerian-employees-punching-bags (accessed 23 November 2013).

Sahara Reporters (2013). Labour movements picket, install workers union in foreign companies that deny workers' welfare. 8 October. Available from: http://saharareporters.com/2013/10/08/photonews-labor-movements-picket-install-workers-union-foreign-companies-deny-workers (accessed 11 December 2013).

Smith, D. (2011). Chinese mining firms in Zambia under fire for mistreating workers. *The Guardian*, 3 November. Available from: http://www.theguardian.com/global-development/2011/nov/03/chinese-mining-zambia-mistreating-workers (accessed 14 December 2013).

Smith, D. (2012). Workers claim abuse as China adds Zimbabwe to its scramble for Africa. *The Guardian*, 2 January. Available from: http://www.theguardian.com/world/2012/jan/02/china-zimbabwe-workers-abuse (accessed 12 December 2013).

Sun, Y.I. (2013). Impressions on labour practices in Chinese factories. *Nigeria News Beat*, 10 October. Available from: http://nigerianewsbeat.com/impressions-labour-practices-chinese-factories (accessed 16 July 2015).

Taylor, I. (2009). *China's new role in Africa*, Boulder: Lynne Rienner.

The Economist (2010). The world's biggest economy dating game: when will China overtake America? 16 December. Available from: http://www.economist.com/node/17733177 (accessed 2 February 2014).

The Economist (2011). The Chinese in Africa: trying to pull together. 20 April. Available from: http://www.economist.com/node/18586448 (accessed 14 December 2013).

The Punch (2012). China factory unrest, fresh headache for Foxconn. 26 September. Available from: http://www.punchng.com/business/international-business/china-factory-unrest-fresh-headache-for-foxconn-report/ (accessed 12 December 2013).

Wade, A. (2008). Time for the West to practice what it preaches. *New African*, March, p. 20.

Wang, F. (2010). China's population destiny: the looming crisis. *Brookings's Current History*. September Available from: http://www.brookings.edu/research/articles/2010/09/china-population-wang (accessed 22 December 2010).

Wells, M. (2011). China in Zambia: trouble down in the mines. *Huffington Post*, 21 November. Available from: http://www.hrw.org/news/2011/11/21/china-zambia-trouble-down-mines (accessed 12 December 2013).

Wenping, H. (2007). The balancing act of China's Africa policy. *China Security*, 3(3): 23–40.

Wilke, S. (2011). U.S. and China should avoid 'Thucydides Trap'. *Belfer Center Newsletter*, Spring. Available from: http://belfercenter.ksg.harvard.edu/publication/20814/us_and_china_should_avoid_thucydides_trap.html. (accessed 17 March 2011).

World Bank (2011). *Atlas of global development: a visual guide to the world's greatest challenges* (3rd edn). Washington, DC: World Bank and Collins.

Xinhua (2014). China-Africa ties to enter new era. *China Daily*, 6 May. Available from: http://www.chinadaily.com.cn/world/2014livisitafrica/2014-05/06/content_17487946.htm (accessed 10 July 2014).

Yang, Z. (2011). A real opportunity for the West as China looks abroad. *Financial Times*, 5 April. Available from: http://www.ft.com/cms/s/2/022f4a66-5ec9-11e0-8e7d-00144feab49a.html#axzz3fsBYSmMU (accessed 14 April 2011).

Yao, Y. (2010). The end of the Beijing consensus: can China's model of authoritarian growth survive? *Foreign Affairs*, 2 February. Available from: https://www.foreignaffairs.com/articles/china/2010-02-02/end-beijing-consensus (accessed 24 March 2011).

Yucheng, L. (2012). China's relations with the world at a new starting point. Speech. China Institute of International Studies (CIIS) Forum, Beijing, China. 10 April. Available from: http://www.fmprc.gov.cn/mfa_eng/wjdt_665385/zyjh_665391/t925181.shtml (accessed 8 January 2014).

10. On the transformative capacity of private fair labour arrangements

Ceren Pekdemir, Pieter Glasbergen and Ron Cörvers

1. INTRODUCTION

Violations of labour law and regulations continue to persist in the 21st century. In 2013 alone, the world witnessed the collapse of Rana Plaza, an eight-storey commercial building, and numerous fires at manufacturing sites in Bangladesh (Burke, 2013), to mention only a few disastrous examples. While violations of fair labour standards occur throughout the world, they are predominant in manufacturing countries and could be prevented through compliance with national and international labour standards.

The International Labour Organization (ILO) is a United Nations (UN) agency devoted to the promotion of social justice and internationally recognised human and labour rights. It is the most authoritative norm- and standard-setting body on the international level. It has a tripartite governing structure, meaning that workers and employers have an equal voice with governments in its deliberations. In voting procedures, governments offset worker and employer voting capacity because each member country is represented by two government delegates, an employer delegate, and a worker delegate. The core rights have been established in a total of 189 conventions, and deal with issues including child labour, forced labour, non-discrimination and equal pay, freedom of association and collective bargaining. Member countries become subject to the ILO's regular supervisory system responsible for ensuring that ratified and binding conventions are applied. Enforcement of the conventions relies upon the jurisprudence of domestic courts, as there are no international courts on labour rights.

A major shortcoming in the influence and power of the ILO is that it lacks enforcement mechanisms. The agency can register complaints against entities that are violating international rules. However, it does not impose sanctions on governments due to the principle of non-intervention in nation-state sovereignty and the influence of national self-interests on international institutions (Scherer and Smid, 2000). As a result, conventions are far from being fully institutionalised and core labour rights are still extensively violated in many parts of the world (Helfen and Sydow, 2013).

The inability to enforce labour rights at the international level is a modern-day problem characteristic of a world that is globalised in its production processes. With the advance of economic liberalisation there has been a shift in sourcing practices by large corporations as they source from networks of global suppliers without legal ties (Barrientos and Smith, 2007). Commodities sold by brands and retailers in the developed world are often produced in long supply chains in which those at the bottom of the system incur cuts to their labour costs. The complexity of the supply chain and the manner in which the options of many of its actors are constrained epitomises a structural injustice (Young, 2006). Complicity to this structural problem is vast as some producers purposefully violate labour laws or are negligent. International brands, and suppliers or contractors who pressurise producers, contribute to cutting labour costs while largely escaping responsibility for unfair labour conditions in supply chains. Southern governments compete for a 'favourable' investment climate which comprises low taxes and minimal regulation (Young, 2004). Consumers also sustain unfair labour practices as they remain unaware or are ignorant of the conditions in which commodities are produced or feel unable to change this. The problem is hence embedded in modern-day consumerism and economic sourcing models and is sustained by the scale of the problem (from local to global), the displacement of human rights responsibilities to manufacturing countries wanting economic prosperity (North and South divide), and the lack of regulatory authorities and enforcement mechanisms of national and international institutions (institutional incapacity). A facilitating factor to the lack of enforcement of fair labour by public actors is that within the neoliberal agenda public issues are increasingly left to private parties. While social relations within supply chains are politicised and conflicts on the normative principles for determining responsibility for social conditions are contested (Macdonald, 2014), neoliberal ideas, rules and practices have become dominant in many domestic and international policy domains, in which faith is placed in free markets and the accompanying political agenda of removing impediments to flows of capital. The prolongation of unfair labour practices within the 21st century is hence a structural problem for which responsibility not only lies with all the actors, but also with the political and institutional structures that sustain the system.

Within this political environment private nongovernmental initiatives for fair labour have arisen from the mid-1990s onwards (Bartley, 2007) to fill the gap left by national governments that do not implement and enforce the standards of the ILO. These arrangements may be multi-stakeholder in nature when they are partnerships including actors from both civil society and the business domain, also referred to as intersectoral partnerships (Bitzer et al., 2012) or cross-sector partnerships (Selsky and Parker, 2005). They may be intra-sectoral when they are constituted of partners solely from civil society or the market domain. These arrangements are involved in regulatory activities that are voluntary in nature, and in this way they transform the nature of existing regulation (O'Rourke, 2003). Seeking to function along the lines of outsourced production, their strategies may encompass setting standards, providing training for businesses, monitoring the implementation of standards, certifying factories, and accrediting certification programmes. Within the private domain, there are at present numerous private arrangements which are involved with various modes of regulation for fair labour on the transnational level. The result is a rather pluralist governance system, in which each of these initiatives tries to gain competitive edge and market share (Derkx and Glasbergen, 2014).

The effectiveness of these private arrangements has been called into question, and recent accounts have been critical about their governance potential (Locke et al., 2009; Marx, 2008). In this chapter we argue that this ineffectiveness should not be understood as a consequence of individual arrangements, but as originating from some characteristics of the system of arrangements as a whole, which impairs the transformative capacity of private arrangements in the issue field. We define transformative capacity as the ability to bring about substantial change in (un)fair labour practices. To analyse the transformative capacity of the system of arrangements, we will develop an analytical perspective that incorporates three dimensions: a structural-organisational, a normative-cognitive, and a collaborative-relational one (section 2). After an explication of our research methods (section 3), we analyse the system on these dimensions (sections 4–6). The last section offers overall conclusions of the study and formulates some suggestions to improve the system.

2. ANALYTICAL PERSPECTIVE

In this chapter we take a systemic view on the private fair labour governance system. This view is based upon the closely connected governance system (Burns and Stöhr, 2011a, 2011b; Guéneau, 2007; Jentoft et al., 2007) and organisational field approach (Dingwerth and Pattberg, 2009; Machado-da-Silva et al., 2006; Smith and Fischlein, 2010). The governance system approach has its roots in governance theory and addresses questions of governability regarding public issues. Its main premise is that no single organisational entity has the capacity to handle governing challenges effectively. Therefore, governance theory places the solution of these problems in the network of public and private actors that have a stake in the issue. The organisational field approach has been developed in organisation theory. It is based on the observations that organisational entities may fulfil similar roles, may recognise each other and may engage with each other. Because these actors are involved in a network of organisations, its main premise is that opportunities and limits to individual behaviour will be created, while the network as a whole may handle issues that the actors individually cannot. Both approaches have in common that they take an observable field of institutional life as their starting point. These institutions consist of organisational entities that relate both to an issue and each other. The qualification 'institutional' refers to the fact that participation of the organisations in the issue field is, at least in the short term, rather stable. Another commonality is that both approaches recognise relationships on three levels of analysis.

On the first level, it is considered that the organisational structure of the institutionalised field is structured by the activities of participants in the same dialogue. The activities directed towards the achievement of the issue and the actors' respective organisational aims, including task allocation, responsibilities and coordination, shape the organisational structure and possibilities for action of the issue field. On the second cognitive and normative level, actors in such an institutionalised area are considered participants in the same dialogue or discussion, although variations may occur in their commitment to specific perspectives, problem definitions, or strategies to solve them. The third level of analysis regards an institutionalised field as a dynamic identity. Here it is assumed that through their strategic responses towards the issue and each other, the actors are able, to a certain extent, to induce changes in the institutional characteristics of the issue field. It is anticipated that participants in the same dialogue will most likely develop some specific relationships to each other: they will interact, collaborate and form alliances, although it is also possible that (coalitions of) actors develop a more hostile and adversarial relationship.

In our study of the private fair labour governance system we have translated this systemic view into three operational dimensions to evaluate their characteristics:

- The first dimension refers to structural-organisational relationships and focuses on definitions of roles, responsibilities and leadership in the issue area.
- The second dimension refers to normative-cognitive relationships and focuses on the extent to which visions related to the standards for fair labour are shared by the participants in the issue area.
- The third dimension refers to dynamism in the system and focuses on the collaborative-relational capacity of the actors in the field, understood as their inclination to collaborate for concerted change.

Empirically, the boundaries between the three dimensions are not always clear-cut, as some characteristics enforce reaction in other dimensions or integrally span boundaries. The dimensions are meant as a conceptual tool to evaluate system characteristics.

3. RESEARCH METHODS AND DATA

This chapter is based on a literature study, semi-structured in-depth interviews and online desk research of information available in 2013. The literature study comprised literature on partnerships and collaborative arrangements for sustainable development, governance and governance systems, with particular attention given to transnational regulatory arrangements for fair labour.

The interviews were conducted with collaborative arrangements of both an intra-sectoral and multi-stakeholder nature. Examining the private governing arrangements as a system includes the setting of boundaries. The criteria for incorporating arrangements into the analysis were that arrangements must: (a) have the improving of fair labour as their main priority; (b) have been explicitly engaged with regulatory activities such as standard setting; and (c) have a transnational scope. A list of arrangements was established based on the literature study and online desk research, which was then complemented with the fair labour arrangements mentioned by our interviewees. More than 20 arrangements were recognised to be involved in regulatory activities for fair labour, but only half of these met the criteria of having fair labour as its main concern and having a transnational scope. In total ten transnational private regulatory arrangements were examined, out of which seven interviews were conducted with representatives of the arrangements (BSCI, CCC, FLA, FWF, SAI, WRAP and WRC) and one ILO expert. All of the private arrangements are not-for-profit nongovernmental organisations (NGOs) and all except for the CCC partner with businesses to enhance compliance with fair labour practices.

The following arrangements have been incorporated into the governance system analysis:

- Business Social Compliance Initiative (BSCI), multi-sector focus;
- Clean Clothes Campaign (CCC), focus on the garment industry;
- Electronic Industry Citizenship Coalition (EICC), focus on electronics;
- Ethical Trading Initiative (ETI), multi-sector focus;
- Fair Labor Association (FLA), multi-sector focus;
- Fair Wear Foundation (FWF), focus on the garment industry;
- Global Social Compliance Programme (GSCP), multi-sector focus;
- Social Accountability International (SAI), multi-sector focus;
- Worldwide Responsible Accredited Production (WRAP), focus mainly on the garment industry;
- Worker Rights Consortium (WRC), focus mainly on the garment industry.

While several arrangements focus on multiple sectors and industries, overall, the garment industry and sewn products receive greatest attention by the main arrangements.

In addition to the interviews, the analysis was complemented through online desk research, and the various secondary sources consulted on the arrangements included their websites, codes of conduct, partnership and/or project reports, and annual reports.

The arrangements were introduced from the mid-1990s onwards; with the exception of the CCC, as its establishment can be traced back to 1989, although they only developed a model code in 1998. The arrangement that was initiated most recently has been the GSCP in 2006. This indicates that the private regulatory frameworks on fair labour took off from the mid-1990s and reasonably stabilised around 2006.

4. THE STRUCTURAL-ORGANISATIONAL DIMENSION

The structural-organisational dimension of the fair labour system focuses on the manner in which the governance system is structured by the activities of the arrangements. The definitions of roles, responsibilities and leadership in the issue area shape the system structure and affect possibilities for action by the arrangements. The characteristics we analysed are the stakeholder representatives included in governance boards, the roles arrangements take regarding businesses, accountability of the arrangements, and views on leadership.

4.1 Stakeholder Compositions

The arrangements we studied are governed by different sets of stakeholders. Some are multi-stakeholder, including actors from civil society such as universities and unions, and from the market domain, including companies and industry associations, while others are intra-sectoral, including only civil society or market actors. Independence is reinforced in cases where arrangements have a multi-stakeholder structure as the different actors possess a more representative collection of motivations and a fuller array of complementary competencies. Private actors bring diverse interests and values, expertise and operational capacities together. Among other functions, civil society actors may contribute operational capacities for collecting, disseminating and analysing information, provide input to agenda-setting and policy development processes, assess conditions and monitoring compliance with agreements, and advocate (environmental) justice (Gemmill and Bamidele-Izu, 2002). Next to economic and management expertise (Van Huijstee et al., 2011) business participation is expressed to strengthen the operational capacities for agenda setting, norm promotion and monitoring (Abbott and Snidal, 2009). While different competencies may be reconciled, the representation of these sectors presents contesting institutional demands, since they are guided by different incongruent core logics (for instance an economic versus a social rationale) (Parker and Selsky, 2004; Van Huijstee et al., 2011).

A critical example of stakeholder representation is the composition of the governance boards. Members of the governance board have ultimate access to decision-making procedures. Board members are reflective of whose point of view is considered since members of the board of directors act on behalf of the organisation's constituents, whether they are from the state, market domain or civil society. Among other responsibilities, nonprofit board responsibilities are described as deciding on the organisation's mission and purpose, determining whether its programmes are consistent with its mission and monitoring the effectiveness of these programmes, and adhering to legal and ethical standards and norms (Ingram, 2008). Access to decision-making procedures enhances accountability and legitimacy, and may improve compliance and acceptance of the standards. It is argued that the absence of affected societal actors in the decision-making processes not only constitutes a lack of legitimacy but also poses a danger to the effectiveness of the arrangements (Schouten and Glasbergen, 2011; Zürn, 2004).

Within the different private standard-setting arrangements, we observe an uneven distribution of types of stakeholders who have access to decision-making in the governance boards. Next to collective representation by businesses, NGOs, unions, universities and colleges, there are also individuals on the boards who function in their own expert capacity. Predominantly represented, however, are business and industry representatives (in eight out of ten arrangements). Throughout all the governance boards, direct representation of workers by unions is minimal (in two out of ten arrangements). Having a multi-stakeholder coalition is, for some of the arrangements, a determining factor for accrediting a sustainable value to negotiating labour rights (for four out of seven interviewed arrangements). A multi-stakeholder input in the governance boards is described as moving towards more sustainable change, and a lack of union representatives on the boards is only by a few deemed to diminish the credibility and legitimacy of the arrangements (for two out of the seven interviewed arrangements). The analysis of governance boards shows that within the private governance system for fair labour, workers' rights are currently more proposed by industry stakeholders and the corporate world than by unions.

4.2 Roles

Civil society is a generic label that covers several disparate and often contradictory and competitive forms of organisation and action (Castells, 2008). NGOs involved in global governance can take a variety of roles, including the mobilisation of public opinion, the representation of the voiceless, and service provisioning by delivering technical expertise on particular topics, as well as participating directly in operational activities, monitoring and assessment, and providing expert advice and analysis (Gemmill and Bamidele-Izu, 2002).

The organisations within the private governance system for fair labour share some characteristics but fulfil diverse roles. This was underscored by the representatives and explained in reactionary, dialectic, but primarily functionalist, terms. Even though it remains indeed ambiguous at whose demand new transnational regulatory institutions are established (Biermann et al., 2009), identity formation of organisations may be seen as an inherently social and inter-organisational process, and the creation of new arrangements essentially reactionary to the particular status quo. The representative of the FWF formulated the functionalist argument as follows: 'All the organisations have a role, otherwise they would not exist'.

The representative of the CCC understood the fulfilment of different roles in dialectic terms constituted in a dynamic political arena with purposeful strategies for power. The CCC has a unique position within the private governance system as it does not have corporate members and primarily fulfils a campaigning role by mobilising public opinion and representing the voiceless. The other arrangements are business–NGO partnerships that, as one source of income, provide, for instance, expertise, advice, monitoring and assessment based on membership fees. Nonetheless, there are further variations, for instance the WRC that takes the representation of the voiceless as one of their primary roles.

Although all arrangements underscore their differences, they are also critical of each other's aims. As will be shown in the next subsections, within the business–NGO arrangements there are many variations in standards and enforcement. While some adhere to stringent standards and discontinue membership in case of noncompliance, other arrangements are toothless and merely provide a global platform for promoting the exchange of knowledge. On a strategic level, this question affects just how the arrangements regard themselves as change agents. Do they fulfil a consultancy role for businesses, or do they perform a more public role? Some of the arrangements are criticised for their impetuses towards industry, while others disapprove of naming and shaming businesses and making public attacks on their operating models. In turn, the more critical and stringent arrangements are critical of the least stringent initiatives, lowering the bar for fair labour standards. The representative of the FLA reflected on the different roles:

> Everyone has its role to play and in a spectrum you need the name and shame [arrangements] because they raise a lot of issues, they serve the watchdog function. The threat that they pose forces a lot of companies to get out of their comfort zone and start thinking about social responsibility . . . But then you also need [arrangements] where the companies that decide to do something need to go. . . . I do get worried though that some of the organisations devalue the currency. . . . They make it harder for other groups who are trying to raise standards.

4.3 Accountability

Even though public opinion may at times influence the strategic course of the private arrangements, those based on the monitoring and assessment of businesses are not directly affected in their relationships with businesses. The reasons for this rest on shortcomings in accountability structures. First of all, the arrangements themselves do not have to fear the purchasing power of consumers. The monitoring arrangements do not have consumers as clientele, but businesses. In fact, the more pressure is applied to businesses, the likelier the chance that a business will opt for membership to a certifying or monitoring fair labour arrangement of their choice. Closely connected to the purchasing power argument lies a second argument, which is that the arrangements that fall within the scope of this research do not certify products, and correspondingly do not fear damage to their reputation on defectively certified products. Even accountability for audits is diffuse. For example, with the collapse of the Rana Plaza complex in Bangladesh in April 2013, with a death toll of 1129, BSCI social audits were performed in two of the factories in the complex. The audits did not include building construction or integrity. Also in the case of the fire in Ali Enterprises in September 2012 in Pakistan, where nearly 300 workers died, the certification body that issued the certification to the company was accredited by the Social Accountability Accreditation Services (SAAS), an accreditation agency used by both BSCI and SAI. While these and other tragedies have received considerable attention, insufficient private certification practices have received rather limited attention from civil society at large. Other arrangements within the governance system are critical of accreditation and certification practices and comment that more responsibility should be taken (according to three out of the seven interviewed arrangements). There is, however, no mechanism by which arrangements that outsource services are held accountable. In the current configuration of the governance system there are thus several identifiable problems that pertain to its accountability structures.

4.4 Ascribed Leadership

Related to the fact that accountability is largely lacking and in the absence of a body that sanctions these organisations, we observe that there is also not one authority that leads or guides the arrangements. The private arrangements consider different public authorities to be relevant and influential for the issue field of fair labour, including: the ILO (e.g. conventions, subdivisions and programmes); the UN (e.g. Guiding Principles on Business and Human Rights as endorsed by the Human Rights Council); the EU (e.g. Corporate Social Responsibility Strategy); and negotiations and agreements made on a national or local level (e.g. the Bangladesh Fire and Safety Protocol). Amongst these, the ILO is considered to be the most authoritative standard-setting body. It serves as a reference point for the arrangements as its conventions, recommendations and jurisprudence are generally appreciated. Some of these works are translated into standards, trainings, and other instruments as employed by the arrangements.

While the former UN Secretary-General's Special Representative for

Business and Human Rights, John Gerard Ruggie, has been recognised as having played an influential role, particularly with regard to his proposition of the framework on the UN Guiding Principles on Business and Human Rights in 2008, our research reveals that strong leadership qualities are currently not ascribed to any institution or person. Even though the ILO is considered to be the most authoritative standard-setting body, within the governance system there is not one leading arrangement that shows or sets out how the private arrangements can or should direct their efforts. What's more, due to its tripartite structure, the private arrangements feel that they have very little, if any, influence on the ILO. The ILO does not employ preferential or specifically accommodating services for the private arrangements. However, there are more structural problems that inhibit the ILO from being perceived as a leader by the arrangements. Firstly, the ILO is considered to be almost a victim of its own democracy as a tripartite body. Member states, but also the employer and worker federations, can restrict its ability to act. Secondly, because it is a tripartite organisation change occurs slowly and incrementally. Thirdly, there is a heavy focus on the national context, and the tripartite structure is seen to mainly serve the national levels, whereas many of the private arrangements are involved in global supply chain activities.

Overall, the characteristics of the structural-organisational dimension show that the representation of market actors, particularly in relation to the more limited direct representation of workers, represents an uneven distribution of stakeholder representativeness. There is a further divide on the role arrangements take on businesses, from a more supportive and consultative role to an adversarial one. Since the arrangements do not certify commodities they do not fear reputational damage or accountability demands from consumers for ineffective enforcement of private standards. Finally, there are currently no leadership qualities ascribed to any private or public institution.

5. THE NORMATIVE-COGNITIVE DIMENSION

Although variations may occur in commitment to specific perspectives, problem definitions or strategies to solve them, the normative-cognitive dimension of the fair labour governance system refers to the extent to which visions related to the standards for fair labour are shared by the participants in the issue area. We analysed the provisions in the standards, means of enforcement, and views on public and private responsibility for effective compliance to standards.

5.1 Standards

Standards set by the private arrangements are based on public regulations, primarily those established by ILO conventions, other human rights frameworks, and, in some arrangements, the benchmark of conduct must only be in line with national and local laws. The standards are typically incorporated into codes of conduct, and they stipulate the minimum norms and rules to which the arrangements envision that companies comply with, and on which performance of the supply chains can or must be evaluated. They are written statements in which a commitment to a conduct is expressed. Information about the codes must therefore be communicated externally to become known for businesses, suppliers and consumers. Ordinarily, many codes fall within the realm of general business ethics with no implementation methods, but businesses that adopt codes of conduct by the standard-setting arrangements, adopt them with the intention to apply them transnationally, particularly as sourcing guidelines (Diller, 1999) in which the code applies to other enterprises in the value chain which are not directly owned, operated or controlled by the business having adopted the code.

Codes related to labour standards were originally quite diverse, but are considered to have converged around the same ILO core standards and principles at the turn of the 21st century (O'Rourke, 2003). Even though it is evident that all are inspired by the same core principles, the statements and details incorporated within the provisions vary considerably.

In our analysis, several issues concerning the key provisions of the different arrangements come to the fore. Here we provide several examples. On the key issue of child labour, WRAP challenges the minimum age law of the ILO of 15 (unless the legal minimum is 14 which needs to be in accordance with the ILO developing country exceptions) by stipulating the age of 14 as a minimum. Even though the BSCI does refer to the ILO and UN Conventions, the minimum age is omitted from the provision. On the key issue of freedom of association the EICC, GSCP and WRAP refer to 'lawful' rights or the rights in accordance with 'local laws', which restricts the human right to freely associate and bargain collectively. On the key issue of wages, WRAP and the EICC refer to wages in compliance to local laws but leave out any provisions on living expenses, basic needs and discretionary income. The BSCI states that employers are encouraged to provide compensation in cases where the legal wage does not cover living expenses, but this remains provisional. On the issue of hours of work, WRAP ignores the ILO Conventions by referring to a country's law. On the issue of employment relationships, the BSCI, EICC, WRAP and WRC do not have any codes. The analysis not only shows that there is clear diversity in the codes of conduct but also shows there is ambiguity about the ILO being considered as an authoritative model code.

5.2 Enforcement Mechanisms

Similar diversity was also found in the enforcement of the standards. Enforcing standards is a means through which the arrangements want to accomplish their goals. Additionally, it also signifies strategic efforts as choices made on the enforcement of standards define how member companies will be treated and how producers in the supply chains will be affected. Systems for implementing and evaluating compliance to codes of conduct are critical to the credibility of the codes endorsed by the standard-setting arrangements (O'Rourke, 2003). Out of the ten standard-setting arrangements in our analysis, seven verify whether businesses implement the respective standards, out of which, three use certification. There is great diversity concerning the actual verification of the implementation of the standards, as arrangements vary on aspects such as who conducts the audits, which aspects of compliance are monitored, how noncomplying members or producers are treated, and whether they make audit results or noncompliant members public.

Our analysis of the enforcement mechanisms reveals that only the ETI does not require that companies have third-party auditing – that is, audits carried out by independent organisations outside the company and its supply chain to verify whether they meet standards, even though the ETI does make validation visits to verify management performance. All other monitoring organisations do commit businesses to third-party auditing, whether the arrangements coordinate audits themselves or have certification bodies for SA8000 management systems. Auditing of standards related to actual performance requires that companies demonstrate changed practices and have not just put a management system in place (Conroy, 2007). Performance-based standards therefore provide more assurance to businesses down the supply chain and to consumers that a company's fair labour management meets the standard. The FLA, FWF, WRAP and WRC require that auditors visit factories and actually verify standard implementation.

Further distinctions are found regarding noncompliance of members and producers. WRAP is the only arrangement that directly audits producers without necessitating membership involvement of brands. In case of noncompliance they do not certify the factory. The ETI, FLA and SAI terminate brand membership to their organisation in cases of noncompliance. They hold their own members accountable for failing to address noncompliance within their own management system or for failing to terminate relations with a noncomplying producer. The BSCI, FWF and the WRC, on the other hand, assign responsibility for noncompliance at the producing level, and take into consideration whether to continue or discontinue relationships between producer and brand at the brand level. Whether this is out of consideration for brand autonomy or for fear that workers might be worse off without jobs, they ultimately hold producers accountable for noncompliance, and not the brands at the end of the supply chain. Similar strategic considerations can be found in keeping audit results or noncompliant members confidential or making them public. Publicising may be regarded as a punishment as it can have a detrimental effect on business performance and does not improve the situation of workers. Nonetheless, not making results public also has detrimental effects in that unfair labour practices may continue, thus also not improving the situation of the workers.

5.3 Views on Responsibility

While the arrangements aspire to improve labour conduct, there is wide acknowledgement that responsibility and capacity to solve the issue is diffuse and rests on everyone, from states, intergovernmental agencies, businesses, trade associations, NGOs and unions, to consumers. None of the arrangements considered their own organisation as bearing the most responsibility in resolving unfair labour conduct. Most often responsibility was placed with businesses and with states.

Reasons for businesses to carry this responsibility firstly derived from the consideration that labour rights abuses happen specifically because of the way brands and retailers do business. Placing severe price pressures and strict deadlines on manufacturing suppliers necessarily puts a negative burden on labour. Secondly, the solutions to unfair labour practices must be grounded on business principles to be effective. Addressing the business motivations that drive the incentives that sustain unfair labour practices is argued to be more successful in getting rid of the problem. Brands and retailers would need to commit to working with certified manufacturers, and this is projected to create incentives for the rest of the manufacturers.

Ensuring commitment to ethical sourcing through the force of law is the main reason why states are envisioned to regulate the private domain. The failure of business compliance is seen as the responsibility of the state. Many national institutions are considered at a loss due to limited capabilities because global supply chains are transnational. Next to the fact that arrangements consider many states to fail at regulating the labour market, international institutions in turn do not have the ability to regulate the global supply chain. The arrangements, in their own operational capacities, try to force business actors to deliver public goods. Interestingly, the regulatory activities by the private arrangements were placed at an intermediate level between businesses and states, though the responsibility to alleviate unfair labour conduct was ultimately placed at the door of state and business conduct.

Overall, the characteristics of the normative-cognitive dimension show that there are different visions of the adaptation of core conventions and principles as set by international institutions, and diverse approaches in enforcement methods. Furthermore, final responsibility to solve unfair labour conduct is primarily given to businesses and public institutions rather than taken by themselves as intermediaries.

6. THE COLLABORATIVE-RELATIONAL DIMENSION

The final dimension of the system refers to the collaborative capacity of the actors in the field, understood as their inclination to collaborate for concerted change. This has been examined on two levels of analysis: firstly, the extent to which the private arrangements cooperate with core international institutions; and secondly, how and to what extent the arrangements collaborate with each other.

6.1 Relationships Between the ILO and Private Arrangements

As previously discussed, different international public authorities are considered to be relevant and influential for the work of the private arrangements. Nonetheless, relationships and cooperation between private and public arrangements are seldom formalised, nor do they occur habitually. Consultation or collaboration with the ILO is stated to be project driven and not embodying a larger affiliation. Examples provided were consultation and training in the leather sector in Ethiopia by WRAP, consultation and adoption of the fair wage concept by the FLA, or the provision of a neutral chair by the ILO for the steering committee of the Bangladesh Accord to which the CCC and WRC are witness signatories. The Accord on Fire and Building Safety in Bangladesh was designed in 2013 by Bangladeshi and international unions, together with other civil society labour groups, including the WRC and CCC. It was signed by over 50 international brands and retailers, who agreed upon a five-year commitment to invest in safer factories. Among other provisions, the accord includes independent inspections by experts, public reporting, mandatory repairs and renovations financed by brands, and a binding contract to make all commitments enforceable. Public support by the ILO of the Bangladesh Accord is considered by the WRC and CCC to have advanced their efforts. With the exception of one arrangement, the arrangements are not frequently in contact with the ILO, nor do they expect to be. The mandate of the ILO is widely considered to precede engagement with the private arrangements.

6.2 Collaboration Between the Arrangements

At present, attempts for enduring collaboration have hardly been found within the private governance system. The arrangements collaborate with a small selection of other arrangements, and efforts are initiated on an individual basis depending on ideological and circumstantial reasons. The ideological argument refers to like-mindedness or as one representative (WRC) stated: 'we collaborate with organisations we feel make similar commitments and have similar enforceability mechanisms'. It was particularly considered that the operating models between industries led arrangements, and organisations without worker representatives were too distinct for real collaborative efforts to take off. Circumstantial motivations refer to factors such as whether arrangements are involved in the same projects, particular countries or regions, brands, factories, or thematic topics such as the living wage concept. Collaboration is particularly valued in cases where duplication of effort is decreased, for example running training on freedom of association or fire and safety. The type of content exchanged is primarily informative, advisory and supportive.

Most of the collaborations are intangible exchanges and take place along informal lines of communication. The only tangible exchanges between the arrangements were noted in those instances where the partners were represented in the governance board, and in cases of joint projects between different standard-setting and monitoring partnerships that are formalised, with, for instance, a memorandum of understanding. From the interviews it became apparent that the latter does not occur often. The most common type of collaboration was along informal lines, such as attending consultation rounds convened by one of the arrangements, attending the same seminars or webinars and congresses, and direct lines of personal communication such as email correspondence and telephone conversations.

While collaborative efforts were perceived as valuable and the arrangements were open for more efforts to be undertaken, they recognised that next to a common ideological or circumstantial purpose, two of the biggest constraints were time and being understaffed. This was also reflected in a more strategic attempt at collaboration that had been explored in the past with the initiation of the Joint Initiative on Corporate Accountability and Workers' Rights in 2003, when a total of six arrangements (CCC, ETI, FLA, FWF, SAI, WRC) convened as a first formalised effort between the different organisations to collaborate. Supported by grants from the European Commission and the US State department, the project was initiated to determine whether and how the participating arrangements could enhance efficiency and effectiveness (Derkx and Glasbergen, 2014). It was an attempt to establish a metagovernance arrangement, or, as it was broadly defined, establishing an 'organisation of self-organisation' (Sørensen, 2006). In an effort to maximise the effectiveness of the regulatory approaches, reduce duplication of efforts, explore possibilities to cooperate and share learning the initiative conducted a 'trial project' in Turkey where they wanted to test various aspects of the collaborative effort. The project ran until 2007 and has not evolved into an active organisational structure or platform in use today. In several studies (Derkx and Glasbergen, 2014; Glasbergen, 2013) it is explicated that the initiative has been valuable as a learning experience and that it was an important first step towards cooperation. However, it was not very effective in its efforts to change company policy or in achieving actual improvements in the Turkish context. These aggravations spilled over into the convergence element of the collaboration, and also complicated relationships between the Joint Initiative's members. The lack of coordinated effort shows that these hurdles have not been surmounted.

The characteristics of the collaborative-relational dimension show that public-private interaction is limited, and although the private arrangements cooperate with each other, this lacks clear coordination and occurs for ideological and circumstantial reasons.

7. CONCLUSIONS

In this chapter we have identified system characteristics of the fair labour governance system which we operationalised on three dimensions. On the structural-organisational dimension, the distribution of representatives across governance boards on the whole includes more industry representation, and the roles the arrangements take on regarding businesses varies. There are certain identifiable shortcomings in relation to accountability structures, and there is no leadership in the governance system. On the normative-cognitive dimension, many variations exist in the provisions taken up in the standards and in their enforcement. While responsibility to solve unfair labour was considered diffuse, final responsibility to solve unfair labour was not placed with the arrangements in the private governance system, but primarily at state or corporate level. On the collaborative-relational dimension we found that private actors generally have sporadic collaboration with core international labour institutions. While the arrangements share knowledge and expertise to some degree with other arrangements that have similar operational models, the incentive to collaborate is weak, and, as a result, collaboration is largely uncoordinated and limited.

We argue that the fragmentation recognizable on the three dimensions impairs the transformative capacity of the governance system of the fair labour issue field. While there are several arguments for why the existence of diverse regulatory arrangements may be positively assessed, including the potential for innovation and covering niche or different parts of the market, our findings indicate that high levels of fragmentation from a systemic point of view brings limited potential for structural change. Even though the potential for transformative capacity is present as arrangements are, to varying degrees, actively involved with standard setting, monitoring, training and education, systemic change has not occurred. As one representative stated: 'Arguably [the industry] is just as bad, just as dangerous as it was 10 years ago when all these programmes had just started'. While positive results are noticeable regarding the ground work, particularly in the dissemination of training, implementing complaints mechanisms, and generally in creating awareness about all the different labour rights and conditions, a sense of frustration across the arrangements was noticeable regarding the effectiveness of the work. In particular, the existence of more lax approaches undermines the efforts of more stringent approaches. Whether this contributes to the confusion on the ends of businesses and civil society at large, it certainly offers businesses the opportunity to choose the stringency level of standards and audits.

The new fulfilment of global corporatism raises serious questions about the representativeness of corporatist arrangements, and the extent to which they function as instruments of co-optation rather than representation. One important characteristic that supports this is the predominant representation of industry and corporate interests in decision-making processes and the scarce direct representation of workers. Furthermore, since the distribution of arrangements has reasonably stabilised and remained secure, the incentive to change conduct is low. The predominant focus on the garment sector and sewn products limits the potential for change across sectors. In addition, lacks in accountability structures, particularly for the certifying arrangements, is a system characteristic that sustains the problem of diffuse responsibility. Certification of commodities could be one solution. However, regulatory arrangements are currently not able to guarantee a supply chain that is completely fair. As long as the public or private transnational governance system cannot guarantee fair labour nor effectively penalise noncompliance, only individuals will be held accountable and no systemic transformations will occur.

The failure to effectively alleviate fair labour violations on an international level by governments and intergovernmental agencies has not been solved hitherto by the private transnational arrangements in the governance system. This raises questions about the effectiveness of the governance system given that its characteristics do indicate problems related to the fragmentation of the system. Example of this are: the variety amongst the private actors themselves, the lack of accountability and the uncoordinated efforts amongst various arrangements, and weak public–private links. Without more coherence the transformative potential of the arrangements may not be accomplished. More structured intergovernmental support would advance the efforts of the private arrangements, as, in addition to expertise and support, leadership could be provided and authoritative leverage would be brought to the table. A private implementation institution of the ILO could, for instance, by means of authority and capacity lending, fill this governance gap. Without addressing these issues, the transformative capacity of the private fair labour governance system will remain challenging.

REFERENCES

Abbot, K.W. & Snidal, D. 2009. The governance triangle: Regulatory standards institutions and the shadow of the state. In: Mattli, W. & Woods, N. (eds) *The Politics of Global Regulation*. Princeton, NJ: Princeton University Press.

Barrientos, S. & Smith, S. 2007. Do workers benefit from ethical trade? Assessing codes of labour practice in global production systems. *Third World Quarterly*, 28, 713–729.

Bartley, T. 2007. Institutional emergence in an era of globalization: The rise of transnational private regulation of labor and environmental conditions. *American Journal of Sociology*, 113, 297–351.

Biermann, F., Pattberg, P., Van Asselt, H. & Zelli, F. 2009. The fragmentation of global governance architectures: A framework for analysis. *Global Environmental Politics*, 9, 14–40.

Bitzer, V., Glasbergen, P. & Leroy, P. 2012. Partnerships of a feather flock together? An analysis of the emergence of networks of partnerships in the global cocoa sector. *Global Networks*, 12, 355–374.

Burke, J. 2013. Bangladesh factory fires: Fashion industry's latest crisis. *The Guardian* [Online], 8 December. Retrieved from: http://www.theguardian.com/world/2013/dec/08/bangladesh-factory-fires-fashion-latest-crisis (accessed 3 February 2014).

Burns, T.R. & Stöhr, C. 2011a. The architecture and transformation of governance

systems: Power, knowledge, and conflict. *Human Systems Management*, 30, 173–194.
Burns, T.R. & Stöhr, C. 2011b. Power, knowledge, and conflict in the shaping of commons governance. The case of EU Baltic fisheries. *International Journal of the Commons*, 5, 233–258.
Castells, M. 2008. The new public sphere: Global civil society, communication networks, and global governance. *The ANNALS of the American Academy of Political and Social Science*, 616, 78–93.
Conroy, M.E. 2007. *Branded! How the 'Certification Revolution' is Transforming Global Corporations*. Canada: New Society Publishers.
Derkx, B. & Glasbergen, P. 2014. Elaborating global private meta-governance: An inventory in the realm of voluntary sustainability standards. *Global Environmental Change*, 27, 41–50.
Diller, J. 1999. A social conscience in the global marketplace? Labour dimensions of codes of conduct, social labelling and investor initiatives. *International Labour Review*, 138, 99–129.
Dingwerth, K. & Pattberg, P. 2009. World politics and organizational fields: The case of transnational sustainability governance. *European Journal of International Relations*, 15, 707–743.
Gemmill, B. & Bamidele-Izu, A. 2002. The role of NGOs and civil society in global environmental governance. In: Esty, D.C. & Ivanova, M.H. (eds) *Global Environmental Governance: Options and Opportunities*. Princeton, NJ: Yale School of Forestry and Environmental Studies.
Glasbergen, P. 2013. Legitimation of Certifying Partnerships in the Global Market Place. *Environmental Policy and Governance*, 23, 354–367.
Guéneau, S. 2007. Certification as a new private global forest governance system: The regulatory potential of the Forest Stewardship Council. Conference 'Non-State Actors as Standard Setters: The Erosion of the Public-Private Divide', Basel Institute on Governance, Basel, 8–9 February.
Helfen, M. & Sydow, J. 2013. Negotiating as institutional work: The case of labour standards and international framework agreements. *Organization Studies*, 34, 1073–1098.
Ingram, R.T. 2008. *Ten Basic Responsibilities of Nonprofit Boards*, 2nd edn. Washington, DC: BoardSource.
Jentoft, S., Son, T.C.V. & Bjørkan, M. 2007. Marine protected areas: A governance system analysis. *Human Ecology*, 35, 611–622.
Locke, R., Amengual, M. & Mangla, A. 2009. Virtue out of necessity? Compliance, commitment, and the improvement of labor conditions in global supply chains. *Politics & Society*, 37, 319–351.
MacDonald, K. 2014. *The Politics of Global Supply Chains*. Cambridge: Polity Press.
Machado-da-Silva, C.L., Filho, E.R.G. & Rossoni, L. 2006. Organizational fields and the structuration perspective: Analytical possibilities. *BAR. Brazilian Administration Review*, 3, 32–56.
Marx, A. 2008. Limits to non-state market regulation: A qualitative comparative analysis of the international sport footwear industry and the Fair Labor Association. *Regulation & Governance*, 2, 253–273.
O'Rourke, D. 2003. Outsourcing regulation: Analyzing nongovernmental systems of labor standards and monitoring. *Policy Studies Journal*, 31, 1–29.
Parker, B. & Selsky, J.W. 2004. Interface dynamics in cause-based partnerships:

An exploration of emergent culture. *Nonprofit and Voluntary Sector Quarterly*, 33, 458–488.

Scherer, A.G. & Smid, M. 2000. The downward spiral and the U.S. model business principles. Why MNEs should take responsibility for the improvement of world-wide social and environmental conditions. *Management International Review*, 40, 351–371.

Schouten, G. & Glasbergen, P. 2011. Creating legitimacy in global private governance: The case of the Roundtable on Sustainable Palm Oil. *Ecological Economics*, 70, 1891–1899.

Selsky, J.W. & Parker, B. 2005. Cross-sector partnerships to address social issues: Challenges to theory and practice. *Journal of Management*, 31, 849–873.

Smith, T.M. & Fischlein, M. 2010. Rival private governance networks: Competing to define the rules of sustainability performance. *Global Environmental Change*, 20, 511–522.

Sørensen, E. 2006. Metagovernance: The changing role of politicians in processes of democratic governance. *The American Review of Public Administration*, 36, 98–114.

Van Huijstee, M.M., Pollock, L., Glasbergen, P. & Leroy, P. 2011. Challenges for NGOs partnering with corporations: WWF Netherlands and the Environmental Defense Fund. *Environmental Values*, 20, 43–74.

Young, I.M. 2004. Responsibility and global labor justice. *Journal of Political Philosophy*, 12, 365–388.

Young, I.M. 2006. Responsibility and global justice: A social connection model. *Social Philosophy and Policy*, 23, 102–130.

Zürn, M. 2004. Global governance and legitimacy problems. *Government and Opposition*, 39, 260–287.

11. Compliance opportunities and the effectiveness of private voluntary standard setting – lessons from the global banana industry

Dennis Klink

1. INTRODUCTION

In an era of 'governance without government' (Rosenau and Czempiel 1992), the emergence of 'private authority' (Hall and Biersteker 2002) has become a pivotal study object (see also Chapter 10, this volume). The role of multinational companies (MNCs) and their attempts to self-regulate through Corporate Social Responsibility (CSR) instruments such as voluntary private standard setting represents an important element within that field (Bartley 2007; Locke 2013; Vogel 2008). Considering this background, the chapter focuses on MNCs in the global banana industry, a sector with a 'dark history' regarding human and labor rights violations (Striffler and Moberg 2003). As a response to stakeholder pressure, most banana MNCs have adopted voluntary certification programs regarding working conditions and environmental practices (Liu 2008). However, civil society organizations (Feral and Fischer 2006; Pier 2002) as well as academics (e.g. Harari 2009; Robinson 2010a) have skeptically evaluated these initiatives and criticize the lack of effectiveness. This chapter argues that private standard setting in the banana industry is contested because empirically we can witness significant differences between the level of standard adoption and that of standard implementation. In other words, all banana MNCs have endorsed and committed themselves to various voluntary social and environmental certification systems at the central company level. Moreover, those systems represent key elements of their CSR policies. Nonetheless, the relatively ambitious adoption agenda is contrasted by rather selective standard implementation figures across different supply-chain countries. Put differently, when comparing the implementation statistics of different banana-producing countries we can observe that despite countries being integrated into MNC supply chains in similar ways some locations show significantly lower certification numbers than others.

This finding draws attention to the domestic conditions in individual supply-chain countries since differences regarding certification numbers are located at the country and not so much at the company level. Based on this observation, I develop an analytical framework that draws on institutional theory, and more precisely the comparative capitalisms literature (Jackson and Deeg 2006). In line with scholars that have made similar arguments (Bartley 2010; Locke 2013), the approach emphasizes that institutional characteristics in producing countries are the major elements that drive or constrain CSR implementation. Companies evaluate those factors and prefer to promote and implement standards at those locations where the most promising opportunities to reach compliance with standard requirements exist. This proposition is further developed by assessing the linkages between four institutional arenas – public business regulations, compliance culture, labor market characteristics, and education of the workforce – and the implementation results of the most widespread certification system in the banana sector, GLOBAL GAP. Furthermore, I evaluate the assumed institutional mechanisms by drawing on empirical material from the two largest producing countries, Ecuador and Costa Rica.

The chapter is organized in the following way. First, I will give a brief overview of the global banana industry and the role that social and environmental standards (in short CSR standards) play in the sector. Afterwards, I discuss the theoretical framework of the chapter, which is based on the comparative capitalism (CC) literature. The next two sections of the chapter are concerned with analyzing the effects of the four institutional characteristics discussed earlier on the implementation of CSR standards across the nine largest banana supply chain countries. At first this is done by assessing each variable individually. While this procedure provides some interesting first explanations, the second part of the analysis focuses on building country clusters based on different combinations of the four institutional conditions. The last section of the chapter concludes and discusses some further implications regarding the effectiveness of business self-regulation through private standard setting.

2. THE GLOBAL BANANA INDUSTRY

With approximately 25 percent of production volume being exported, bananas are the world's most exported fresh fruit (Liu 2008: 2). Having reached an all-time high of 16.5 million tons in 2012 (FAO 2014), banana-export production is of substantial economic importance for certain developing countries. Market structures make bananas a typical 'cash crop' linked to an established South-North export system, meaning that they are almost exclusively produced in developing countries and then mainly exported to European and North American markets. MNCs from importing countries are the key players in that system.

Due to geographical and climatic conditions, profitable banana production is only possible in certain areas that are almost exclusively located in developing countries. Moreover, banana export production is concentrated in a few large producing countries, which are predominantly located in Latin America. High levels of concentration are also prevalent at the level of importing countries where Europe, the United States, and Japan account for two-thirds of worldwide banana imports. As their domestic markets are relatively small, producing countries are highly dependent on expectations that originate from US and European markets (e.g. CSR commitments).

For the analysis that follows, I will focus on the nine largest banana-producing countries. Together they produce almost 80 percent of the globally exported fruit. Those nine countries also predominantly cater to the US or EU markets, a fact which theoretically exposes them to the CSR discourse taking place there.

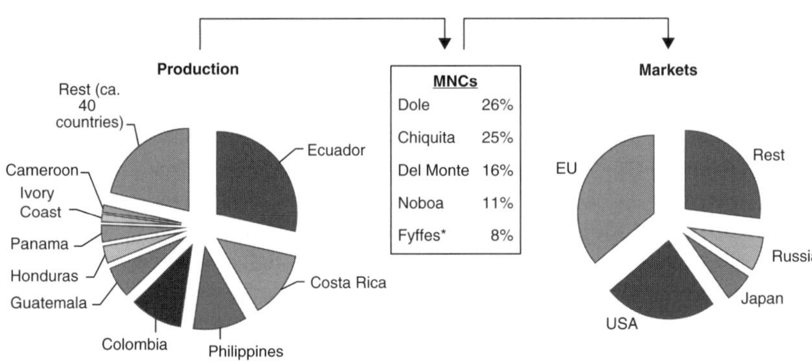

Note: * In March 2014, Chiquita and Fyffes announced a merger. According to industry sources, Chiquita is willing to pay US$526 million for the Irish trader. ChiquitaFyffes would become the largest banana MNC and further consolidate the industry's oligopolistic structure. Due to antitrust issues the merger is still pending.

Source: Author's own calculations based on FAOSTAT(2013).

Figure 11.1 The global banana industry at a glance

3. THE ROLE OF BANANA MNCs

In the banana commodity chain, MNCs function as producers, exporters and/or importers of fruit (Arias et al. 2003: 68–70). Over the years, this strategy has enabled them to exercise control over various parts of the commodity chain thereby reaping benefits from the most profitable areas while outsourcing those with higher risks to smaller business actors. Today, MNCs operate their own plantations but usually procure the majority of fruit from 'independent' producers (Arias et al. 2003: 68; van de Kasteele and van der Stichele 2005: 18). The key to power, however, is their dominance over banana exports (UNCTAD 2009). In that context, MNCs function as gatekeepers for producers that are trying to access profitable overseas markets. They are important brokers and intermediaries (Arias et al., 2003: 70), a position resulting from their centuries-old experience in organizing and managing the complexities of banana production and transportation in a reliable manner. This has led to the development of a sector in which two-thirds of the world market is controlled by three companies. Moreover, the five largest companies together account for more than 80 percent of world market share (see Figure 11.1). In a nutshell, MNCs are not only the most important and influential actors in the banana sector, they are also key to spreading and promoting private voluntary standard systems.

4. BANANA EXPORT PRODUCTION AND THE RISE OF PRIVATE VOLUNTARY STANDARD SETTING

Banana export production is labor intensive and subject to a very price-sensitive market (Robinson 2010b: 286). Fruit quality – not defined in terms of nutritional value or taste but based on the absence of bruises, black spots and deformations – is the most important requirement in banana production (Wells 2003: 320). In that context, the perishable nature of the banana has created an industry that relies on high levels of process organization. Companies have a time frame of 21 days from harvesting to the moment when the banana becomes an inedible mush. Within that time frame, many work steps such as harvesting, washing, impregnating, boxing, shipping, etc., are necessary for ensuring that the fruit enters consumer markets on time and in good quality. In that system, the low mechanization potentials and the susceptibility of the plants to diseases make wages, working hours and agrochemicals key production resources. Particularly in those issue areas, banana companies have been criticized for their business practices.

From a historical perspective, the majority of MNCs in the sector have been involved in scandals or accused of corporate irresponsibility.[1] In fact, they represent typical examples of cases where foreign companies have shown irresponsible business behavior across various 'host countries'. 'Flexibilization' and deregulation of labor (Martínez Valle 2004), gender discrimination (Prieto-Carrón 2006), low wages and unpaid overtime (Humbert 2011), and the widespread use of child labor (Pier 2002) on 'agricultural killing fields' (Sass 2000) represent only some of the most prominent examples on the list of unsustainable business practices that have traditionally been used to guarantee profitable production systems (Striffler and Moberg 2003).

Interestingly, the banana sector has also undergone some incremental changes concerning the management of such issues during the last 20 years. Some authors argue that after having realized that exploitative corporate behavior 'threatens the banana's happy market image as a tasty, nutritious, funny, sunny and sexy fruit' (Gonzalez-Perez and McDonough 2005: 7) all big banana companies have introduced sustainability programs and CSR policies. Company-own codes of conduct and voluntary social and environmental certification systems are the most important instruments in that context. Today, the most common certification schemes are GLOBAL GAP (approximately 48 percent of world exports), Rainforest Alliance (18 percent) and SA 8000 (6 percent). Furthermore, there are niche standards such as Fair Trade (3 percent) and organic certifications (3 percent).[2] Within the last 10–15 years, these systems have become increasingly popular amongst MNCs. A closer look at the central company level furthermore reveals that CSR adoption is more or less equally distributed across MNCs.

---

1 Chiquita, for instance, experienced a public relations disaster when in 1998 the *Cincinnati Enquirer*, a local newspaper from the city where the corporate headquarter was based at that time, published a story about the company's unethical business practices. Amongst other issues, the article accused the company of having bribed Colombian paramilitary groups, poisoning workers and avoiding taxes and unionization of workers through 'secretly controlled scores of ostensible independent companies' (Taylor and Scharlin 2004: 19/20). Dole and also Del Monte have a similar history and often engaged in the very same practices (Feral et al. 2006; Klink 2015).

2 There are no definite numbers available concerning the exact volume of certified fruit. Therefore, the figures mentioned above represent estimates that are taken from Liu (2008) and Potts et al. (2010) or calculated based on industry sources.

Table 11.1 *CSR standard adoption by MNCs*

	Code of Conduct	Global Gap	Rainforest Alliance	SA 8000	ISO14001	Organic	Fair Trade
Chiquita	+	+	+	+	−	+	−
Dole	+	+	+	+	+	+	−
Del Monte	+	+	+	−	+	−	−

Source: Author's own elaboration based on Chiquita Brands (2012), Dole Food Company (2011), Fresh Del Monte (2012).

Table 11.1 implies that CSR adoption in the banana sector is relatively effective among MNCs. However, the picture is quite different when we shift our perspective from company-owned plantations to those that are operated by nominally 'independent' producers. Here, a closer look at the implementation figures at the producing-country level shows that although MNCs have committed themselves to ambitious CSR policies, they only promote private voluntary standards very selectively across countries. To illustrate this point, I will use the example of GLOBAL GAP, the most widespread standard system in the banana sector.[3]

Figure 11.2 shows the GLOBAL GAP certified area (in percentage of national supplier-owned production area) across the nine largest banana-producing countries.

Hence, the certification landscape in the global banana industry is characterized by two patterns that seem to contradict each other. At the global (*adoption*) level, the leading MNCs in the sector commit themselves to ambitious CSR policies based on private standard systems (Table 11.1). They also implement these CSR standards in the supply chain. However, they do this in a very selective way (*implementation level*). Moreover, the discrepancies between certain supplier countries is relatively large, indicating that some countries seem to be much more 'attractive' for standard

[3] GLOBAL GAP is the acronym for Global Good Agricultural Practice. The standard system originated from an initiative created by European retailers in 1997 under the name EUREP GAP. The principal intention was to harmonize the existing private health and food safety standard systems of the participating retailers under one umbrella standard. The new collaborative system represented 'a highly ambitious internal agenda that combines auditing of food safety standards with protocols for sustainable food production' (Campbell 2005: 2). From a technical point of view, GLOBAL GAP covers four main areas, which are: food safety, environmental protection, occupational health and safety, and animal welfare. For a detailed history of the standard system see Campbell (2005).

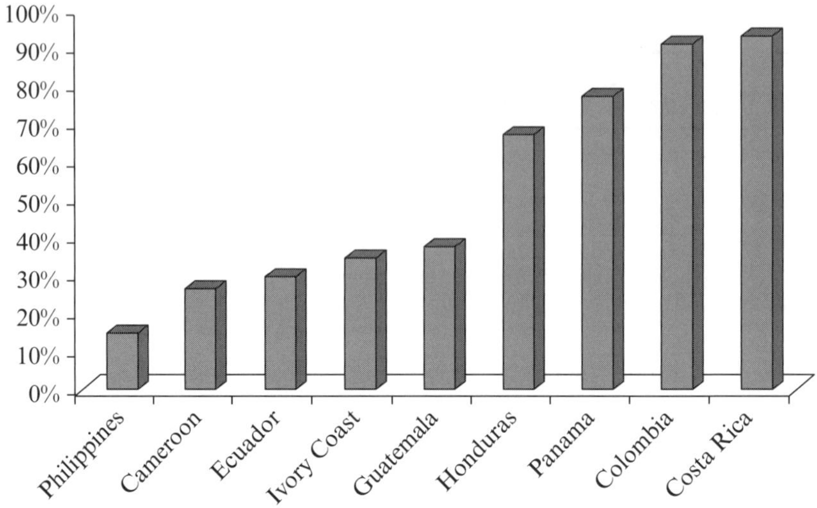

Source: Calculated based on industry sources and personal communication.

Figure 11.2 Implementation of GLOBAL GAP on supplier plantations

implementation than others (Figure 11.2). This finding suggests that adoption and implementation are likely to follow different logics of action. The following section further elaborates on this idea by developing an explanatory model that is based on institutional theory and a multi-level perspective on transnational CSR standard setting.

5. TOWARDS A THEORETICAL FRAMEWORK FOR EVALUATING TRANSNATIONAL CSR STANDARDS

All companies that do not exclusively produce in, source from, or sell to domestic markets are exposed in one way or another to multiple institutional environments. This is certainly the case for MNCs, which are – by definition – active in various countries and markets around the globe. Moreover, for MNCs countries have different functions. One can distinguish at least between two groups: countries in which a product is sold (importing countries) and countries in which this product is produced (producing/exporting countries). Such a model of functional division is prone to significant power asymmetries. Nevertheless, it has not been sufficiently systematized how and to what extent these factors impact CSR

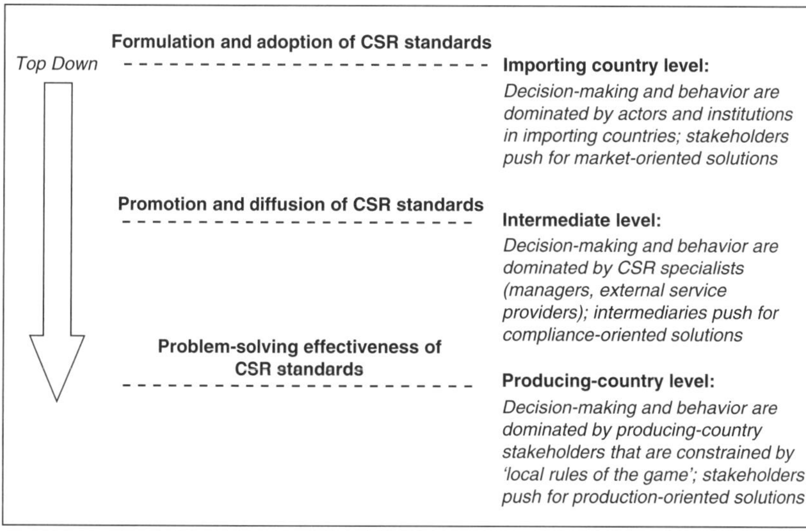

Figure 11.3 Transnational CSR as a multi-level top-down process

adoption, diffusion and implementation. By arguing that transnational CSR first and foremost represents a hierarchical, top-down chain of activities that begins in importing countries and ends in exporting countries (and more precisely at the level of production), the model takes this issue into account. Additionally, the approach is built on the idea that CSR instruments are subject to consecutive development stages. This offers the possibility of analytically disaggregating the effectiveness question into various dimensions. Figure 11.3 displays a model that is based on those considerations.

For evaluating the effectiveness of transnational CSR standard setting, I consider three principal levels: the adoption level, the diffusion level and the problem-solving level. I argue that on each level a distinctly different logic of action dominates actor behavior. That is because stakeholders on each level are predominantly concerned with *one* specific element of a CSR policy's development.

Formulation and adoption of CSR policies usually takes place at the importing-country level. Here, the most important questions are how successfully CSR instruments can be integrated into existing market structures. Will key market participants (consumers, investors, etc.) give sufficient credibility to the instrument? Can legal and public relations risks be mitigated or avoided through CSR adoption, and does it enhance the company's financial performance?

A completely different logic of action is present at the producing-country level. Here, CSR instruments alter the existing business practices and impact important parameters by changing the costs of production. The principal logic that dominates this level features production-oriented solutions in its center. Hence, the most important questions for actors in producing countries might be to what extent CSR standards interfere with established mechanisms of organizing and coordinating regular work flows. Therefore, production-level conditions largely determine the adaptation costs of certification and with that the attitude of stakeholders towards transnational CSR standards.

Finally, the intermediate level is shaped through its position in between the two other levels. CSR experts and professionals such as CSR managers, certification specialists, auditors and other service providers are the dominant players here. Their main objective is to implement what has been decided upon at the level of adoption. Hence, they are responsible for the diffusion of CSR standards throughout the supply chain. During that process, they tend to promote implementation at those locations that show the highest likelihood for success. This creates the situation that some producing countries might offer more favorable conditions for the formal implementation of CSR standards than others. As a result, the dominant logic at the intermediate level is driven by the opportunities to achieve formal compliance with CSR standards. I argue that the quality of those *compliance opportunities* is primarily shaped and determined by institutional characteristics in supply-chain countries. Thus, I draw on institutional theory for identifying and conceptualizing compliance opportunities.

6. INSTITUTIONAL THEORY AND THE COMPARATIVE CAPITALISMS (CC) LITERATURE

Often institutions are referred to as 'the rules of the game in a society' (North 1990: 3). Various institutionalist schools draw on this basic concept. One of them is the Comparative Capitalisms (CC) literature (Jackson and Deeg 2006). Broadly speaking, the CC literature is primarily interested in how and what kind of institutional effects impact economic outcomes (Amable 2003; Hall and Soskice 2001b; Hollingsworth et al. 1994; Whitley 1999). Furthermore, a key feature of this literature is that it goes beyond analyzing economic outcomes as a function of market mechanisms and/or formal policies. Rather 'economic action is viewed as a special case of social action' (Jackson and Deeg 2006: 11). This idea refers to the concept of 'institutional embeddedness' (Granovetter 1985). Decisions and actions of economic actors are not only determined by pure market considerations or regulative constraints and incentives but are seen as being mediated through institutional characteristics that encompass a broader set of social and cultural non-market factors. Together, those elements create a distinct logic of economic action, which, in the end, makes 'societies differ in their "coordination" procedures' (Amable 2003: 51). Behind that background, the CC literature also assumes the existence of a 'competitive institutional advantage' that leads to different firm strategies (Hall and Soskice 2001a: 36). Broadly speaking, the CC literature has identified a number of key institutional features that shape economic behavior and firm strategies at the level of national business systems (Whitley 1999). I borrow four of them and apply them, in a slightly modified way, in this study. Table 11.2 outlines those features as well as the corresponding causal mechanisms and the indicators that I applied to measure them.

These four institutional features are hypothesized to impact the quality of compliance opportunities. The next section further develops these assumptions through the application of simple correlations performed on the nine largest banana-producing countries. It shows that each selected variable is subject to correlational patterns with the GLOBAL GAP certification numbers across countries. However, these relationships are not statistically perfect. Put differently, individual variables have only limited explanatory power in this context. Since a core element of CC literature relates to viewing institutions not as isolated factors but as features that can complement and enhance each other's effectiveness (Jackson and Deeg 2006: 12), I further build country clusters based on institutional conditions. Beyond that, I evaluate the explanatory power of the causal mechanisms (Table 11.2) by discussing the situation in reference to the two largest producing countries (Ecuador and Costa Rica). The purpose of this step is to demonstrate that potential relationships between institutional variables and certification outcomes do not occur randomly but are based on causality. For this part, I draw on further macro-level indicators as well as on empirical data gathered during fieldtrips to the respective countries.[4]

[4] During two fieldtrips to Ecuador (January–March 2012) and Costa Rica (February–April 2013), interviews with MNC representatives, NGOs, government officials, plantation owners and managers, workers and further experts were conducted and later analysed for this study.

Table 11.2 Institutional mechanisms and measurement

Institutional arena	Mechanism	Indicator and sources
Public business regulations	Compliance with national law is a basic requirement of all CSR standards. In that context, the 'business-friendliness' of public labor regulations becomes an important factor determining the adaptation costs of standard implementation. Countries with business-friendly regulations will have an advantage over those that are characterized by a more protective and stringent legal framework.	'Regulatory quality', World Bank Governance indicators (Kaufmann et al., 2009)
Compliance culture	Compliance culture refers to the extent to which business activities are executed in a formalized way. It is linked to prevalent norms of trust in formal authorities, regulations, contracts, etc. The implementation of CSR standards is based upon the formalization of various aspects of coordination (written working contracts, formalized payment procedures, etc.). These require a strong compliance culture that supports the formalization of business practices instead of preventing them.	'Rule of law', World Bank Governance indicators (Kaufmann et al., 2009)
Labor market characteristics	The existence of 'CSR-sensitive' groups within a national workforce can create challenges (i.e. costs) for CSR implementation. Often CSR standards specifically target such groups (e.g. women, children, migrants). If those groups have a strong presence in national labor markets, compliance with CSR standards can create significant adaptation costs making a country less attractive for standard implementation. At the same time, MNCs perceive those countries as high-risk locations from a public relations point of view. This incentivizes them to follow a low-profile strategy in order to avoid stakeholder exposure.	Female employment in agriculture (World Bank 2013)
Education and professionalism	In order to reach compliance with CSR standards a certain degree of education and professionalism among key implementation actors (e.g. plantation managers, workers, etc.) is necessary. Monitoring and reporting systems, standardized internal mechanisms of labor coordination as well as training for workers are necessary components for successful implementation. Therefore, countries with a more educated workforce are more likely to create favorable compliance opportunities in the eyes of MNCs.	Spending on education, Human Development Index (UNDP 2011)

7. PUBLIC BUSINESS REGULATIONS

There are two principal reasons why business regulations, in particular those that regulate labor, are crucial in the context of CSR standard implementation. First, the banana industry is labor-intensive and wage-sensitive, a fact that makes labor regulations a crucial parameter determining the price of one of the most important production resources. Second, a basic requirement for the successful implementation of all private standard systems is compliance with national law. This can lead to the situation that in some countries compliance with CSR standards is easier to reach because the basic requirements for certification are less stringent. The idea that the legal environment might matter for standard implementation has been introduced by scholars before (see e.g. Marx and Cuypers 2010). In line with these studies, I use the Regulatory Quality Indicator from the World Bank Governance Indicator data set, which captures 'perceptions of the ability of the government to formulate and implement sound policies and regulations that permit and promote private sector development. (Kaufmann et al. 2009: 6). Figure 11.4 shows the results for the relationship between business-friendly regulations and the implementation of CSR standards.

In Figure 11.4, we can observe a group of high performers with business-friendly legal frameworks (Costa Rica and Panama) and an

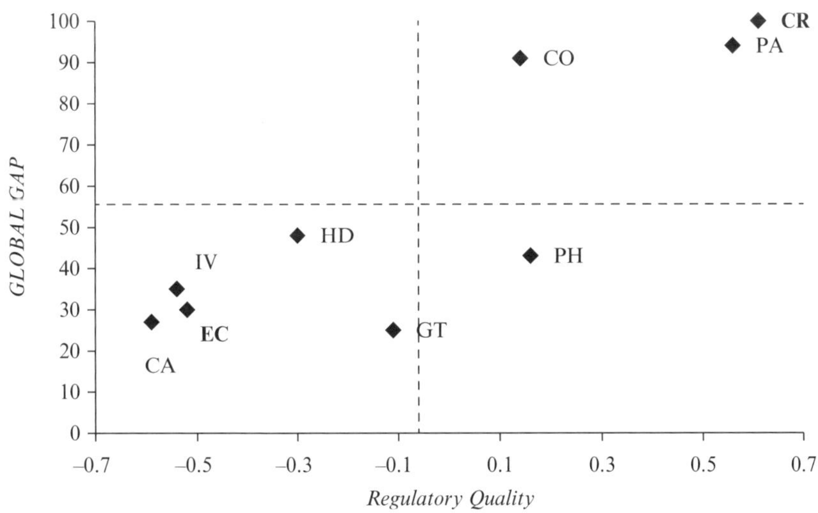

Figure 11.4 Public regulations and GLOBAL GAP implementation on supplier farms

opposing group of low performers with business-unfriendly regulations (Ecuador, Ivory Coast, Honduras and Cameroon). However, three countries (Colombia, the Philippines and Guatemala) are not very well represented by the explanation. This tells us that, as an indicator, business regulations alone cannot fully explain the picture. Before I discuss this in more detail, I now will briefly highlight the role that differences in business regulations play for those cases that are in line with the explanation. As mentioned before, I will draw on the examples of Ecuador and Costa Rica.

In both countries' national labor codes we can observe a number of crucial differences. In Costa Rica, the maximum work time is 48 hours per week. Compared to other banana-producing countries, redundancy costs are relatively low (19 weeks of salary for the entire process of dismissing an average worker).[5] By law Costa Rican workers are only entitled to ten days of paid holiday and the statutory regulations on mandatory overtime are relatively liberal (US Department of State 2012b). In contrast, the Ecuadorian labor code stipulates a maximum working time of 40 hours per week, 15 days of paid annual leave, the prohibition of mandatory overtime, and that voluntary overtime must not exceed 12 hours per week. Moreover, with 36 weeks of salary for dismissing an average worker, the country shows the highest redundancy costs across the nine largest banana-producing countries (US Department of State 2012a).

In sum, we can argue that business regulations in both countries vary distinctively for issues that are crucial for producing bananas. We could now argue that Ecuador clearly has a competitive disadvantage compared to Costa Rica. In reality, however, it is the largest producer of export bananas and a country that functions as a key supplier for all MNCs. How is this possible? The second institutional feature can provide an answer to this question.

8. COMPLIANCE CULTURE

Regulations can only have the intended effect if business actors and workers comply with them. Although quite trivial, in the case of voluntary certification this basic statement should not be underestimated. I use

---

[5] For redundancy costs, I use the definition proposed by Botero et al., which encompasses 'the equivalent in pay of the sum of the notice period, severance payment and any other mandatory penalty directly related to the dismissal of the worker' (Botero et al. 2004: 13).

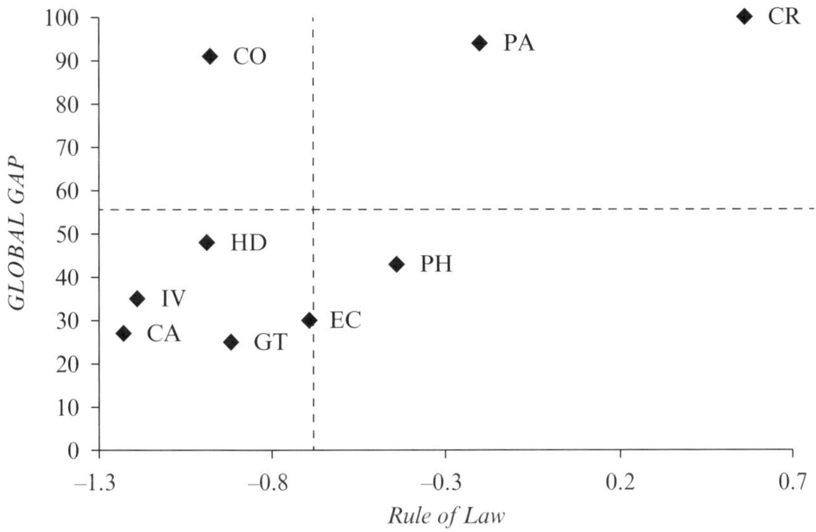

Figure 11.5 Compliance culture and GLOBAL GAP implementation on supplier farms

the Rule of Law[6] indicator to assess a country's compliance culture in reference to the GLOBAL GAP results (see Figure 11.5).

Again, we can observe a group of countries with very low values on both dimensions (Ecuador, Ivory Coast, Cameroon and Honduras). Furthermore, their position is consistent with the one in Figure 11.4. The same result, just mirrored from the lower left to the upper right quadrant, occurs for Costa Rica and to a smaller extent for Panama. We can conclude that the three countries with low implementation results have unfavorable business regulations *and* a weak compliance culture, whereas the two high performers also show high values on both dimensions. However, for Colombia we can observe a significant discrepancy between *business regulations* and *compliance culture*. This indicates that both dimensions are not identical and that we cannot use compliance culture as a (functional) substitute for business regulations (or vice versa). Nevertheless, as the examples of Costa Rica and Ecuador show, both are closely related to each other.

---

6 The indicator captures 'perceptions of the extent to which agents have confidence in and abide by the rules of society, and in particular the quality of contract enforcement, property rights, the police, and the courts, as well as the likelihood of crime and violence' (Kaufmann et al., 2009: 6).

In the area of working conditions and labor rights, a typical manifestation of a weak compliance becomes visible in high levels of labor informality (Schneider 2009; Schneider and Karcher 2010). Here, Costa Rica and Ecuador differ significantly. Moreover, they represent extreme examples in the context of Latin American countries. Next to Chile (38 percent), Costa Rica has the third smallest informal sector (41 percent), whereas in Ecuador more than two-thirds of the economically active population is part of the informal economy (Rinne and Sánchez-Páramo 2008: 354). The size of the informal sector is important for both banana production and certification.

Producers have traditionally been dealing with the seasonal character of the industry by hiring and firing workers flexibly and on a short-term basis. In that respect, the relatively stringent public labor regulations in Ecuador represent a severe burden to national suppliers. It is very costly to lay off banana workers formally because severance pay is high. In contrast, the more flexible labor market regulations in Costa Rica create lower barriers for business owners to employ workers through formal contracts. Based on this mechanism, Schneider and Karcher have argued that Latin American countries with protective and 'labor-friendly' public regulations are usually characterized by large informal sectors (Schneider and Karcher 2010: 634). This view is consistent with the Ecuadorian case. In fact, the 'business model' of the Ecuadorian production system is grounded in the approach of operating virtually outside the public legal framework (Pier 2002). In contrast, the situation in Costa Rica is much more favorable for standard implementation. That is not only because the country's informal sector is much smaller, but also because the quality of the existing enforcement mechanisms is higher. Statistically, every labor inspector in Costa Rica covers a workforce of 7,000 workers, whereas in Ecuador this number goes up to 26,300 (US Department of State 2012a, 2012b). Although, the labor inspector/workforce ratio is a crude measurement for the quality of rule enforcement, it is very likely that such a huge gap has an effect on a country's compliance culture. A weak and fragmented public enforcement regime represents an important feature of an institutional environment in which labor issues are coordinated rather informally. However, these baseline conditions make it also more difficult, hence costly, for standard systems to be implemented and monitored in the long run. Based on this mechanism, I argue that local actors in countries with a weak compliance culture will show high levels of resistance in the face of transnational certification programs.

9. LABOR MARKET CHARACTERISTICS

Certain features in national labor markets vary significantly across producing countries. I have argued that for understanding CSR standard implementation it is necessary to pay attention to those groups within national labor markets that would receive particular attention within the process of certification. In this chapter, I will focus on female workers as an example of a 'CSR-sensitive' group.[7] Depending on the country, there is a tendency to assign flexible and low-paid jobs to female banana workers (World Banana Forum, 2012). Since all CSR standards entail clauses that deal with gender equity issues, the amount of women on a plantation might become an important issue during the certification process. I use figures regarding female employment in agriculture (World Bank 2013) to capture this dimension on a macro level. I assume that a high dependency on agricultural work amongst women increases the likelihood that this group will face precarious or de-facto unregulated working conditions. This would result in significant additional costs and makes resistance to CSR standards more likely where certification systems are introduced. I therefore argue that high levels of women employed in agriculture will lead to low CSR standard implementation results. Figure 11.6 displays this relationship.

Figure 11.6 confirms the initial hypothesis that an increase in CSR-sensitive groups leads to a decrease in CSR standard implementation. With 27 percent and 23 percent of female laborers pursuing agricultural work, I consider Ecuador and the Philippines countries with comparably high shares. Although slightly beyond the threshold, Guatemala (18 percent) also falls into that category. That is also because in the two African countries significantly more women participate in the national workforce than in any other country. On the other hand, in Costa Rica (4 percent), Colombia (5 percent) and Panama (7.3 percent) few women are employed in agriculture and CSR standard implementation reaches high numbers. However, in particular the case of Honduras violates the explanation. At 10 percent we find almost as few women in the agricultural sector as in Panama (7.3 percent). Nevertheless, the country's certification figures (48 percent) are more similar to the ones in Ivory Coast (35 percent) or the Philippines (43 percent). I will discuss this point in the last part of the chapter in more detail and compare the situation in Costa Rica and Ecuador first.

---

[7] Further examples for CSR-sensitive groups could be child laborers or migrant workers.

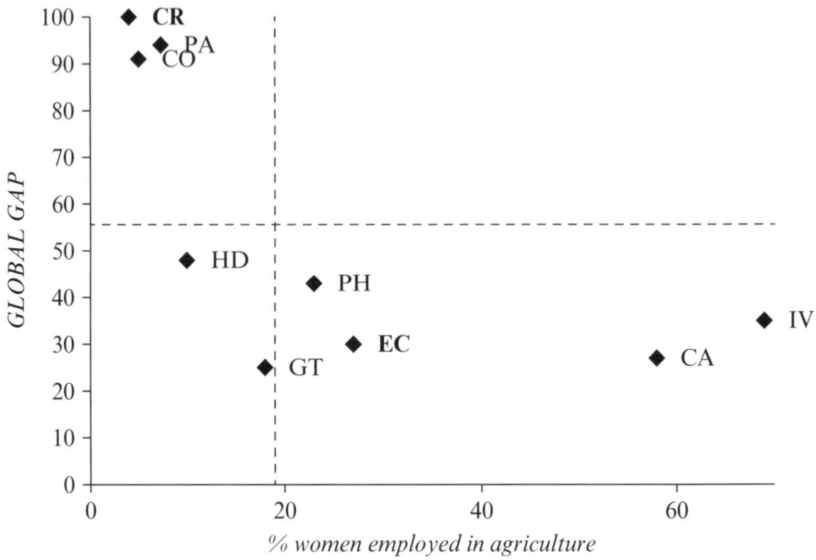

Figure 11.6 CSR-sensitive groups and GLOBAL GAP implementation on supplier farms

The role of female labor in agriculture differs significantly between Costa Rica and Ecuador. In Ecuador women are perceived as cheap laborers that are assigned 'inferior' tasks, which are badly paid. What makes the implementation of CSR standards even more difficult is the problem that women are usually employed informally (Striffler 2002: 201). In contrast, there are no significant differences in employment arrangements between male and female workers in the Costa Rican banana industry. What does that mean for the process of standard implementation? Compared to Costa Rica, integrating a substantial amount of (female) laborers working in non-compliance with labor regulations would not only lead to short-term adaptation costs but also to a permanent increase in labor costs. I therefore argue that Ecuadorian suppliers show much more resistance against certification programs since they would severely constrain their economic competitiveness.

10. EDUCATION AND PROFESSIONALIZATION

The level of education and professionalization impacts the ability to individually process and to collectively manage the requirements of

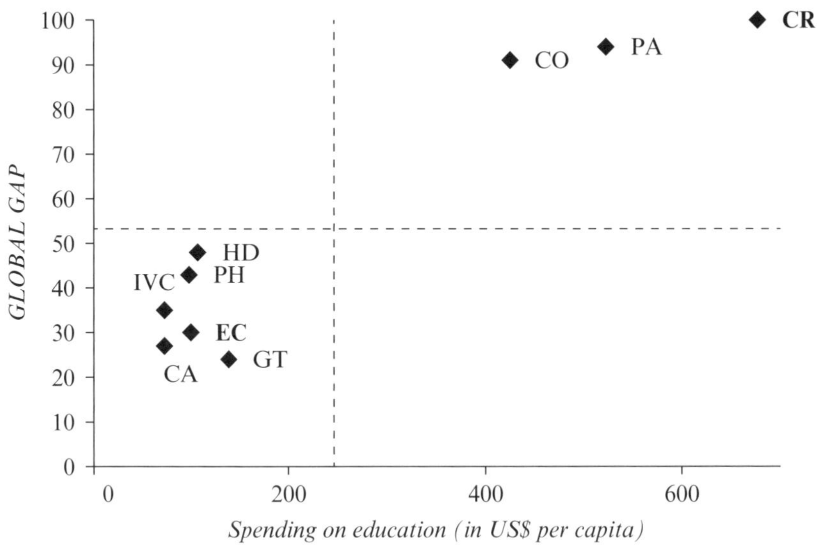

Figure 11.7 Education and professionalization and GLOBAL GAP implementation on supplier farms

CSR standards. I use national spending on education as an indicator for displaying institutional differences in that area (UNDP 2011).

Figure 11.7 shows a strong relationship between the level of education and CSR standard implementation results. All countries with high spending on education have a high certification record (Costa Rica, Colombia and Panama). Conversely, all countries with low spending also show low values for the implementation of Global GAP (Ecuador, Philippines, Guatemala, Honduras, Cameroon and Ivory Coast). Consistent with the finding from the first three institutional arenas, Costa Rica is part of the group of high performers, whereas Ecuador is a clear member of the low performing group. Now how do differences in the level of education and professionalization impact the implementation of CSR standards in those countries?

Under closer examination, Ecuador and Costa Rica differ significantly in the educational coverage, educational quality and opportunities that the education system can offer students and graduates to further their professional careers. Additional indicators show that there is a relatively large gap concerning literacy rates (CR 96.2 percent; EC 84.2 percent), enrolment in secondary education formats (CR 100 percent; EC 80 percent) and the percentage of the population with at least secondary education (CR 53.6 percent; EC 36.6 percent) between both countries (UNDP 2011;

World Bank 2012). These figures highlight the poor performance of the Ecuadorian system. Moreover, it is important to note that in Ecuador low levels of education are especially prevalent in rural areas, which are precisely the zones where banana production takes place (Parandekar et al. 2002: 145). In contrast, the Costa Rican educational system reads like the opposite example and strongly contrasts the low-quality system in Ecuador. The country's good performance can be seen as the result of 'the government interest to maximize the strategic objective of the educational system' (Fischel Volio 1992: 148). More importantly, Costa Rica was able to ensure that rural areas would not fall behind in the process of increasing educational coverage (Reimers 2006: 471).

11. THE FOUNDATIONS OF FAVORABLE AND UNFAVORABLE INSTITUTIONAL ENVIRONMENTS

The last section demonstrated that individual institutional conditions can explain selective standard implementation for certain locations while they represent less convincing solutions for others. One way to deal with this issue is viewing institutional conditions as interconnected and not as isolated explanatory factors. I therefore propose to cluster the nine cases under observation based on the relative presence or absence of each institutional condition.[8] This procedure allows for identifying at least three different types of institutional environments: ideal-typically favorable systems, ideal-typically unfavorable systems, and in-between systems. The results of this categorization are presented in Table 11.3.

Table 11.3 shows the distribution of the values of the four institutional conditions across the nine largest supply chain countries and in reference to their respective GLOBAL GAP certification rates (last column to the right). The clustering process reveals that those countries that show business-friendly public regulations, a strong compliance culture, the absence of CSR-sensitive groups in national labor markets, and high levels of education and professionalization amongst the workforce have

[8] This idea very much follows a set-theoretical logic, which has been introduced into social science research most prominently within the scope of Qualitative Comparative Analysis (QCA) (Ragin 1987, 2008). By 'relative' presence or absence, I mean that I conceptualize the value of a condition in reference to a predefined threshold. In this case, I use the mean across all condition values. In other words, if a condition value lies below this mean, the condition is interpreted as if it was absent. Conversely, if it is above the mean it is treated as being present.

Table 11.3 Favorable and unfavorable institutional environments for the implementation of CSR standards

	Business-friendly public regulations	Strong compliance culture	High share of CSR-sensitive groups in national labor markets	High levels of education and professionalization	Certification rate
Ideal-typically favorable institutional environment					
Costa Rica, Panama	present	present	absent	present	high (CR 100%/ PA 94%)
In-between environments					
Colombia,	present	absent	absent	present	medium-high (91%)
Honduras,	absent	absent	absent	absent	medium-low (48%)
Philippines	present	present	present	absent	medium-low (43%)
Ideal-typically unfavorable institutional environment					
Ivory Coast, Ecuador, Cameroon, Guatemala	absent	absent	present	absent	low (IV 35%; EC 30%; CA 27%; GT 24%)

the highest certification rates (Costa Rica and Panama). In contrast, the institutional environments in those countries with the lowest certification rates (Ivory Coast, Ecuador, Cameroon and Guatemala) are characterized by the opposite condition values. Hence, they represent the inversion of favorable institutional environments.

The mapping procedure becomes more interesting when we look at in-between countries. Here, Colombia, which also performs relatively well (although not as well as Costa Rica and Panama), shares three out of the four conditions that constitute favorable environments. Public regulations are business-friendly, CSR-sensitive groups do not form an important element of the labor market and the workforce is relatively well educated and professional. However, Colombia faces serious problems when it comes to the country's compliance culture. Here, its institutional environment is much closer to countries such as Honduras and Guatemala (see Figure 11.5). As a result, it does not reach as high a certification as found in Costa Rica or Panama.

Honduras represents another case of an in-between country. It shares the absence of the business-friendly legal framework (although we can already observe a small gap here in the raw data), the weak compliance culture and the low level of education and professionalization with an ideal-typically unfavorable institutional environment. However, for CSR-sensitive groups, the differences become larger and Honduras moves more toward becoming a favorable institutional environment. This becomes visible in the country's modest certification record (48 percent GLOBAL GAP). Summed up, Honduras shares three of the four conditions that characterize the lower end of the certification landscape in the banana sector. It is therefore able to offer slightly better compliance opportunities and consequently shows a higher certification rate than Ecuador, Ivory Coast, Cameroon and Guatemala.

Finally, there is the case of the Philippines, which is crucial for a number of reasons. Here, we observe the presence of a business-friendly legal framework and a strong compliance culture. However, these favorable conditions are contrasted by low levels of education and the prevalence of CSR-sensitive groups. Hence, the Philippines represent something like a tie: two favorable conditions versus two unfavorable ones. How does this combination of institutional conditions materialize in the country's certification record? At first, and as expected, the GLOBAL GAP certification rate is significantly higher (43 percent) compared to those countries with four unfavorable conditions. However, it is slightly lower than the figure in Honduras, which shares three of the four unfavorable conditions and also one more than the Philippines. Hence, the Philippines and Honduras are interesting because both cases contain information about the importance of the selected individual conditions. We can now argue that at least for the Philippines and for Honduras, female participation in agricultural labor markets seems to be more important in determining the quality of compliance opportunities than business regulations and compliance culture.

How can that finding be explained? At first, the Philippines seems to have a solid advantage due to its business-friendly legal framework and its modest compliance culture. Certainly, this will make the process of implementation easier compared to implementation in Honduras. However, the high share of female workers in agriculture hints at an employment and recruitment system that disadvantages women strategically.[9] CSR standard implementation would then create high adaptation costs since female workers are institutionally disadvantaged through established (and legally accepted) business practices. However, once CSR standards are implemented it is more likely that gender policies will de-facto be respected due to the country's modest compliance culture. From the perspective of a local supplier, certification would then lead to a significant and stable increase in costs creating local economic disadvantages and finally resistance. We can argue that because of this particular interplay of institutional conditions in the Philippines, the business-friendly legal framework and the modest compliance culture do not have such a strong effect in leading to a more favorable institutional environment and, hence, a higher certification rate.

12. CONCLUSION

In this chapter, I provide an answer to the question why transnational CSR instruments, such as social and environmental certification systems, are promoted and implemented inconsistently across global supply-chain countries. The argument is based on the idea that compliance opportunities (the opportunities to reach compliance with CSR standards) are the main drivers behind standard implementation. To illustrate this claim, the chapter focuses on the global banana industry and the two largest supply-chain countries, Ecuador and Costa Rica. The results show that countries characterized by business-friendly public regulations, a strong compliance

[9] In the Philippines, a common practice is, for instance, the use of pregnancy tests before female workers are hired (CTUHR 2013: 40). While this procedure is legally accepted it would be rather difficult to maintain on certified plantations since those need to comply with private gender equity and anti-discrimination norms.

culture, an absence of CSR-sensitive groups in national labor markets and high levels of education and professionalization amongst the workforce constitute favorable institutional environments for the implementation of CSR standards. In contrast, unfavorable environments are built upon the inverse conditions.

At first, the study confirms those voices in the literature that find mixed effectiveness results and approach social and environmental standard setting with a good degree of skepticism (Barrientos and Smith 2007; Liubicic 1999; Rodriguez-Garavito 2005). The empirical realities found in unfavorable institutional environments seem to resonate with this literature. Moreover, there is a slight hint of irony in the chapter's broader finding that those countries in which the improvement of labor conditions and environmental practices is needed most, receive the lowest attention from standard setters.

However, concluding that CSR standards are completely ineffective would be a misleading final remark, too. In contrast, the chapter suggests that under certain (institutional) conditions, CSR standards can have a positive effect. In other words, there might be an 'institutional threshold' that determines not only the likelihood of standards implementation but also their effectiveness in contributing to better working conditions. Although it is clear that more large as well as small N research is needed to verify and further specify the propositions made here, the four institutional features represent a first proposal for approximating this threshold.

For countries that are located above that line, CSR standards might, indeed, represent helpful tools. However, even in such scenarios we should not expect them to lead to substantial 'net improvements' in social and environmental conditions. That is because private standard implementation occurs most likely where the existing public regulations as well as the dominant social conventions and norms have already created comparably decent conditions (e.g. in Costa Rica). Hence, private standards do not add much from a pure regulatory point of view. Nevertheless, they might lead to stabilizing and further institutionalizing the existing norms. Why? Through CSR standards companies expose themselves to additional transnational monitoring mechanisms that complement the domestic ones. Private inspection systems operate with a stick and carrot mechanism (access to high quality markets, removal of certificate, etc.) that is driven by importing country actors (e.g. retailers). In supply-chain countries, those are often considered more respected authorities than the local ones. Under such conditions, importing-country expectations might support and further promote the institutionalization process of domestic norms that show a certain congruency with transnational standards. However, in that scenario we should not consider CSR standards instruments of 'business self-regulation', but rather we should view them as elements of an emerging system of 'public-private co-regulation'.

REFERENCES

Amable, Bruno. 2003. *The Diversity of Modern Capitalism*. New York: Oxford University Press.
Arias, Pedro, Cora Dankers, Pascal Liu and Paul Pilkauskas. 2003. *The World Banana Economy 1985–2002*. Rome: Food and Agriculture Organization of the United Nations.
Barrientos, Stephanie and Sally Smith. 2007. 'Do Workers Benefit from Ethical Trade? Assessing Codes of Labour Practice in Global Production Systems'. *Third World Quarterly* 28(4): 713–29.
Bartley, Tim. 2007. 'Institutional Emergence in an Era of Globalization: The Rise of Transnational Private Regulation of Labor and Environmental Conditions'. *American Journal of Sociology* 113(2): 297–351.
Bartley, Tim. 2010. 'Transnational Private Regulation in Practice: The Limits of Forest and Labor Standards Certification in Indonesia'. *Private Regulation in the Global Economy* 12(3): 1–34.
Botero, Juan C., Simeon Djankov, Rafael La Porta and Andrei Shleifer. 2004. *The Regulation of Labor*. Washington DC: World Bank.
Campbell, Hugh. 2005. 'The Rise and Rise of EurepGAP: European (Re) Invention of Colonial Food Relations?' *International Journal of Sociology of Food and Agriculture* 13: 1–19.
Chiquita Brands. 2012. *Annual Report 2012*. Cincinnati: Chiquita Brands.
CTUHR. 2013. *The Labour and Environmental Situation in Philippine Banana Plantations Exporting to New Zealand*. Oakland: Oxfam New Zealand.
Dole Food Company. 2011. America *Annual Report 2011*. Westlake Village: Dole Food Company.
FAO. 2014. *Banana Market Review and Banana Statistics 2012–2013*. Rome: Food and Agriculture Organization of the United Nations.
FAOSTAT. 2013. 'Banana Production Statistics'. http://www.fao.org/index_en.htm (May 31, 2013).
Feral, Maude, Helge Fischer, Jesper Nielsen and Alistair Smith, with Stephen Coats. 2006. *Dole Behind the Smoke Screen: An Investigation into Dole's Banana Plantations in Latin America*. Geneva: IUF.
Fischel Volio, Astrid. 1992. 'Costa Rica: Education and Politics – A Historical Perspective'. In *Education, Policy, and Social Change: Experiences from Latin America*, eds. Daniel A. Morales-Gómez and Carlos Alberto Torres. Westport: Praeger, 141–56.
Fresh Del Monte. 2012. *Annual Report 2012*. Coral Gables: Fresh Del Monte.
Gonzalez-Perez, Maria-Alejandra and Terrence McDonough. 2005. 'Bananas Ethical Quality: Multi-Stakeholders, Corporate Social Responsibility and Corporate Governance'. *CISC Working Paper* (21): 1–18.
Granovetter, Mark. 1985. 'Economic Action and Social Structure: The Problem of Embeddedness'. *American Journal of Sociology* 91(3): 481–510.
Hall, Rodney Bruce and Thomas Biersteker. 2002. 'The Emergence of Private Authority in the International System'. In *The Emergence of Private Authority in*

Global Governance, eds. Rodney Bruce Hall and Thomas Biersteker. Cambridge: Cambridge University Press, 3–22.

Hall, Peter A. and David Soskice. 2001a. 'An Introduction to Varieties of Capitalism'. In *Varieties of Capitalism: The Institutional Foundations of Comparative Advantage*, eds. Peter A. Hall and David Soskice. Oxford: Oxford University Press, 1–70.

Hall, Peter A. and David Soskice, eds. 2001b. *Varieties of Capitalism: The Institutional Foundations of Comparative Advantage*. New York: Oxford University Press.

Harari, Raúl. 2009. *Labour, Environment and Health in Ecuadorian Banana Production*. Quito: Corporation for the Development of Production and the Working Environment (IFA).

Hollingsworth, Roger J., Wolfgang Streeck and Philippe C. Schmitter, eds. 1994. *Governing Capitalist Economies: Performance and Control of Economic Sectors*. Oxford: Oxford University Press.

Humbert, Franziska. 2011. *Bittere Bananen*. Berlin: Oxfam Deutschland.

Jackson, Gregory and Richard Deeg. 2006. 'How Many Varieties of Capitalism? Comparing the Comparative Institutional Analyses of Capitalist Diversity'. *MPIfG Discussion Paper* 06(2).

Kaufmann, Daniel, Aart Kraay and Massimo Mastruzzi. 2009. *Governance Matters VIII: Aggregate and Individual Governance Indicators*. Washington DC: World Bank.

Klink, Dennis. 2015. 'Dole and DBCP Legacy'. In *Business and Society: Ethics and Stakeholder Management*, eds. Archie B. Carroll and Ann K. Buchholtz. Mason, OH: South Western, 618–23.

Liu, Pascal. 2008. FAO Commodity Studies, *Certification in the Value Chain for Fresh Fruits: The Example of Banana Industry*. Rome: FAO.

Liubicic, Robert J. 1999. 'Corporate Codes of Conduct and Labeling Schemes: The Limits and Possibilities of Promoting International Labor Rights through Private Initiatives'. *Law & Policy in International Business* 30(1): 111–58.

Locke, Richard. 2013. *The Promise and Limits of Private Power: Promoting Labor Standards in a Global Economy*. Cambridge, New York and Melbourne: Cambridge University Press.

Martínez Valle, Luciano. 2004. 'Trabajo Flexible En Las Nuevas Zonas Bananeras de Ecuador'. In *Efectos Sociales de La Globalización: Petróleo, Banano Y Flores En Ecuador*, eds. Raúl Harari et al. Quito: CEDIME, Abya-Yala, 129–56.

Marx, Axel and Dieter Cuypers. 2010. 'Forest Certification as a Global Environmental Governance Tool: What is the Macro-Effectiveness of the Forest Stewardship Council?' *Regulation & Governance* 4: 408–34.

North, Douglas C. 1990. *Institutions, Institutional Change and Economic Performance*. Cambridge, New York and Melbourne: Cambridge University Press.

Parandekar, Suhas, Rob Vos and Donald Winkler. 2002. 'Ecuador: Crisis, Poverty, and Social Protection'. In *Crisis and Dollarization in Ecuador: Stability, Growth, and Social Equity*, eds. Paul Beckermann and Andrés Soliman. Washington DC: World Bank, 127–76.

Pier, Carol. 2002. *Tainted Harvest: Child Labor and Obstacles to Organizing on Ecuador's Banana Plantations*. New York: Human Rights Watch.

Potts, Jason, et al. 2014. *The State of Sustainability Initiatives Review*. Winnipeg and London: International Institute for Sustainable Development.

Prieto-Carrón, Marina. 2006. 'Corporate Social Responsibility in Latin America: Chiquita, Women Banana Workers and Structural Inequalities'. *Journal of Corporate Citizenship* 21: 85–94.

Ragin, Charles. 1987. *The Comparative Method: Moving Beyond Qualitative and Quantitative Strategies*. Berkeley: University of California Press.

Ragin, Charles. 2008. *Redesigning Social Inquiry: Fuzzy Sets and Beyond*. Chicago: University of Chicago Press.

Reimers, Fernando. 2006. 'Education and Social Progress'. In *The Cambridge Economic History of Latin America: Volume II – The Long Twentieth Century*, eds. Victor Bulmer-Thomas, John H. Coatsworth and Roberto Cortés Conde. Cambridge, New York and Melbourne: Cambridge University Press, 427–80.

Rinne, Jeffrey and Carolina Sánchez-Páramo. 2008. 'Labor Market and Civil Service in Ecuador'. In *Revisiting Ecuador's Economic and Social Agenda*, eds. Vicente Fretes-Cibils, Marcelo Giugale and Eduardo Somensatto. Washington DC: World Bank.

Robinson, Pamela. 2010a. 'Do Voluntary Labour Initiatives Make a Difference for the Conditions of Workers in Global Supply Chains?' *Journal of Industrial Relations* 52(5): 561–73.

Robinson, Pamela. 2010b. 'Responsible Retailing: The Practice of CSR in Banana Plantations in Costa Rica'. *Journal of Business Ethics* 91(S2): 279–89.

Rodriguez-Garavito, C.A. 2005. 'Global Governance and Labor Rights: Codes of Conduct and Anti-Sweatshop Struggles in Global Apparel Factories in Mexico and Guatemala'. *Politics & Society* 33(2): 203–333.

Rosenau, James N. and Ernst-Otto Czempiel, eds. 1992. *Governance without Government: Order and Change in World Politics*. Cambridge: Cambridge University Press.

Sass, Robert. 2000. 'Agricultural "Killing Fields": The Poisoning of Costa Rican Banana Workers'. *Environmental and Occupational Health* 30(3): 491–514.

Schneider, Ben Ross. 2009. 'Hierarchical Market Economies and Varieties of Capitalism in Latin America'. *Journal of Latin American Studies* 41(3): 553–75.

Schneider, Ben Ross and Sebastian Karcher. 2010. 'Complementarities and Continuities in the Political Economy of Labour Markets in Latin America'. *Socio-Economic Review* 8(4): 623–51.

Striffler, Steve. 2002. *In the Shadows of State and Capital: The United Fruit Company, Popular Struggle, and Agrarian Restructuring in Ecuador, 1900–1995*. Durham: Duke University Press.

Striffler, Steve and Mark Moberg, eds. 2003. *Banana Wars: Power, Production, and History in the Americas*. Durham: Duke University Press.

Taylor, Gary and Patricia Scharlin. 2004. *Smart Alliance: How a Global Corporation and Environmental Activists Transformed a Tarnished Brand*. New Haven and London: Yale University Press.

UNCTAD. 2009. 'Information on Bananas'. http://www.unctad.info/en/Infocomm/AACP-Products/COMMODITY-PROFILE---Banana/ (accessed May 31, 2013).

UNDP. 2011. 'Human Development Index'. http://hdr.undp.org/en/data (accessed January 14, 2014).

US Department of State. 2012a. *Country Report on Human Rights Practices for 2011: Ecuador*. Washington DC: United States Department of State/Bureau of Democracy, Human Rights and Labor.

US Department of State. 2012b. *Country Reports on Human Rights Practices for*

2011: Costa Rica. Washington DC: United States Department of State/Bureau if Democracy, Human Rights and Labor.

Van de Kasteele, Adelien and Myriam van der Stichele. 2005. 'Update on the Banana Chain'. *Paper Presented at the II International Banana Conference*, Brussels.

Vogel, David. 2008. 'Private Global Business Regulation'. *Annual Review of Political Science* 11(1): 261–82. http://www.annualreviews.org/doi/abs/10.1146/annurev.polisci.11.053106.141706 (accessed March 23, 2011).

Wells, Allen. 2003. 'Conclusions: Dialectic Bananas'. In *Banana Wars: Power, Production and History in the Americas*, eds. Steve Striffler and Mark Moberg. Durham and London: Duke University Press, 317–34.

Whitley, Richard. 1999. *Divergent Capitalisms: The Social Structuring and Change of Business Systems*. Oxford: Oxford University Press.

World Banana Forum. 2012. 'Diagnosis on the Labour Rights Situation in the Global Banana Industry: Paper on Discrimination'. In *Paper Presented at the World Banana Forum*, Guayaquil, 1–5.

World Bank. 2012. 'Education Statistics'. http://databank.worldbank.org/data/views/variableselection/selectvariables.aspx?source=education-statistics-~-all-indicators#

World Bank. 2013. 'World Bank Open Data'. http://data.worldbank.org/ (August 13, 2011).

12. The 'Accord for Fire and Building Safety in Bangladesh' in response to the Rana Plaza disaster

Juliane Reinecke and Jimmy Donaghey

1. INTRODUCTION

On 24 April 2013, in the Savar suburb of Dhaka, Bangladesh, the Rana Plaza building complex which housed several garment factories employing over 3,000 workers collapsed, leaving 1,129 dead and over 2,000 injured. The building had seen four floors added without planning permission and was originally built as a shopping complex and office block – not a factory hub housing 3,000 workers and their machines. On the day prior to the collapse, large cracks had appeared in the building and, with the exception of the garment factories, all other parts of the building had been closed that day. After the collapse, it quickly emerged that firms based in the hub comprised a checklist of Western household names in the textile industry, including Benetton, Primark and Walmart. Very quickly and in a way reminiscent of the controversy surrounding Nike's issues with child labour in its supply chains,[1] public opinion in the developed world became sensitised to what was happening in the supply chains of these brands. While strictly speaking these brands had no legal obligation to take care of their garment workers, pressure grew on these companies to take responsibility for the incident. Within weeks of the disaster, a host of leading textiles brands had signed up to the 'Accord for Fire and Building Safety in Bangladesh' (the Accord), which was unprecedented both due to its legally binding nature in committing brands to pay into a central inspection regime and maintain purchasing volumes from Bangladesh for two years, as well as being an agreement between over 180 Western brands, two Global Union Federations (GUFs) and four social movement organisations. This chapter uses the Accord as an exploratory

[1] Locke, 2013.

case study, drawing on empirical research carried out by the authors to examine the governance of labour rights in supply chains, particularly with respect to how production-based power and consumption-based power was used to establish this novel collective agreement.

As explored in Chapter 10, the governance of labour rights within global supply chains is an issue which has attracted increased attention.[2] In particular, with the increased fragmentation of production across often multiple borders, the ability and often willingness of states to engage in meaningful regulation has decreased, leading to gaps in the enforcement of international labour rights. Instead, a multitude of private governance initiatives have emerged.[3] With governance shifting from the national to the global level, there is a need to understand the mechanisms that drive labour governance in global supply chains. As will be elaborated on below, significant effort has gone into analysing initiatives to improve labour conditions,[4] yet little work to date has considered the interface between labour-driven and consumption-driven mechanisms of private labour governance. In a previous piece we developed a conceptual framework for understanding this interface (see Figure 12.1).[5] In particular, we highlighted that while there are both labour-driven and consumption-driven initiatives, within the context of global supply chains, more attention on initiatives that bring together labour- and consumer-based actors is warranted. This chapter seeks to further develop this framework by empirically examining one such initiative and draw out key lessons of how the complementarity between consumer and labour-driven governance can be a generator of significant initiatives in developing greater regulation of work within supply chains. The example of the Accord is particularly informative, as developed below, since neither unions nor social movements had the capacity to create unilaterally such an agreement, but were able to form an alliance which was sufficiently complementary to overcome their shortcomings.

2. LABOUR-DRIVEN APPROACH TO GLOBAL LABOUR GOVERNANCE

The labour-driven approach to global labour governance is rooted in the study of industrial relations, with a focus on the role of trade unions and

---

[2] Hassel, 2008; Donaghey et al., 2014; Meardi & Marginson, 2014.
[3] Bernstein & Cashore, 2007; Hassel, 2008; O'Rourke, 2006.
[4] E.g. Locke, 2013.
[5] Donaghey et al., 2014.

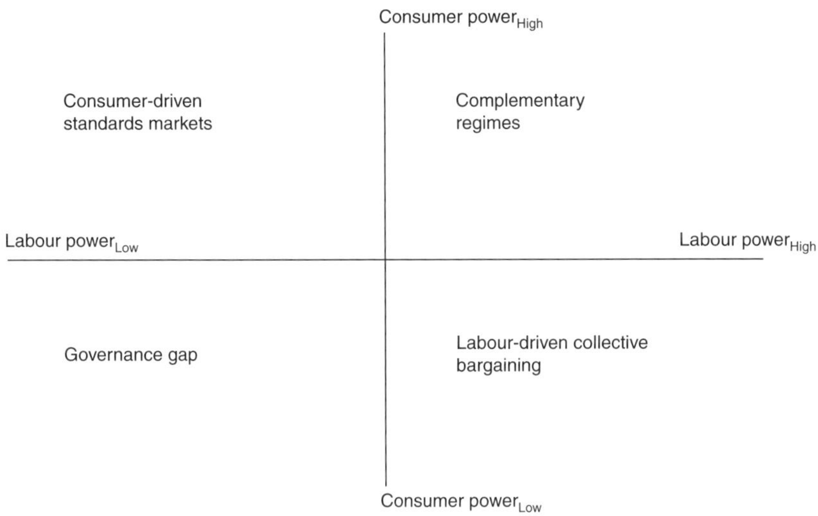

Source: Adapted from Donaghey et al., 2014.

Figure 12.1 Regimes of global labour governance

collective bargaining and the ways in which these have been a driving force in protecting labour rights and improving working conditions in industrialised countries. In the context of supply chains, particular emphasis is placed on International Framework Agreements (IFAs), which have emerged as one of the main mechanisms in global supply chains for regulating labour through negotiated, collective agreements between individual corporations and Global Union Federations (GUFs).[6] In terms of content, IFAs generally focus on procedural issues such as the recognition of national unions, who then negotiate more detailed substantive terms and conditions.[7] However, beyond these IFAs, little attention to date has been paid to other mechanisms where the influence of the international labour movement has helped to regulate international employment relations within supply chains.

While for a long time, trade union internationalism was aspirational in nature, the increased internationalisation of employment relations has highlighted a number of key challenges for unions.[8] Wright's division of structural power and associational power provides a useful lens to conceptualise

[6] Hammer, 2005; Nitorou, 2012.
[7] Hammer, 2005.
[8] Croucher & Cotton, 2009; Hyman, 2005.

the power bases of the pre-production mechanisms available to trade unions. Structural power can be defined as 'power that results simply from the location of workers within the economic system'.[9] Thus, structural power effectively refers to how labour is positioned vis-à-vis other actors and interests within the economic system, including institutions such as legal frameworks, employer structures and the physical location of work: the greater the potential of labour to affect the production process the more power it exerts.

The associational power of labour can be defined as 'the various forms of power that result from the formation of collective organizations of workers', such as trade unions.[10] Thus, within the supply chain context, associational power is contingent on the relationships between supplier-firm unions and lead firm unions, the degree of unity among unions, and the ability of unions across a supply chain to coordinate in solidaristic actions. GUFs have partly taken this role to coordinate actions at the supranational level. However, the affiliation of a local trade union to a GUF does not necessarily translate into local compliance with core labour rights.[11] Differences in perceptions regarding local strategies and international campaigns but also differences in political orientations can result in inter-union conflicts and therefore in the absence of a shared collective identity between (and within) the global and the local groups of labour.[12] Also, the concentration of resources on national employment relations has meant that GUFs have often been lacking in basic resources that are necessary to build a more strategic perspective.[13]

To sum up, in terms of both structural and associational power, achieving cross-border regulation of the employment relationship has proved increasingly difficult. Nevertheless, among non-state actors, unions remain the only representatives of economically-based and institutionally organised labour, with a potentially important role in the production of global labour governance institutions.

3. CONSUMPTION-DRIVEN APPROACH TO GLOBAL LABOUR GOVERNANCE

The consumption-oriented approach to labour governance in supply chains has its roots in organisational and CSR-related scholarship,

---

9 Wright, 2000: 962.
10 Wright, 2000: 962.
11 Niforou, 2012.
12 Anner et al., 2006.
13 Cotton & Gumbrell-McCormack, 2012.

which has focused on how NGOs and social movement activists expose the involvement of Western corporations in exploitative behaviour in developing economies.[14] Facing a critical mass of consumers who have started to include ethical issues in their evaluations of products and services, brand-name retailers and manufacturers see their reputation and image at risk from exposure to violations of labour rights in their supply chains. This change has been facilitated not least by the changing strategies of non-governmental organisations (NGOs), faith groups, student organisations, and human rights activists, who have increasingly mobilised consumers to use their power, at the end point in the global supply chain, to put pressure on MNCs.[15] Campaigns, such as the student-led anti-sweatshop protests against Nike, exposed the complicity of MNCs in human rights abuses, in industries from rug weaving in South East Asia to cocoa farming in Africa.[16] In particular, initiatives based on consumption often take as their leverage point the brand image of those corporations which source products from suppliers who have questionable labour standards.[17] The consumption-driven approach has seen a range of different private labour standards emerge, from unilateral codes of conduct[18] to multi-stakeholder standards that involve the participation of NGOs and MNCs.[19] Standards emerging from consumption-based pressures have in common that they are often monitored through social auditing, and attaining a standard is used as a marketing tool to highlight the ethical stance of the brand.

On the one hand, consumption-based campaigns may encourage consumer boycotts of goods such as the 1970s and 1980s boycott of goods due to Apartheid in South Africa.[20] The mere threat of exit may suffice to alert companies to avoid inflicting damage on the ethical reputation of their brands.[21] On the other hand, consumer activism has moved from 'a morality of reaction' against socially offensive corporate behaviour to a 'buycott' strategy, where consumers positively choose brands based on the extent to which they are perceived to engage in ethical behaviour, such as organic food or Fairtrade labelled goods.[22] One weakness of such

---

14 Den Hond & de Bakker, 2007.
15 King & Pearce, 2010.
16 Bartley, 2007.
17 Bartley, 2003.
18 Locke, 2013.
19 Fransen & Kolk, 2007.
20 Soule, 1997.
21 Bartley, 2007.
22 Nicholls & Opal, 2005.

an approach is that the companies targeted by social movements, NGOs and the media are not necessarily those engaged in the most offensive and least responsible behaviour, but rather those most vulnerable to societal exposure.[23]

What is clear from the above is that in terms of actors, processes and outcomes, while there are multiple lines of development of both production-based and consumption-based labour rights, there are clear weaknesses across the board. What has attracted surprisingly little attention to date has been examination of initiatives which involve both consumption- and production-based power. Yet, the role of customers in supply chains need not be unidirectional: The interactions between consumers and producers can potentially be complementary.[24] However, the circumstances when both production- and consumption-based mobilisation for labour rights can produce synergies in supply chain labour governance is unexplored empirically. This chapter seeks to use an exploratory case study to investigate the question of how production- and consumption-based power can interact to produce private labour governance in global supply chains.

4. THE ACCORD FOR FIRE AND BUILDING SAFETY IN BANGLADESH

After China, Bangladesh is the second largest textile producing economy, with over 5,000 factories employing approximately four million, mainly female, workers, producing goods primarily for the developed world. Since the textile sector evolved in 1976, it has dwarfed all others with $21.5bn (approximately 80 per cent of total) in annual exports and 13 per cent of GDP, according to 2012/13 figures. For Western corporations, Bangladesh provides cheap produce from primarily Bangladeshi-owned factories, thus removing these brands from legal liability over labour abuses. Factories typically prepare garments for multiple buyers, with many factories preparing for multiple buyers. The Bangladeshi garment sector has, according to the Workers' Rights Consortium, the lowest minimum wage for garment workers in the world: $43 per month/21c per hour. From the mid-2000s onwards, increasing attention was drawn to labour issues within the Bangladeshi fabrics sector. In particular, a series of deadly incidents focused attention on the poor quality of the buildings which housed garment factories. Building and fire safety

23 Lange & Washburn, 2012.
24 Compa, 2004, 2008; Heery, 1993.

were often lacking, with buildings often having locked exits and upward extensions built on top of existing structures.

The Accord is an agreement between global union federations and over 180 retailers and brands from 20 countries in Europe, North America, Asia and Australia. Unlike Corporate Codes of Conduct and IFAs, the Accord is a legally binding agreement where all signatories agree that arbitration awards or enforcement of fees may be pursued in their national legal system. Companies commit to maintaining their purchasing volumes in Bangladesh for two years. Making a long-term commitment is needed to benefit workers and provide incentives for suppliers to invest in safety improvements. In terms of legal obligations, companies agreed to pay an annual fee on a sliding scale of up to $500,000 for five years. This includes safety training as well as inspections by qualified safety inspectors and, if necessary, remediation measures to implement corrective actions and carry out structural repairs or renovations. Committed to transparency, all supplier factories and inspection reports will be made publically available.

The Accord also has a number of other novel features. First, unlike IFAs, which are generally made between one MNC and GUFs, the Accord covers multiple employers. Secondly, the Accord has a tripartite governance system. The agreement is governed by a Steering Committee with equal representation chosen by the trade union signatories and company signatories. An Advisory Board involves brands and retailers, suppliers, government institutions, trade unions and NGOs. The International Labour Organization (ILO) acts as the independent chair. In addition, the Accord has its own secretariat to administer the process and to employ inspectors for the factories. Finally, there is a complaints procedure which has a legally binding arbitration system. As an aside, many North American brands have refused to sign up and 26 have formulated an alternative called 'the Alliance'. This effectively is a multi-company code of conduct, which is only legally binding in annual fees and originally did not involve any representatives of labour, but it is beyond the focus of this chapter.

Because of its wide scope and the multiple actors involved, the story of the emergence of the Accord is built around a number of key actors constitutive of the 'labour caucus', including campaign organisations and GUFs. While the labour caucus is comprised of both unions and campaign groups, the unions are the parties to the agreement and the campaign groups are witness signatories. In terms of unions involved, once Rana Plaza occurred, the emphasis shifted onto creating a proper collective agreement with IndustriALL and UNI Global, being the unions involved. IndustriALL was formed in 2012 with the merger of three existing federations with the International Textile, Garment and Leather

Workers' Federation, as the organisation which drew its membership from the relevant workers in Bangladesh, with IndustriALL thus providing the link to Bangladeshi unions. UNI Global organises in the services sector and represents retail workers in developed economies. This was of particular significance as it signified a shift to developed world brands. Thus a rather clear division of labour existed between the two global union federations, who acted in a co-operative fashion.

In terms of direct involvement with the Accord, four campaign organisations were involved. First, the Clean Clothes Campaign, founded in 1989, is a federation of more than 200 nationally-based campaign organisations who campaign on labour issues within the apparel sector; see, for example, its UK-arm 'Labour behind the Label'. Secondly, the Workers' Rights Consortium is a labour rights monitoring organisation founded in 2001 to campaign for no sweatshop products within Universities in the US. The third and fourth NGO signatories are the International Labour Rights Federation in the US and the Maquila Solidarity Network in Canada. While these were the campaign groups who were actively involved in the negotiation of the Accord, three online campaign groups, Change.org, Avaaz.org and SumofUs.org, launched campaigns against companies sourcing from Bangladesh.

5. FINDINGS

5.1 Creating the Accord – The 'Boiling Pot' Moment

Three disasters prior to Rana Plaza stood out in terms of bringing conditions in the Bangladeshi garment sector to the fore. First, in 2005, the Spectrum disaster killed 64 and injured 80 when illegally-built floors on top of an existing building collapsed. In December 2010, a fire broke out which killed 29 workers in the That's It Sportswear factory, which produced for GAP, Abercrombie and Fitch and Target, amongst others. Then, in November 2012, the Tazreen fire caused 112 confirmed deaths. While the media attention captured by these fires was not high, they provided an important spur to action amongst campaign groups. Following these disasters, pressure began to grow on brands that there had to be something done about fire and building safety in Bangladesh. In particular, the Workers' Rights Consortium and the Clean Clothes Campaign, along with the Ethical Trading Initiative, played a major role in developing the 'Memorandum of Understanding' (MoU). The MoU was an initiative targeted at a number of large buyers from Bangladesh to sign up to committing resources into developing greater safety in factories.

For the MoU to come into existence it required four companies to sign up and make a financial commitment of $500,000. By mid-April 2013 only two companies, Tschibo (Germany) and PVH (USA), had signed up. Simultaneously, under the auspices of the Global Social Compliance Program, an industry-led organisation, a number of retailers and brands, including Walmart, Tesco, Carrefour and Migros, called for a collective approach to a social auditing programme on fire and building safety in Bangladesh. For the labour caucus, this social auditing programme was seen as 'far too industry biased and very much about a service delivery to industry and not about engaging, we felt, with the wider issues, political dimension, with workers' rights', as a respondent from an NGO noted.

A meeting was due to take place in Germany on 29 April, at which the German Development Agency (GIZ), the Ethical Trading Initiative, IndustriALL, campaign groups and a number of European and American brands were going to review the two programme proposals and discuss whether the two approaches could be merged and whether there was enough common ground for a joint programme. The meeting was expected to be, according to a Labour campaigner 'very much sort of your traditional paradigm' where 'we'd all sit in meetings and we might have a few phone calls'. However, five days prior to the meeting, the Rana Plaza disaster occurred, which was, to quote one interviewee, 'a game changer'. The GIZ meeting, which was 'already in everyone's diary', became a critical juncture.

The Rana Plaza collapse demonstrated the limits of the prevailing social auditing paradigm, which companies had increasingly adopted to manage social and/or reputational 'risks' in their supply chains. Prior to Rana Plaza, a number of the unions and campaign groups, but particularly UNI Global, had become involved in social auditing programmes with Bangladesh. However, both campaigning groups and unions had become frustrated with existing social auditing approaches. A GUF respondent noted that the 'system of social auditing had failed because if it had delivered then we wouldn't have had disasters like that'. At least two of the factories in the Rana Plaza complex had been audited and certified by the Business Social Compliance Initiative. The compliance-based approach of social auditing was seen to have clearly failed to prevent the series of industrial accidents in Bangladesh and had fuelled the determination of the labour caucus to call for alternative solutions. Thus, the labour caucus decided to 'together create a bigger push towards the brands and retailers to finally take their responsibilities', as a GUF interviewee recalled.

After Rana Plaza, momentum behind the MoU gathered pace, but no longer was a voluntary contribution sought: the focus shifted onto developing a legally binding collective agreement. In particular, according to interviewees, IndustriALL used the meeting to signal that it intended to take a lead role in developing the process. IndustriALL's position was strongly supported by the campaign groups in the labour caucus. The serious nature of the disaster concentrated minds in the labour caucus on achieving more unity of purpose. While in earlier negotiations around the MoU, 'the unions and the labour rights groups weren't entirely on the same page', a campaigner acknowledged, the labour caucus now united behind a joint, single task. Now 'they all got behind this. This is the right document, this is the time', as an observer put it. This joint position of trade unions and campaign groups created a powerful 'pressure cooker' or 'boiling pot moment', as one interviewee described it. The labour caucus used their united position to call for companies to sign the Accord by 15 May. This deadline became a key point in building momentum, as a participant in the meeting remembered, 'as soon as that [deadline] became public it became a public commitment . . . this became a drop-down deadline for something to be signed by somebody'.

The Accord was described as an evolution 'behind the scenes', from the 29 April meeting, when IndustriALL called on companies to sign the MoU, to the deadline of 15 May. The MoU text was taken as a basis to negotiate the Accord. But despite pressure from brands to soften the agreement, campaign groups and trade unions stood firm that the agreement should be binding – a key obstacle for some companies when it came to signing.

A key feature of the thinking within the labour caucus was that the serious nature of the disaster provided a unique, yet limited, window of opportunity where they had to act fast in order to develop a meaningful agreement. Due to the firm stance of the labour caucus, the MoU morphed into a proposal for a legally binding agreement. Based on negotiations amongst unions and brands, three key changes were integrated into the Accord. First, the Accord made reference to the Bangladeshi National Action Plan, a significant addition for companies who were reluctant to take sole responsibility in place of the Bangladeshi government. Second, the ILO agreed to act as neutral chair, lending legitimacy to the Accord. Third, brands urged the amendment of the 'governance piece which was also not really company friendly' to create equal representation, according to a company interviewee.

The Accord was celebrated by both campaigners and unions as a unique achievement, a 'sea-change' or a 'paradigm shift'. As a steering committee member put it, the Accord was seen as a unique opportunity to do exactly what many of the previous multi-stakeholder initiatives, such as Social Accountability International or the Fair Wear Foundation, were not able to do. The lead-in to 15 May saw unions, campaign groups and NGOs using their influence to try to get companies to sign up. Below we will explore how complementary leverage points of labour and consumption power were used in this process.

5.2 Leverage Points of Unions and Campaigning Groups

Of the companies who signed up early to the Accord, a key feature is that both IndustriALL and UNI Global used their existing relationships to leverage these companies into signing. It is thus notable that the first companies to sign, H&M followed by Inditex, Tesco and Primark, all recognised and had pre-existing relationships with unions. In particular, the fact that UNI Global, the global union federation covering retail workers in developed countries, had become involved meant that UNI Global could use their relations with both Inditex and H&M, with whom they had IFAs, to convince them to sign up to the Accord. Existing relationships with unions paved the way for negotiations, as a respondent from UNI Global confirmed: 'It was easier for us to talk and convince companies to sign the Accord that we already had relationships with, than convincing companies that you only just talk[ed] to for the first time in your life.' GUFs could thus position themselves as strategic partners for collaboratively 'resolving some of these intractable supply chain problems' in partnership with companies, rather than as opponents.

However, despite the initial signing up of a number of those brands with established relationships with the unions, in a sector (retail) with limited union penetration, density and coverage, the ability of unions to use their influence to get companies to sign up was rather limited. IFAs, the unions' main instrument, also carry a structural problem inherent in their nature: IFAs are generally organised through one union in a given sector. Yet the increasingly complex nature of supply chains means that workers at different points in the chain may be, at least theoretically, covered by different GUFs. In addition, in terms of associational power, the level of remoteness of retail workers relative to the manufacturing workers was seen as a particular challenge. Throughout the labour caucus specific challenges in the Bangladeshi context were highlighted by interviewees. In particular, union fragmentation, with 37 union federations sharing 6 per cent density in the ready-made garment sector, an immature system of industrial relations, and political corruption all meant that traditional labour resources for enabling the development of agreements was curtailed.

In the context of weak power in the hands of labour at the production end of the supply chain, the role of campaign groups and their focus on consumption became ever more important in the process. The key leverage point of campaigning groups was creating a reputational risk to companies by damaging, or threatening to damage, their brand image through repeated negative publicity. The threat of negative campaigns was a powerful factor in pushing companies to sign up to the Accord initially, as well as increasing the number of corporate signatories. In particular, the campaign organisations at various points threatened or actually started campaigns to force companies to sign up. Given that, as a campaign group interviewee said, 'most brands, retail companies, only consist of their image', campaigning groups could influence how this image appeared in the minds of consumers. This brand image was seen to be an accumulation of images over time, where the glorious images created by brand marketers competed with counter-images showing the darker sides of production relations that campaigners made visible. For instance, campaign groups were successful in getting PVH to sign the initial MoU as the brand needed, as they put it, 'a defence against this big bad publicity that they were about to get' by the exposé 'High Fashion, Deadly Factories' by ABC News, a US-based news channel, in March 2012, in which the founder of one of their flagship brands, Tommy Hilfiger, was confronted backstage at New York Fashion week over the company's involvement in the That's It Sportswear factory, where a fire resulted in the deaths of 29 workers. Tommy Hilfiger, together with other brands that were involved, including H&M and Kohl's, had pledged $37,500 each towards a fund for the relatives of those who had died in the accident, but did little else as news attention faded. Campaigners explained their strategy as being to focus attention on one visible brand name company. Other brands would witness what happened to their competitor and try to avoid a similar exposure.

In specific cases, campaigning groups revert to the 'short-term strategic kind of boycotting' of specific brands in specific markets. For instance, they leverage support from college and university students to target specific brands, such as Adidas and Fruit of the Loom, who cannot afford to alienate consumers in this key strategic market. While many companies were severely shocked by the disaster and, as a multi-stakeholder platform director explained, 'actually most of the CSR folk would have signed up, you know, immediately', the challenge was to convince commercial teams and senior management, and here is where public pressure played a role in lifting labour rights violations from mere ethical to strategic concerns.

5.3 Complementary Power of Unions and Campaign Organisations

Overall, the Accord was perceived as a unique step, and the fact that more than 180 brands signed up had not been expected by the labour caucus. Respondents from unions, campaign groups and companies all agreed that this was achieved not due to union or campaign groups having unilateral effects but due to synergies and complementarities built up between the various groupings. The complex nature of the ready-made garment sector supply chain meant that both structurally and associationally, unions were weak in their capacity to deliver meaningful collective bargains alone. Thus, the knowledge and contacts of campaign groups in particular provided a vital resource to unions in order to pressurise Western brands to act.

Within the process, there developed a division of labour between the various participants in the labour caucus, but particularly between UNI Global, IndustriALL, the WRC and the CCC. In particular, IndustriALL was the GUF covering workers in the ready-made garment (RMG) sector in Bangladesh, and UNI Global represented workers in the retail sector. The WRC provided research and up-to-date information on the industrial sector within Bangladesh. The Clean Clothes Campaign, while providing some on-the-ground assistance in Bangladesh, was heavily involved in campaigning against brands in developed economies. Email campaign groups, such as change.org, sumofus and avaaz, while not part of the inner circle, could often add what one e-campaigner described as 'surge capacity . . . that can really push something over the line'. In some cases, e-campaigns were stopped after the initial test phase, and before rolling them out to their wider email list. The 'implied threat' of a big public campaign was sufficient as it 'just really increases the pressure on those decision makers', a campaigner confirmed. But that alone would not have been sufficient in developing a solution. Thus, one respondent went on to argue that 'unions knowing about negotiation, not just campaigning, was the important counter point'.

The way in which the first signatories to the Accord were pushed to sign it illustrates the way in which union power and campaigning power came together in complementary ways. Unions and labour organisations both had distinctive leverage points that they brought to bear on companies. Convincing the first signatory 'was the big barrier to get anyone to sign', as a campaigner recalled. Both H&M and Inditex were identified as 'obvious targets'. H&M was the single largest buyer from Bangladesh while Inditex was the largest textile company in the world. Unions leveraged their existing relationships with H&M and Inditex. IndustriALL had an IFA with Inditex, and UNI Global had an IFA with H&M.

H&M, however, was rather exceptional because, as a Swedish brand, the high level of density in membership made it an outlier within the retail sector (according to the company, 63 per cent of H&M employees worldwide are covered by collective bargaining agreements). Within H&M, there was close co-operation between GUFs, with UNI Global targeting

H&M directly and IndustriALL targeting other parts of the supply chain. This involved a mix of tactics, including online campaigns, and also the more direct threat of putting pressure on H&M through industrial means. Invited by UNI Global, the Swedish retail union, Handels, used its relationship with H&M to open a dialogue at the company's Swedish headquarters. In addition, GUFs together with Swedish unions published an advertisement in one of Sweden's biggest newspapers to urge garment companies to sign the Accord.

Moreover, campaign groups leveraged existing brand vulnerabilities to push H&M to sign. The company had been the subject of a year-long campaign over its failure to pay a 'living wage' in Cambodia, leading to H&M being called to answer questions in the Riksdag, the Swedish parliament. In addition, the campaign groups targeted H&M through online campaigns. For instance, Avaaz, a progressive global campaign group, collected over 1.2 million signatures to pressure H&M to sign the agreement. Even if H&M signed before the fully-fledged campaign had started, it was widely agreed that, in the words of an e-campaigner, 'having that implicit threat helped focus minds'. Yet, in H&M, the threat of industrial action also existed, as a union activist noted: 'if H&M had not responded to our, to . . . all the methods that we were applying, then the unions in Sweden would have been prepared to use their members in Sweden to increase the pressure. But we never had to go that far.'

Thus, the combination of strong unionisation and an IFA, alongside a brand which was taken to task on another issue, led to them being identified as being vulnerable and in need of improving their brand image. Moreover, discussions with H&M focused on highlighting the advantage that being the first signatory would bring to their brand. In particular, targeting a leading brand-name company was viewed as potentially leading to a domino effect of other brands signing up. Indeed, once the Accord had gained momentum, and a critical number of brands had signed up, it got to a 'tipping point' situation where companies followed their peers in signing because 'no one wants to be left out', as a CSR manager from a signatory brand explained. Even companies with small or even no volumes from Bangladesh were reported to have signed to show symbolic commitment. Moreover, with a large number of signatories, many brands recognised that 'actually this is a good business proposition all of a sudden', as an NGO respondent put it. As the otherwise large burden of inspection and remediation costs were shared by a large number of collaborating companies – financial contributions were pegged to 1 per cent of annual sourcing from Bangladesh – the Accord came to be seen as 'the best place to be for your business to manage risks'.

In sum, the different leverage points exercised by a united labour caucus, described as both 'cajoling and pressurising' companies into the Accord, created a 'pressure cooker' that tipped the balance of power from an industry-led social auditing proposal, which companies proposed initially, to unprecedented support for a binding agreement between corporations and global labour. While unions were the key actors in negotiations and maintaining dialogue, the noise created by campaign groups was seen as vital in creating an implicit threat of reputational damage.

5.4 Divergence in the Labour Caucus

While for the most part, the four key organisations in the labour caucus maintained highly co-operative relations, issues did arise in terms of both the priorities and tactics employed by the differing groups. One campaign group member encapsulated this in stating, 'obviously *we*'re [campaign groups] always getting frustrated that they [unions] don't move quickly enough. And *they*'re always getting frustrated that we act without thinking it through.' The campaign to get Edinburgh Woollen Mill to sign the Accord revealed some of the differences within the labour caucus. Trade unions and campaign groups were planning a joint campaign against Edinburgh Woollen Mill which had been highly resistant to signing up to the Accord and had refused to pay compensation for victims at the Tazreen factory as it was disputing that their clothes were made in that factory.

Unions and campaign groups planned demonstrations outside a number of Edinburgh Woollen Mill stores across the UK on the 24th of November 2013, which marked the first anniversary of the Tazreen fire, to mobilise consumers to demand that the company sign the Accord. However, just a few days before the planned action, Edinburgh Woollen Mill, aware of the reputational damage it risked, contacted the TUC to inform them that they were willing to sign the Accord. The TUC saw this as a victory as the demand to sign up to the Accord was met. The union publicly commended Edinburgh Woollen Mill for signing the Accord, even though the issue of compensation for Tazreen victims was outstanding. For campaign groups, the fact that the TUC called off the campaign and 'put out statements congratulating Edinburgh Woollen Mill' was perceived as 'very frustrating'.

At other times, aggressive campaigning against the brands with whom unions were in negotiations was perceived as hindering the dialogue. Campaign groups were sometimes seen as 'too much on the outside' to show sensitivity and to understand the need to maintain an environment in which dialogue was possible. In particular, the relationship with online campaign organisations in targeting brands was much less coordinated, at times creating tensions. In some cases, brands 'threatened to walk away from the Accord if they were publicly campaigned at', as a campaigner explained, which put them in the difficult position of maintaining pressure without overdoing it. These examples highlight the delicate balance that needs to be struck between campaign groups supporting the process of negotiating agreements with companies through actual and implicit threats, on the one hand, and not negatively impacting sensitive negotiation processes through alienating companies on the other hand.

6. DISCUSSION: THE ROLE OF CONSUMPTION RELATIONS IN GOVERNING PRODUCTION RELATIONS

Previous work has been traditionally separated in different strands of literature to focus on the power dynamics of either production actors putting pressure on employers or consumption actors putting pressure on brands. Moreover, interests between consumers and workers are typically seen to be conflicting, with consumers putting downward pressure on prices or the idea of customer sovereignty being utilised by management as a mechanism of control over workers.[25] What have attracted much less attention are examples of where the interests of customers/consumers can be complementary to those of workers.[26] This chapter highlights a need for a better understanding of these dynamics in a context of complex supply chains where traditional trade union tactics are no longer the driving force in governing working conditions and defending labour rights, and where consumers have come to the fore as important pre-production actors. Integrating consumption and production into the conceptualisation of power relationships puts a much greater emphasis on understanding how relationships amongst actors can influence power dynamics. The analysis of the intersection between trade unions and campaigning groups produces insights about these dynamics that lead us to re-examine how labour rights may be promoted in global value chains.

The key insight presented is that consumption- and production-based power can be symbiotic and that distinct power resources may become transformed and re-worked through complementary relationships. Extending Wright's (2000) notion of associational power, this chapter suggests that the complementarity between campaign groups is the

[25] Korczynski & Ott, 2004.
[26] Cutcher, 2004; Heery, 1993.

source of 'inter-associational power'.[27] The findings suggest that such inter-associational power, that is, power resources of campaign groups and trade unions becoming aligned in a quasi-association, was vital in driving change and making companies take responsibility beyond their legal duties.

Campaign groups' ability to mobilise public pressure played a key role in creating an actual or implicit threat to brand reputation – lifting the issue of labour rights violations from a merely ethical to a strategic concern. Whereas unions mobilise workers to withdraw their labour power from the production process, campaign groups mobilise consumers to withdraw their social and affective investments in brands in ways that interfere with the reproduction of a distinctive brand image as envisaged by corporate brand managers. As brand value has become a significant economic factor, or intangible asset, in the global economy,[28] campaigns that threaten brand image could be seen to disrupt the productive process of branding. But the logical response by corporations to attacks on their reputation has been to safeguard their image. Such consumption-oriented motivations have often led to symbolic and compliance-centric approaches that focus more on corporate risk management than substantive issues.[29] Trade unions, and GUFs in particular, may use public pressure to enable the development of production-based power where workers are weak. Simultaneously, trade unions have enjoyed greater legitimacy as the representatives of global labour within companies than campaign groups. They are thus critical in transforming consumption-based power directed at reputation into production-based power.

Together, campaign groups and trade unions presented a coordinated networked approach to promoting labour governance in which both leverage points came together. Trade unions' diminishing capacity to mobilise workers at the starting point of the global supply chains was compensated by campaign groups' ability to mobilise consumers at the end point of the supply chains. While we previously hypothesised that high labour and high consumer power would lead to complementary relationships, in this example, while labour was institutionalised in many of the Western brand signatories to the Accord, it was weak in the context of the Bangladeshi workers. Thus, the existence of complementary relationships in this case was based around parties having different levels of power at different points in the supply chain. Yet, union power was not simply the ability to

27 Wright, 2000.
28 Lury & Moor, 2010.
29 Locke, 2013.

threaten production. In this case it was drawn from the legacy of having established relationships with many of the Western brands. The campaign groups' limited legitimacy with the brands they campaigned against was compensated by trade unions' pre-existing relationships and their negotiation skills. In particular, the findings highlight three main leverage points where unions could mobilise consumption-based power. First, *past* labour-related campaigns against brands built up negative public sentiment and created critical vulnerabilities in brand reputation. Vulnerable brands were perceived to be more susceptible to the threat of renewed action and more eager to repair their damaged reputation through positive publicity. Second, actual campaigns effectively took advantage of the media storm in the aftermath of Rana Plaza to mobilise consumers against selected target brands. Campaign groups would often channel all their energy against one single well-known brand name company to act as a deterrent to other companies. Third, one of the most powerful leverage points campaign groups used was the dormant potency of reputation damage as a powerful threat. Many campaigns, such as against H&M, Edinburgh Woollen Mill and the Arcadia group, never actually materialised: their planning was enough to make companies turn around while allowing them to save face by appearing to be proactive rather than merely caving in to activist demands.

7. CONCLUSION

The Accord is unique in its binding nature. As an institution, it has created a mechanism to enable and commit companies without legal duties to take responsibilities for global labour rights. The consumption end of the global supply chain makes financial and resource commitments to improve labour conditions at the production end. Can this integration between consumption and production actors provide a new model for driving global labour governance? The ready-made garment industry, partly because of outsourcing production and the role of consumer brands, has been the arena where experiments in private labour governance first began to emerge. The garment industry has seen the emergence of codes of conduct in the 1990s, followed by various forms of social auditing programmes championed by NGOs and industry groups alike.[30] The scale of Rana Plaza was unprecedented, and the dynamics that led to the Accord and its 180+ corporate signatories must be seen as a rather unique

---

[30] Fransen, 2012.

case. A critical enabling factor was that both campaign groups and trade unions had a clear and shared sense of purpose, which reflected the scale of the Rana Plaza disaster as well as the history of previous factory fires and building collapses in Bangladesh. This allowed them to unite behind the single task of negotiating the Accord as a binding agreement to improve fire and building safety. However, symbiotic relationships like this do not pre-exist and are likely to be fragile and subject to ongoing interactions amongst actors that may lead to re-negotiation of positions.

Another enabling factor was that trade unions and campaign groups had a relatively clear understanding about their division of roles. Campaign groups thus accepted the unions' role as the representatives of workers, who were thus full signatories to the Accord, whereas campaign groups were witness signatories with limited influence over the steering committee. In private labour standards, campaign groups have often transformed into the key actor of standards setter within a multi-stakeholder governance system where unions had become only one among many stakeholders, such as in Fairtrade or the Fair Labour Association.[31] Notwithstanding the exceptional scale that contributed to its emergence, the Accord has set a new standard and provided a new template in designing an institutionally binding arrangement that may be relatively easily transferred to a new sector, a new country or a new set of demands. The Accord has also demonstrated to the labour caucus what they can achieve when they stand united, and may thus serve as a model for future collaborations. This may also involve the re-organisation of organised labour. The involvement of both UNI Global and IndustriALL forged a connection between the start and the end point of the global supply chain by bringing together their existing relationships with retailers in consumer countries and textile workers in Bangladesh.

REFERENCES

Anner, M., Greer, I., Hauptmeier, M., Lillie, N., & Winchester, N. (2006). The industrial determinants of transnational solidarity: Global interunion politics in three sectors. *European Journal of Industrial Relations* 12(1), 7–27.

Bartley, T. (2003). Certifying forests and factories: States, social movements, and the rise of private regulation in the apparel and forest products fields. *Politics & Society* 31(3), 433–464.

Bartley, T. (2007). Institutional emergence in an era of globalization: The rise of transnational private regulation of labor and environmental conditions. *American Journal of Sociology* 113(2), 297–351.

---

[31] Fransen & Kolk, 2007.

Bernstein, S. & Cashore, B. (2007). Can non-state global governance be legitimate? An analytical framework. *Regulation & Governance* 1(4), 347–371.
Compa, L. (2004). Trade unions, NGOs, and corporate codes of conduct. *Development in Practice* 14, 210.
Compa, L. (2008). Corporate social responsibility and workers' rights. *Comparative Labor Law & Policy Journal* 30, 1.
Cotton, E. & Gumbrell-McCormick, R. (2012). Global unions as imperfect multilateral organizations: An international relations perspective. *Economic and Industrial Democracy* 33(4), 707–728.
Croucher, R. and Cotton, E. (2009). *Global Unions, Global Business*. Hendon: Middlesex University Press.
Cutcher, L. (2004). The customer as ally: The role of the customer in the finance sector union's campaigning. *The Journal of Industrial Relations* 46(3), 323–336.
Den Hond, F. & de Bakker, F.G. (2007). Ideologically motivated activism: How activist groups influence corporate social change activities. *Academy of Management Review* 32(3), 901–924.
Donaghey, J., Reinecke, J., Niforou, C. & Lawson, B. (2014). From employment relations to consumption relations: Balancing labor governance in global supply chains. *Human Resource Management* 53(2), 229–252.
Fransen, L. (2012). Multi-stakeholder governance and voluntary programme interactions: Legitimation politics in the institutional design of Corporate Social Responsibility. *Socio-Economic Review* 10(1), 163–192.
Fransen, L.W. & Kolk, A. (2007). Global rule-setting for business: A critical analysis of multi-stakeholder standards. *Organization* 14(5), 667–684.
Hammer, N. (2005). International framework agreements: Global industrial relations between rights and bargaining. *Transfer* 11(4), 511–530.
Hassel, A. (2008). The evolution of a global labor governance regime. *Governance* 21(2), 231–251.
Heery, E. (1993). Industrial relations and the customer. *Industrial Relations Journal* 24(4), 284–295.
Hyman, R. (2005). Shifting dynamics in international trade unionism: Agitation, organisation, bureaucracy, diplomacy. *Labor History* 46(2), 137–154.
King, B.G. & Pearce, N.A. (2010). The contentiousness of markets: Politics, social movements, and institutional change in markets. *Annual Review of Sociology* 36(1), 249–267.
Korczynski, M. & Ott, U. (2004). When production and consumption meet: Cultural contradictions and the enchanting myth of customer sovereignty. *Journal of Management Studies* 41(4), 575–599.
Lange, D. & Washburn, N.T. (2012). Understanding attributions of corporate social irresponsibility. *Academy of Management Review* 37(2), 300–326.
Locke, R.M. (2013). *The Promise and Limits of Private Power: Promoting Labor Standards in a Global Economy*. Cambridge: Cambridge University Press.
Lury, C. & Moor, L. (2010). Brand valuation and topological culture. In: M. Aronczyk & D. Powers (eds) *Blowing up the Brand*. New York: Peter Lang, pp. 29–52.
Meardi, G. & Marginson, P. (2014). Global labour governance: Potential and limits of an emerging perspective. *Work, Employment & Society* 28(4): 651–662.
Mosley, L. (2011). *Labor Rights and Multinational Production*. New York: Cambridge University Press.

Nicholls, A. & Opal, C. (2005). *Fair Trade: Market-Driven Ethical Consumption*. London: SAGE.
Niforou, C. (2012). International framework agreements and industrial relations governance: Global rhetoric versus local realities. *British Journal of Industrial Relations* 50(2), 352–373.
Niforou, C. (2013). International Framework Agreements and the democratic deficit of global labour governance. *Economic and Industrial Democracy* 35(2), 367–386.
O'Rourke, D. (2003). Outsourcing regulation: Analyzing nongovernmental systems of labor standards and monitoring. *Policy Studies Journal* 31(1), 1–29.
O'Rourke, D. (2006). Multi-stakeholder regulation: Privatizing or socializing global labor standards? *World Development* 34(5), 899–918.
Soule, S.A. (1997). The student divestment movement in the United States and tactical diffusion: The shantytown protest. *Social Forces* 75(3), 855–882.
Wright, E.O. (2000). Working-class power, capitalist-class interests, and class compromise. *American Journal of Sociology* 105: 957–1002.

13. The International Labour Organization, multinational enterprises, and shifting conceptions of responsibility in the global economy

Yossi Dahan, Hanna Lerner and Faina Milman-Sivan

1. INTRODUCTION

In his first report since being appointed Director-General of the International Labour Organization (ILO) in 2012, Guy Rider declared a need to reform and renew the institutional features of the ILO.[1] In particular, the Report identified the ILO's engagement with enterprises as one of the four institutional features most in need of such reform. It acknowledged the ILO's inadequacy in attending to the contemporary realities of the world of work. One distinctive feature of these new realities, which is significantly transforming the way work is organized today, is the rise of multinational enterprises (MNEs) and their operation via international supply chains, which the Report singled out as being 'one particular area worth examining'.[2] The urgency of addressing the relations between MNEs and the ILO is a product of both the severity of the abuses that occur within international supply chains and the ILO's feeble response to the violation of core rights within these structures.[3] The Rana Plaza tragedy in Bangladesh in April 2013 underscored this urgency. In this

[1] ILO, ILC, *Report of the Director-General*, Report 1(A) Towards the ILO Centenary: Realities, Renewal and Tripartite Commitment, ILC.102/DG/1A (2013).

[2] Ibid., para. 140.

[3] The DG Report acknowledged that the ILO has been the 'object of pointed criticism for having failed to take up its own responsibilities' in this regard. Ibid., para. 141.

incident, more than 1100 workers died due to unsafe working conditions, which eventually led to the collapse of their factory, illustrating the vital need for greater ILO involvement in protecting the rights of workers in transnational supply chains. Moreover, the ILO's role in facilitating the signing of the Accord on Fire and Building Safety in Bangladesh (the Accord) – a groundbreaking, legally binding agreement for the implementation of a safety-improvement program in the Bangladeshi readymade garment industry[4] – is evidence of its potential for systemic, proactive, ex-ante engagement with the new 'super employers'[5] of the world.

International or global supply chains have profoundly transformed production methods worldwide and the labor conditions of production workers. Global supply chains (GSCs), often referred to as global production chains, are complex transnational networks of businesses that operate collectively to procure, manufacture, and distribute a family of related products.[6] In labor-intensive industries, such as the apparel industry, toys industry, and electronics, these supply chains are often buyer-driven.[7] Namely, global buyers (brand companies and retailers) play a central role in coordinating the complex activities of a product, accomplishing everything – from conception through distribution to consumers – without direct ownership. So although global buyers do not own any of the factories involved in the production and distribution of the relevant products, they typically wield significant control over the specification of the final product and generally dictate the profits allocation within the production chains. This is acknowledged in the term 'global value chain', which emphasizes the unequal distribution of profits within a chain, affecting in particular suppliers from developing countries.[8] International production and trade in the global era occurs, to a large extent, 'in various kinds of

---

4 See: http://www.bangladeshaccord.org (last visited: 14 August 2014).

5 C. Estlund, *Corporate Self-Regulation and the Future of Workplace Governance*, 84 Chicago-Kent Law Review, 617 (2009).

6 J. Henderson, *Global Production Networks and the Analysis of Economic Development*, 9 Review of International Political Economy, 436–464 (2002); M. Christopher, Logistics & Supply Chain Management: Strategies For Reducing Cost And Improving Service (London: Financial Times Professional Limited, 1998).

7 Gary Gereffi, John Humphrey and Timothy Sturgeon, *The Governance of Global Value Chains*, 12 Review of International Political Economy, 78–104 (2005).

8 Olivier Cattaneo, Gary Gereffi and Cornelia Staritz, *Global Value Chains in a Postcrisis World: Resilience Consolidation and Shifting End Markets*, in Olivier Cattaneo et al. (eds) Global Value Chains in a Postcrisis World: A Development Perspective (Washington: The World Bank, 2010), pp. 3–20, p. 18.

coordinated networks, which are economic structures that lie *between* the conceptual poles of markets and hierarchies'.[9] Within these flexible and partly hierarchical structures of transnational production, many workers are in a state of 'structural disempowerment', as they are unable to control opportunities and resources or compel external decision-makers to take responsibility for maintaining workers' well-being.[10] Labor-intensive industries, where production is outsourced rather than conducted through direct foreign investment,[11] are particularly susceptible to violations of production workers' basic labor rights.

Given these global economic realities, the question of the scope, and appropriate nature, of the responsibilities borne by powerful MNEs in GSCs for labor-related abuses down their supply chain has become particularly pressing. The 2013 ILO Director-General (DG) Report powerfully and persuasively argues that prioritizing its relations with MNEs should be one of the ILO's key institutional reforms. However, the Report offers very little in terms of concrete suggestions for such reform, and the measures undertaken to date by the ILO have yet to reveal an inherent commitment to substantial reform. Although the organization declared 'engagement with enterprises' as one of its centennial projects, the content of the reforms required for such engagement remains unclear. The DG Report refrained, for example, from recommending reconsideration of the ILO's tripartite representational structure, to assess whether it provides MNEs with adequate representation.[12] Instead, the Report suggested that the ILO could provide better services to corporations in the field of corporate social responsibility (CSR).

Yet, historically, the ILO has been ambivalent regarding CSR. For several years, employers' groups have been resisting even scheduling a discussion on international supply chains and CSR at the ILO conferences, with the topic only recently scheduled for discussion, for the first

---

[9] Ibid., at 4.

[10] Young, I., *Responsibility and Global Justice: A Social Connection Model*, 23 SOCIAL PHILOSOPHY AND POLICY, 102–130 (2006); Macdonald, K., *Globalizing Justice within Coffee Supply Chains? Fair Trade, Starbucks and the Transformation of Supply Chain Governance*, 28 THIRD WORLD QUARTERLY, 793–812 (2007).

[11] On the implications of outsourcing as opposed to direct foreign investment into labor, see Layna Mosley, LABOR RIGHTS AND MULTINATIONAL PRODUCTION (New York: Cambridge University Press, 2011).

[12] For objections to this proposal, see discussions conducted within the ILO Governing Body following the publication of the Report. ILO, GB, *ILO Engagement with The Private Sector*, 20th Session, Geneva, 13–27 March 2014, GB.320/INS/5/1, para. 4.

time, at the upcoming 2016 conference.[13] Moreover, the ILO Governing Body (GB) has expressed concerns that CSR belongs to the realm of private standards setting.[14] Accordingly, the Governing Body has reiterated the need to strengthen and promote the ILO Tripartite Declaration of Principles concerning Multinational Enterprises and Social Policy (the MNE declaration),[15] which has had only a marginal impact, at best, on business practices since its adoption in 1977.[16] Tellingly, the Governing Body seems to have completely disregarded the most intriguing suggestion in the DG Report, namely, that the ILO assist in the implementation of what promises to be the most influential initiative in the field of MNEs' responsibility to date: the Guiding Principles for Business and Human Rights, written by John Ruggie (the Ruggie Principles), as unanimously endorsed by the United Nations (UN) Human Rights Council in 2011.[17]

The Ruggie Principles outline the responsibilities of business enterprises in preventing human rights violations during the course of their business activities, throughout their supply chains. In the context of labor standards, the Ruggie Principles reiterate the expectation that companies monitor their global supply chains to at least prevent violations of the ILO's four core labor rights. This document is the most recent attempt to internationalize the regulation of human rights, and was accepted by the UN Global Compact framework as a guide to its participants in fulfilling their commitments.[18]

Many have lauded the significant breakthrough of the recognition in the Guiding Principles of MNEs' responsibility for human rights violations throughout their chains of supply. Yet empirical evidence shows that private self-regulation has had limited impact on the labor standards

---

[13] ILO, GB, *Minutes of the 319th Session of the Governing Body of the International Labor Office*, 319th Session, Geneva, 16–31 October 2013, GB.319/INS/2; GB.319/PV/Draft, paras 5–35.

[14] DG Report, para. 138.

[15] ILO, GB, *ILO Engagement with The Private Sector*, 20th Session, Geneva, 13–27 March 2014, GB.320/INS/5/1, para. 4.

[16] ILO, Tripartite Declaration of Principles concerning Multinational Enterprises and Social Policy (Geneva, Nov. 1977).

[17] Special Representative of the Secretary-General on the Issue of Human Rights and Transnational Corporations and Other Business Enterprises, *Guiding Principles on Business and Human Rights: Implementing the United Nations 'Protect, Respect and Remedy' Framework*, 19, U.N. Doc. A/HRC/17/31 (Mar. 21, 2011) (by John Ruggie).

[18] See: https://www.unglobalcompact.org/docs/issues_doc/human_rights/Resources/GPs_GC%20note.pdf (last visited: 5 January 2015).

in global production chains.[19] Richard Locke argues that for a system of private voluntary regulation to be effective and sustainable, support and facilitation from public authoritative, rule-making institutions are vital.[20] As one such public international institution, the ILO certainly has the potential to significantly facilitate the success of initiatives like the Guiding Principles framework. Playing such a role, however, would require comprehensive reform of the ILO's approach to private enterprises and international supply chains and MNEs' responsibilities to uphold workers' rights.

The central claim put forth in this chapter is that the ILO should rethink its understanding of the very concept of responsibility, which currently rests on an outdated conception of statist responsibility that is unsuited to the structure of the global economy. Under this statist conception, the nation-state is either the sole or primary agent bearing responsibility towards workers within the member states' jurisdiction. As explored in section 2, the statist conception also underpins the ILO's structure and enforcement mechanisms. It will be argued in this chapter, however, that recent economic, political, and legal developments across the globe require that the ILO allocate responsibility for workers' rights not only to states but also to empowered private non-state actors, such as MNEs. Given the ongoing erosion of nation-states' ability to regulate and enforce even a minimum level of labor standards, the ILO should view MNEs in particular as at least partially responsible for enforcing labor rights within their chains of production.

As an alternative to the statist conception of responsibility, we propose that the ILO adopt a novel conception of *shared* responsibility, which we term *the labor connection model of shared responsibility*. Under this model, responsibility for remedying unjust working conditions in the global labor market is borne by a complex set of agents and institutions that participate in global production, including MNEs.[21] We are, of course, aware of the potential conceptual as well as pragmatic and political difficulties that our

---

19 Richard Locke, The Promise and Limits of Private Power: Promoting Labor Standards in a Global Economy (Cambridge: Cambridge University Press, 2013).

20 Ibid.

21 Additionally, under certain circumstances, responsibility should be assigned to the states in whose territories these brands or the corporation headquarters reside. This issue, however, is beyond the scope of this chapter. See Yossi Dahan, Hanna Lerner and Faina Milman-Sivan, *Shared Responsibility and the International Labor Organization*, 34 Michigan Journal of International Law 675–743 (2013). The following analysis of the ILO and its statist conception of responsibility draws heavily on the study in this article.

proposed model might pose, particularly given the recent unprecedented crisis in the ILO supervisory system, which has put the Organization's continued operation in jeopardy for the first time since its establishment.[22] However, as we show in this chapter, the 'seeds' of the shared responsibility model have already been planted in existing ILO mechanisms and procedures.

Our discussion proceeds as follows, in three stages. Section 2 discusses how the statist conception of responsibility has underpinned the ILO structure from the very outset and continues to be deeply embedded in its supervisory system. Section 3 then presents our proposed labor connection model of shared responsibility, which rests on four principles by which responsibility for workers' rights should be allocated amongst the various actors and institutions that participate in global production. Lastly, Section 4 suggests some practical measures to be taken within the ILO in order to implement the regulatory ideal of the shared responsibility model, focusing in particular on the Organization's supervisory system and corporations. In this context, we will show that the values underlying our proposed model are already present in the ILO's supervisory system.

2. THE ILO: A STATIST MODEL OF RESPONSIBILITY

An underlying premise of the ILO's norm-generating and monitoring procedures is that the nation-state is the basic unit of deliberation and decision-making. Under the statist model, legally, states are the key actors responsible for and benefactors of implementing workers' rights. Not even the unique structure of representation that characterizes most of the ILO's organs – namely, the tripartite structure comprised of representatives of governments, employers, and workers – undermines the dominance of the statist model, since the participation of non-governmental interests (namely, the interests of employers and employees) is channeled through their state. Take, for example, the structure of the International Labour Conference (the Conference), which is the body that sets the ILO's broad policies, often referred to as the ILO parliament. The Conference is comprised of four representatives from each of the ILO member states, two of whom are governmental delegates and two non-governmental delegates,

[22] Lee Swepston, *Crisis in the ILO Supervisory System: Dispute over the Right to Strike*, 29 The International Journal of Comparative and Industrial Relations, 199–218 (2013).

representing, respectively, the employers and employees of each of the member states.[23] While the ILO Constitution requires that the appointments of nongovernmental representatives (i.e., workers and employees) be decided in conjunction with local industrial organizations, it is the state itself that nominates representatives of its functional interests in its territory. The ILO organizational structure excludes all other interests and functional groups beyond workers and employees,[24] and fails to afford representation to the particular interests of MNEs who dominate international supply chains.[25]

The ILO's adherence to the statist model is also exemplified in the nature of its standards. ILO standards – namely, Conventions (the primary proclamations of labor standards) and Recommendations (nonbinding labor standards) – are formulated to create obligations for member states. States, thus, are the only legal bearers of responsibility for the violations of labor rights as they are the only actors expected to ratify and comply with these standards. Each state retains full discretion whether to ratify and, thereby, be legally bound by the Conventions and Recommendations produced by the ILO.

The rest of this section will focus on the ILO's Supervisory System. Compliance with ILO standards is supervised through two separate, yet complementary, systems, both of which showcase the statist model of responsibility: (1) a regular reporting system, based on the submission of national reports in fixed intervals as to the member state's compliance with its legal obligations; and (2) a procedure for submitting complaints regarding particular violations, open to a wide variety of players.

2.1 The Regular Reporting System

The ILO's statist model is clearly evident in its reporting system in a variety of ways. Only states are obligated to submit reports, and the state is the only legal subject monitored under the procedure. Additionally, the nature of the information that states are required to provide reflects

---

[23] Constitution of the International Labour Organization, art. 3(1), June 28, 1919, 49 Stat.2712, 15 U.N.T.S. 35 [hereinafter ILO Constitution].

[24] These include, for example, the interests of migrants, religious groups, women, and agricultural workers. For further discussion, see Faina Milman-Sivan, *The Virtuous Cycle: A New Paradigm for Democratizing Global Governance through Deliberation*, 30 Comparative Labor Law & Policy Journal, 801–834 (2009).

[25] Gerry Rodgers et al., The ILO and the Quest for Social Justice, 1919–2009 (Ithaca, NY: Cornell University Press, 2009).

statism. Member states are key players in the monitoring process and are obligated to submit periodic reports on ratified Conventions. Workers' and employers' associations participate in the process via article 23(2) of the ILO Constitution, whereby they may submit comments to their state's report, pointing, for example, to discrepancies between law and practice. Although allowing these comments can be understood as a move toward shifting responsibility from the state to its functional organizations, such comments are discretionary rather than mandatory. They are also submitted on a national basis: each organization comments on its own government.

The statist model is similarly reflected in the nature of the work of the Committee of Experts on the Application of Conventions and Recommendations (CEACR or Committee of Experts), the body that is in charge of analyzing states' reports, which can be characterized as *semi-legal*.[26] This legal orientation correlates with the CEACR's composition: 20 prominent apolitical jurists who are expected to act in an objective and neutral manner in their evaluations, a departure from the tripartite structure common to many ILO bodies.

The legal subject at the center of the Committee of Expert's operations is the individual state. The CEACR, in its assessment of state compliance, mostly engages in a legal analysis of legal discrepancies, while neglecting violations in practice. This focus on law, rather than on the practical application of the norm, necessarily directs attention to state authorities, as they are the generators of law, rather than to the two partners in the labor relations, employees and employers, who operate on the ground. Accordingly, the CEACR's key products are conclusions and comments (observations and direct requests), which are directed solely at the individual state under review. Notices of good practice of states, indicating a sort of 'best practices', generally follow similar lines.

2.2 Supervision Procedures Based on Complaints and Representations

At first glance, the complaints procedures seem to be as reflective of the statist model as the regular reporting system they supplement, for they are similarly focused on the state as the sole actor responsible for upholding legal obligations under ratified Conventions within its territory. Article 24 of the ILO Constitution, which governs the representations procedure,

---

[26] The legal character of the CEACR is relevant here insofar as it indicates the use of a statist model. It was this 'legal nature' of the committee that was disputed in the recent 2012 supervisory system 'crisis.' See Swepston *supra* note 22.

one of the procedures within the complaint system, explicitly refers to the failure of a member state to comply with a ratified Convention 'within its jurisdiction'.[27]

The complaints and representation system allows for several complaints procedures: a representation when filed by industrial organizations; and a complaint when member states can charge another member state with violating its obligations under a ratified Convention. In severe and rare cases a full-scale investigation is launched through the Commission of Inquiry or the Fact-Finding and Conciliation Commission on Freedom of Association – the comparable body in cases that involve freedom of association.

Once a representation – that is, a complaint alleging an International Labour Standards (ILS) violation – has been submitted and deemed receivable, the ILO Governing Body (GB) can establish a tripartite committee to report on the case. The committee's investigation is focused on revealing any possible responsibility on the part of the territorial state for the alleged wrong, once again underscoring the centrality of the statist model. Where the government's response is not deemed satisfactory, the GB is authorized to take various measures against the state. Complaints regarding freedom of association violations are referred to the Committee on Freedom of Association (CFA) and follow approximately the same procedures.

In the most severe and persistent cases, the GB can decide to launch a full-scale investigation by constituting a Commission of Inquiry, a quasi-judicial body[28] that conducts thorough examinations of the law and the practice at hand.[29] The Fact-Finding and Conciliation Commission on Freedom of Association (FFCC) is the comparable body in cases that involve freedom of association.[30]

The legal subject of the Commission of Inquiry's investigation is always the individual state, again manifesting the statist model, which is apparent

---

[27] Constitution of the International Labour Organization, art. 24, June 28, 1919, 49 stat. 2712, 225 Consolidated Treaties and International Agreements (CTIA) 373 [hereinafter ILO Constitution].

[28] The Commission of Inquiry has several features of a quasi-judicial body: it is composed of three legal experts acting in their personal capacities; its reports do not have to be approved by the Conference and are directly submitted to the relevant state; and the Director-General automatically publishes all of the Commission's reports.

[29] The Commission of Inquiry is not bound by strict procedural regulations, and its members are free to set new rules in accordance with the Constitution and the custom established by previous Commissions.

[30] Lars Thomann, Steps to Compliance with International Labour Standards (Springer, 2011), p. 125.

in other features of the Commission's procedure as well. The Commission report is directed at ascertaining the responsibility of the individual state for the matter at hand and gives detailed recommendations that only the state is obligated to fulfill. The report is based on a substantial investigation, which usually includes visits to the site and witness hearings. The on-site visits, however, require the consent of the state in which the investigation is being conducted.

Under Article 33 of the ILO Constitution, when a member state continuously refuses to implement the recommendations in a Commission of Inquiry report or ICJ decision, the GB can take action to secure compliance. This authority was invoked for the first (and, thus far, only) time in ILO history in 2000, when the GB initiated measures against Myanmar in order to end forced labor in the state. In this context, too, the state was the primary entity assigned responsibility for workers' rights, while the multinational corporations that were involved and could have been considered culprits (notably TOTAL)[31] were never officially deemed a party to be investigated. In the face of contradictory evidence as to the corporations' involvement in profiting from the forced labor, the Commission of Inquiry concluded that it could come to no finding on the matter due to its inability to visit Myanmar.[32] It can be assumed that had key private companies been officially considered potential culprits along with the state, more rigorous efforts could have been made to verify the facts.

To sum up, this section has demonstrated how and in what form the statist model dominates the supervisory system and other key operational functions of the ILO. However, recent global economic, political, and legal developments mandate a new conception of responsibility. In the next section, we present such an alternative conception of shared responsibility.

3. SHARED RESPONSIBILITY AND LABOR

The notion of shared responsibility is increasingly arising with respect to various spheres of life, in both legal and philosophical contexts. From

---

[31] For a description of TOTAL's involvement in Myanmar, see, e.g., Ryan Tiz, *Searching for a Corporate Liability Standard Under the Alien Tort Claims Act in Doe v. Unocal*, 82 Or. L. Rev., 559, 562–63 (2003).

[32] ILO Governing Body, *Measures, Including Action Under Article 33 of the Constitution of the International Labour Organization, to Secure Compliance by the Government of Myanmar with the Recommendations of the Commission of Inquiry Established to Examine the Observance of the Forced Labour Convention*, 1930 (No. 29), GB.277/6, 277th Sess. (Mar. 2000), pp. 452.

a legal perspective, the need to address the new complex economic and social realities by extending the scope of responsibility has been recognized in several recent court decisions on both the national and transnational levels, in the areas of tort law, environmental law, and human rights law.[33] When we use the term 'shared responsibility' in the context of labor rights, we mean that the responsibility to remedy the unjust conditions suffered by workers anywhere in the world does not necessarily rest with only one particular state or particular actor, but, rather, could be shared by a variety of different actors and institutions, especially where international supply chains are involved. In contrast to earlier models of shared responsibility, such as, for example, those developed by Iris Young[34] and Margot Salomon,[35] our model offers a more suitable response to the realities of the global labor market faced by international labor regulators and enforcement organizations.[36]

Under our proposed shared responsibility model, responsibility for remedying the unjust conditions of workers in the global era is shared, albeit unequally, amongst the various actors that participate in the global labor markets. These include actors on the interactional level (for example, employers, private companies, subcontractors, and consumers) and actors on the institutional level (for example, states and international organizations).[37] On both levels, assigning responsibility for workers' welfare is an intricate and complex task. In what follows, we outline four principles to guide the allocation of this responsibility.[38]

---

[33] Oren Perez, Ecological Sensitivity and Global Legal Pluralism (Oxford: Hart Publishing, 2004), ch. 6 (regarding the doctrine of 'direct liability' introduced by the UK Supreme Court); Margot E. Salomon, Global Responsibility for Human Rights: World Poverty and the Development of International Law (Oxford: Oxford University Press, 2007); Ariel Porat, *Collective Responsibility in Tort Law*, 23 Mishpatim, 311, 322–25 (2004) (regarding the doctrines of 'market share liability' and 'enterprise liability' in US tort litigation).

[34] Iris Marion Young, Responsibility for Justice (Oxford and New York: Oxford University Press, 2011), pp. 120–21.

[35] See Salomon *supra* note 33, at 99–100.

[36] This model is based on the 'labor connection model' we developed in a previous article. See Yossi Dahan, Hanna Lerner and Faina Milman-Sivan, *Global Justice, Labor Standards, and Responsibility*, 12 Theoretical Inquiries L., 117 (2011).

[37] Richard W. Miller, Globalizing Justice: the Ethics of Poverty and Power (Oxford: Oxford University Press, 2010), pp. 60–62.

[38] These four principles draw heavily on Christian Barry's work. See Christian Barry, *Global Justice: Aims, Arrangements, and Responsibilities*, in Toni

3.1 The Connectedness Principle

The principle of connectedness is based on the premise of the existence of a special relationship between people and of the special moral obligation that derives from this relationship. As Christian Barry defines it, the principle of connectedness can be construed in two different ways: the one, in terms of shared identity (e.g., membership in a community, nation, or tribe) and the other, in terms of participation in a joint activity (e.g., collaborating in the production of a certain product). In the labor sphere, connectedness through a joint activity is usually recognized by states through the legal regulation of labor relations, namely, by creating an intricate web of mutual responsibilities and rights, in which workers enjoy special protection and status. In contrast to general transactional contracts, labor contracts are considered relational contracts.[39] Whereas transactional contracts usually refer to a one-time exchange of goods or money, the parties to relational contracts develop long-term relationships that are based on trust and solidarity and greatly exceed the terms of the original arrangement.[40] A labor connection, therefore, generates special commitments between the participants in the joint activity of production, which are similar to what is described in the philosophical literature as 'associative duties'.[41]

The question of which actors should be regarded as engaging in the joint activity defined in terms of 'labor connection' is one of the central dilemmas of global labor today. The expansion of the global chain of production beyond state borders and the emergence of new modes of production have led to a legal reality in which the traditional definition of employer–employee relations can no longer serve as the sole criterion for determining the degree of connectedness between parties. Iris Young argues, for example, that participants in the 'joint activity' of sweatshops should include consumers, fashion designers, and local

Erskine (ed.) CAN INSTITUTIONS HAVE RESPONSIBILITIES? (Basingstoke: Palgrave Macmillan, 2003), pp. 218, 227–31.

39 A transactional contract is of short duration, relates to a precise transaction of money and goods (usually a one-time-only exchange of an easily commoditized good for cash), and includes no element of altruism and little or no future cooperation.

40 Robert C. Bird, *Employment as a Relational Contract*, 8 U. PA. J. LAB. & EMP. L., 149, 151 (2005); Ian R. Macneil, *Contracting Worlds and Essential Contract Theory*, 9 SOC. & LEGAL STUD., 431, 432–33 (2000).

41 Samuel Schaffler, BOUNDARIES AND ALLEGIANCES: PROBLEMS OF JUSTICE AND RESPONSIBILITY IN LIBERAL THOUGHT (Oxford: Oxford University Press, 2001), pp. 48–65.

municipalities.[42] While we agree with Young that such actors should bear some degree of responsibility for remedying the unjust labor conditions in sweatshops, consumers and fashion designers should be held less responsible than actors that more directly participate in what we term the labor connection (i.e., chain of production), such as manufacturers and subcontractors.

Under the principle of connectedness, within global production chains, direct employers bear greater responsibility with respect to workers than the brands. Similarly, in the ILO context, the government in whose jurisdiction a violation occurs bears greater responsibility under the principle of connectedness than the government in whose jurisdiction the brand resides.

3.2 The Capacity Principle

The capacity principle refers to the ability of agents to rectify the unjust conditions of workers.[43] Several factors can determine this capacity, including scope of influence, that is, the number of workers whose labor conditions could be improved by the actions of the particular agent or institution.[44] Capacity can also be measured by the extent of political and economic power an actor wields to operate on both the institutional and interactional levels. On the institutional level, actors may affect the rules of global trade or impact the structure of global institutions so as to remedy unjust working conditions around the world. As has been discussed in Chapter 3, for instance, the EU and the US can also draw on the strength of their respective power positions in the international community and can impose unilateral sanctions linked to labor standards. Thus, under the principle of capacity, the world's powerful states seem to bear greater responsibility than the weaker states to remedy unjust work conditions.

---

42 Iris Young, *Responsibility and Global Justice: A Social Connection Model*, 23 Soc. Phil. & Pol'y, 102, 123–25 (2006).

43 For capacity as a principle that will assist in identifying responsible agents see, for example, David Miller, National Responsibility and Global Justice (Oxford: Oxford University Press, 2007), pp. 103–104. Compare with Young's use of 'power,' Young, Responsibility for Justice, *supra* note 34, at 123–52.

44 This use of the term 'influence' is different from John Ruggie's use. See Special Representative of the Secretary-General on the Issue of Human Rights and Transnational Corporations and Other Business Enterprises, *Promotion and Protection of All Human Rights, Civil, Political, Economic, Social and Cultural Rights, Including the Right to Development: Clarifying the Concepts of 'Sphere of Influence' and 'Complicity'*, 7–8, 14–15, U.N. Doc. A/HRC/8/16 (May 15, 2008) (by John Ruggie).

On the interactional level, MNEs exert control over the workers' conditions without direct ownership through a variety of processes, including conceptualization, design, and quality control.[45] In addition, major MNEs in buyer-driven industries have wielded total control over pricing and could influence workers' conditions by more balanced pricing.[46]

Lastly, the capacity of agents and institutions is contingent on how the desired standards and norms to be implemented are defined and the nature of the agent that bears responsibility. To illustrate, although MNEs could have the ability to enforce health and safety regulations throughout their global production chains, they may be less capable of efficiently eliminating child labor.[47]

3.3 The Beneficiary Principle

Under the beneficiary principle, the more a particular private or public actor benefits from a violation of labor rights, the greater its responsibility toward workers. In the context of global labor, we believe that benefit should primarily refer to economic gain, and, thus, it would be plausible to assume that both states and MNEs could be deemed responsible under this principle. For example, in the context of international chains of production, MNEs benefit more from production conducted in unjust conditions in developing states than do the subcontractors and managers of the local factories.[48] MNEs, thus, should bear greater responsibility

---

45 Jeroen Merk, *Jumping Scale and Bridging Space in the Era of Corporate Social Responsibility: Cross-border Labour Struggles in the Global Garment Industry*, 30 THIRD WORLD QUARTERLY, 599, 601 (2009).

46 Don Well, *Too Weak for the Job: Corporate Codes of Conduct, Non-Governmental Organizations and the Regulation of International Labour Standards*, 7 GLOBAL SOCIAL POLICY, 51, 55 (2007).

47 MNEs could refrain from employing children in their and their suppliers' factories, yet this could worsen the children's conditions in certain circumstances. In order to eradicate child labor effectively there should be comprehensive social and economic policies in place, such as, for example, the establishment of a comprehensive schooling system and other social services (child allowances, pensions, access to credit, etc.). These measures could give children access to education and thereby free them from the need to work for subsistence, and could only be provided by public agents such as the state. Effective policies for eradicating child labor are hotly debated. See, e.g., Drusilla K. Brown, Allan V. Deardorff and Robert M. Stern, *Child Labor: Theory, Evidence, and Policy*, in Kaushil Basu et al. (eds) INTERNATIONAL LABOR STANDARDS (Oxford: Blackwell Publishing, 2003), p. 195.

48 S. Prakash Sethi, SETTING GLOBAL STANDARDS (Hoboken, NJ: John Wiley and Sons Inc, 2003), pp. 58–59.

than the subcontractors to remedy the unjust labor conditions in local factories where labour rights violations are known to be taking place.

One feasible way of calculating benefits is to assume that the volume of production serves as a good estimate of benefits. Accordingly, economic benefit can provide a relatively exact measurement of the benefit exacted by each actor. This was, in fact, the method employed by the Accord in Bangladesh, whereby the share each individual company contributes to ensure the funding of the Accord correlates to its volume sourcing from Bangladesh, relative to the annual volume of other company signatories.[49] Similarly, the Alliance for Bangladesh Worker Safety – a five-year undertaking which was founded by North American apparel companies, retailers, and brands in 2013 in order to improve workers' safety – calculates its members' contributions using a tiered fee structure, based on the previous year's dollar volume of exports of apparel products from Bangladesh.[50]

3.4 The Contribution Principle

The extent of contribution to an outcome is a standard principle in ascertaining moral and legal liability, but its exact meaning requires further clarification. Christian Barry provides one possible application of the principle of contribution: 'agents [are] responsible for addressing acute deprivations when they have contributed, or are contributing, to bringing [those situations] about'.[51] In the labor context, this translates into agents' responsibility for remedying unjust labor conditions that they are contributing, or have contributed, to bringing about. In other words: 'A's conduct did not merely allow a causal sequence that had antecedently put B under threat of acute deprivation to play out, but rather initiated, facilitated or sustained it.'[52]

A complete application of the principle of contribution to unjust work conditions would require a detailed empirical investigation. For example, where networks of production are involved, the ILO could determine whether brands have pressured the other members of the network to violate the law, either directly or indirectly. In many labor-intense industries,

---

[49] This is subject to a maximum contribution of $500,000 per year for each year of the term of the Accord. See http://www.bangladeshaccord.org/faqs/ (last visited: 19 July 2014).

[50] See: http://www.bangladeshworkersafety.org/files/Alliance-Action-Plan-Package-FINAL.pdf (last visited: 19 July 2014).

[51] Christian Barry, *Applying the Contribution Principle*, 36 METAPHILOSOPHY, 210, 211 (2005).

[52] Ibid.

however, the principle of contribution may turn out to be less helpful than in other legal situations of ascertaining legal liability. This is because the labor rights violations that occur in these industries are usually a systemic part of production, occurring on a regular basis and without any particular unexpected change in the time or scope of the production orders from the MNE or core company. The principle of contribution, therefore, would be insignificant in such situations. Instead, it would increase the responsibility of MNEs when they have made a business decision that forces their affiliates to change their regular labor policies and commit human rights violations. This would include cases in which last-minute changes are made to the design of a product or the volume of a particular order is suddenly increased, in turn compelling suppliers to force workers to work long overtime hours to meet production quotas.

4. APPLICATION OF THE FOUR PRINCIPLES IN THE FRAMEWORK OF THE ILO

The shared responsibility model should be understood as a regulatory ideal, an objective to which the ILO should aspire. It would require significant reforms in the ILO's operation, the specifics of which should be worked out internally. In this section, we will merely offer several preliminary suggestions for such reforms. Our underlying assumption, as explicated below, is that the ILO already embodies values that are close to the shared responsibility ideal, especially relative to other international organizations. A conscious move toward an ideal of shared responsibility, however, entails a political will that is currently not discernible in the ILO.[53]

Our proposal proceeds in two stages. The first stage is to identify the potential actors that should be considered responsible for remedying unjust labor conditions according to the four principles of shared responsibility just defined in section 3. As we demonstrate, this process leads to the allocation of responsibility for workers' rights among key actors that are overlooked by the existing supervisory systems: (1) states other than the state in whose territory the labor rights are violated; and (2) powerful MNEs that participate in global production chains. In the second stage,

[53] This is best exemplified in the recent 2012 crisis in the supervisory system, see Swepston *supra* note 22. See also, Mark Barenberg, *Sustaining Workers' Bargaining Power in an Age of Globalization*, EPI Briefing Paper No. 246 (Econ. Pol'y Institute, Washington, DC), at 19 (Oct. 9, 2009); Guy Standing, *The ILO: An Agency for Globalization*?, 39 DEV. & CHANGE, 355, 380 (2008).

we elaborate on the particular procedures within the supervisory system that should be reformed for trans-border enforcement of labor standards.

4.1 Expanding the Scope of the Actors Responsible for International Labor Standards

The ILO identifies two types of violations of labor standards. One type is legislative in nature, which we accordingly term 'legal violations', namely, an inadequacy in the legal scheme in a given country. In such cases, the territorial state clearly bears responsibility for the violation and its amendment. There is, however, a second type of violation, which we term 'practice violations', where workers' rights are violated in practice. In such cases, actors other than the territorial state may bear responsibility for the violation. While the territorial state always bears some degree of responsibility for violations within its borders, the ILO should not automatically assume that other states or private employers are without responsibility. Indeed, in practice violation cases, the ILO should identify and assign legal responsibility to key actors according to procedures that we propose, shortly, as part of the reformed supervisory system.

In addition to identifying the responsible actors, the four principles of responsibility can assist in determining how the responsibility should be allocated among them. Pragmatic considerations seem to imply that the ILO should focus on several main candidates for sharing responsibility. For example, once a supply or distribution chain is identified, the ILO should engage with the most powerful player in the chain. Thus, the ILO could set a guideline whereby for each production chain, it assigns responsibility only to the MNE that is the relevant global buyer and sets aside other smaller identifiable players. This could be rationalized by an underlining assumption that it is usually global buyers that will be held responsible under all four principles of responsibility. It is also important to note however, that the shared responsibility model does not 'reduce' the responsibility of the territorial state, which would remain the key actor responsible for any violation within its territory. Others could, in appropriate cases, merely share this responsibility. One example of such cases is when MNEs perform state-like functions, especially in the developing world.[54]

This expansion of the scope of actors that could bear responsibility for labor standards to state actors other than the territorial state for actions

[54] Stepan Wood, *The Case for Leverage-Based Corporate Human Rights Responsibility*, 22 Business Ethics Quarterly, 63–98, 76 (2012).

that occur outside of their jurisdiction and, to private actors raises a set of conceptual problems. Imposing responsibility on private entities could prove to be controversial, according to traditional international law.[55] In recent years, however, proponents of strengthening corporate social responsibility and holding multinational enterprises more accountable have argued that corporate social responsibility codes should be transformed into legally binding standards and that corporations could participate in protecting human rights.[56] The imposition of responsibility on private corporations has also found expression in international documents, such as the Universal Declaration of Human Rights and in national domestic legal systems. International labor law, in particular, is often regarded as a prime example of a legal regime that imposes legal and moral responsibilities on corporations.[57] This is expressed, for example, in the manner in which some ILO Conventions are worded, placing direct duties on corporations.[58]

4.2 The ILO's Supervisory System: Proposals for Reform

We now proceed to some initial concrete proposals for legal reforms that would enable the incorporation of private bodies (and non-territorial states) into the ILO's existing governance framework – its reporting system and complaints procedures. We begin by pointing to the existing features that already lay the groundwork for the implementation of the shared responsibility model.

4.2.1 Initial signs of a shared responsibility model: the reporting system

Incorporating shared responsibility into the ILO's reporting system would entail a radical change in how the Committee of Experts operates. Such

---

[55] We have discussed objections to extending the responsibility of states beyond their jurisdiction elsewhere – see Dahan, Lerner and Milman-Sivan, *supra* note 21.

[56] See, e.g., Surya Deva, REGULATING CORPORATE HUMAN RIGHTS VIOLATIONS: HUMANIZING BUSINESS (London: Routledge: 2013). A significant development in this matter occurred in 2014, when the UN Human Rights Council adopted the 'Elaboration of an International Treaty' Resolution (Ecuador Resolution). The Ecuador Resolution provides for the establishment of an open-ended intergovernmental working group with the mandate to elaborate an international legally binding instrument on transnational corporations and other business enterprises with respect to human rights.

[57] Steve R. Ratner, *Corporations and Human Rights: A Theory of Legal Responsibility*, 111 YALE LAW JOURNAL, 443, 478–79 (2001).

[58] E.g., Convention Concerning Occupational Safety and Health and the Working Environment, art. 16.1, June 22, 1981, 1331 U.N.T.S. 279.

a reform would be advanced by two general measures with respect to the ILO's supervisory process. First, the ILO would have to further harmonize compliance with its core standards (or even with some other basic minimum of standards) among its member states. This would require authorizing the Organization to intensify supervision of its core standards regardless of whether a member state has ratified the relevant standards, thus narrowing states' discretion regarding which standards legally bind them to some agreed-upon minimum. Second, the shared responsibility model would entail expanding and deepening the involvement of workers' and employees' organizations in the supervisory process. This enhanced participation could require modification of the type of information requested of the states in their ILO annual reports.

Traces of these two approaches can already be detected in the current reporting system and the Committee of Experts' mode of operation. Elements of the ILO reporting system reflect a push toward harmonization of the Organization's norms among its member states that shifts away from the statist model in several respects. One such element is a unique reporting requirement whereby member states are required to report on the degree of their compliance with obligations set forth in Conventions they have yet to ratify. This reporting requirement departs from the international law principle that states have absolute discretion in determining the standards that bind them. The authority to impose such a legal obligation, rather extraordinary in the international legal system, derives from Article 19 of the ILO Constitution,[59] which empowers the Organization to monitor unratified Conventions and recommendations. This authority can be understood as undermining states' sovereignty for the purpose of contending with problems of interstate cooperation and coordination, and thus in line with the model of shared responsibility.[60]

This deviation from the principle of state sovereignty is manifested in the reporting system in two central exceptions to the general rule that states are legally bound only by standards they have ratified. The first exceptional procedure is the General Survey. Every year, the GB chooses an issue on which all member states are obligated to report, whether or not they have ratified the Conventions that address the subject matter at hand. In their reports, the states are called upon to elaborate on current practice in their jurisdiction regarding the issue at hand and on the obstacles to ratification of the Conventions. The General Survey creates a worldwide

---

[59] Article 19 of the ILO Constitution, ILO Constitution, *supra* note 27.

[60] Laurence R. Helfer, *Monitoring Compliance with Unratified Treaties: The ILO Experience*, 71 L. & CONTEMP. PROB., 193, 195 (2008).

overview of the issue, which is published in the General Survey as a part of the Committee of Experts' annual report.

Secondly, the ILO reporting duties impose certain procedures on member states' internal ratification process that may indicate movement toward the greater harmonization of norms. Under the ILO Constitution, member states must submit any new instrument adopted by the International Labor Conference to their relevant national political bodies for serious consideration of ratification and/or implementation of the standards set forth within. The states have one year to report that this duty has been met and that the Convention was brought before the competent legislative authority for approval. In addition, if the national legislature has refused to ratify, the states are required to justify this refusal and indicate whether the state intends to use alternative means for implementing the relevant labor standards. This is an extraordinary and unprecedented procedure, for states are requested to submit to their legislature legal instruments that were not necessarily endorsed by their own relevant authorities.[61] This reporting obligation represents a further shift away from full and complete state sovereignty, toward the international harmonization of norms and a departure, as such, from the statist model.

Several aspects of the reporting system also embody the aspiration to expand the scope of actors involved in the supervisory system. There is explicit deviation from the statist model in Article 23(2) of the ILO Constitution, which requires all governmental reports to be communicated to the national representative organizations, which in turn make their own observations as to the factual situation on the ground.[62] Moreover, the ILO has recently deepened the involvement of its functional organizations in its reporting system by assigning greater weight to their reports. In 2006, the Governing Body established guidelines for the proper treatment of comments received from employers' and workers' organizations concerning the application of a ratified Convention in a non-reporting year.[63] These guidelines are aimed at ensuring that the Committee of Experts will be able to address serious violations of legal obligations, even in non-reporting years. They provide that the Committee may request states to

[61] At its inception this procedure was described as innovative and bold. Int'l Labour Office, *International Labour Organisation: The First Decade* (1931), 268–69 [hereinafter *The First Decade*].

[62] Article 23(2) of the ILO Constitution, ILO Constitution, *supra* note 27.

[63] Int'l Lab. Conf., 99th Sess., *Report of the Committee of Experts on the Application of Conventions and Recommendations*, 77, (2010), available at http://www.ilo.org/wcmsp5/groups/public/@ed_norm/@relconf/documents/meetingdocument/wcms_123424.pdf.

report outside their regular cycle when employers' or workers' organizations have directed its attention, via their comments, to severe violations of a ratified Convention.

Certain elements of the functioning of both the CEACR and Conference Committee can be described as better conforming to the shared responsibility model. For example, since 2005, the Conference Committee has stressed the link between technical assistance and the standards-related activities of the supervisory bodies, in a manner that is aligned with the notion of shared responsibility. Thus, the supervisory system will highlight cases where technical assistance will be particularly helpful in ensuring compliance with labor standards. This promotional focus follows an implicit understanding that individual states should not always be held fully responsible for their failure to comply and in fact are in need of external help to act in accordance with their legal obligations. The follow-up to the 1998 ILO Declaration on Fundamental Principles and Rights at Work was similarly designed to complement the ILO's supervisory procedures in a promotional manner.

4.2.2 Initial signs of a shared responsibility model: the complaints system

The ILO complaints process, like its reporting system, reflects seeds of the two objectives described above. The first objective – the need to broaden the legal consequences of violating core standards – is most fully advanced in the framework of the ILO's freedom of association norm. This is manifested in the exceptional procedure that provides that allegations of an infringement of freedom of association can be filed against states that have not ratified the relevant Convention. This procedure was introduced in the 1950s and underscored at the time the unique nature of freedom of association was enshrined in the ILO Constitution as a customary norm.[64]

---

[64] Nicolas Valticus, *Once More about the ILO System of Supervision*, in Niels Blokker and Sam Muller (eds) Towards More Effective Supervision by International Organizations (Dordrecht: Martinus Nijhoff, 1994), p. 106. The ILO Constitution is the legal basis for this understanding of the norm. This procedure is commonly used, and over 2500 cases have been examined since its inception, see, Thomann, *supra* note 30, at p. 128. Its jurisprudence, set forth in a digest published at regular intervals, is supplemented by the occasional decisions of the Fact-Finding and Conciliation Commission on Freedom of Association, and is closely related to that of the Committee of Experts, which also provides a periodic General Survey on freedom of association. See ILO, Freedom Of Association: Digest Of Decisions And Principles Of The Freedom Of Association Committee Of The Governing Body Of The Ilo (5th rev. edn, 2006).

Yet the ratification status of freedom of association Conventions is not without significance. In allegations of a severe violation by a member state that has ratified the relevant Conventions, the Governing Body can refer the matter to the FFCC to investigate the claim. In contrast, when the alleged violation is by a non-ratifying state, the state's participation in the inquiry is voluntary, for its explicit consent is necessary for the matter to be referred to the FFCC.[65]

The second objective – the need to include non-state actors in the supervisory process – already finds expression in the representations procedure. Indeed, any industrial organization (usually workers' organizations) can submit a representation, regardless of the organization's size or national affiliation or whether it is a local, national, or international organization. The only requirement for qualifying as a complainant is that the GB determines it to be an 'industrial organization'. In order to prevent any manipulation of the definition by the national state involved, the ILO specifically provides that in determining an organization's eligibility, the Governing Body is not bound by definitions endorsed by the national authorities of the state where the organization resides, but rather should make an objective evaluation according to its own rules. The principle of inclusive participation is further served by allowing international organizations that have affiliates with a direct interest in the alleged violation to serve as complainants. This rather inclusive procedure opens up the possibility of representations being submitted by regional organizations, such as the Latin American Central of Workers (CLAT) and the Latin American Federation of Trade Workers (FETRALCOS),[66] and international organizations, such as the International Confederation of Free Trade Unions, which has in fact filed several representations.[67]

A further indication of the acceptance of the values of the shared responsibility model is that it is possible for several organizations to coordinate

---

[65] Nicolas Valticos and Geraldo Von Potobsky, INTERNATIONAL LABOUR LAW (Kluwer Law & Taxation Publishers, 2nd edn, 1995), p. 297.

[66] These organizations cooperated and together alleged a non-observance by Venezuela of the ILO Employment Policy Convention, 1964, http://www.ilo.org/dyn/normlex/en/f?p=1000:50010:0::NO::P50010_ARTICLE_NO:24 (last visited: 18 Feb. 2013).

[67] A few examples include: in 1991 an alleged non-observance by Yugoslavia of the ILO Discrimination (Employment and Occupation) Convention, 1958; in 1994, an alleged non-observance by Myanmar of the ILO Forced Labour Convention, 1930; and in 1996, an alleged non-observance by France of the ILO Labour Inspection Convention, 1947 and the ILO Social Policy (Non-Metropolitan Territories) Convention, 1947. These represent merely a few examples of the extensive participation of the ICFTU in the ILO's activities.

and file a joint representation. In addition, industrial organizations are not restricted to submitting representations only regarding violations that have occurred in their own states, but rather regarding violations in any state; they can even submit representations regarding several states in conjunction, something that has already been done in practice. Thus, for example, the representation procedure allows for a Turkish workers' union to allege a violation by the Dutch government toward Turkish workers who worked in the Netherlands.[68] These features of the representation procedure, which usually go unnoticed, enable the ILO to address labor rights violations that occur in the framework of cross-border economic activity. It seems no coincidence that recent years have witnessed an increase in the submission of representations.

In sum, then, much in the same way as the reporting system, the complaints system exhibits distinct signs of a shift toward a shared responsibility model. The implications of this shift, we will show below, can be extended to other mechanisms of the ILO standard supervisory system.

4.2.3 Proposed reforms toward a shared responsibility model: the reporting system

How can the ILO progress beyond these initial stages toward a more comprehensive model of shared responsibility? Most significantly, the CEACR should expand the scope of actors to which it assigns responsibility. Namely, when it detects practical labor rights violations, it should no longer assume automatically that the sole actor responsible for the violation is the state in whose territory the violation occurred. Rather, it should weigh assigning responsibility to other states as well as to private bodies, by applying the four principles of responsibility allocation and making an initial assessment of each actor's degree of responsibility.

In addition, the CEACR should expand the information it gathers. Thus, for example, it could try revising its questionnaires to request information that goes significantly beyond a description of the state's legal reality and instead (or also) provides a picture of actual labor rights protection. The ILO should further consider allowing the CEACR to receive reports directly from civic organizations and workers' unions that are not necessarily the most representative organizations.[69] After

[68] In 2006 the Confederation of Turkish Trade Unions (TURK-IS) filed a representation against the Netherlands alleging non-observance by the Netherlands of the Equality of Treatment (Social Security) Convention, 1962 (No. 118).

[69] CEACR's ability to examine such information should be considered. This suggestion should be implemented incrementally, as civil society often lacks the accountability mechanisms needed to ensure the accuracy of the information.

concluding its assessment, the Committee could summarize its initial findings in a report to the Conference Committee, similarly to current practice.

Naturally, such changes to the operation of the CEACR would yield parallel modifications to the functioning of the Conference Committee, as they would have to address MNEs. The proceedings of the Conference Committee should address directly all the actors identified by the CEACR in every particular case. The Conference Committee's considerations for choosing cases for discussion and follow-up should thus be transformed accordingly. Some amendments to its discussion procedures will be indispensable, particularly in cases where one of the actors is a private body. For example, observations, when warranted, could also be published with regard to private entities, as in the case of states. Allowing observations against MNEs or other private employers would incentivize workers' organizations and civic organizations to include relevant information about violations that targets particular employers.

4.2.4 Proposed reforms toward a shared responsibility model: the complaints system

To fully integrate the shared responsibility model, where a state has not yet ratified core Conventions, the ILO would need to waive the requirement of state consent currently necessary before the FFCC may initiate an investigation, as is the case with the CFA procedure. The CFA's current mandate to investigate cases without the involved states' consent, even if they have not ratified the relevant Conventions, should be extended to the other three core rights – the right to be free of forced labor, the right to equality at work, and the right to be free of child labor– a move that has been advocated by Bob Hepple, for example.[70] From a practical perspective, the CFA's and FFCC's existing procedures, with the necessary modifications, could serve as a model in adapting the representations procedure, and could also inform new Commission of Inquiry procedures for initiating investigations regardless of ratification status. In fact, the representations procedure already borrowed procedural rules from the ILO legislative bodies that supervise the freedom of association norm.[71] One concern that could arise, of course, is the possibility of abuse

---

[70] Bob Hepple, *Does Law Matter? The Future of Binding Norms*, in George P. Politakis (ed.) PROTECTING LABOUR RIGHTS AS HUMAN RIGHTS: PRESENT AND FUTURE OF INTERNATIONAL SUPERVISION (Geneva: ILO, 2007), pp. 221, 229.

[71] See the GB's decision to accept the procedural rules that apply to cases of freedom of association as guidelines that would assist in resolving disputes as to procedural quandaries that relate to the procedure of representations under Article 24. See Comm. on Legal Issues and International Labor Standards,

of the procedure by an increase in politically motivated complaints. A possible solution to this problem could be found in the current mandates of the ILO supervisory bodies. These bodies have been accorded discretion as to whether to receive or reject complaints.[72] Similar discretion could be applied to determine the preliminary question of the responsibility of non-territorial states according to the four principles of shared responsibility. The supervisory bodies also have ample experience dealing with complex matters. The CFA, for example, requires that all complaints be submitted in writing with evidence to support the allegations made therein. It is required to determine complicated preliminary questions, such as whether the industrial organization that submitted the complaint was qualified to do so. Accordingly, the CFA is authorized to determine whether the complainant has a 'direct interest' in the case; in cases of complainants where the international organizations lack consultative status with the ILO, the CFA must determine whether the national affiliates of the particular organization are directly affected by the allegations. Similar initial rules of receivability could be instituted to determine whether the non-territorial states in question are prima facie appropriate parties for investigation.

The Commission of Inquiry has also had experience with investigating allegations made against private bodies, even though such bodies have never been official subjects of investigation. When the Commission has found a corporation to be 'of a special position' with regard to the case, it has not hesitated to investigate it. Thus, for example, in investigating a complaint filed by Ghana against Portugal claiming a violation of the 1957 Abolition of Forced Labour Convention (No. 105), the Commission of Inquiry communicated with and investigated allegations against concerned corporations.[73] In this case, the Witwatersrand Native Labour Association Ltd. was involved in recruiting workers from Mozambique to work in mines in South Africa and thus was called upon by the

---

Governing Body, *Possible Improvements in the Standards Related Activities of the ILO: Proposals Regarding Submission to the Competent Authorities and the Representation Procedure*, GB292/LILS/1(Rev.), 291st Sess. (Mar. 2005).

[72] The CFA, for example, may reject a complaint on several bases. See ILO, *Special Procedures for the Examination in the International Labour Organization of Complaints Alleging Violations of Freedom of Association – Annex 1*, at para. 38.

[73] Comm'n Appointed under Article 26 of the Constitution of the ILO to Examine the Complaint Filed by the Government of Ghana Concerning the Observance by the Government of Portugal of the Abolition of Forced Labour Convention, 1957 (No. 105), Rep., para. 720, O.B. XLV(2), Supp. II (Apr. 1962) [hereinafter Portugal's Report].

Commission 'to send a duly accredited representative to give evidence at its second session concerning the conditions of recruitment and employment of the labour concerned'.[74] Further, the complainants had pointed to particular private enterprises in their allegations: the Diamond Company of Angola was accused of employing a quarter of its workers under forced labor, while the Benguela Railway Company was accused of being partly maintained by forced labor, as were various other European-owned plantations.[75] The Commission of Inquiry established appropriate procedures for investigating the companies, which cooperated with the investigation.[76] The companies provided information and sent representatives to the Commission's sessions to present relevant statements.[77] In the case of most of the companies deemed relevant to the investigation, the Commission also visited the work sites and met and interviewed workers.[78] This is one instance of actual ILO experience that exemplifies the Organization's ability to develop procedures for investigating private entities as well as non-territorial states.

Implementing the shared responsibility model would also require that all actors deemed responsible for labor rights violations be subject to the ILO's sanction scheme, including private bodies and non-territorial states in the appropriate circumstances. The wording of Article 33 of the ILO Constitution, which sets forth the most severe sanctions the Organization can impose, does not necessarily preclude the ILO from making such reforms. The Article provides that the GB may recommend to the International Labour Conference 'such action as it may deem wise and expedient to secure compliance'. There is nothing in this wording that rules out sanctions against private bodies or sanctioning several countries in tandem.[79]

---

74 Ibid., 25.

75 Ibid., 23.

76 The general managers of the private companies concerned were invited and gave evidence before the commission, as can be evidenced by the list of witnesses, see ibid., 43–44.

77 Ibid.

78 Ibid., 61–62, 64–77.

79 The wording of Article 33 was amended in 1946, and the particular reference to economic sanctions deleted. Economic sanctions, however, are not ruled out as such. See Francis Maupain, *The Settlement of Disputes within the International Labour Office*, 2 J. Int'l Econ. L., 273, 284 (1999). It can be similarly argued that the Article's wording does not preclude sanctions against private entities.

5. CONCLUSION

In this chapter, we have argued that the ILO should not assign sole legal responsibility for remedying the unjust conditions of workers in the global labor market to the states in whose territory the labor rights violations occur. Rather, additional actors, public and private, should also share in the legal responsibility for remedying these conditions, including powerful MNEs. Resting on an interdisciplinary approach, which combines normative-philosophical and empirical-legalistic perspectives on international labor standards, this chapter has outlined a proposed reform of ILO procedures and mechanisms, particularly in the supervisory structure. Full and comprehensive implementation would likely mandate sweeping reform of the entire ILO operational and institutional structure, including its tripartite structure and norm-generating procedures, and not just its supervisory system. Our model could therefore represent an aspiration: toward reducing the discrepancy between the actors that are morally responsible for ensuring workers' core labor rights and the actors that shoulder the legal responsibility for doing so under the current ILO approach.

The notion of shared responsibility in the sphere of global labor has been gaining support in recent years from various scholars and activists, who advocate this approach as a solution to human rights violations in transnational chains of production and to the 'accountability gap', namely, the ineffectiveness of states in addressing these violations in the global economy. Several schemes emphasizing shared responsibility among different actors, such as states, MNEs, international organizations, and local and international unions, have been recently published, two of which are particularly noteworthy.[80] One proposal suggests setting up an international legal framework for combating human rights violations in transnational chains of production, in a Convention to be adopted by states as well as corporations.[81] As Karin Lukas notes, in the proposal,

---

[80] These proposals go beyond the debate as to how the ILO should address the International Framework Agreement, which will be discussed in 2016. International Framework Agreements are yet another important path to promote workers' rights that the ILO is hesitant to explore. Paragraph 14 of the DG plan of action formulated pursuant to the discussions on social dialogue at the 102nd Session (June 2013) of the International Labour Conference states that the ILO should increase its 'engagement with multinational enterprises (MNEs) and global union federations (GUFs) in the field of social dialogue'. Nevertheless, the subject is hotly debated, as exemplified by recent discussions in the Governing Body, see, ILO, draft minutes of the 319th session of the Governing Body, para. 356 (2013).

[81] See A. Reinisch, *The Changing International Legal Framework for Dealing*

there is a precedent for this, as companies can already be held liable for environmental harms at the international level. Moreover, this human rights Convention could be supplemented by 'an international court of human rights that would adjudicate complaints once national avenues have been exhausted or are seen as ineffective to bring about justice for TNCs' human rights violations'.[82] A second proposal, authored by Sune Skadegaard Thorsen and Signe Anderson, advocates a race-to-the-top approach, through the creation of CSR risk-free sourcing and investment zones: 'By creating a regulatory race to the top, local authorities as well as local suppliers within a zone will benefit from the attraction of international buyers looking for CSR risk free sourcing and investment.'[83] This shared responsibility framework would assign a central role to the state and local authorities in a partnership that would include MNEs, civil society organizations, and buyers, while giving a significant role to development cooperation agencies as facilitators of the process. In our view, although the ILO is not defined strictly as a development cooperation agency, it can make an important contribution to such a partnership with its expertise and technical assistance on issues of labor rights.

Clearly, additional conceptual and empirical study is called for to develop a comprehensive and effective system of responsibility allocation among the various private and public actors in the global labor market. Further practical considerations will have to be taken into account in the effort to counter the political pressure likely to be brought to bear by powerful private actors such as MNEs. Nevertheless, as shown in this chapter, our proposal for incorporating a conception of shared responsibility into the very structure of the ILO seems both morally justified and practically plausible.

---

with Non-State Actors, in P. Alston (ed.) NON-STATE ACTORS AND HUMAN RIGHTS (Oxford: Oxford University Press, 2005), p. 82.

[82] See K. Lukas, *Human Rights in the Supply Chain: Influence and Accountability*, in Radu Mares (ed.) THE UN GUIDING PRINCIPLES ON BUSINESS AND HUMAN RIGHTS (Leiden, the Netherlands: Brill Nijhoff, 2012), p. 166.

[83] See Sune Skadegaard Thorsen and Signe Anderson, *Remodeling Responsible Supply Chain Management*, in Radu Mares (ed.) THE UN GUIDING PRINCIPLES ON BUSINESS AND HUMAN RIGHTS (Leiden, the Netherlands: Brill Nijhoff, 2012), p. 146.

14. Conclusion: which way to enforcement?

Glenn Rayp, Axel Marx and Jan Wouters

The protection of labour rights is becoming increasingly complex in a world characterised by transnational supply chains, mobile capital and mobile people. In recent decades we have witnessed the development of an intricate web of political and legal initiatives on the issue of the global protection of labour rights, independent from established multilateral initiatives such as the International Labour Organization (ILO). These initiatives include trade-related initiatives, supply-chain oriented private initiatives by NGOs or firms, and unilateral actions by civil society actors. The contributions in this book provide an analysis of the present state of the most significant initiatives and how they impact global labour governance. A central question throughout the contributions concerns the enforcement of these initiatives. In this conclusion we aim to summarise, from a comparative perspective, the findings and proposals of the individual chapters around the issue of enforcement. In doing this we will make a distinction between state-driven public initiatives, mainly through trade-related measures, and private-driven initiatives.

Before we proceed we would like to note, however, that the contributions are as relevant about the subjects they explicitly discuss as they are regarding at least one on which they remain silent. This we want to clarify first. No chapter indeed mentions, in whatever context, the possibility of automatic improvement of labour protection and the respect of core labour standards as a consequence of economic growth and development, an argument proposed by several free trade advocates. At least before the financial crisis of 2007–2008, the world economy was characterised by a high growth rate, according to historical standards, over the previous 25 years, in which we saw the development of new and large countries, China in particular (and the BRICS and MICs in general). Yet, none of the authors is seemingly confident that economic development will also entail social development, improved labour protection in particular, despite this being a common belief in some literature. Considering the findings by Marx et al. in Chapter 2 they may have good reasons for remaining careful about the prospects of a spontaneous upward convergence in labour protection. Updating and extending the series by Kucera and Mosley of the ratification and protection of the ILO conventions on the core labour standards mentioned in the Fundamental Principles and Rights at Work, Marx et al. (Chapter 2) find a continuing *fall* of the protection level, though less marked in the new millennium compared with the two last decades of the previous one. In addition, the reported fall has the pattern of a global shock, affecting countries of all income levels, that is, poor as well as rich countries, industrialised as well as developing countries. In this respect, the data do not suggest convergence in social protection, even towards the mean. Given the continuous economic growth in the same period, the correlation between the evolution in protection of core labour standards and economic development can therefore be expected to be weak. In discussing potential explanations of this fall, or at least stagnation in the protection of core labour rights, the authors admit that the trend can be influenced by better and more monitoring mechanisms, which result in a structural increase in the number of reported violations. However, they indicate that it cannot be excluded that trends in the world economy, like globalisation and technological change, may be less favourable for labour and put a strain on labour protection. Marx et al.'s figures provide a compelling argument for taking the question of enforcement seriously, as the other authors in this book do, given that they suggest that despite the substantial multi-level initiative taking in the field of global labour governance, not much progress in the protection of core labour standards has been achieved.

1. INTERNATIONAL LABOUR NORMS AND THEIR ENFORCEMENT AT THE INDIVIDUAL STATE'S LEVEL

The contributions by Brown (Chapter 5), Velluti (Chapter 3) and Van den Putte (Chapter 4) consider the inclusion of labour protection in the social dimension of unilateral or bilateral external economic and trade policy initiatives by the US or the EU, which makes clear that it is in particular these countries that promote this strategy (in addition to Canada). In this respect, Brown distinguishes a US from an Asian perspective on the social dimension of free trade agreements (FTAs) or bilateral investment treaties (BITs). In particular, intra-Asian bilateral or regional FTAs or BITs, which have developed quite substantially in the recent years, generally do *not* include a social dimension or clauses concerning the protection of labour rights. The US perspective, in contrast, is characterised as seeking to embrace and promote commitments to ILO core labour standards as embodied in the ILO Declaration on Fundamental Principles and Rights at Work, either promotional, pre-ratification conditional, or by providing enforcement mechanisms for states and investors for alleged trade or labour violations. Hence, dispositions for enforcement are, at least comparatively, well elaborated in the recent treaties and agreements concluded by the US. Yet, Brown notices that dispute settlement provisions do not apply separately for labour but for trade violations as well and that the access to dispute settlement is restricted for interested third parties. In addition, Brown asks whether a number of inadequacies in the way labour protection is included in bilateral treaties might reduce their effectiveness in advancing labour standards. First, he remarks that the US refers to the ILO Declaration, rather than the ILO Conventions and therefore he remains sceptical as regards their enforceability. Next, it is unclear to what extent the dispute settlement mechanisms effectively allow the enforcement of labour obligations. For example, Brown observes that complaints filed under trade agreements (other than NAFTA/NAALC), activated since 2008, have led to only six cases filed up to June 2012. Third, only states and individual investors are entitled to bring claims; not third parties such as non-governmental organisations, unions and labour groups. And, finally, while nations are expected to enforce labour standards, much less (voluntary) commitment is expected from corporations. Because advancement of labour protection is confined to the nations within the boundaries of their domestic law, the leeway for cross-national companies in respecting labour standards remains substantial. Regarding this last point, Brown suggests the introduction of mandatory International Framework Agreements that would oblige companies to follow international corporate social responsibility standards.

The discussion of the EU initiatives to include labour protection and a social dimension in external policy by Velluti shows some remarkable differences with the US approach. Velluti points to the strategic partnership between the EU and the ILO over the last decade. In its promotion of labour rights and social dialogue, the EU refers to the European social model as well as the ILO labour standards. Recent EU external policy initiatives indicate the growing importance of the adoption and implementation of ILO standards. This is especially clear in the unilateral trade policy initiatives by the EU, such as the GSP (Generalised Scheme of Preferences), GSP+ and the Everything But Arms (EBA) schemes, where market access advantages are made conditional upon the respecting of ILO labour standards, assessed by, amongst others, ILO reports. Yet, Velluti argues that enforcement of ILO labour standards through these policies may be affected by inconsistencies and selectivity in the application of the scheme. Not all countries, comparable in terms of labour rights violation, are denied access to the GSP scheme, which may suggest that, with these schemes, the EU aims at other (foreign policy) objectives than ensuring the protection of labour rights. Velluti stresses the role of the EU Parliament, which insists upon the Commission to monitor more strictly compliance with ILO labour standards. In addition to its strengthened institutional position since the Lisbon Treaty, the EU Parliament may have a considerable impact on the position of the Commission in this matter, given the large consensus amongst its members on the inclusion of labour standards and the social dimension in trade and development policy, although from (or perhaps because of) different perspectives and political interests (that is, from a social, economic as well as a human rights discourse), as argued by Van den Putte. Though subjacent divergences in points of view may always weaken its resolution, one may expect that, given the common interest in labour standards that Van den Putte indicates, the EU Parliament takes a firm position in this matter. In any case, Velluti concludes by pointing to the reformed GSP law that the EU adopted, aimed at: (i) strengthening the impact of the GSP scheme; (ii) reinforcing the incentives for the respect of core human and labour rights, environmental and good governance standards; (iii) reversing the burden of proof on the beneficiary country (which is expected to demonstrate its compliance with its binding undertakings); and (iv) making the withdrawal mechanism faster and more efficient.

Concerning the inclusion of labour protection clauses in the bilateral trade agreements of the EU, Velluti refers explicitly to the 'involvement and influence of the EU Parliament in the conclusion of trade treaties' (as well as to the institutional changes as a results of the Lisbon Treaty) to explain 'some level of commonality as to the substantive standards and the institutional set-up envisaged'. However, she also notes some obstacles in the effective implementation and enforcement of the labour clauses included in the trade or development treaties: weaknesses in the coherence in the EU's external policy, as the Member States take different positions on the trade–labour linkage and not all Member States are fully compliant with ILO Conventions, or because different sets of provisions coming from different schemes overlap.

This process of interaction, tension and contradictions between different actors involved on different levels of governance is also scrutinised in the contribution by Frank Hendrickx and Pieter Pecinovsky (Chapter 6). They discuss the internal EU policies in the context of the new EU (austerity) initiatives and the tension these policies create with other commitments such as those to fundamental labour rights as formulated by the ILO and the Council of Europe. They frame this debate in an assessment of how coherent internal policies are in light of external commitments (that is, external coherence), and raise the issue of which level of governance has the authority to induce others to change their policies. In the current situation, they argue, it seems that neither the ILO, nor the Council of Europe is capable of imposing their views on the EU. Moreover, Hendrickx and Pecinovsky note, the Union's Member States are bound by the ILO's conventions, the European Social Charter and the ECHR, but the EU is not bound by them directly. What emerges is a complex set of interactions, and in their words networked legal orders, in search of suitable governance mechanisms which are not based on hierarchy but on co-existence. How these governance mechanisms should work and whether they contribute to a better enforcement of labour rights is an outstanding question.

2. INTERNATIONAL LABOUR NORMS AND THEIR ENFORCEMENT AT THE LEVEL OF PRIVATE ACTORS

A second set of contributions focuses on the role of private actors in global labour governance. In their contribution, Zandvliet and van der Heijden (Chapter 8) note that: 'If the ILO was able to ensure full compliance with the entire international labour code there would be no need to look for alternative enforcement mechanisms.' In addition, like Brown, they observe that additional public policy initiatives to enforce the international enforcement of (basic) labour protection, does not close all the loopholes in application. Therefore, individual firms, in particular multinational corporations, are increasingly addressed directly to adopt basic principles of labour protection on a voluntary basis, beyond and complementary to the domestic legal framework of the countries where they operate, by means of a code of conduct that reflects corporate social responsibility (CSR). Despite the divergence in commitments within as well as between codes of conduct, just like between unilateral codes and initiatives that involve the stakeholder community, Zandvliet and van der Heijden note that CSR codes tend to include gradually more references to international labour law. They conclude that most CSR initiatives at present recognise all the core labour standards in addition to health and safety standards. In addition, the use of standardised normative documents or reporting templates increase the reliance on international norms. In this way, ILO standards remain highly relevant for CSR codes, and private initiatives, in adopting ILO labour standards, can become genuinely complementary to public regulations, either those of international organisations such as the ILO or from subsidiary public unilateral or bilateral schemes. Based on these observations, they argue for distinguishing CSR as a 'privatisation of public standards', in which nations and international institutions can and should keep a steering function, from privatisation as a mere introduction of private standards.

Pekdemir, Glasbergen and Cörvers (Chapter 10), however, are more sceptical of this 'privatisation of public standards' and argue that private labour standard arrangements as a system are characterised by structural weaknesses. Their analysis focuses on private multi-stakeholder monitoring schemes and proceeds along three dimensions. The first refers to structural-organisational relationships and considers definitions of roles, responsibilities and leadership in private labour standard codes. They notice that the representation of stakeholders in governance boards of private labour standard schemes, and hence decision making, differs substantially. In particular, industry and business representatives tend to outnumber (direct) workers' representatives and therefore 'workers' rights are currently more proposed by industry stakeholders and the corporate world than by unions'. In addition, accountability in the monitoring schemes is lacking because, among other factors, they depend on business for the demand of their services, rather than on consumers. Finally, they point to the absence of an authority that guides the arrangements.

The second dimension consists of the normative-cognitive relationships, regarding which they verify the presence of a common vision of labour standards among the participating stakeholders in the monitoring schemes. In line with the finding also mentioned by Zandvliet and van der Heijden, they acknowledge that the labour standard codes in the arrangements converge to ILO core labour standards and principles. Yet, according to Pekdemir, Glasbergen and Cörvers the stringency of specific labour standards still varies between these systems as well as the verification mechanisms (audits) of the implementation of these standards. Concerning the latter there is variation concerning who bears the responsibility for the monitoring, which aspects of the codes are monitored, and how non-complying firms are treated (that is, the presence and absence of sanctioning). On the third dimension, defined as the collaborative-relational capacity of the actors (the extent of co-operation), Pekdemir, Glasbergen and Cörvers find that the arrangements they analysed are not frequently in contact with the ILO, let alone structurally linked. Moreover, while some co-operation between the systems is present, systematic co-ordination between the schemes is not, which is partially explained by ideological differences. Therefore, the labour standard schemes remain highly fragmented, which limits the potential for structural change. To improve the effectiveness of private schemes, the authors recommend a more structural support from intergovernmental institutions.

The limited effectiveness of these private schemes is illustrated by the contribution of Dennis Klink (Chapter 11). One could argue that Klink adds another dimension to those indicated by Pekdemir, Glasbergen and Cörvers. His cross-country analysis on the adoption of GLOBALGAP in the banana sector shows an unequal and incoherent adoption of these private standards across countries. He explains this in terms of 'compliance opportunities', that is, the institutional characteristics that determine the opportunity to reach compliance. 'Countries characterized by business-friendly public regulations, a strong compliance culture, an absence of CSR-sensitive groups in national labor markets and high levels of education and professionalization amongst the workforce constitute favorable institutional environments for the implementation of CSR standards.' Therefore, private standard adoption is more likely where the existing public standards, as well as the dominant social conventions and norms, have already created comparably decent conditions. 'Hence, private standards do not add much from a regulatory point of view.'

Pekdemir, Glasbergen and Cörvers' suggestion of a more structural support or involvement of intergovernmental institutions in private labour standard schemes is taken up by Dahan, Lerner and Milman-Sivan (Chapter 13) who explore how the ILO could play a more active role in CSR. A key issue here, according to them, is the notion of responsibility (in labour issues), which is constitutive for ILO governance. The definition of this notion should shift from a purely 'statist' concept (in which the nation is the main if not the only responsible agent in labour issues) to a concept of 'shared' responsibility, implying that the responsibility in labour issues is imputed to a number of agents and institutions along the entire production process, in particular when production is internationally structured, as in global value chains. Shared responsibility is defended and would therefore be determined based on the principles of connectedness, capacity (the ability to exert an influence on labour conditions), benefit (the extent to which agents gain from unjust working conditions) and contribution. In addition to this observation, and hence arguing that these four principles, constitutive for the notion of shared responsibility, are already implicitly present in the values that the ILO embodies, Dahan, Lerner and Milman-Sivan formulate a strategy to bring ILO governance more in line with the principle of shared responsibility and to strengthen the involvement of private agents. Their first suggestion is to expand the scope of the actors responsible for international labour standards beyond the state, that is, the agents that should be considered responsible for infractions of labour standards, based on the four principles of shared responsibility. Secondly, they propose reforming the reporting and complaints system. The authors recommend, first, that the ILO should harmonise compliance with the core labour standards, by intensifying the supervision of its standards, whether states have ratified them or not (in order to reduce problems of international co-ordination and co-operation), and, second, that workers' and employees' organisations should be more deeply involved in the supervisory process.

This idea of a deeper involvement of workers' organisations in the global governance of labour is further developed in the contribution by Koch-Baumgarten and Kryst (Chapter 7), who indeed point to how trade unions, up to now mostly neglected as a relevant *global* actor, can contribute to global labour governance. According to the authors, trade unions have at their disposal four institutional assets in this respect. First, given their network, trade unions can engage in traditional and implicit forms of lobbying through the direct communication channels they have with national governments and international organisations. Second, most trade unions that operate at the firm or sector level are organised in general union federations that, as well as providing support, allow them to share information and co-ordinate strategies. Third, given their popular basis, trade unions can increase the democratic content and the representativeness of international politics, together with and complementary to NGOs that operate at a more general level. Fourth and finally, trade unions are a crucial party in collective bargaining at the aggregate (macro-economic), sector or firm level, and therefore control an important leverage for the respect and implementation of labour standards.

Koch-Baumgarten and Kryst point to different mechanisms through which trade unions could be integrated in global labour governance. In this context they, as Brown, point primarily to the potential of International Framework Agreements that specifically require characteristics that are part of trade unions' competences: strong employee representation with direct access to the companies' headquarters and a culture of social dialogue and trust between management and workers' representatives. Finally, the authors see evidence in support of their argument, in particular, in the role unions play in the transnational collective bargaining system of the International Transport Workers' Federation as well as in the Clean Clothes Campaign, alongside and interconnected with the broader-scoped NGO network. Building on this and the important role of unions in enforcing labour rights, Juliane Reinecke and Jimmy Donaghey (Chapter 12) detail another mechanism in which unions play a key role, namely the 'Accord for Fire and Building Safety in Bangladesh', which is an independent, legally binding agreement between brands and trade unions designed to work towards a safe and healthy Bangladeshi ready-made garment industry. They argue that the Accord is unprecedented in its binding nature and hence constitutes a very interesting case study to further investigate this type of collaboration between employers and unions.

Returning to the initial question from which these concluding observations started, if we were to summarise all the contributions in one bottom line, it is the strong focus in the conclusions of deeper direct involvement of workers' representative organisations which seems the most common denominator. Yet, Tobi Oshodi, in Chapter 9, on the social conflicts and the working conditions in Chinese MNEs in Sub-Sahara Africa, points to a new dimension in global labour governance, as a result of the continuous unbundling of the world economy. Just like international trade in goods and services, foreign direct investment has become a multi-dimensional phenomenon with, in addition to the already common investment flows between industrialised countries and from industrialised to developing or newly industrialised countries, at present substantial investment flows from newly industrialised countries to industrialised or developing countries. If private labour arrangements have emerged in particular because the traditional tripartite approach from a statist perspective became less adequate for an economy characterised by global or, at least, transnational value chains, then, given the geographically diverse origins and ownership of the value chains, it will become increasingly important to take into account the cultural differences in these value chains, with all their implications and – additional – complexities for global labour governance.

Index

Abbott, K. 29, 215
Abolition of Forced Labour Convention, 1957 (No. 105) 13
Accord for Fire and Building Safety in Bangladesh (The Accord) 10, 163, 223, 257, 258, 262–4, 275, 279, 292, 313
  creating 264–7
  emergence of 263–4
  novel features 263
  scope of agreement 263
accountability 32, 148, 170, 179, 214, 215, 217–19, 225–7, 266, 300, 304, 305, 311
Africa
  China as largest trading partner 197
  Decent Work Agenda, fostering in 191, 199–204
  labour practices and China 197–9
  three realities of China in 193–7
African Caribbean and Pacific countries (ACP) 57, 200
African Union (AU) 191, 200
African Union Extraordinary Summit of Heads of State and Government on Employment and Poverty Alleviation in Africa in Ouagadougou in 2004 200
agriculture, and female employment 240, 245, 246, 251
Alert Mechanism Report (AMR) 125
Alston, P. 45, 46, 57, 68, 93, 172, 188
Alter, K. 29
Anner, M. 155, 157, 161, 260
Annual Reports on the Violation of Trade Union Rights (ITUC) 17
Article XX GATT 46
ASEAN *see* Association of Southeast Asian Nations (ASEAN)
Asia
  future growth 84
  scope of 83, 84
  trade agreements 6, 84
    Asia–US social dimension provisions 104–7
    bilateral investment treaties 104
    compared to US perspective 114–15
    free trade agreements 6
    inter-Asian social dimension provisions 108–11
    pivoting towards Asia 116–17
Asian Development Bank (ADB) 97–100
Association Agreements 55, 56–7
Association of Southeast Asian Nations (ASEAN) 58, 97, 100, 101, 102, 103
  ASEAN + 3 countries 102
  ASEAN + 6 countries 99, 103
  ASEAN Economic Community 98
associational power 259–60, 272–3
austerity initiatives 6, 141–5
Australia 83–4
Austria 23

BALPA (British Airline Pilots' Association) 140–41
bananas 9–10
  export production 233–6
  global industry 231–3
  rise of private voluntary standard setting 233–6
Banda, Rupiah 198
Bangladesh
  Accord for Fire and Building Safety in Bangladesh (The Accord) 10, 163, 262–7
  Alliance for Bangladesh Worker Safety 292
  Bangladeshi National Action Plan 266

garment sector 262
Rana Plaza disaster *see* Rana Plaza disaster, Bangladesh (2013)
unions 264
Barry, C. 289
Bartels, L. 46, 50, 52, 53, 54, 56, 57, 58, 59, 61
Bartley, T. 150, 170, 211, 230, 231, 261
Belarus 50
beneficiary principle 291–2
Bhagwati, J. 68
bilateral and regional trade agreements 3, 14
EU context 54–60
labour provisions in EU agreements 56–60
shift in focus 54–6
bilateral investment treaties (BITs) 6, 83, 84, 90, 93, 103–5, 107, 112–14, 307
boycotts of goods 261, 268
BRICS countries 306
British Airline Pilots' Association (BALPA) 140–41
Brown, D.K. 67, 68, 291
Brown, R.C. 6, 29, 89, 90, 104, 113, 307, 308, 310, 313
Brunei Darussalam 28
BSCI (Business Social Compliance Initiative) 214, 265
business regulations 243
business self-regulation 165, 166, 231, 253
Business Social Compliance Initiative (BSCI) 214, 265

Cambodia 52, 60
campaigning groups
complementary powers of unions/ campaign organizations 268–71
and trade unions 273–4
leverage points 267–8
see also trade unions
Canada 39, 71, 84, 87, 94, 110, 114, 307
Maquila Solidarity Network 264
trade agreements 87, 88, 95, 104, 105, 106, 109
capacity principle 290–91
cash crops 232
Caspary, D. 73
CCC *see* Clean Clothes Campaign (CCC)
ceiling effect 173
Central America 71
EU–Central America Association Agreement 55, 56, 57, 58
certification 10, 250
bodies 218, 221
environmental schemes 230, 251
numbers 231, 239
programmes and schemes 9, 14, 211, 230, 234, 244, 246
rates 248, 250, 251
systems 230, 231, 234, 245, 251
Charter of Fundamental Rights of the European Union 42, 129, 131, 134, 140, 145, 146
China 195, 197–9
Chinese Africana 191, 194, 196, 204
Chinese domestica 191, 194, 195, 204
Chinese internationa 191, 194, 195–6, 204
Chinese Non-Ferrous Metals Mining Corporation (CNMC) 204
Cingranelli-Richards (CIRI) Human Rights indicators 14, 16, 18, 38
civil fostering of Decent Work Agenda 9, 200, 203
Clean Clothes Campaign (CCC) 8, 214, 217, 223–5, 264, 269, 313
trade unions and collective bargaining power 151, 161–2
CLS *see* core labour standards (CLS)
codes of conduct 234, 261
international labour standards 171, 176, 177, 185
private fair labour arrangements 214, 220, 221
protection of international labour rights 14
trade unions and collective bargaining power 150, 158, 159, 162, 163, 164
CoE *see* Council of Europe (CoE)
coherence
austerity experience 141–5
and economic governance 137–9
employment policy and flexicurity 135–7

external 6, 7, 139–45
internal 6–7, 129–39
in international labour law 172–4
social and economic Europe 129–31
terminology 120
Viking and *Laval* case law 119, 131–4, 139–41
collaborative arrangements 213
collaborative-relational dimension
collaboration between arrangements 224–5
ILO and private arrangements 223–4
collective bargaining 150–69
and freedom of association *see* freedom of association and collective bargaining (FACB)
maritime shipping 159
see also trade unions
Colombia 39, 56, 64, 71, 234, 250
Canada-Colombia Trade Agreement 88
Chile-Colombia Trade Agreement 86
compliance and private standard setting 234, 242, 243, 245, 247, 250
EU-Colombia and Peru Trade Agreement 55, 56, 58, 73, 75, 76, 77
US-Colombia Trade Agreement 88
colonialism 199
Commission for Labour Cooperation (CLC) 95
Committee of Experts on the Application of Conventions and Recommendations (CEACR) 29, 37, 59, 178, 285, 295, 296, 297, 298
economic governance and labour rights 140, 141
Committee on Freedom of Association (CFA) 37, 144
Committee on International Trade (INTA) 71, 79
Common Commercial Policy (CCP) 5, 42
Communication on Promoting Core Labour Standards and Improving Social Governance in the Context of Globalization (2001) 54
Communication on Trade, Growth and World Affairs (2010) 53
Compa, L. 161, 262
comparative capitalism (CC) 231, 238–40
competitive institutional advantage 239
competitiveness frame 68, 69, 74, 75, 76, 77, 79
complaints systems, shared responsibility model 298–300, 301–3
complex multilateralism 152
compliance
culture 242–4
and effectiveness of private standard setting 230–56
labour market characteristics 245–6
compliance culture 243
compliance gap 3
Comprehensive Economic Partnership Agreement (CEPA) 100, 101
conditionality 86–7
Confederal Group of the European United Left – Nordic Green left (GUE) 70, 73, 76–7, 78, 79
Confederation of Greek Civil Servants' Trade Union (ADEDY) 142
connectedness principle 289–90
consumer power 10, 150, 153, 259, 273
consumption-oriented approach 260–62, 272–4
contribution principle 292–3
convenience hypothesis 171–2
Convention Against Torture (CAT), 1984 51
Convention on the Rights of the Child (CRC), 1989 51
Cooperation Agreements 55, 56
cooperative activities 87
co-regulation 253
core labour standards (CLS) 2, 6, 37
and enforcement 306, 307, 308, 310, 311, 313
ILO standards and CSR mechanisms 175, 176, 177, 189
international trade agreements, comparative perspective 83
social dimension provisions and external trade relations 44, 46, 47, 51, 58

social trade, post-Lisbon era 63, 67, 77
United States perspective 89–90
corporate social responsibility (CSR) 3, 8, 9, 42, 73, 89, 113, 150, 170–72, 270, 280, 281, 291, 295, 305, 308, 310–12
and international labour law 172–82
judicial and non-judicial enforcement of commitments 182–8
theoretical framework for evaluating transnational standards 236–8
transnational standard setting 237
US transparency requirements 186
Corrective Action Plan (CAP) 126
Cörvers, R. 9, 311, 312
Costa Rica 10, 242, 244, 246, 248, 250
Cotonou Partnership Agreement (CPA) 57
Council of Europe (CoE) 6, 7, 309, 310
EU economic governance and labour rights 118–20, 132, 139–43, 145, 147–9
Country Specific Recommendations (CSRs) 122, 128
Court of Justice of the European Union 119, 125, 131, 139, 140, 146, 147
Critical Frame Analysis (CFA) 66, 69–71
CSR standard implementation 241, 245, 247
Cyprus 16, 126–7

Dahan, Y. 11, 282, 288, 295, 312
De Sarnez, M. 72
Decent Work 2, 49, 51, 56, 116, 193
and labour standards 45–8
Decent Work Agenda (DWA), 2000 9, 47, 58, 191, 192–3
in Africa 191, 199–204
civil fostering 9, 200, 203
social dimension provisions and external trade relations 45–8
strategic objectives 192
Declaration on Fundamental Principles and Rights at Work (ILO), 1998 2, 13, 68, 111, 172, 298, 308
labour rights under international trade agreements, comparative perspectives 89–90, 91–2, 93
social dimension provisions and external trade relations 45, 46, 57
Declaration on 'Social Justice for a Fair Globalization' (2008), ILO 2
deep and comprehensive free trade agreements (DCFTA) 58
Delors, J. 122, 136
Demir and Bavkara v. Turkey 140, 174
Deng Boqing 199
development 2, 6, 52, 76, 192, 193, 196, 198, 241
economic 2, 56, 67, 69, 76, 77, 78, 79, 84, 307
human resources/human capital 107, 109, 112
policy 215, 237
social 48, 56, 69, 78, 79, 306
social dimension provisions and external trade relations 46, 47, 54, 57
sustainable *see* sustainable development
and trade 57, 101, 309
diffuse responsibility 226
discourse 6, 47, 232, 309
social trade, post-Lisbon era 66, 68, 70, 75
displacement hypothesis 170–71
dispute settlement 55, 57, 86, 87, 89, 90, 94, 101, 112, 113, 308
Doha Development Round 45
Doha Ministerial Conference (2001) 45
Donaghey, J. 10, 258, 259, 313
Draft Norms on the Responsibilities of Transnational Corporations and Other Business Enterprises with regard to Human Rights 181–2, 183
DWA *see* Decent Work Agenda (DWA)

EAP (Economic Adjustment Programme) 127
Earl of Dartmouth (EFD) 74
EBA (Everything But Arms) scheme 5, 43, 52, 308

Ebert, F. 167, 174
ECB (European Central Bank) 127
ECHR (European Convention of Human Rights) *see* European Convention of Human Rights (ECHR)
ecological fallacy problem 16
Economic Adjustment Programme (EAP) 127
Economic and Monetary Union (EMU) 118, 122, 123, 124, 146
economic development frame 69, 76–8
economic governance, EU
  Albany approach 133
  and European semester 121–2
  immunity approach 134
  instruments and frameworks 122–6
  and internal coherence problems 137–9
  and labour rights 118–49
    possible criticisms from perspective of 127–9
  mechanism 120–21
  and Member States in crisis 126–7
  monitoring instruments 137
  Schmidberger doctrine 133
  and social trade in post-Lisbon era 71–8
  Treaty on the Functioning of the European Union 64, 120, 121, 123, 126, 128, 129, 131, 132, 134, 136, 137, 146
  'triangle' of Council of Europe, ILO and EU 119, 120
economic partnership agreements (EPAs) 29, 44, 58, 59, 99, 100–101, 103, 109–12, 114, 115
ECR (European Conservatives and Reformists) 70, 76
ECtHR *see* European Court of Human Rights (ECtHR)
Ecuador 10, 246, 248
Edinburgh Woollen Mill 271, 274
EDP (Excessive Deficit Procedure) 123, 124
education 246–8
EFD (Europe of Freedom and Democracy) 70
effectiveness 9, 10, 42, 43, 59, 113, 164, 211, 308
  private arrangements 215, 216, 225, 226, 227, 311
  private standard setting 230–56
EFSF (European Financial Stability Facility) 126
EFSM (European Financial Stabilisation Mechanism) 126
Egels-Zandén, N. 161, 163, 164
EICC (Electronic Industry Citizenship Coalition) 214
EIP (Excessive Imbalance Procedure) 126
Electronic Industry Citizenship Coalition (EICC) 214
employee networks 157, 159
employment policy, EU 135–7
Employment Title 135
empty signifier 70, 80
EMU (Economic and Monetary Union) 118, 122, 123, 124, 146
Energi Yapi Yol Sen case 139, 140
enforcement mechanisms 7, 57, 118, 147, 172, 184, 209, 210, 244, 306–14
  level of individual states 307–10
  level of private actors 310–14
  private fair labour arrangements 221–2
  social dimension provisions 87
  US model frameworks 94
EPAs (economic partnership agreements) 58, 99, 100–101, 111–12, 114
EPP (European People's Party) 65
Ethical Trading Initiative (ETI) 178, 214, 264, 265
EU-CARIFORUM 58, 59
EU–Central America Association Agreement 55, 56, 57, 58
EUCFR *see* EU Charter of Fundamental Rights (EUCFR)
EU Charter of Fundamental Rights (EUCFR) 129, 131, 134, 140, 145, 146
  social dimension provisions and external trade relations 42, 46, 47
EU–Colombia and Peru Trade Agreement 55, 56, 58, 73, 75, 76, 77

EU-Korea Free Trade Agreement 105
Europe 2020 120, 121
Strategy on Smart Inclusive and Sustainable Development 47–8
Europe of Freedom and Democracy (EFD) 70, 74–8
European Central Bank (ECB) 127, 149
European Commission 66, 139, 182
Annual Growth Strategy 122
Troika *see* Troika
European Committee of Social Rights (ECSR) 132, 142–4
European Conservatives and Reformists (ECR) 70, 73, 74, 76
European Convention of Human Rights (ECHR) 7, 29, 139, 140, 146, 147, 310
Protocol No. 1 143
European Court of Human Rights (ECtHR) 139–40, 143, 146, 147, 173–4, 188
European Court of Justice (ECJ) *see* Court of Justice of the European Union
European Financial Stabilisation Mechanism (EFSM) 126
European Financial Stability Facility (EFSF) 126
European Parliament (EP) 5, 52, 148
Critical Frame Analysis of relevant EP resolutions and legislative files 69–71
and social trade in post-Lisbon era 63–82
justifications for social trade 67–9
necessary to ensure level playing field/social progress 71–8
European People's Party (EPP) 65
European Social Charter 7, 29, 140, 142, 147, 148, 187, 310
European Union (EU)
bilateral and regional trade agreements 54–60
labour provisions in 56–60
shift in focus 54–6
Court of Justice *see* Court of Justice of the European Union
economic governance
instruments and frameworks 122–6
labour rights, possible criticism from perspective of 127–9
mechanism 120–22
and Member States in crisis 126–7
EU Agenda for Change for Development Policy 48
EU Strategy on Promoting Human Rights and Democracy 48
internal coherence problems 129–39
unilateral regulatory globalization 48–54
evaluation 50–54
Generalised System of Preferences 48–50
see also European Parliament (EP)
Everything But Arms (EBA) scheme 5, 43, 52, 308
Excessive Deficit Procedure (EDP) 123, 124
Excessive Imbalance Procedure (EIP) 126

FACB index 15–20, 23, 32
construction 28
data collection and methodology 17–18
relationship with other human rights indicators 19–20
sample 18–19
Fact-Finding and Conciliation Commission on Freedom of Association (FFCC) 286, 299, 301
A Fair Globalization: Creating Opportunities for All (WCSDG) 14
Fair Labour Association (FLA) 214, 217, 221, 223, 225
fair labour governance 209–29
fair trade 64, 234, 235, 280
Fair Wear Foundation (FWF) 213, 214, 216, 221, 222, 225, 266
Fairtrade 261, 275
female employment
and agriculture 240, 245, 246, 251
FFCC (Fact-Finding and Conciliation Commission on Freedom of Association) 286, 299, 301

Fiscal Compact 122, 124, 125
FLA (Fair Labour Association) 214, 217, 221, 223, 225
flexicurity 137
Forced Labour Convention, 1930 (No. 29) 13
fragmentation 172–4, 226, 227, 258, 267
frames
  competitiveness 68, 69, 74, 75, 76, 77, 79
  definition 67
  human rights 68, 69, 74, 75, 76, 78, 220
  social development 69, 76–8
  see also Critical Frame Analysis (CFA)
Frederick, Kenneth 197
free trade agreements (FTAs) 6, 18, 64, 83
  deep and comprehensive free trade agreements (DCFTA) 58
  EU-Korea Free Trade Agreement 58, 77, 104, 105
  evolution and spread (USA) 88–9
  Model Free Trade Agreement (Model FTA) 90, 91, 92, 93, 94, 113
  North American Free Trade Agreement (NAFTA) 94, 95–6, 112
  social dimension provisions, evolution of labour rights in 85
  United States 88–9
  US-Korea Free Trade Agreement (KORUS) 6, 84, 91, 105, 106
free trade area 101
Freedom House Civil Liberties (FH – CL) 19, 38
Freedom House Human Rights indicators 14, 16, 20
freedom of association 2, 131, 144, 162, 286
  and collective bargaining *see* freedom of association and collective bargaining (FACB)
  ILO standards and CSR mechanisms 171, 173, 178, 179, 180, 181, 183, 185
  labour rights under international trade agreements, comparative perspective 87, 89, 90, 91, 92
  private fair labour arrangements 209, 220, 224
  and responsibility 298, 299, 301
  social dimension provisions and external trade relations 45, 46, 50, 51
  Universal Declaration of Human Rights 15–16
freedom of association and collective bargaining (FACB) 4, 13, 13–41, 46
  evolution of protection 21, 22
  index *see* FACB-index
  rights protection trends since 1985 20–27
    country scores 24–5
    difference by law and practice 27
  rights violations 35–6
  see also Freedom of Association and the Protection of the Right to Organize Convention (ILO, No 87); Right to Organize and Collective Bargaining Convention (No 98)
Freedom of Association and the Protection of the Right to Organize Convention, 1948 (No. 87) 13, 15, 17, 51, 141
FTAs *see* free trade agreements (FTAs)
FWF (Fair Wear Foundation) 213, 214, 216, 221, 222, 225, 266

General Agreement on Tariffs and Trade (GATT) 51, 63
  Article XX 46
General Federation of Employees of the National Electric Power Cooperation (GENOP-DEI) 142, 143, 144
general social norms 54
Generalised System of Preferences (GSP) 5, 42, 48–50
Generalised System of Preferences Plus (GSP+) 14, 63
  social dimension provisions and external trade relations 42–3, 47, 49, 51
GENOP-DEI and ADEDY v. Greece 143, 144

Glasbergen, P. 9, 211, 216, 225, 311, 312
Global Compact (UN) 3
global corporatism 226
Global Good Agricultural Practice (GlobalGAP) 10, 231, 234–6, 239, 243, 246–8, 250
global governance theory 212
global intergovernmental labour regulation 157
Global Jobs Pact (2009) 48
global labour governance 8, 259
  complex and hybrid-like 155–64
  consumption-oriented approach 260–62
  institutional factors of trade unions in 155–7
  labour-driven approach 258–60
  trade unions and collective bargaining power 150–69
Global North 6
Global Reporting Initiative (GRI) 179
Global Social Compliance Programme (GSCP) 214, 220
global supply chains (GSCs) 9, 10, 222, 279, 281
  Rana Plaza disaster, Bangladesh (2013) 258, 259, 262, 273
Global Union Federations (GUFs) 7, 153–4, 257, 259, 263, 264, 304
GlobalGAP *see* Global Good Agricultural Practice (GlobalGAP)
globalization, unilateral regulatory 48–54
governance
  governing through trade 4, 5
  labour rights 3
  multi-stakeholder initiatives 275
  private *see* private governance
  systems 213
  'without government' 230
GRI (Global Reporting Initiative) 179
Group of European Greens/European Free Alliance (Greens/EFA) 70, 72, 73, 75, 77, 78, 79
Group of the Alliance of Liberals and Democrats for Europe (ALDE) 70
Group of the Progressive Alliance of Socialists and Democrats (S&D) 70, 76, 77
GSCP (Global Social Compliance Programme) 214, 220
GSCs *see* global supply chains (GSCs)
GUE *see* Confederal Group of the European United Left – Nordic Green left (GUE)
GUFs (Global Union Federations) 7, 153–4, 257, 259, 263, 264, 304
Guidelines for Multinational Enterprises (1976), ILO 2, 3
Guiding Principles on Business and Human Rights (2011) 176, 218, 219, 281

H&M 267, 269–70, 274
Hafner-Burton, E. 3, 63, 79
Hendrickx, F. 6, 7, 134, 309, 310
Hénin, J. 73
Hepple, Bob 43, 44, 172, 188–9, 301
Hoekman, B. 29–30
Honduras 251
HRC (Human Rights Committee) 173, 188
Hu Jintao 199
human rights
  human rights based norms 54
  Human Rights indicators 14, 16, 18, 20, 38
  social norms as 68–9, 74–6
  trade-labour linkage 43
human rights clause 50, 55, 57, 59, 61
Human Rights Committee (HRC) 173, 188
human rights frame 68, 69, 74, 75, 76, 78, 220
Human Rights Watch 198, 202, 203
human rights-based norms 54

ICCPR *see* International Covenant on Civil and Political Rights (ICCPR)
Iceland 23–4
IFAs *see* International Framework Agreements (IFAs)
ILO *see* International Labour Organisation (ILO)
IMF (International Monetary Fund) 126, 127, 149, 157, 194

Inclusive Development International (IDI) 52
India 64, 66, 71, 73, 79, 99, 101, 109, 200
Inditex 267, 269
industrial relations systems 157
  see also shadow of industrial relations system
IndustriALL 162, 163, 263, 264, 265, 266, 267, 269, 270, 275
institutional change 309
Institutional Covenant on Economic, Social and Cultural Rights (ICESCR) 173
institutional embeddedness 239
institutional environments
  foundations of favourable and unfavourable 248–51
institutional theory 231, 236, 238–40
INTA (Committee on International Trade) 71, 79
internal coherence problems, EU *see* coherence problems, EU
International Confederation of Free Trade Unions 16
International Convention on Civil and Political Rights 29
International Convention on Economic, Social and Cultural Rights 29
International Covenant on Civil and Political Rights (ICCPR) 3, 29, 51, 173
International Framework Agreements (IFAs) 4, 7–8, 178, 259, 304, 308, 313
  supply chains 259
  trade unions and collective bargaining power 151, 158–9
International Labour Conference 93, 181, 283, 303, 304
international labour law, fragmentation and coherence in 172–4
international labour norms, US model frameworks 91–3
International Labour Organisation (ILO) 278–305
  Action Plan (2010) 2
  Committee 141, 144
  Constitution 1, 45, 285
  Conventions
    Abolition of Forced Labour Convention, 1957 (No. 105) 13
    Core Conventions 49, 92, 149, 171, 223, 301
    Forced Labour Convention, 1930 (No. 29) 13
    Freedom of Association and the Protection of the Right to Organize Convention, 1948 (No. 87) 13, 15, 17, 51, 141
    Right to Organize and Collective Bargaining Convention, 1949 (No. 98) 13, 15, 16, 17
  core labour standards *see* core labour standards (CLS)
  Declaration on Fundamental Principles and Rights at Work (1998) *see* Declaration on Fundamental Principles and Rights at Work (1998)
  Declaration on 'Social Justice for a Fair Globalization' (2008) 2
  establishment (1919) 1, 10
  Freedom of Association cases 17, 37
  Governing Body (GB) 286
  Guidelines for Multinational Enterprises (1976) 2, 3
  labour standards and decent work at 45–8
  Philadelphia Declaration (1944) 2
  and private arrangements 223–4
  Reports of the Committee on Freedom of Association 16
  role 10–11
  shared responsibility principles, application in framework of 293–303
  standards and CSR mechanisms 170–89
  supervisory system 8, 17, 37, 209, 295
  trade agreements, framework and perspective on 85–7
  Tripartite Declaration of Principles concerning Multinational Enterprises and Social Policy (ILO MNE Declaration) 2, 175, 185

tripartite structure 158, 209, 219, 280, 283, 285, 286, 304
International Labour Rights Federation, US 264
international labour standards 1, 5, 8, 42, 119, 172, 209, 286, 312
actors responsible for, expanding scope 294–5
aims 13
and CSR mechanisms 170–89
economic governance and labour rights 139, 140
privatization 8, 311
violation 44
voluntary appropriation of public norms 174–80
International Monetary Fund (IMF) 126, 127, 149, 157, 194
International Organization for Standardization (ISO) 179, 189
international rights, protection 13–41
International Textile Garment and Leather Workers' Federation (ITGLWF) 162, 263–4
International Trade Union Confederation (ITUC) 17, 26, 37, 39, 40, 162
International Transport Workers' Federation (ITF) 151, 160, 161
intersectoral partnerships 211
Ireland 23
ITF (International Transport Workers' Federation) 151, 160, 161
ITF and FSU v. Viking Line (*Viking*) 119, 131–4, 139–41
ITGLWF (International Textile Garment and Leather Workers' Federation) 162
ITUC (International Trade Union Confederation) 17, 26, 37, 39, 40, 162

Japan-Singapore Economic Partnership Agreement (JSEPA) 101
Jenks, W. 173
Jintao, H. 199
Joint Initiative on Corporate Accountability and Workers' Rights 225

Kasky v. Nike 185
Kennan, J. 53
Kenner, J. 44, 46, 47, 57
Klink, D. 9–10
Koch-Baumgarten, S. 7, 8, 150, 151, 152, 153, 154, 155, 156, 158, 159, 160, 161, 313
KORUS *see* US-Korea Free Trade Agreement (KORUS)
Koufaki and ADEDY v. Greece 143
Kryst, M. 7, 8
Kucera, D. 4, 15, 16, 17, 18, 35, 37, 39, 307

Labour Affairs Council 106
labour caucus 263, 265, 266, 267, 268, 269, 271–2, 275
Labour Cooperation Mechanism 106
Labour Cooperation Mechanism of Understanding (MOU) 86, 110–11, 114
labour governance
global *see* global labour governance
as sparse patchwork of global regulations 151–4
labour market characteristics 245–6
labour rights
and economic governance (EU) 118–49
enforcement 4, 176, 308, 310
governance 3
protection 1–12
international rights 13–41
labour standards
and decent work at ILO 45–8
enforcement of rights and standards 4, 176, 308, 310
fair 209, 217
improved 53
private 261, 275
public 189
transnational 47
see also core labour standards (CLS); international labour standards
labour-driven approach, global labour governance 258–60
Lange, B. 77, 262
Laval un Partneri v. Svenska (*Laval*) 119, 131–4, 139–41

LDCs (Least Developed Countries) 32, 49, 52–3
leadership, ascribed 218–19
Least Developed Countries (LDCs) 32, 49, 52–3
legitimacy 42, 50, 60, 129, 140, 149, 163, 165, 215, 216, 266, 273, 274
  external 66, 79
Lerner, H. 11, 282, 288, 295, 312
Levi, M. 30
Lithuania 16, 17
Locke, Richard 282

Maastricht Criteria 123, 125, 142
Maastricht Protocol on Social Policy (1991) 131
Macroeconomic Imbalance Procedure (MIP) 122, 125, 127
Maquila Solidarity Network, Canada 264
Martin, D. 77
Martin, O. 174
Marx, A. 4, 14, 29, 88, 211, 241, 306, 307
Mathieu, J.F. 66
Maupain, F. 45
mechanism for complaints and dispute settlement 86
Members of the European Parliament (MEPs) 64, 70
Memorandum of Understanding (MoU) 47, 127, 139, 179, 224, 264
  Labour Cooperation Mechanism of Understanding (MOU) 86, 110–11, 114
MEPs (Members of the European Parliament) 64, 70
Meriga, M. 201
metagovernance 225
Meunier, S. 4
MFN (Most Favoured Nation) treatment 51, 53
Mikolasik, M. 72
Milman-Sivan, F. 11, 282, 284, 288, 295, 312
Ming Dynasty, China 195
Mingas, R. 203
MIP (Macroeconomic Imbalance Procedure) 122, 125, 127
Mitro Repo 72
Model Bilateral Investment Treaty (Model BIT) 90, 91, 92, 93, 95
Model Free Trade Agreement (Model FTA) 90, 91, 92, 93, 94, 113
Mosley, L. 4, 15, 16, 17, 18, 20, 21, 26, 29, 31, 37, 38, 39, 40, 307
Most Favoured Nation (MFN) treatment 51, 53
Movement for Multi-Party Democracy (MMD), Zambia 198
multilateralism, complex 152
multinationals 157, 159, 194, 196, 197
  multinational companies (MNCs) 30, 230, 232, 233, 234, 235, 236, 240, 242, 261
  multinational corporations 157, 159, 175, 287, 310
  multinational enterprises (MNEs) 2–4, 278, 280–82, 284, 291–2, 293, 294, 301, 304, 305, 314
multi-stakeholder initiatives 9, 311
  and Bangladesh 261, 266, 275
  ILO standards and CSR mechanisms 178, 185, 189
  private fair labour arrangements 211, 213, 215, 216
  see also stakeholders
mutually assured destruction of economy (MADE) 195
mutually assured destruction of society (MAD) 195
Myanmar (Burma) 45, 50

NAALC (North American Agreement on Labour Cooperation), NAFTA 95–6, 112
NAFTA *see* North American Free Trade Agreement (NAFTA)
National Administrative Office (NAO) 96
National Contact Points (NCP) 87, 185
National Reform Programmes 118, 121, 122, 127–8
national unionism 150
NCPs (National Contact Points) 87, 185
Netherlands 186–7
New Partnership for African Development (NEPAD) 193

NGOs (non-governmental organisations) 7, 8, 261
and Africa 202–3
coalitions 161, 163
and trade unions 151, 156
Nicolaïdes, K. 4
Nigeria 198, 199, 200, 201, 202, 203, 204
Pax Nigeriana 199
Nigerian Labour Congress (NLC) 202
non-governmental organisations *see* NGOs (non-governmental organisations)
non-state actors 3, 7, 8, 9, 10, 11, 260, 282, 299
African 191–2, 200
Africa and China 193, 198, 199, 203, 204
plurality of 152–3
trade unions and collective bargaining power 150, 152, 153, 154, 161, 164–5, 166
noodle bowl of overlapping agreements 6, 98
normative-cognitive dimension, private fair labour arrangements 219–23
enforcement mechanisms 221–2
responsibility 222–3
standards 220–21
norms
Draft Norms on the Responsibilities of Transnational Corporations and Other Business Enterprises with regard to Human Rights 181–2, 183
general social 54
individual labour norms, enforcement at individual states' level 307–10
integrated international labour 91–3
public 8, 174–80
social *see* social norms
social governance 54, 67
North American Agreement on Labour Cooperation (NAALC), NAFTA 95–6, 112
North American Free Trade Agreement (NAFTA) 94, 95–6, 112
North-South agreements 86
Nye, J. 154

Obama, B. 90
observership 44
occupational safety and health 92, 96, 179, 181, 182, 184, 235
OECD Guidelines for Multinational Enterprises (OECD Guidelines) 2, 3, 175, 182, 185
see also Organisation for Economic Cooperation and Development (OECD)
Olusegun Obasanjo 199
open method of coordination 130
Orbie, J. 50, 54, 55, 63, 64–5, 66, 67, 69, 80
Organisation for Economic Cooperation and Development (OECD) 4, 174–5
non-EU countries 21–2
see also OECD Guidelines for Multinational Enterprises (OECD Guidelines)
organisational field 212
Oshodi, T. 8, 194, 196, 197, 314
Owolabi, A. 201, 202

Pacific Four (P-4) *see* Trans Pacific Strategic Economic Partnership/ Pacific 4 (P-4)
Panama 250
partnerships 9, 111, 211, 213, 217, 224
Partnership Agreements 55
Pax Nigeriana 199
Pecinovsky, P. 6, 7, 309, 310
Pekdemir, C. 9, 29, 311, 312
performance-based standards 221
Peru 56, 71, 87, 88, 101, 107, 110, 114
EU–Colombia and Peru Trade Agreement 55, 56, 58, 73, 75, 76, 77
workers' rights 16, 17
Philadelphia Declaration (1944) 2
points of engagement 9, 191–2, 194, 200, 202
points of exit 9, 191, 194, 200, 203
post-ratification conditionality 87
pre-ratification conditionality 86–7
Primark 267

private arrangements 9, 211, 213, 217, 218, 219, 220, 227
collaboration 224–5
and ILO 223–4
private authority 230
private fair labour arrangements
analytical perspective 211–13
collaborative-relational dimension 223–5
enforcement mechanisms 221–2
normative-cognitive dimension 219–23
research methods and data 213–14
stakeholder compositions 215–16
structural-organisational dimension 214–19
private governance 9, 10, 29, 150, 151, 155, 156, 158, 163, 164, 165, 216, 217, 224, 226, 258
private regulation 8, 161, 165
private standard setting 158, 216
and banana export production 233–6
and compliance opportunities 230–56
private standards 8, 171, 189, 219, 252, 281, 311, 312
privatization of international labour standards/public norms 8, 311
process standards
social norms as 68–9, 74–6
production power 10
production-consumption interface 10
professionalization 246–8
promotional labour provisions 86
public business regulations 241–2
public good 170, 223
public norms 9, 174–80
public regulation 8, 189, 220, 310, 312
compliance opportunities and private voluntary standard setting 241, 244, 248, 249, 250, 251, 252
ILO standards and CSR mechanisms 170, 172, 189
public-private co-regulation 253

Qualitative Comparative Analysis (QCA) 248

Rana Plaza disaster, Bangladesh (2013) 75, 163, 209, 218, 257–77, 278, 279
see also Accord for Fire and Building Safety in Bangladesh (The Accord); Bangladesh
Rayp, G. 13
RCEP (Regional Comprehensive Economic Partnership) 98, 99
ready-made garment (RMG) 10, 267, 269, 274, 313
REC (regional economic communities) 200
Regional Comprehensive Economic Partnership (RCEP) 98, 99
regional economic communities (REC) 200
Regulatory Quality Indicator 241
Reinecke, J. 10, 313
reporting systems
shared responsibility model 295–8, 300–301
responsibility
diffuse 226
normative-cognitive dimension 222–3
shared *see* shared responsibility principles
statist responsibility model 283–7
see also corporate social responsibility (CSR)
Rider, Guy 278
Right to Organize and Collective Bargaining Convention, 1949 (No. 98) 13, 15, 16, 17
Roddick, Anita 170
Ruggie, J. 176, 177, 181, 188, 219, 281, 290
Ruggie Principles 281
Rule of Law indicator 243

S&D (Group of the Progressive Alliance of Socialists and Democrats) 70, 76, 77
SAAS (Social Accountability Accreditation Services) 218
SABMiller 171
safety standards 75, 182, 189, 197, 235, 310

SAI (Social Accountability International) 213, 214, 218, 221, 225
Sainjion report (1994) 63
Salomon, M. 288
SAP (Social Action Programme) 130
Schlyter, C. 72–3
Schömann, Isabelle 178
shadow of hierarchy 155, 157, 160, 161, 163, 165
shadow of industrial relations systems 157, 159, 160, 165
shared responsibility principles 11, 287–93
  application in ILO framework 293–303
  beneficiary principle 291–2
  capacity principle 290–91
  complaints systems 298–300, 301–3
  connectedness principle 289–90
  contribution principle 292–3
  initial signs of a shared responsibility model 295–300
  proposed reforms towards shared responsibility model 300–303
  reporting systems 295–8, 300–301
Simmons, B. 3, 14, 26
Six Pack legislation 118, 122, 123, 124, 125, 128, 138, 146
  see also Two Pack legislation
Social Accountability Accreditation Services (SAAS) 218
Social Accountability International (SAI) 213, 214, 218, 221, 225
Social Action Programme (SAP) 130
social clauses 5, 29, 44, 45, 54, 59, 63, 65, 67, 68, 150, 157, 163
social development frame 69, 76–8
social dimension provisions
  Asian perspective 114–15
    Asian FTAs 103
    Asia–US 104–7
    inter-Asian social dimension provisions 108–11
  characterization 85–7
  conditionality 86–7
  cooperative activities 87
  enforcement mechanisms 87
  EU context
    bilateral and regional trade agreements 54–60
    unilateral regulatory globalization 48–54
  external trade relations 42–62
  of free trade agreements, evolution of labour rights in 85
  promotional activities 86
  social trade in post-Lisbon era (European Parliament position) 63–82
    justifications for social trade 67–9
  trade-labour linkage *see* trade-labour linkage
  US perspective 89–94, 112–13
social governance norms 54, 67
Social Movement Unionism 155–7
social norms
  as process standards or as human rights 68–9, 74–6
  trade and non-trade issues 67
  whether link with trade necessary and desirable 67–8, 72–4
social trade 5
  concept 65
  Critical Frame Analysis of relevant EP resolutions and legislative files 69–71
  justifications for 67–9
  necessary to ensure level playing field/social progress 71–8
  in post-Lisbon era (European Parliament position) 63–82
  whether link with social norms necessary and desirable 67–8, 72–4
  see also social norms
solidarity 129
South Korea 19, 40, 55, 77, 94, 99, 100, 108, 109, 114
Spectrum disaster (2005) 264
spill-over effects 130
Sri Lanka 51, 107
Stability and Growth Pact (SGP) 123
stakeholders
  accountability 217–18
  ascribed leadership 218–19
  compositions 215–16

roles 216–17
see also multi-stakeholder initiatives
standard implementation 221, 230, 240, 244, 246, 248, 251, 252
corporate social responsibility 241, 245, 247
standards
core labour see core labour standards (CLS)
international labour and corporate social responsibility 170–89
voluntary appropriation of public norms 174–80
labour standards and decent work at ILO 45–8
performance-based 221
private fair labour 220–21
private voluntary setting of 230–56
process, social norms 68–9, 74–6
Stassen, L.J.A.J. 79
statist responsibility model 283–7
regular reporting system 284–5
semi-legal states' reports 285
supervision procedures 285–7
see also International Labour Organisation (ILO)
Stevens, C. 53
structural power 259–60
structural-organisational dimension
private fair labour arrangements 214–19
supervisory system, ILO 8, 209, 295
Supervising Reports 17, 37
supply chains 186, 210, 220, 221, 222, 227, 230, 235, 238, 252, 257, 258, 260–61
complex 272
global 9, 10, 222, 258, 259, 262, 273, 279, 281
individual supply-chain countries 231
international 30, 278, 280, 282, 284, 288
large countries 248, 251
MNC 231
ready-made garment (RMG) 269
transnational 279
Survey of Violations of Trade Union Rights 37–8
sustainable development 48, 49, 50, 51, 56, 57, 58, 64, 76, 77, 80, 105

tariffs 53
Tazreen fire (2012) 264, 271
Tesco 267
textile industry 257
third party auditing 221
TPP see Trans-Pacific Partnership
trade
external trade relations 42–82
governing through 4, 5
linking social issues to policy 5
social
justifications for 67–9
in post-Lisbon era (European Parliament position) 63–82
trade-labour linkage see trade-labour linkage
trade agreements
Asian perspective 84, 96–112
Asia–US social dimension provisions 108–11
bilateral investment treaties 104
compared to US perspective 114–15
economic partnership agreements 111–12
evolution 96–104
pivoting towards Asia 116–17
bilateral and regional trade agreements (EU context) 54–60
comparative differences regarding social dimensions provisions (Asia vs US) 112–15
free trade agreements see free trade agreements (FTAs)
ILO framework and perspective 85–7
international 83–117
labour provisions in EU agreements 56–60
North-South 86
observations 115–16
and social dimension provisions
Asian perspective 104–11, 114–15
US perspective 89–94, 112–13
United States perspective 84, 88–96
evolution and spread of FTAs 88–9

model provisions 89–94
North American Agreement on Labour Cooperation (NAALC) 95–6, 112
trade unions
and campaigning groups 273–4
leverage points 267–8
and collective bargaining power 150–69
complementary powers of unions/campaign organizations 268–71
cooperation 150, 151, 152, 154, 160
global labour governance 258–9
global policies 153
influence, components and networks 157–64
institutional factors 155–7
leverage points 267–8
lobbying 155, 165, 313
and NGOs 151, 156
rights 64, 75, 162, 164, 175
Survey of Violations of Trade Union Rights 37–8
traditional strongholds 153
see also global labour governance
trade-labour linkage
debate 43–4
labour and WTO 44–5
labour standards and decent work at ILO 45–8
Trans Pacific Strategic Economic Partnership/Pacific 4 (P-4) 106, 110, 111, 114
Transatlantic Trade and Investment Partnership (TTIP) 88
transnational governance 227
transnational networks 8, 159, 279
Trans-Pacific Partnership (TPP) 89, 106, 107, 110, 114
Treaty of Amsterdam (1997) 135
Treaty of Lisbon (2009) 42, 62, 64, 72, 134, 145, 309
Treaty on European Union *see* Treaty on the Functioning of the European Union
Treaty on Stability, Coordination and Governance 124
Treaty on the Functioning of the European Union (TFEU) 5, 42, 52, 64, 145
economic governance and labour rights 120, 121, 123, 126, 128, 129, 131, 132, 134, 136, 137, 146
social chapter 131, 132
tripartite alliance 152–3
Tripartite Declaration of Principles concerning Multinational Enterprises and Social Policy (ILO MNE Declaration) 2, 175, 185
tripartite structure 263, 314
and ILO *see under* International Labour Organisation (ILO)
Troika 127, 144–5, 149
Economic Adjustment Programmes 142
Turkmenistan 50
Two Pack legislation 122, 124
see also Six Pack legislation

UN Convention on the Rights of All Migrant Workers 60
UNI Global Union 163, 263, 264, 265, 267, 269, 270, 275
unilateral action 3
unilateral regulatory globalization (EU context)
evaluation 50–54
Generalised System of Preferences 48–50
United Nations Global Compact 3, 158, 159, 176, 281
United States
Alien Tort Statute 187
CSR transparency requirements 186
International Labour Rights Federation 264
model provisions 89–94
compared to Asian perspective 112–13
enforcement mechanisms of model frameworks 94
integrated international labour norms, model frameworks 91–3
State Department Country Reports on Human Rights Practices 16, 17, 37
trade agreements 84, 88–96
evolution and spread of FTAs 88–9

Model Provisions 89–94
North American Agreement on Labour Cooperation (NAALC) 95–6, 112
Universal Declaration of Human Rights 15–16, 295
Urgent Appeals 162
Uruguay Round (1986–94) 44
US-Cambodia Textile Agreement 60
US-Korea Free Trade Agreement (KORUS) 6, 84, 91, 105, 106
Uzbekistan 50

Van den Putte, L. 5, 6, 54, 55, 67, 69, 80, 307, 309
Van der Heijden, P. 8, 29, 310, 311
Velluti, S. 5, 29, 307, 308, 309
Verloo, M. 67
Vienna Convention on the Law of Treaties 174
Vogel, D. 3, 150, 158, 230
voluntary appropriation, of public norms 174–80

Wade, A. 196, 199
WCSDG (World Commission on the Social Dimension of Globalization) 14, 32, 57
Weinblum, S. 66
White Paper on Growth Competitiveness and Employment 136
Worker Rights Consortium (WRC) 178, 214, 262, 264
Workers' Rights Consortium 264
World Bank 3, 21, 157, 194, 245, 248
Governance Indicator data set 240, 241
World Commission on the Social Dimension of Globalization (WCSDG) 14, 32, 57
World Trade Organization (WTO) 44, 63, 79, 85, 97
and labour 44–5
Ministerial Conference in Seattle (1999) 44
Ministerial Conference in Singapore (1996) 44
Worldwide Responsible Accredited Production (WRAP) 213, 214, 220, 221, 223
Wouters, J. 4, 5, 44, 62, 88, 306
WRAP (Worldwide Responsible Accredited Production) 213, 214, 220, 221, 223
WRC (Worker Rights Consortium) 178, 214, 262, 264
Wright, E.O. 259–60, 272

Xin Shunkang 204

Young, I. 288
Yucheng, Le 190

Zambia 198, 201
Zandvliet, R. 8, 29, 310, 311
Zimbabwe 202
Zürn, M. 216